Wisconsin
VOTES

Wisconsin VOTES

An Electoral History

ROBERT BOOTH FOWLER

THE UNIVERSITY OF WISCONSIN PRESS

This book was published with the generous support of the
EVJUE FOUNDATION, INC.,
the charitable arm of *The Capital Times*.

The University of Wisconsin Press
1930 Monroe Street, 3rd Floor
Madison, Wisconsin 53711–2059

www.wisc.edu/wisconsinpress/

3 Henrietta Street
London WC2E 8LU, England

Library of Congress Cataloging-in-Publication Data
Fowler, Robert Booth, 1940–
Wisconsin votes : an electoral history / Robert Booth Fowler.
p. cm.
Includes bibliographical references and index.
ISBN 0-299-22740-5 (cloth : alk. paper) — ISBN 0-299-22744-8 (pbk. : alk. paper)
1. Voting—Wisconsin. 2. Elections—Wisconsin. I. Title.
JK6092.F69   2008
324.9775—dc22   2007040020

CONTENTS

ILLUSTRATIONS

MAPS

TABLES

PREFACE

I have long been fascinated by the history of voting in Wisconsin. In the 1980s I became interested in turning my fascination into a serious project and began encouraging some of my students at the University of Wisconsin–Madison to explore the voting behavior—current, historical, or both—of their hometowns, which often were in Wisconsin. From their experiences as young researchers, I started learning about some of the challenges and opportunities ahead of me were I to undertake this history.

In the mid-1990s I decided to begin the project in earnest, though it had to fall in the occasional free spaces between teaching, other research and writing, family, and the rest of life. By 2002 I was able to concentrate on the project, and by then a good deal of my basic electoral research was done. The story of the research and writing I detail in Appendix B, the methodology essay. There I lay out the various steps and sometime missteps that I took as I pursued various aspects of the project.

I want to be clear from the start that this is a story—a story of the voting history of Wisconsin. My focus tends to be on gubernatorial and presidential voting, though not exclusively. It is not a political history of Wisconsin, though inevitably I discuss the electoral history of various key players, or a general history of Wisconsin, a task others have accomplished so well and from which, as my notes and text reveal, I have benefited greatly, or a technical essay in quantitative analysis. This is a story about electoral behavior—who won and lost, what the voting patterns were, and what we might learn from the voting results. It builds less from newspapers and secondary accounts than from detailed study of city, village, and town (usually termed "townships" in other states) voting results—from the actual votes, not somebody or other's opinion at the time or today. It engages all sorts of ethnic, economic, and, sometimes, religious data over Wisconsin's history, and it recounts the interactions of voters and voting, parties and key politicians, and the ethnic and socioeconomic realities in the state over time with recognition that Wisconsin is and has inevitably been part of the larger nation and its political development. Along the way I have had a lot of fun and learned much about the story of Wisconsin voting behavior. I hope this book's readers will find the subject as fascinating and as rewarding as I did.

ACKNOWLEDGMENTS

The list of people who helped me in this journey is long. I must acknowledge the members of the Election Study Project, who were major contributors during the project and who, in some cases, also greatly helped me later on: Chris Chapp, Austin King, Kelly Morrow, Erich Mussak, and Nicolas Mink. Jackie Ballweg provided our wonderful setting. Avraham Fox was there for me at the start. Clayton Nall was absolutely essential to this book. Adam Briggs guided me into Marathon County, Rob Yablon into Milwaukee. Dave Boyd, Leon Epstein, Mike Felber, and Ray Taffora all helped me understand Wisconsin voting behavior and politics. Heather Hartwig Boyd, Marc Ratkovic, and Ben Fowler helped with the numbers. Dennis Dresang and Ed Miller caught important oversights and errors. Alice Honeywell helped with everything. To each and all, including the staff at the University of Wisconsin Press, I am deeply, deeply grateful. They helped me see a dream come true.

Wisconsin VOTES

1 From Statehood to Lincoln's Election

WISCONSIN WAS ADMITTED to the Union as a state in 1848, and its citizens voted in their first presidential election that year. General Zachary Taylor, famous for his service in the Mexican-American War, was elected president as a Whig. Although it was Wisconsin's first year of official statehood, settlement by whites had begun well before 1848. White explorers were active in Wisconsin by the seventeenth century, but it was not until the Black Hawk War of 1832, in which whites established their ascendancy, that Wisconsin became open for widespread settlement. In 1836 Wisconsin became a territory of its own rather than a part of other territories, and in the 1840s the serious flood of immigrants to Wisconsin began. Records from 1830 showed 3,245 white people living in what is now Wisconsin; by 1836 there were close to 12,000; by 1840, 30,945; and by 1846, 155,000. By 1850 there were 305,391 white and 635 African American residents. The number of American Indians by 1850 was roughly 10,000.[1]

In 1848 Wisconsin had three distinct regions of settlement. The first was the mining area of the southwest, which, with its supply of lead, had attracted settlers by the 1820s. Many Cornish migrants, willing to mine the lead, as well as a fair number of American southerners from Kentucky, Tennessee, and southern Illinois moved to the region. Second was the southeastern part of the state along the Lake Michigan shore, populated by a high number of native-born settlers, often of British descent, many from New York and New England. This settlement pattern explained Wisconsin's early reputation as New York's daughter state. The third region, which grew rapidly, was the extensive farmland on the west and north sides of the lake—good farming territory in the "wilderness." More and more Germans and immigrants of other nationalities moved to these seemingly vast and fertile areas that covered much of south and central Wisconsin. They made Wisconsin a remarkably productive agricultural state in surprisingly quick order, and they were to play an important role in the state's electoral history.[2]

As immigrants flooded into Wisconsin in the 1840s, the push for statehood grew just as rapidly as the state's population. However, the way was not entirely smooth as there were many clashing forces and interests. There were arguments over who could get the most from the government, especially cheap land, and there were rival personalities and competing regions. Other issues concerned how much attention should be shown to mining interests, where the state capital should be located, the appropriate role for foreign immigrants, and, in the 1840s, the proper shape of the state constitution. One effort to pass a constitution in 1846 was defeated at the polls. In 1848 another effort received voter endorsement, and with the quick approval of the U.S. Congress in 1848, Wisconsin became a state.

A first issue that needs to be addressed in a history of Wisconsin voting is who could vote in the new state and who could not. The 1848 constitution carefully outlined in Article II who had voting rights. Native-born white males headed the list, a stance that put Wisconsin firmly in the democratic movement of the time. Suggestions for a property qualification for voting—or for office holding—never got a serious hearing. More radical was the provision that white males who were foreign-born and not U.S. citizens could also vote. While this provision was not in accord with the 1836 law originally establishing the Wisconsin territory, it was supported in the territorial law of 1844. Then the Wisconsin legislature allowed all free white males to vote, citizens or not, if they had lived in Wisconsin at least three months. In 1845 the required time period was extended to six months, and aliens seeking to vote had to intend to become U.S. citizens.

The wide-open provision of the Wisconsin Constitution of 1848 allowing resident aliens to vote was one of the two most discussed suffrage standards in the 1847–48 constitutional convention. Some Whigs opposed the provision, well aware that many of the foreign immigrants to the state leaned toward the Democrats. They argued that voting was a privilege and that its exercise belonged only to those who were already citizens. More negatively, opponents spoke of immigrants' ignorance about American government and insisted, therefore, that they should not be voting. Proponents celebrated American liberties and democracy and argued that they should be shared with all (white males) who came to live in Wisconsin. These proponents won because the spirit of the convention was inclusive and democratic, the Democratic Party was powerful in these years, and the protests of German immigrants who feared they might be excluded from suffrage were heard.[3]

The adoption of this rule made a huge difference in the size of the electorate at this time, since some 36 percent of the (male) residents in Wisconsin in 1850 were foreign-born. It also made a substantial difference in materially aiding the Democratic Party, as this chapter later explains. This arrangement did not end after just a few years, either. It lasted until 1908, when the constitution was amended to require that by 1912 only those residents of Wisconsin who were U.S. citizens could vote. This amendment reflected not only rising unease in Wisconsin over "others" who were not yet politically integrated but similar fears nationally. Also, the Republican Party, especially, had no investment in an alien resident voting provision, which they suspected—often correctly—benefited the Democrats much more than it did them. It also was an indication that the greatest flood of migrants into Wisconsin was now in the past. The Irish, Germans, and Scandinavians had, for the most part, settled already, long ago, and many Wisconsinites were their children, even their grandchildren, most of them born in the state and thus citizens. True enough, there were other immigrants still coming after the turn of the century, but the numbers did not match the surge from the 1840s to the 1880s. By 1910 the number of foreign-born residents had fallen to 22 percent and continued to slowly and steadily decline.[4]

The 1848 Constitution did require all eligible males, whether native-born or resident aliens, to be state residents for one year. The idea, which was much debated at the constitutional convention, was that such a residency requirement would ensure that every voter was at least somewhat acquainted with Wisconsin ways before he could vote. It also represented a compromise with those who were reluctant to allow noncitizens to vote. It guaranteed that people with no connection to the state—an issue at that time when Wisconsin was still a frontier society—would not be deciding its fate at the ballot box.[5]

This rule was predictable, but there was something much more surprising in Article II's extension of the vote to some of Wisconsin's American Indians. This decision provoked no serious discussion in the convention, despite what one might expect in those days of often bitter strife between whites and American Indians. One provision authorized voting by all "civilized persons of Indian descent" who were no longer connected with any tribe—that is, American Indians who had more or less melded into the general population. There is no information on how many such American Indians there were in 1848 (ca. 1,000 in 1860) or if any did in fact subsequently vote.

The second group of American Indians the constitution enfranchised were those who were already citizens or who later were made citizens by the

U.S. Congress. There was only one tribe in Wisconsin that had citizen status in 1848 and thus could vote, the Brothertowns. Their pre-1848 history is long and complicated, as it is for all American Indians in nineteenth-century Wisconsin, and not all accounts quite agree. But it is agreed that in the 1830s the Brothertowns received from the U.S. government a reservation in Wisconsin of about 23,000 acres and chose to allot this land to individual plots rather than hold it communally (which resulted in the land being lost to foreclosures and tax sales). The act of allotment, encouraged by the national government, led Congress to grant the Brothertowns U.S. citizenship, though it is unknown how many Brothertowns there were in 1848 or, again, if any actually voted.[6]

The government's idea was that when American Indians chose allotments, they were operating in a culture of individual property-holding similar to white culture. This made them somehow closer to "real" (white) Americans and thus merited granting them U.S. citizenship.

The rest of the American Indians in Wisconsin were, for a variety of reasons, in different situations than the Brothertowns and were not citizens in 1848 and could not vote. Over time, during the nineteenth century, a number of tribes and groups of American Indians in Wisconsin did shift to the allotment arrangement (leading to the loss of about half of reservation lands) and were granted citizenship. In 1924 Congress made all American Indians U.S. citizens, which in Wisconsin guaranteed all the right to vote. In some other states this did not follow, since the U.S. Constitution reserves to states the right to decide who may vote. Indeed, it was not until after World War II that all American Indians in the United States could vote.[7]

The other, and equally important, side of the discussion of the electorate in 1848 Wisconsin revolves around who could not vote. Women could not vote, and their status was not subject to serious discussion at the 1848 convention. Also, aside from the Brothertowns, few American Indians could vote, and no blacks could vote. The few blacks in the state in 1848, almost certainly far fewer than 1,000, had, for the most part, been brought in (or their parents had) as slaves by white southerners who came to the southwest Wisconsin lead region earlier. But by 1848 there were no slaves in Wisconsin, and slavery was illegal.

At the 1848 convention the question of black suffrage was a major subject of contention, while the issue of American Indian or women suffrage was not. Many efforts were made at the convention to gain suffrage for black males by one means or another, but they uniformly failed. Some radical voices in the state on this issue denounced the final constitutional document for just this reason. The convention's compromise was the provision that at any time the state could expand the constitution's suffrage provisions—if the voters then approved—thus intentionally leaving the door open for advocates of black voting rights.[8]

The issue hardly died in the 1848 constitutional convention, and the Wisconsin legislature scheduled a referendum on black suffrage in 1849. This referendum duly passed, the triumph of an idea that was certainly radical for its time and quite inconceivable in such neighboring states as Illinois or Indiana. The 1849 vote demonstrated that the southwest mining areas (home to many transplanted southerners) and German American settlements within the state rejected black suffrage, while Yankee settlements and strong Whig areas generally supported black enfranchisement.

However, the Wisconsin Constitution at the time was interpreted by the State Board of Canvassers as holding that this referendum, one that attracted less than one-third of the voters who cast ballots in the simultaneous governor's race, was null and void on the grounds of low participation. Thus black suffrage did not take place in Wisconsin in 1849. And as things turned out, that decision marked the end of any realistic chance for such suffrage in the state until after the Civil War. In 1865 another referendum took place, and Wisconsin voters indicated that they were not ready for black suffrage. But in 1866 the Wisconsin Supreme Court ended debate on that matter, holding in *Gillespie v. Palmer* that the 1849 vote was valid and had been in 1849. Thus, the court ruled, black males could now vote and, moreover, should have been able to since 1849.[9]

In its territorial years and in the statehood year of 1848, most citizens who could vote were Democrats and, in terms of national politics, Wisconsin was a Democratic Party state. It was a northwestern state in a frontier phase, which in these decades of the nineteenth century guaranteed that it was heavily Democratic. Support for a Jacksonian Democratic, rough-and-ready "people's" politics was strong in frontier states from Wisconsin to Alabama; the Whig Party was often seen as the party of stuffy and privileged eastern elites. In Wisconsin, though, the resistance of the national Democratic Party to internal improvements was a major limiting factor for the party. People wanted development, including an economic infrastructure, such as canals and roads, and this ran against the national Democratic Party's opposition to big government programs.

Too much significance should not be attributed to Wisconsin's overall Democratic allegiance at the beginning of statehood. The Democratic Party in Wisconsin was little more than a set of factions, more devoted to their self-interests than usual, even for political parties of that era. There was no coherent political party operating in Wisconsin, Democratic or Whig. Indeed, party labels were often just thinly veiled covers for what was really a politics of private interest maneuvering.[10]

THE ELECTORAL SYSTEM FROM 1848 TO 1860

Democratic and factionalized at the beginning of statehood in 1848, Wisconsin became a solidly Republican state by 1860, leaving far behind its Democratic Party heritage. In these years, Wisconsin also became a battleground for a variety of third parties and a center for the many turbulent issues that rent pre–Civil War politics in the United States: prohibition, the extension of slavery and slavery itself, political corruption, immigration, and ethnic antagonisms, to name a few. The fluid politics of voting in pre-1860 Wisconsin could not have been more dramatic or more contentious.[11]

Scholars have studied this period in other states, especially in the Midwest, and Wisconsin politics and voting results fit comfortably within the general pattern of upheaval, change, and apparent instability in the larger region. Everywhere the issues of slavery and its expansion, immigration and ethnic-religious tensions, and alcohol and prohibition were active and brought on destabilizing conflicts. As a consequence, the Democratic and Whig parties faced serious challenges to their unity and integrity as more or less cohesive parties. The eventual result was the death of the Whig Party and profound weakening of the Democratic Party. And everywhere in Wisconsin, as in the rest of the Midwest, the contentious issues proved to be tightly connected to ethnic and religious allegiances and alliances, and therefore structured voting behavior, more than did anything else, including party loyalty or economic class. The politics of issues, so interwoven with ethnicity and religion, produced the resulting electoral volatility that occurred between 1848 and 1860.[12]

Yet the voting results from 1848 to 1860 reveal a narrative that is, in many ways, also about stability. It remained true in this era that most voters in Wisconsin located themselves within two major voting blocs. The labels of each sometimes changed, and the forces pushing each did change, but basic voting behavior was often constant. And while many groups voted the same way much of the time, and while in the end the Republicans came out on top, Wisconsin was not a one-party state. At no time in the nineteenth century, in fact, despite the state's eventual reputation as a one-party state, was there an absence of stable, close electoral conflict.

THE ELECTION OF 1848

The first election in which Wisconsin participated as a state was that of 1848. No election in this entire period produced more upheaval. Whig candidate Zachary Taylor was elected president in 1848, defeating Lewis Cass, the Democratic candidate, and Martin Van Buren, a former president but by then the candidate of the Free Soil Party.[13] Cass carried Wisconsin, consistent with its brief Democratic tradition, though he received only 38 percent (15,001 votes) of the state's vote (Taylor 13,747 and Van Buren 10,418).

The startling figure was the Free Soil Party vote, and it hinted at what was to come in the decades ahead as Wisconsin shifted away from the Democrat Party. Van Buren was a former Democrat, and his and the Free Soil Party's efforts reflected the growing unease in the nation over slavery and focused specifically on opposing the expansion of slavery, a sentiment that had been building for a long time. It came out of a deep dislike of the practice of slavery and a strong sense that the institution of slavery threatened the livelihood of free whites.[14]

While to conventional Whigs and loyal Democrats in Wisconsin the Free Soil Party was pretty radical, to some in the antislavery movement in Wisconsin it was no true descendant of the Liberty Party of 1840, which had bravely opposed all slavery in the United States. But the Liberty Party failed at the polls, and its story is not especially central to Wisconsin's electoral history because its brief moment came long before statehood. But it was a harbinger in Wisconsin and elsewhere of the growing public concern over the institution of slavery and its expansion.[15]

Nonetheless, in 1848 most Liberty Party voices supported the Free Soil Party, doing so often with reluctance but understanding that this was their best option for the moment. This helped the Free Soil Party garner its impressive 26.6 percent of the state vote and, at least as noteworthy, pick up one seat in Congress. The party garnered 10 percent of the national vote, which was also significant given that it was not even on the ballot in the southern states. Wisconsin was the third highest Free Soil state following only Vermont and Massachusetts. New York was very close behind Wisconsin. The vote percentages for the Free Soil Party were all the more impressive given that it asked dissident Whigs to vote for a former Democratic president even as rebellious Democrats were asked to vote for a Democrat known to be a political schemer whom they did not trust.[16]

At the heart of the Free Soil appeal was its opposition to the expansion of slavery as the matter came to a head over the Wilmot Proviso. This proposed federal law held that in no territory acquired from the Mexican American War of 1846–48 would slavery be allowed. The proposal ultimately failed, even though in Wisconsin both the Whig and the Democratic parties approved it, well aware that opposition to the advance of slavery—and slavery itself—was spreading in Wisconsin. Their shared stance undercut the Free Soil effort in Wisconsin and made it more difficult. The fact that the Free Soil Party in Wisconsin criticized all slavery did help its cause with the small cohort of former Liberty Party backers. In any event, both "mainstream" parties united to oppose a campaign and a party that focused on the divisive issues of slavery.[17]

Van Buren may have been an especially effective candidate to carry the Free Soil banner. Although many antislavery Whigs felt uncomfortable with such a nominee, and the Whig Party tried hard to show that Free Soil leaders were simply just another group of Democrats, some Whigs were prepared to vote for Van Buren. These Whigs were engaged more with the issue of slavery expansion than Van Buren's Democratic past. Meanwhile, Van Buren was able to do what other critics of slavery had not, penetrate into Democratic circles in the North, foreshadowing the exodus from the Democratic Party in the years ahead as the slavery issue grew in prominence.

Yet perspective is needed here. Most Democrats and most Whigs did not defect. Henry Dodge, for example, a prominent Wisconsin Democratic politician, turned down the chance to run as Van Buren's s vice presidential candidate because of his continuing loyalty to the Democrats. Still, there were losses signified not just by Van Buren himself but also by the eventual Free Soil vice presidential candidate, New Englander John P. Hale. Hale was a former Democrat who had become disillusioned by the annexation of Texas as a slave state and went on to a turbulent political career in and out of the Senate. He died a Republican.[18]

While the Democrats tried hard in Wisconsin to link their candidate, Cass, with the popular opposition to slavery expansion, this did not work well. Cass's own caution and the realities demanded by a national Democratic Party, which was strong in the South, interfered. Cass was not terribly popular in Wisconsin (even though he was from neighboring Michigan) because he adhered to the national Democratic policy of opposing internal improvements that many Wisconsin Democrats fervently wanted. Yet Cass did win Wisconsin, and the Democratic Party's strength continued down the ballot as Democrat Nelson Dewey had no trouble winning the governorship over Whig John Tweedy 19,875 to 14,621. The Free Soil candidate, Charles Durkee, did poorly, partly because Dewey also opposed the expansion of slavery. No one in either the Whig or Democratic parties at the Wisconsin state level needed to defect.[19]

Given the volatile situation of Wisconsin electoral politics of the 1840s, it would be easy to assume that the Free Soil Party phenomenon, which seemed to fade from the national and state picture almost immediately after the election of 1848, was merely a blip, that it signified very little. At first that seemed correct, because after the Compromise of 1850 most U.S. citizens, including in Wisconsin, appeared to breathe a sigh of relief in the hope that the slavery disputes had come to an end. Wisconsin Whigs regained some energy, and the Democrats also saw the return of many who had voted Free Soil in 1848. Moreover, the Free Soil Party in Wisconsin veered away from a focus on the slavery expansion question and by 1853 was more involved in temperance and prohibition issues, though such endeavors were wastes of time in hard-drinking Wisconsin. However, the Free Soil uprising of 1848 was significant. After all, the Compromise of 1850 did not last long, and on the horizon lay a far more permanent and effective party, the Republican Party, and the end of slavery through bloody battle.[20]

The patterns of the 1848 presidential and gubernatorial votes in Wisconsin were quite similar, even though the presidential vote was much closer and the Free Soil Party fared better. The Democrats ran best in Milwaukee and the many counties to the west and north of Milwaukee that were already largely occupied by German American farmers. They also did well in the southwestern mining areas where many citizens had come from the upper South and were committed Democrats. The Whigs also did well there, where many miners were of British origin or descent. The Whigs carried Mineral Point, for example. The Whigs' greatest strength was in southeastern Wisconsin, settled first by Yankee easterners, firmly mainline Protestant (and non-Lutheran) and uneasy over (other) immigrants making their way to the state, especially Catholics, whether German or Irish. The center of Free Soil strength was in Walworth, Waukesha, and Rock counties in southeastern Wisconsin, often paralleling areas of Whigs strength, which suggests that a good portion of Van Buren's support in the state came from disaffected antislavery Whigs.

Thus in the parts of Dodge County that were increasingly German, Cass ran very well. In the heavily Protestant German towns of Herman, Hustisford, and Lebanon, for example, he won easily. The story was the same in the mixed religious German town of Emmet in Dodge County as well as in the German Roman Catholic town of Shields. However, in town after town in rural Walworth County, a part of Wisconsin where German Americans, Catholics, and even Democrats were few, Van Buren swept to victory. Here was the center of a fervent antislavery Protestantism already well established in a county that was to become the most Republican in Wisconsin for the next 150 years.[21]

Apart from the fight over black suffrage, Wisconsin seemed calm during the election of 1849. The Free Soil Party was no longer a serious factor. The main result of the vote was the predictable reelection of Democratic Governor Nelson Dewey. The vote was 16,649 for pioneering leader Dewey (who was to end his life in poverty, implicated in business frauds and disowned by family and friends) and 11,317 for Whig candidate Alexander Collins. Collins was a typical antislavery Wisconsin Whig. Warren Chase, the Free Soil Party candidate, got 3,761 votes. Chase was the most interesting of the three. A former Democrat, he was a character known for his militant anti-Christian stance and was a devotee of Fourierist social planning. He eventually left Wisconsin for what he thought might be a more propitious life in California.

While the 1849 vote was a return to the stable pre-statehood pattern, ongoing tensions over slavery resurfaced when the Wisconsin legislature censured U.S. Senator Isaac Walker because he failed to stand up for the Wilmot Proviso. Originally from Virginia, Walker started out as a Democrat opposing the extension of slavery, but his later waffling on the issue guaranteed his failed reelection in Wisconsin.[22]

The Compromise of 1850 attempted to be a national resolution on slavery issues. It protected slavery in southern territories while forbidding it in northern ones, and among its many complicated provisions, it provided for the return of escaped slaves. Given the general antislavery sentiments in the state, it is no surprise that all of Wisconsin's members of Congress, in all parties, opposed it. But while the compromise soon failed and proved to be a pathetic illusion, at first it did bring a certain national respite from the issues surrounding slavery. While this was true even in Wisconsin to an extent, it did not prevent the election of a Whig governor in 1851.

Leonard Farwell was an earthy Madison real estate agent who won by the narrowest of margins with the support of both Whigs and Free Soil partisans. One factor explaining Farwell's victory was distaste for the previous administration, which was widely believed to be corrupt. The election was not a referendum on national issues, but it was historic: it brought the first non-Democrat to the governorship in Wisconsin. The Democratic candidate, Don Upham, who was a lawyer and mayor of Milwaukee, collected 21,812 votes to Farwell's 22,319. It was in Democratic Milwaukee where Farwell showed surprising strength, probably a result of Mayor Upham's personal unpopularity.

Ironically, Farwell's term as governor was also rife with corruption scandals. And although the scandals do not appear to have involved him personally, the corruption in his administration did seriously tarnish his reputation. He later left Wisconsin for the Patent Office in Washington before joining the business world in Chicago and then Missouri.[23]

A far more accurate and more important indicator of Wisconsin's preferences in the early 1850s came in the presidential election of 1852. Held under the false glow of the Compromise of 1850, this election pitted New Hampshire Democrat Franklin Pierce against Whig General Winfield Scott of Mexican War fame. Pierce won easily in Wisconsin, as he did across the nation.[24]

The Wisconsin vote was 33,658 for Pierce and 22,210 for Scott. Pierce carried thirty-one of the thirty-five counties. John Hale received 8,814 votes as the Free Soil candidate. In an era in which candidates stayed at home, Hale was unusual in that he campaigned hard across the North and even visited southeast Wisconsin in his doomed presidential effort. Hale garnered what was a considerable percentage of the state vote, 13.6 percent, in a time when most citizens did not want to address the issue of slavery in any form. Given that his national vote was only 4.9 percent, the much larger Wisconsin showing demonstrated that even in a moment of quiet, the question of slavery had not gone away in the state.[25]

Still, the overall picture of Democratic strength was reaffirmed in the election of 1853 when Democrat William A. Barstow was elected governor in a contest that had little to do with antislavery and a great deal to do with temperance and prohibition. Originally from Connecticut, Barstow was a Waukesha merchant who was hostile to prohibition but cagily waffled in the election campaign. He faced a new (and short-lived) party, the People's Party, which was formed of many Whigs, Free Soil adherents, and some Democrats. The People's Party's candidate was Edward Holton, whose program stressed advancing prohibition in Wisconsin. This cause was a national one at the time, and it had great support from many of those leading the antislavery, or anti–extension of slavery, crusade in Wisconsin. Reformers in those days were commonly involved in both issues. Barstow also faced what was left of the Whig Party. The Whig candidate, Henry S. Baird, was a Green Bay lawyer, originally from Illinois, who had little support. Democrats received 30,405 votes for governor, the People's Party 21,886, and the Whigs merely 3,304, making it an easy victory for the Democrats. The renewed Democratic strength came as an answer of sorts to the temperance reform efforts that Democrats opposed, efforts that had swept up a part of the Wisconsin electorate if only for that brief moment.[26]

The entire issue of drinking in Wisconsin—then as now—involved much controversy, which sometimes waxed and sometimes waned but rarely quieted completely. Easterners, Yankees so-called, brought the cause to heavy-drinking Wisconsin in the 1830s. The first Wisconsin temperance society was founded in 1839 in Walworth County, a country named, in fact, for a New York State temperance leader. At all times the movement's greatest strength lay in southern Wisconsin, in areas originally settled by Yankees from the East. Methodist and Congregational Protestant churches were often the centers of agitation on the issue.

One important organization involved was the Sons of Temperance. Its Wisconsin branch was formed during 1846–47 and was joined by a Daughters of Temperance auxiliary in 1849. It was militantly active in the temperance cause in the late 1840s and into the 1850s, though it always had to deal with a certain suspicion emanating from many Protestant religious groups because it was a secret organization. In the 1850s it underwent a serious decline as the issue faded and because it chose to exclude blacks from membership, a move that alienated other reformers.

In the late 1840s temperance elements had some party support, certainly within the Whig and antislavery parties but even within the Democratic Party, as long as prohibition itself was not the goal. The cause had some success, achieving its first victory in 1849 with the commencement of state regulation of bars and later, in 1851, with a much-tightened licensing bill for taverns. Its greatest advance came in 1853 when a statewide referendum on the issue of prohibition carried 27,519 to 24,109. Eventually this vote resulted in the passage of a statute to prohibit the sale, not the manufacture (Wisconsin was already important in that business), of alcohol. Democratic Governor Barstow vetoed the 1855 bill, and for the moment the issue died as antislavery matters took center stage again.[27]

Predictably, the vote in 1853 closely paralleled the Democratic versus People's/Whig party division. Milwaukee, already a great center of German American culture, voted 77 percent against prohibition, while southeastern Yankee centers such as Walworth County supported it. The connections between the Democratic vote and support for prohibition were unmistakably negative in Milwaukee, Kenosha, and Waukesha.[28]

The results revealed how clearly voting in Wisconsin reflected the cultural-ethnic divisions of the pre–Civil War period (and long after, as we will see). From the beginning, temperance measures, not to speak of prohibition, had little support from the growing numbers of immigrants to Wisconsin from Germany—and most everywhere else. Any mention of the issue always alienated this part of the Wisconsin population, which by the 1850s was already becoming an important part of the state electorate. Ethnic loyalties around the drink issue were strong, reflecting different cultural traditions about drinking, a fact that was well understood at the time. Thus areas in Wisconsin in 1853 with many Yankee immigrants strongly supported prohibition in 1853, while German immigrant areas were even more strongly opposed to it. Efforts to discern evidence of economic or class measures correlating with the vote have proven useless, an early sign that class far from routinely trumped other matters in much of Wisconsin's voting history.[29]

The issue of drinking was part of a set of reforms that engaged many Wisconsinites in this period and that also included tackling slavery and its expansion. While the quarreling over alcohol did not last long as a central concern in the 1850s, memories of its dangers as an issue lingered in political strategists' minds. Thus, knowing how divisive it could be, the newly formed Republican Party of the middle and later 1850s steered carefully away from the matter; besides, the party had its own explosive issue in its opposition to the expansion of slavery. The logic was simple: Why needlessly antagonize the growing numbers of immigrants and their sons, especially those from Germany, on a matter that was hardly first in minds of the emerging Republican leadership?[30]

The moment of crisis on the antislavery issue came in 1854 when the Kansas–Nebraska Act first was considered and then passed in Congress, nullifying part of the Compromise of 1850 by providing that all new states could decide by popular vote whether or not to allow slaveholding. Promoted by Democrats, including the leading Democrat of the age, Senator Stephen Douglas of Illinois, it aroused a storm of dissent in northern states such as Wisconsin. It raised the possibility of expanding slavery into northern and western areas of the nation where the Compromise of 1850 had forbidden slavery.

In this climate a huge uproar in Wisconsin also occurred over the liberation of a slave, Joshua Glover, from slave catchers, in Milwaukee in March 1854. This event resulted in all sorts of legal and political actions and disputes. While Sherman Booth, a prominent leader of the effort to free Glover, was eventually discredited (though not convicted) for seducing a young maid in his family's service, this scandal did not affect the struggle over the Glover affair in the courts. Eventually, the Wisconsin Supreme Court declared that the part of the Compromise of 1850 that allowed the capture of slaves who fled to free states was unconstitutional. The majority's controversial argument focused on issues of when a trial by jury was required, but the larger signifi-cance of the court's decision illustrated the fact that the antislavery forces were now invoking state court decisions and states' rights claims to back up their views on the slavery issue—just as the slaveholding states had been doing. Disunion was in the air on all sides.

The meaning of all the controversy swirling in 1854 and after was straight-forward: slavery was an explosive issue, one that more and more Wiscon-sinites were confronting, even though few of them had ever seen a black person. During this period the politicians of the Wisconsin Democratic Party struggled to contain the issue, which they knew was becoming more and more alive in Wisconsin. They insisted on the importance of law and order as opposed to antislavery vigilante activism and invoked frank racism, de-scribing blacks in harshly negative language and working hard to stir up fears of miscegenation.[31]

The most important consequence of all the uproar was the birth, growth, and reach of the Republican Party. Several places claim to be the place of origin of the national party, Michigan and Wisconsin vying especially ardently. What there is no doubt about is that Wisconsin was one center of the movement. In 1853 Whig A. E. Bovay started the process of forming a new party in Ripon, Wisconsin, with a series of meetings around the state followed by the official establishment of the party in Wisconsin on July 13, 1854, in the Wisconsin Assembly chambers. This formalization demonstrated how far the fledgling party had grown in a year in Wisconsin, since it was not until 1856 that the party was seriously established in all the northern states. A good deal is known about those first organizing delegates, particu-larly that they were overwhelmingly mainline Protestants, with hardly a Catholic or Lutheran to be found among them. They were generally from elite occupations, such as law and business, and had incomes well above aver-age. Few were farmers, even though farming was the occupation of the vast majority of males in the state.[32]

From the beginning the tone of the Republican Party was evangelistic and moralistic. A part of that mindset was expressed in the Republicans' argu-ment that the old parties were pernicious entities, mere associations for vul-gar personal and group economic gain coupled with the insistence that the Republican Party would be different. This was also an integral theme during the emergence of the Republican Party in Michigan. The Republican Party certainly was different in its frank opposition to the Kansas–Nebraska Act as well as to any other possibility for the expansion of slavery, though the party avoided calling outright for slavery's abolition.

Meanwhile a great help to the fledgling Republican Party in Wisconsin was the national Democratic Party, because by the early 1850s it was the party of choice for most southern slave states and those northerners who favored letting each state decide on slavery by popular vote. The national Democratic Party was also helpful to the Republicans because of its opposition to internal improvements—such as canals—and free, or virtually free, land for settlers. The national Democratic Party of that age was hostile to a powerful and active government, and the Wisconsin party continued to pay a price for it.

A good number of early Wisconsin Republicans favored some form of political rights for free blacks. This was undoubtedly a radical position, as was their widespread sentiment that the South deserved punishment for its sins, including the sin of slavery, though Republican reformers were not free from the racism so pervasive in the Democratic Party. Above all else, however, Republicans felt that there was a southern conspiracy to control the United States and promote their evil practice of slavery everywhere. This was the great moral issue, and on it Republicans were united and determined to thwart the South.[33]

In addition to contributing to the formation of the Republican Party, the 1854 Kansas–Nebraska Act had other consequences in Wisconsin. What was left of the Whig Party in the state collapsed, the People's Party came to an end, and a fair number of Democrats who were against slavery or its expansion became Republicans. Unlike much of the rest of the North, however, Wisconsin was unusual because in the 1850s the Know-Nothing Party did not play a huge role in the founding of the Republican Party in the state. The Know-Nothings' relative weakness in Wisconsin was undoubtedly linked to the fact that its hostility to immigrants just did not work politically in a state so composed of immigrants of all kinds. The composition of the Republican Party in Wisconsin in 1854 was estimated to be one-fourth old Free Soiler, two-fifths former Whigs, and one-fifth or more ex-Democrats.[34]

The results of the 1854 legislative and congressional elections were distinctly unfavorable to the Democrats, a defeat that was a sign of their future. While Democratic Governor William A. Barstow *appeared* to win reelection in 1855, this proved to be an illusion, as evidence of considerable corruption came to light. Barstow resigned in 1856, and the indicators of a triumph of the Republican Party in Wisconsin were suddenly unmistakable.[35]

In fact, Barstow was not personally corrupt, but his three-person electoral counting board was. It manipulated the returns for governor in 1855 and counted out the actual winner, Republican Coles Bashford. This was only

the last of a long series of failures in the Barstow regime, all of which contributed to Barstow's defeat, including rigged bidding for the new insane
asylum and questionable school land sales. Bashford was the ultimate bene-
ficiary. He was an Oshkosh lawyer and a newly minted Republican who had
come to Wisconsin first in 1850. Yet it took action by the Wisconsin Supreme
Court for Barstow to accept defeat, leading the way for Bashford to become
governor. In him the Republicans had their first win, one that was to be
repeated over and over in the contest for the state's elected leadership. In the
years 1857 to 1930, Republicans won all but three times.[36]

A complication of the historic campaign was the attempt of the Know-
Nothings, so powerful nationally in the mid-1850s, to get involved in Wisconsin. Their effort did not get very far. Of course the Democrats, so dependent
on immigrants and Catholics, had no sympathy for the movement since it
was all about hostility to immigrants and was aggressively anti-Catholic.
But the new Republican Party steered clear also, just as it avoided getting
caught up in the quarrels between prohibitionists and their antagonists.
The Republicans' strategic response was well calculated. Sure to get the votes
of those sympathetic with prohibition and Know-Nothingism anyway, they

Coles Bashford, governor 1856–58
(Wisconsin Historical Society, WHi-2537)

could hardly afford to alienate potential voters who disagreed with these groups as the party sought to establish itself. And, after all, while the election of 1855 was a major and really stunning Republican breakthrough, it was a narrow victory. The rest of the statewide Republican ticket lost (for the last time in decades).[37]

The 1856 election in Wisconsin generated spectacular excitement. Under John C. Frémont all the diverse forces moving into the Republican Party had a candidate for president they were happy to support. Frémont had no political baggage from the past; he had an excellent reputation as an explorer of America; and he was definitely opposed to the expansion of slavery. His campaign in Wisconsin and elsewhere in the North (there was no Republican campaign in the South) was framed in classic American terms as a quest for liberty. This did not necessarily mean liberty for slaves, though slavery was universally denounced; but it certainly meant total opposition to any extension of slavery. Above all, it meant a celebration of the free labor and free states of the North and a stinging critique of the ominous, freedom-denying activities of the South. Indeed, the campaign often "became in the eyes of its participants a crusade to save freedom."[38]

Frémont was helped in Wisconsin and elsewhere by the all-out fight in Kansas in 1856, a violent war between pro- and antislavery forces. This murderous contest brought home how serious the stakes had become since the passage of the Kansas–Nebraska Act. The Republicans saw that freedom, especially northern freedom, was in a deadly contest with an advancing slavocracy. While some former Whigs were reluctant to join the Republicans fearing (correctly) that disunion would be the result of Republican victory, other elements that could have caused trouble proved quiescent. This was true of Know-Nothings nationally and in Wisconsin. Prohibition and immigration issues faded into the background, and even the "shocking" rumor that Frémont was a Roman Catholic quieted soon enough.[39]

Democrat James Buchanan swept much of the nation on his road to victory in 1856, but in Wisconsin Frémont won easily with 55.6 percent of the two-party vote.[40] He ran well in traditional Whig areas and in places where the Free Soil Party had been relatively successful in 1852, thus carrying Walworth County in southeast Wisconsin, the very epicenter of Yankee reformism and Hale's strongest county in 1848, by about a 3 to 1 margin. He swept through Rock County (neighbor to Walworth) by more than 2 to 1. Rock was one of the few counties where Whig Winfield Scott did well in the 1852 presidential voting. It was the same story in Grant, Richland, and Waupaca counties, all Whig oriented.

Buchanan ran very well in the Democratic areas of 1852, most heavily settled by German Americans, winning, for example, Washington County 3 to 1, carrying every town in that county. The result was the same in German Ozaukee County, where Buchanan won 6 to 1, again carrying all the towns, and in Milwaukee, where Buchanan rolled up 71.5 percent of the vote.

Yet this kind of comparison can go only so far. After all, in 1852 Franklin Pierce, the Democratic nominee, received a majority of Wisconsin votes, his total greater than the Whig and Free Soil numbers combined. In 1856 things had changed. Frémont, heir to the Whig and Free Soil votes, got 55 percent of all votes. The popularity of the new Republican Party now clearly outpaced the appeal of the Whigs and the Free Soilers in 1852. Dane County provides a good illustration. In 1852 the Democrats easily captured Dane County with 60.6 percent of the vote, with the Whigs getting 31.3 percent and the Free Soilers 8.1 percent. But in Dane, as in most Wisconsin counties by 1856, matters had shifted. The Democratic vote there fell to 46.3 percent, while the Republicans pulled in 53.7 percent (despite Democratic Madison's vote of 58 percent for Buchanan).

In other words, the 1856 Wisconsin outcome was not a matter of some key ethnic or other group somehow swinging dramatically toward the Republicans and making the difference. What happened was a general decrease in Democratic support in many places even though the bases of Democratic strength remained the same: German American Milwaukee County and other heavily German counties surrounding it and along Lake Michigan as well the heavily Irish-, Cornish-, and southern-settled areas in the southwestern mining counties. Much of the rest of the state supported Frémont, often by large margins. Overall the Republican gains over the old Whig/Free Soil elements were not overwhelming, but they were decisive and, as it turned out, permanent enough so that the Republican Party became the new force in Wisconsin.[41]

The succeeding years, through Lincoln's Wisconsin victory, followed what quite rapidly became the established pattern—one of Republican victory, but victory in decidedly competitive elections. In 1857 Republican Alexander Randall was narrowly elected governor, the vote of 44,693 to 44,239 being about as close as one could imagine. (Randall would have won more easily if his Republican predecessor, Coles Bashford, was not entrapped in charges and countercharges of corruption—quite the staple of Wisconsin politics before the Civil War!—regarding favors to railroad interests.) Democrats did win some statewide races, including the post of lieutenant governor, where the well-known liberal German Carl Schurz went down to defeat.

Alexander Randall was born in New York State and came to Wisconsin in his early twenties as a Democrat, one who exemplified that segment of the Democratic Party that eventually shifted to the Republicans over the issue of slavery and helped to form the new Republican majority. He was selected to run largely because the Republicans knew that their coalition was still in the making and they hoped Randall could attract and cement a certain portion of the Democrats to their cause. His instincts were in line with the determined abolitionist camp, and he also had connections with both prohibitionists and nativist forces, though he did not join either group.[42]

The Democrats nominated James B. Cross, a businessman and the mayor of Democratic Milwaukee. A popular and effective speaker, he was a serious opponent, one who was helped by the presence on the ballot of an unpopular referendum on black voting rights. The referendum was soundly defeated, garnering only 36 percent of the votes cast. The Democrats, who expressed clear opposition to the referendum, tried hard to take the entire Republican ticket down over the issue. It was one thing to oppose the extension of slavery, indeed slavery itself; that was a position now popular enough to produce Republican victory. It was something else to endorse black political equality. That simply was not acceptable in Wisconsin, especially in German areas, in 1857.[43]

Alexander Randall,
governor 1858–62
(Wisconsin Historical Society,
WHi-2885)

Two years later, in the 1859 elections, Governor Randall won reelection more easily when he garnered 53 percent of the vote. His opponent, Democrat Harrison Hobart, a Calumet County lawyer, was hurt by continuing controversy over corruption during the Barstow administration and by the Republican assertions that the Wisconsin Democratic Party was merely a puppet controlled by southern slave interests. But Republicans had their own problems following the attempt by John Brown and a few others to free slaves forcibly at Harper's Ferry, which created a backlash against antislavery efforts. Much of the Republican political energy came from the part of the party that saw itself as a movement, as an antislavery crusade, but not one that approved of violence. Its home was in peace-loving Protestant churches.[44]

Thus the stage was set for the crucial national and state elections of 1860. Lincoln's victory in Wisconsin was predictable given that the Democratic Party broke apart in 1860, the Whigs were weaker than ever, and Wisconsin was already a Republican state. And Lincoln did indeed win Wisconsin, garnering 86,113 votes and 56.6 percent of the total. Illinois Senator Stephen Douglas was far behind with 65,021 votes and roughly 42.7 percent of the total, while assorted other candidates won less than 1 percent of the vote.[45]

Lincoln's victory indicated that Republicans were now the majority party in Wisconsin. A realignment had occurred, though this was not completely obvious even in 1860. Succeeding elections showed its truth unmistakably, however, and revealed consistent partisan voting allegiances. Thus there was a far higher association of voting patterns in my representative sample of Wisconsin voting units between 1860 and 1864 than there was between 1856 and 1860 when the new alignment was still emerging.[46]

The size of Lincoln's victory was, however, slightly misleading about the relative strength of the two parties in Wisconsin. Lincoln's margin of victory, like Frémont's in 1856, was larger than what the Republicans could muster in the state races. In those races the results remained close between the two parties (as they were to remain until after the depression of 1893). The point bears repeating: Republican success did not mean Republican dominance. This cannot be overemphasized, since so many accounts of Wisconsin history disregard the existence of opposition Democrats in the last half of the nineteenth century. They did indeed exist and were a constant threat to the Republicans, as the Republican Party at the time knew very well.

One aspect of Lincoln's victory that has long been in dispute questions the degree to which his Wisconsin victory was promoted by German American support. Some have argued that in this period German American voters in the United States shifted in large numbers from the Democratic to the Republican Party.[47] This was not true in Wisconsin at that time, and Wisconsin was by far the most German state in the Union. True, the Republican campaign of 1860 strove to get these votes, explicitly separating themselves from anti-immigrant sentiments and celebrating free white men, free soil, and free labor while skirting any endorsement of black rights. But they had no particular success in Wisconsin with the campaign to win wide allegiance from German Americans. Across the board, with all parts of the electorate, Republicans did a bit better than they had in previous recent state elections, including with some German Protestants, but there was no massive swing

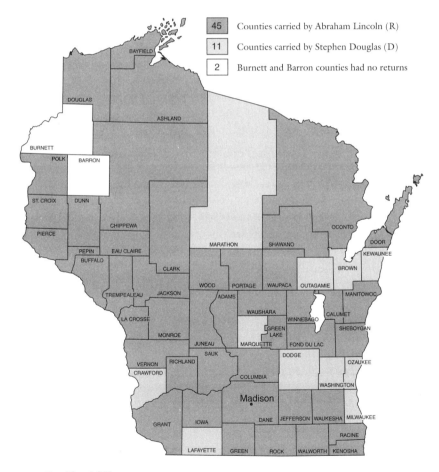

1860 Presidential Vote

to Lincoln. Typical German Protestant areas still voted strongly for Douglas, the Democrat. Thus the town of Herman in Dodge County voted 81.3 percent for Douglas, Lebanon in Dodge County 84 percent, Meeme in Manitowoc County 65.4 percent. In largely German Catholic areas the outcome was the same: Woodville in Calumet County went 68.9 percent for Douglas, Shields in Dodge County 89.9 percent, Calumet in Fond du Lac County 86.1 percent. These margins are hardly ambiguous, though in most cases they were smaller for the Democrats than they had been in earlier elections. There was a marginal shift toward Lincoln among German Americans. Thus Lincoln was unusual as a Republican candidate because of his appeal to this group, but that appeal was still small.[48]

ELEMENTS OF THE VOTE FROM 1848 TO 1860

The geographic dimensions of Wisconsin voting are important to note from the start. In 1849 Milwaukee and the areas around it were the most important single element, but by 1860 growth had taken place in so many parts of southern and central Wisconsin that, temporarily, Milwaukee and southeast Wisconsin were less significant and no longer represented 30 percent of the state vote but, instead, half of that.

Class issues do not appear to have been important. The challenges of measuring class variables and voting are complex, not least in the pre–Civil War period (see Appendix B). This dimension of voting behavior in Wisconsin, especially in these years, has received too little attention, but what attention it has gotten underlines its distinctly secondary role in Wisconsin's voting. Cultural differences and tensions appear to have mattered most.[49]

We do know from census data that property (income data were not then collected) was unequally shared. Thus in 1860, 2 percent of the male population owned 31 percent of property wealth, 40 percent had property worth less than $200, and 30 percent had no property at all. The median was $350. Not surprisingly, real differences existed in the property owned by native versus foreign-born populations, old versus young, settled farmers, German or Yankee, versus the Milwaukee workers and frontier farmers.[50]

We also know from research on wealth distribution and various geographical units in Wisconsin in the early 1850s that relative party strength in areas did vary somewhat according to degrees of affluence. Thus Free Soil places were likely to be more well-to-do than Whig areas, and Whig areas more than Democratic ones. Republican areas also were more affluent than Democratic ones. But affluence does not seem to explain Wisconsin voting; therefore, not surprisingly, relative wealth within individual ethnic groups does not prove to be a good predictor of differences in political choices. For example, German Americans differed greatly in their individual economic positions in Wisconsin at this time, but whatever their economic position, they were generally very Democratic in their voting habits.[51]

Instead ethnic and religious variables are the key to understanding Wisconsin voting behavior during this period.[52] Of course within every ethnic group and every religious perspective there were multiple opinions. Nothing was rigid, nothing was unanimous. Yet the general contours within each major group show considerable stability in what appears to be a highly turbulent period of electoral and party change, which is not surprising since we know that the shift to the Republican Party was a matter of small margins and relatively minor adjustments. The change was of great importance, but it did not reflect change among the majority of voters. The situation among groups and individuals from 1848 to 1860 remained mostly fixed.

Consider first the German Americans, who comprised the most important ethnic group among the state's voters. In the antebellum period they constituted a large proportion of Wisconsin's population. After all, one-third of Wisconsin's population in 1860 was foreign-born, and of that fraction more than 40 percent were German American. (The percentage would probably be higher if those born in Austria and Switzerland were included.) Moreover, their children were numerous in a state where half of all the citizens were either foreign-born or the children of same. Their numbers, as well, were frequently increased by further immigration, a process that continued during much of the nineteenth century.[53]

German Americans, of course, came from many different parts of an area that was not to become a unified Germany until 1870–71. To them, especially in the first generation, the region they came from in Germany mattered. Thus, by way of example, many Germans from Saxony settled in Centerville in Manitowoc County, those from Prussia in La Crosse, those from northern Germany in Dodge County, and those from Rhineland in Fond du Lac County. Immigrants from southern Germany established themselves near the lake in Washington County, while its lake neighbor, Ozaukee County, just north of Milwaukee, became the home of Luxembourgers, who spoke German but did not see themselves as Germans. In short, there was no united German community, even among the majority of German Lutherans in this period. However, while Germans coming to Wisconsin rarely saw themselves, in fact, as "Germans," they soon enough became so, first to non-Germans and then to themselves as they experienced their definition by the larger culture as German and as "other."[54]

Many Germans settled in Wisconsin cities in this period, but by far the greater number of Germans settled on farms, often on good land along Lake Michigan around Milwaukee and elsewhere in southeastern and, eventually, central Wisconsin. These settlers soon produced excellent farming operations. Their practice was to focus on steady farming and to avoid financial speculation, and their economic success in the rural areas they settled was well-known, admired, and sometimes envied.

Germans tended to migrate with and then settle with other Germans, usually from the same region in Germany. This was as true in Milwaukee or Appleton as it was in rural areas. Always there was a tremendous focus on their home country's culture and language, and there was considerable ethnic solidarity. The story of the vibrant German American culture in nineteenth-century Wisconsin is a rich and fascinating one and deserves even more attention than it has received.[55]

The great divide within the German American population of Wisconsin was over religion. At first region of origin was very important, but time softened or eliminated that difference. Time did not, however, diminish the divisive power of religion. There are no exact figures on the religious orientations of the Germans who came to Wisconsin, but a reasonable estimate is that about two-thirds were Protestants. Among Protestants, however, major divisions remained throughout the nineteenth century. Although most were Lutherans, often coming from Prussia or other locations in northern Germany, Lutheranism was not homogeneous. Rather, many types and synods of Lutherans were represented, and these were by no means united in doctrine or spirit. Even today the three primary Lutheran bodies remain separate: the largest, the Evangelical Lutheran Church, an amalgam of many German and non-German Lutherans; the Missouri Synod Lutherans, formed in 1847; and the Wisconsin Lutheran Synod, formed in 1850. In addition to the Lutherans, however, considerable numbers of Protestant Germans came from the Evangelical, Reformed, or Evangelical United Brethren churches. Catholic Germans also came, mostly from Bavaria and other more southern parts of Germany. In short, it was not uncommon for a typical village or area of German settlement to have three very separate churches often in not-so-subtle conflict.[56]

This rarely mattered politically in the years before the Civil War since most Germans steadfastly supported the Democratic Party. The issues were clear. They saw the Whigs, Free Soilers, and then the Republicans as the parties sympathetic to blacks but not immigrants. Many German Americans also felt the other parties were not sympathetic to German ways, specifically their culture of social drinking. The Democrats welcomed the Germans and made clear that they were not a party determined to make German immigrants over to fit some pietistic Yankee model. To be sure, some Lutheran churches opposed drinking and even denied sacraments to tavern operators. Strongly pietistic German Americans could be found. Yet in the dominant German Lutheran culture, drinking in moderation was and remained an integral part of life, part of simply having a good time, and the Democratic Party was supportive of this.[57]

A faction of so-called free-thinking Germans, religious liberals led by Carl Schurz, endorsed the Republican Party, but they were not typical of most Wisconsin German Americans. Their numbers were quite small, and they were decidedly alienated from the rest of the Germans in Wisconsin. Indeed, wherever they were, conflict in the German community was likely to follow. Too much has been made of this tiny minority in contrast to the overwhelming majority of German Americans from the 1840s to the 1860s.[58]

Religious differences, however, came to matter a great deal politically within the German American community. After the Civil War and up until the depression of 1893, there was a slow but steady movement of German Protestants toward the Republican Party, perhaps most clearly in areas where German Lutherans and German Catholics came into contact with one another. Its consequences were monumental for the two political parties in Wisconsin in the second half of the nineteenth century. It meant, first of all, that German Americans were never to obtain the kind of ethnic influence that their large numbers alone might have allowed them to achieve. Over time German American voters split between the two parties, more and more predictably by religious affiliation—Catholic versus Protestant.

As a group, German Americans did not prove to be particularly political. Dutiful citizens, yes, but their culture was not a fertile spawning ground for politicians. The German specialties became and remained hard work, disciplined family lives, and a willingness to enjoy life when work was done. This mattered as the years went by, because while there were to be many successful politicians of German heritage in Wisconsin, the numbers did not approach what they could have been.[59]

The Republican Party needed all the German American votes it could get as the century waned, and it did win over more and more citizens of German Protestant ancestry. The Democrats made gradual gains among other sectors of the population, as demonstrated by Polish Americans when they entered the electorate in sizable numbers late in the century. But the

Democratic Party suffered as many Protestant Germans gradually edged away from what they came to see as the Catholic Democratic Party.

An intriguing sidelight on this topic was the role of the Swiss Germans. They were not numerous, just one German group among several. Many came to Wisconsin before the Civil War and settled largely in Green County, most famously in the New Glarus area. Swiss farming areas were highly successful, and Swiss towns long boasted relatively high incomes as a result. Yet class was no guide to voting behavior here either. From the beginning there was little voting cohesion in Swiss areas, their votes split largely along familiar religious lines: Swiss Catholics leaning Democratic and Swiss Protestants, often of a Reformed rather than Lutheran tradition, leaning Republican. The overall result made Green County mostly, but hardly entirely, Republican.[60]

As evident over and over in this study, the Germans may have been—and have remained—the dominant ethnic group in Wisconsin, but numerous other groups appeared whose voting behavior was important. For example, the Dutch, who came to Wisconsin largely before 1860, were a small but distinctive group that demonstrated, from the start, a cohesiveness that extended to their voting behavior. At first most Dutch immigrants and their children were Democrats, repeating the pattern of most (but not all) immigrants to Wisconsin. This was apparent in two early largely Dutch settlements, Alto in Fond du Lac County and Holland in Sheboygan County. As the Dutch came to predominate there in the late 1850s, these regions became Democratic; however, they switched in the election of 1860 and have never once since—no matter what—voted Democratic for any governor or president.

At first the Democrats were attractive to immigrants and seen as being the party of the cultural and economic outsiders. They were not associated with anti-immigration sentiments and efforts, so voting Democratic made sense in Dutch communities. But by the time of the Civil War, Protestant Dutch areas—and most Dutch were Protestants—had become strongly Republican. This was largely due to their opposition to slavery, though another factor was a rising perception that the Democratic Party was the party of the Catholics, and the Dutch Catholics in particular, and with the Dutch, as with others in that era, there was significant tension over religion. To this day, the most Republican areas in Wisconsin—as elsewhere—are those that were heavily settled by Dutch Protestants. A classic instance of a still significantly Dutch place in Wisconsin is the village of Oostburg in Sheboygan County, where George W. Bush received 84.2 percent of the vote in the

2000 presidential election, a typical result for it and other traditional Dutch-settled locations. In 2004 the pattern was strengthened, so in Oostburg, for example, support for Bush was 85.9 percent.

However, the Catholic Dutch immigrants remained strongly Democratic, and so the Protestant-Catholic divide continued throughout the rest of the nineteenth century within this group. The classic Dutch Roman Catholic Democratic town was Vandenbroek in Outagamie County. Named after the Dutch Roman Catholic priest who founded it, Vandenbroek has seen its Democratic allegiance fade in the twentieth and twenty-first centuries, and Republicans even carrying it. The old Protestant-Catholic divide, once so crucial to understanding electoral behavior, has begun to fade everywhere.[61]

All the discussion of ethnic groups' roles, large or small, in Wisconsin's voting behavior must include consideration of the old-stock Yankee population, often British in origin, who migrated to Wisconsin from the East. The most famous members of this mix were the immigrants from Britain's Cornwall area who played such a significant part in the earliest days of Wisconsin as miners in the southwest part of the state. But even by 1860 they made up only a small part of the British-origin Wisconsin population.

Yankee citizens were overwhelmingly Protestants, commonly Methodist, Episcopalian, or Congregationalist in the long-gone era in which some in these denominations were distinctly evangelical in religion. They were often also evangelical in politics, frequently of a reformist disposition regarding drinking or slavery, and were strongly Whig, Free Soil, or eventually Republican. They were often hostile to Roman Catholicism and its adherents, and there was a good deal of distaste for all foreign immigrants and what they considered the dubious ways of these newcomers. Yankees and other British descendants made up a significant part of Wisconsin's population throughout the nineteenth century; though precise figures are not available, they made up a third or more of the state's population. This group become the very heart of the emerging Republican Party. Throughout the nineteenth century at least 75 percent of Yankee voters were dependably Republican, voters who, as we will see, often entered the voting booth to stand against alien forces and alien cultures.[62]

Yankees, so-called, were not necessarily the same people as those who came to be called "native stock" residents of Wisconsin. Many of the latter were not of British background, even granting how diverse "British" could be. Rather, they were distinct from contemporary immigrants and their children since they came to Wisconsin already U.S. citizens, arriving from other parts of the country, and this distinction had a cultural effect. They tended to be Republicans in their voting behavior, often distinctly uneasy with immigrants, especially Catholics.[63]

While Wisconsin began as a Yankee state, Yankees became increasingly a minority as the century progressed. Nonetheless, they wielded political influence far beyond their numbers and normally commanded the political scene, usually through the vehicle of the Republican Party. Key was their relative political unity, as well as the fact that prominent Yankees became the economic elite of Wisconsin in the nineteenth century. Yankees also had the advantages of greater education, at least at first, which was always a political resource; a familiarity with English, which took each arriving non-Yankee group time to acquire; and a freedom from ethnic enclaves that often were limiting.[64]

The Yankees themselves were diverse in many ways, even in terms of ancestry, though their principal background was likely to be British in one form or mix or another. But everyone understood very clearly that "Yankee" did not include one British ancestry group: the Irish. The Irish were a definite presence in Wisconsin from the beginning of the white settlement and became the second largest group, after the Germans, migrating from abroad to Wisconsin in the years before the Civil War. Many Irish Americans moved frequently, and as a group they were not as oriented to farming as were most other Wisconsinites. Thus they did not establish as many enduring ethnic enclaves as the Germans or Scandinavians, for example. While the Irish transience does not allow as smooth a tracing of the electoral preferences over time, in the nineteenth century in Wisconsin there were some distinctly Irish American communities, though few after that date. A considerable sense of Irish ancestry remains, however, and in the 2000 census of Wisconsin almost 11 percent of Wisconsin residents identified their ethnic background as Irish. So while Irish Americans do not live together today and often did not in the nineteenth century, a sense of Irish ethnic awareness lingers.

Irish voting behavior was consistently Democratic throughout the nineteenth century, both before the Civil War and after. This orientation paralleled Irish American voting behavior throughout the nation in that century and reflected the strong Irish Catholic sense of tension with Yankee (i.e., British) Protestants, usually Republicans, and their culture. Irish Americans knew that Yankees were often hostile toward the Irish, and, naturally, they fiercely resented it. While this animosity was not as common in Wisconsin as it was on the East Coast, the tension was real, and Irish American voting in the state reflected it. A classic example of an Irish community in this era was

Erin Prairie in St. Croix County. In 1860 it cast 94.5 percent of its vote for Democrat Stephen Douglas and against Lincoln.[65]

One other ethnic group that was part of the already complicated mix in the antebellum period was the Belgians. While they were not numerous, they came to Wisconsin in the 1850s and settled largely in southern Door (south of what is now Sturgeon Bay) and Kewaunee counties. They formed there what became the largest rural Belgian settlement in the United States. Walloon-speaking Belgians, they were devoted to the Roman Catholic Church. Yet living as they did in their own rural world, Wisconsin's Belgians had little contact with anti-Catholicism. As a result, they are the prime example in Wisconsin of a Roman Catholic ethnic cluster that was self-consciously alienated neither from the dominant Protestant culture nor from the public schools. It followed that they were by no means dependable Democratic voters. Prior to the Civil War, Democratic margins in Belgian areas were in the 90-percent-plus range for Democratic candidates, but in the war years this ended, and it was common for Belgian areas to vote 75 percent Republican for the rest of the nineteenth century. There were exceptions to this, as evident in several volatile governors' races in the 1870s and in the early 1890s where, in the first instance, Democrats won and in the second they came close.[66]

There is every reason to agree that the years 1848 to 1860 were eventful ones in Wisconsin electoral history. To be sure, not everyone who could vote did. Estimates indicate that for much of the period voter turnout was well lower than it is today in Wisconsin, when more than 70 percent vote in presidential elections. In both the 1856 and 1860 elections, however, and in some in between, voter turnout was as high as 80 percent, which testified to the rising level of political tension as the Civil War approached.[67]

This whole period was one of remarkable excitement and fluidity in Wisconsin electoral politics. Yet it is also true that it evolved toward a situation of narrow Republican control by the late 1850s that was to be the story for the rest of nineteenth century. The reality is that out of the seeming chaos of a dozen or so prewar years came a stability that lasted for half a century and more.

Equally true, voting in Wisconsin in these years was largely determined by what we today would call cultural and moral issues intersecting with ethnic and religious loyalties over such issues as alcohol and the expansion of slavery. At the same time it is important to understand that while there was undoubtedly plenty of religious bigotry at that time (and since), there was little open campaigning that spoke directly in terms of one religion versus another. The tensions were there, but they rarely surfaced in any explicit way, though occasionally open hostility toward one ethnic group or another did. Free Soil Party newspaper editors, for example, did not bother to hide their very real distaste for German and Irish Americans.[68]

Nevertheless, while the tensions were muted somewhat in the campaigns, the party alignments of these years up to 1860 were built on ethnic-religious divisions. The diverse cultures of Wisconsin Germans, Yankees, Dutch, and others were, for the most part, the determining factor at the polls in this era—and thus is what explains Wisconsin voting behavior then and for a long time thereafter.

These differences were complicated but never fell along foreign immigrant versus nonimmigrant lines. After all, the Yankee elements of Wisconsin soon enough had the support of many immigrants, including many Dutch, Norwegian, and Swedish Protestants, while most German Protestants favored the Democrats as they joined most Catholics, immigrants and nonimmigrants alike. Of course these lines were not hard and fast and did not describe the behavior of every individual voter, but they were there even amid all the fluidity. Where economics did matter, such as the general enthusiasm for government to help with economic development in Wisconsin, it did not seem to form on the basis of class differences within the electorate, as there is scant evidence of class voting in pre–Civil War Wisconsin.[69]

2

The Civil War and the Politics It Created

1861–1888

IT IS TOO EASILY ASSUMED that the long years between 1861 and 1888 were dull times for electoral politics. Such was hardly the case, however, and certainly not for Wisconsin. In fact, it was a period of close electoral contests between the Republicans and Democrats and a time of challenges posed by third parties. It was also a time of sometimes intense factionalism within the established parties. Nothing about Wisconsin electoral history in this age was placid. True enough, voting patterns of the 1850s and 1860s persisted, though they were rarely set in concrete. Wisconsin had become a Republican state, one where a Republican machine soon came to operate politics and elections as a business, arranging patronage favors in terms of jobs or economic favors as a standard means of obtaining or maintaining support. Yet Wisconsin was not really a Republican stronghold, especially after the 1860s. By the 1870s voting was close between the two major parties, reflecting national trends. By the 1880s the two parties were in a virtual tie with third-party efforts repeatedly hurting both major parties. The result was an electoral scene that has rightly been characterized as "one of *stability*, not stagnation."[1]

During most of this period Wisconsin remained a farm state, but one with a high degree of mobility among its populace. In 1870 only 20 percent of the population lived in any place with more than 2,500 persons. One-third of that number dwelt in Milwaukee, and only a few other cities had a population over 5,000. Milwaukee was the real growth area, but even it was small, with only 71,000 people in 1870, less than 10 percent of the state's citizens. In just thirty years its population would reach 285,000. Milwaukee's expansion did signal the growth of a different Wisconsin as banks, large-scale industries, and commercial firms moved to Milwaukee.

The major agricultural event of this era was the shift from wheat production to dairy farming, a change that took tight hold by the 1880s but one that did not alter the basic rural character of Wisconsin. Also important, of course, was the lumber business, which was of great significance throughout the 1870s, 1880s, and 1890s in north central and northern Wisconsin and provided work for numerous Wisconsinites, especially immigrants, and made fortunes for those in control of the business.[2]

During this era Wisconsin continued to be a state populated overwhelmingly by immigrants and their children. In 1870 68 percent of Wisconsinites were foreign-born or had one or both parents who were foreign-born.[3] Yet Wisconsin politics during this period, as in others, did not become a battle between immigrants and their children against the rest of the population, though ethnic and religious divisions were still key. Voting behavior was instead grounded in a range of ethnic-religious loyalties not necessarily defined by one's status as an immigrant. At this time groups tended to keep to themselves, and marriage outside the ethnic group was rare. These differing cultures and values led to fierce and lasting party loyalties. The classic analysis, articulated best by Roger Wyman, holds true: electoral politics in Wisconsin between the Civil War and the Progressive Era was "based fundamentally upon ethnic and religious divisions in the population."[4]

Thus the core of Democratic strength remained German Americans, especially Catholics, but it also included, among others, substantial numbers of Irish Americans as well as Catholic Dutch Americans and, in time, Polish Americans. Republican strength lay among Protestant Scandinavian immigrants and their children, Yankees and those of British origin, Dutch Protestants, Belgian Catholics, and increasingly, as the century unfolded, German American Protestants. Indeed, the latter's slow drift toward the Republican Party was essential to that party's victories in this period.[5] Most Catholics, estimated to have been 15–20 percent of the population by 1880 and 25–30 percent by century's end, were Democrats; Protestants, except the divided Protestant Germans, were overwhelmingly Republicans.[6]

While voting behavior was closely and continually linked with ethnic, religious, and cultural divisions, the actual control of the political parties in Wisconsin lay mostly in the hands of the famous Bourbons of the age—big businessmen whose political concerns lay in making money for their particular economic interests. This was particularly true of the Yankee-dominated Republican Party, though it was riven with numerous factional battles as different economic interests clashed. Though major economic forces were long involved with the Republican Party, Wisconsin Republican origins were at first largely ideological, grounded in opposition to the extension of slavery. However, subsidies for railroad and canal interests from the Republican

Congress during the Civil War helped Wisconsin Republicans. Later, other big business interests, which certainly did not always agree—thus the abundance of factionalism among the Republicans—controlled the party and used it for their economic advantage.[7]

It was a rather curious situation in which ethnic-religious divisions created the basic voting patterns in the state, while key business interests in the Republican Party kept Wisconsin on a track that was decidedly pro-business, especially big business. One example of an influential Republican of the era was Matthew Carpenter, who came from Vermont and eventually became a highly successful Wisconsin lawyer and U.S. senator. Intelligent and charming, he began his political career in 1868 as a Radical Republican very critical of southern whites and their resistance to Reconstruction after the Civil War. Before he died in 1881 he had evolved into an ardent pro-business Republican.

An even more famous Republican of the time was the remarkable, semiliterate Philetus Sawyer. Originally from Vermont as well, Sawyer came to Wisconsin as a young man and became hugely successful in the lumber business that was so important to the state in the second half of the nineteenth century. He served ten years in the U.S. House of Representatives (1865–75) and then two terms in the Senate (1881–93). He proved to be a powerful influence in Republican politics for business interests not only in Wisconsin but also in Washington, and he was respected and feared in both places.[8]

FROM 1861 TO 1872

The first decade or so after 1860 was particularly good for the Republicans, but not easy. Lincoln's impressive 56.6 percent of the presidential vote in 1860 was nearly repeated by Louis Harvey's robust victory with 54.2 percent in the gubernatorial election of 1861. His campaign ran on support for Lincoln and opposition to slavery but did not express interest in addressing issues of equality between the races. Originally from Connecticut, this southeastern Wisconsinite defeated Democrat Benjamin Ferguson for the governorship. The campaign was an ugly one, with the Democrats opposing emancipation of the slaves and concentrating on fanning a less-than-noble fear of "Negro mongrelization." Harvey died soon after his election when he fell into a Tennessee river while on an aid mission to Wisconsin soldiers. He was succeeded by Lieutenant Governor Edward Solomon, a German immigrant whom the Republicans had nominated to help them with German American voters.

Then and thereafter Wisconsin Democrats were divided in their sentiments on the war. Many supported it while remaining loyal to the Democratic Party; others were open "Copperheads," opposed to the war, and sometimes

bitterly so. Copperhead strength was real in Wisconsin. A La Crosse publisher, Brick Pomeroy, led the antiwar effort, which was rooted in the Irish
and German American feeling that fighting over slavery and blacks was not
worth anyone's life. In response, Republican denunciation of the Copperheads and their wing of the Democratic Party in Wisconsin was plentiful,
though there was little persecution of individual Copperheads.[9]

By 1862 things were not sanguine for the Republicans. The war was not
going particularly well, the economy was not booming, the draft was in effect,
and feelings of racism were often raw. Fortunately for Governor Solomon,
he did not have to run for election in 1862 since things otherwise did not go
well for the Republicans at the polls in 1862. Democrats gained seats in both
houses of the state legislature, and half the state's six congressional districts
elected Democrats. Indeed, the Democrats received 50.9 percent of the total
vote for Congress. The Republicans did still manage to stay in control of
the state legislature. The election results would have been much worse for
the Republicans overall were it not for the substantial soldier vote, which
went Republican by more than 80 percent, a margin that provoked not a
little suspicion of fraud.[10]

The 1863 elections in Wisconsin, however, turned out well for the party
of Lincoln. The battlefield tide had begun to shift, and the Republican voter
operation to reach Wisconsin soldiers in the field was excellent. James Taylor
Lewis, a Columbus, Wisconsin, lawyer originally from New York, was elected
governor with a record 59.6 percent of the vote. He defeated Democrat
Henry Palmer, a successful Milwaukee lawyer and businessman who had a
great deal to do with the creation of Northwestern Mutual Life Insurance
Corporation. There was a big Republican victory all the way down the ballot line, and the Democrats, who had little to offer except racist prejudice, fell
into serious disarray, splitting into contentious factions.[11]

This did not mean the Democrats went away. In the case of Wisconsin
during the Civil War, these voters continued to be a substantial minority.
In 1864 Lincoln, riding the tide of a war now unmistakably being won and
advantaged by a large soldier vote (82 percent), carried Wisconsin by about
56 percent of the total, a comfortable margin. Yet the Democrats, with candidate General George McClellan, still mustered 44 percent, which was actually a little larger percentage than in 1860.[12]

The draft was intensely unpopular in Wisconsin and even led to riots in the
eastern—German American—part of the state, where there was no love for
Lincoln or his war. McClellan, for example, carried Milwaukee with almost
67 percent of the vote, a substantial improvement from the Democrats' 54

percent in 1860. Democratic Milwaukee mayor Abner Kirby freely denounced Lincoln and the war. Sample German Protestant precincts around the state agreed, giving McClellan an average of 63.5 percent of their votes.[13]

By 1864 voting patterns were well-established and stable between the two parties in most areas of Wisconsin. In my representative sample, Democratic and Republican voting in Wisconsin in 1864 was closely associated with the 1860 vote.[14] This situation, these party loyalties, continued into the post–Civil War years.

In 1865, 1867, and 1869 Republican Lucius Fairchild was elected and twice reelected governor. Fairchild (known as "Lush") was a fascinating figure. From Ohio, he came to Madison a poor student, and then headed to California upon learning of the gold rush. That western experience was his college, and when he returned to Wisconsin he ran for political office as a Democrat, following family tradition. He was elected clerk of court for Dane County in 1858 but was defeated in 1860. Soon after that he enlisted in the army, which transformed him physically (he lost an arm at the Battle of Gettysburg) and politically (he became a committed Republican for whom party and nation were one). Eventually made a general in the war, he was unusually popular with fellow soldiers and, later, many others at home. In 1863 he was elected Wisconsin's secretary of state as a Republican, and his gubernatorial career began in 1866.

Lucius Fairchild, governor 1866–72
(Wisconsin Historical Society, WHi-6601)

Fairchild always ran as a former Union military officer, noting his loyalty and sacrifice for the Union in the Civil War. The Democrats never could compete with Fairchild, who lost his left arm in battle for the nation, and Fairchild never let the Democrats forget their decidedly mixed enthusiasm for the war. To be sure, his opponent in 1865, Harrison Hobart, had an impressive war record of his own. He had been captured by the Confederates, escaped, and then joined Sherman's March to the Sea. But he had both of his arms.

Nor was it easy for such Democratic candidates as Hobart, John Tallmadge (1867), or Charles Robinson (1869) to avoid the fact that Fairchild, as a former Democrat, represented the kind of people whose change of loyalty had consigned their party to minority status. John Tallmadge, a Milwaukee merchant, came the closest to winning in 1869, holding Fairchild to only 51.7 percent of the vote. Charles Robinson did well also, getting 46.8 percent, but the Green Bay publisher, Civil War veteran, and general businessman could not beat Fairchild, who campaigned that year on the importance of Wisconsin getting more internal improvements to make its rivers more navigable. In the end, though, Fairchild also suffered a downfall. It turned out that the ruling elites of the Republican Party in the 1870s and 1880s were not interested in promoting him to the Senate and chose instead more dependable allies of big business.[15]

The most significant feature of the 1865 election was the defeat of yet another black suffrage referendum. It garnered 46 percent of the vote, but the results showed that there was still much opposition, even in Republican circles, to giving blacks full citizenship. For example, while Governor Fairchild carried Madison and Dane County, the suffrage amendment did not. No wonder Fairchild, after endorsing the suffrage amendment, studiously avoided treating it as a major campaign issue, even as his Democratic critics strove to make it one.[16]

Although Fairchild and other Republicans reigned, both in the statehouse and as representatives to Washington, they all won by modest margins. Ulysses Grant won the nation and Wisconsin in his first election for president in 1868 and did better than Fairchild, not surprisingly, given Grant's iconic status as the winning Union general of the Civil War.[17] He got 56.2 percent in Wisconsin as he defeated New York's Horatio Seymour. Grant ran surprisingly well in German Milwaukee, garnering 59 percent of the vote.[18] But my examination of German Protestant rural precincts statewide in shows Seymour still won a minimum of two-thirds of German Protestant voters. Meanwhile, the high association of 1860 and 1868 Democratic and Republican voting in my representative sample of places in Wisconsin underlines again the basic electoral stability in the state.[19]

The early 1870s brought intimations of change in the electoral scene. In 1871 Republican C. C. Washburn, a wealthy La Crosse businessman, was elected governor. His was a spectacular Horatio Alger story involving business failures as well as triumphs before he found great success in the flour business. Washburn also served four and a half years in the Civil War and experienced deep personal tragedy when his young wife had to be committed to an asylum for the rest of her life. Washburn's margin was typical for gubernatorial elections of the time, narrow at 53 percent. His Democratic opponent, James Doolittle, challenged the control of Wisconsin politics by big business and voiced complaints of many in Wisconsin about the arrogance of the railroads, on which most everyone in such an agricultural state was deeply dependent. He also criticized the Republican legislature for its efforts to regulate drinking more tightly, a policy that caused consternation in German Wisconsin. Now issues besides the Civil War and the often futile search for internal improvement money were beginning to surface, though as yet there was no discernable electoral impact.[20]

Nationally, reform elements in the early 1870s were raising their heads, often in the ruling Republican Party. Reformers complained about politics as usual, which was proving to be often corrupt and rarely centered on a broader public interest. These concerns led some national Republicans to turn against the increasingly corrupt Grant administration, in some cases, such as in 1872, even to support eccentric reformer Horace Greeley, Grant's opponent in his second presidential election. This unease on the national scene, however, did not manifest itself at the Wisconsin polls.[21] Grant carried Wisconsin by the usual margin, with 54.6 percent of the electorate supporting him.[22] The Republican and Democratic votes in 1872 correlated closely with their parties' respective votes in previous elections in the 1860s, emphasizing again the electoral system's stability.[23]

THE 1873 SURPRISE AND THE REPUBLICAN RECOVERY

The calm of Wisconsin voting behavior, however, with its close but steady Republican margins, came to an unexpected halt in the 1873 election. Suddenly the Republicans were turned out, and the Reform Party, composed of Democrats and reform Republicans, swept into power. Its candidate for governor, William R. Taylor, unseated Governor Washburn. From Cottage Grove in Dane County, Taylor was a successful farmer who had served on the Dane County Board and for seventeen years had been the county's superintendent

William Taylor and other reformers, 1873 (Wisconsin Historical Society, WHi-24110)

of poor relief. He was well-known as "Farmer Taylor" and had an established appeal.[24]

Taylor received 55 percent of the vote. This victory was really quite astounding. Straight party voting was a way of life in this period, and the majority of Wisconsin voters in the 1860s and early 1870s were reflexively Republican. The Reform Party's victory margin came from defecting Republicans, some unhappy with the national economic recession in 1873, others discontented with a Republicanism grown stale and often corrupt. Versions of the Reform Party popped up in other midwestern states at the same time, including Iowa, Illinois, and Minnesota, a reminder, often needed, that Wisconsin was not, and is not, an island.

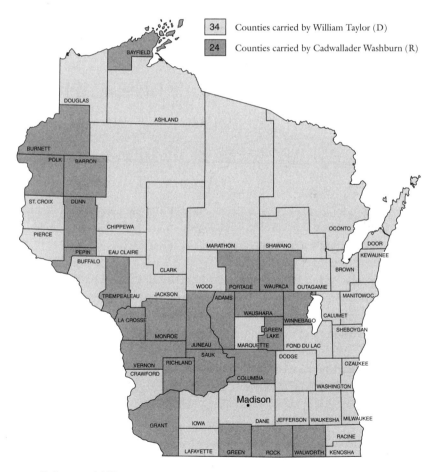

1873 Gubernatorial Vote

Granted, several issues besides discontent with Republican rule and the national economic decline also affected the Wisconsin election. One was the continuing grievances over the railroads, especially their high fees, which the economic recession only aggravated. Taylor knew this situation bothered many farmers, and in his campaign he promised relief. Then there was, once again, the matter of alcohol. In 1872 the Republican Wisconsin legislature had passed the Graham Law, which tried to control the number of bars in Wisconsin, charged a bond of $2,000 for each liquor license, made licensees liable for what happened in their taverns, and set firm penalties for drunken behavior.

Such regulations were not always controversial in themselves, but it was widely understood in Wisconsin that they were an opening wedge for those who sought to curtail drinking in the state, raising the old challenges to German Americans in particular and encouraging them to unite in opposing such regulations and the Republicans who had advanced them. Nor was the Republicans' failure to renominate the German American state treasurer, and select a Norwegian instead, a wise or well-timed move.

Taylor gladly accepted support from beer and alcohol interests (organized as the Wisconsin Association for the Protection of Personal Liberty) as well as some railroad interests, which thought he was a milder reformer than some others waiting in the wings. Most of all, though, Taylor's agricultural credentials appeared to have helped him. He was a former organizer for the then-popular Grange and had been president of the state agriculture society, which was at the time becoming well known and respected in farm circles in this overwhelmingly agricultural state.

The pattern of the vote is noteworthy. One would assume from the fore-going discussion that it was in rural areas that Taylor did better than the usual Democratic candidates. That was certainly the case. This was especially noticeable among the German American Protestant voters who were by no means unanimously in the Democratic camp at that point. A dramatic (and temporary) shift to the Democrats among German American Protestants in rural and small town areas occurred, the average town going for Taylor with 78.4 percent of the vote. Many did so with percentages in the 80s and even 90s. A striking example was the shift in Schleswig in Manitowoc County, which went 99.1 percent for Taylor, an almost 30 percent gain for the Democratic candidate for governor over the 1871 gubernatorial election. But big gains also came in urban areas, where the Depression of 1873, the Graham Law, and the presence of middle-class reform Republicans led to plenty of defections from the Republican ticket. On average, in the larger Wisconsin cities Taylor obtained a record 58.5 percent of the total. The figure in Milwaukee was an overwhelming 79.3 percent for Taylor.[25]

The governor's race of 1875 was particularly interesting because incumbent Taylor fought so hard to stay on. But the Republicans had learned their lessons. They acted as if they had never heard of the Graham Law regulating taverns; they mobilized all railroad interests and investors they could to get rid of Taylor, even though he had proved to be no radical railroad reformer; and they used the lingering recession for their side this time.

The Republicans were also shrewd in choosing their nominee for governor, Harrison Ludington. Ludington was a megarich merchant and lumber businessman, four-time mayor of Milwaukee, and staunch opponent of the Graham Law. Still, Ludington barely made it in with 50.1 percent of the vote, and the rest of the Republican ticket lost for one last time.[26] Analysis of the vote for governor shows how quickly the old Republican pattern resumed. German Protestant areas dropped nearly 8 percent in their Democratic vote, German Catholic areas fell 5 percent, and Milwaukee was some 26 percent less Democratic than it had been in 1873. A comparison of the pre-Taylor 1871 with the 1875 Republican and Democratic vote in my sample also demonstrates how firmly matters had returned to normal.[27]

For decades to follow, Republicans had nothing to do with the alcohol issue. And they certainly did not bring it up during the presidential election of 1876. This famous—or infamous—race in which Republicans and Democrats competed nationally over who could steal the most votes did eventually result in the election of Republican Rutherford Hayes of Ohio to the presidency. He lost the popular vote but won by the narrowest of Electoral College margins. While all the corruption was not a Wisconsin story, the pattern of very close elections in the state was repeated. Hayes eked out a 51.3 percent majority in the two-party vote, running best in nonurban areas, and once again losing Milwaukee.[28]

THE GREENBACKS

One reaction to the turbulent economic times of the 1870s was the surge of support for the Greenback Party, a national party of protest that first appeared in the United States in the 1870s as an expression of farmers' discontent but gradually fused with some urban labor elements. The Greenback Party of the 1870s saw itself devoted to helping farmers, workers, and small businessmen by promoting inflation to cut their indebtedness. Greenbacks wanted to create inflation by greatly increasing the supply of money, thereby making everything cheaper. Their proposed means of doing that was to issue paper money, greenbacks. This idea had a significant champion in Wisconsin in the person of Edward P. Allis, a former Republican and major industrialist who would later become well-known as the founder of Allis-Chalmers Manufacturing Company.

The Greenback Party ran a national campaign in 1876, but its candidate, Peter Cooper, did poorly, and his campaign got lost in the close contest—and a legendary struggle over the election results—between Republican Hayes and Democrat Samuel Tilden. Cooper's national campaign effort came out of a series of independent state campaigns that had preceded it and then, in 1876, paralleled it. In 1877 Greenbacks made an even greater effort, this time entirely in statewide contests. Though in some cases Greenback candidates did much better than they had done in 1876, they routinely lost, ending Republican Party concern over their campaigns and candidates. Wisconsin, as well as other states, saw the Greenback Party at its height in 1877.

In 1877 Allis decided the time had come for him to make his bid for governor on the Greenback ticket. He had to be taken seriously by both parties in an age of economic turbulence; he was too important a figure to be dismissed as loony and irrelevant. The Democrats nominated James A. Mallory, and the Republicans turned to William E. Smith, another Milwaukee businessman and one of the founders of the state Republican Party. In the contest, the "old" issues of 1873 and the former reform Republican–Democratic coalition, already pretty frayed by defeat in 1875, were forgotten. Instead, the two main parties drew on their traditional ethnic and religious loyalists while competing with each other to defend "sound" money and attack the paper money inflation candidacy of Allis. The Republicans assumed that this was a formula for Republican victory if Allis drew equally from partisans of both parties on election day.[29]

And as it turned out, there was no particular connection between areas of Greenback Party appeal and areas of either Republican or Democratic strength. Allis hurt both parties. The Republicans got only 44.8 percent of the three-party total vote while the Democrats did worse at 40.1 percent. Allis received an impressive 14.9 percent, and the Greenbacks elected thirteen members to the Wisconsin Assembly. Allis and the Greenback Party demonstrated the rural and small town origins of Greenback discontent, receiving close to 20 percent of the vote in my sampled rural areas and 23 percent in the smaller cities. But Allis garnered only 9.6 percent of Milwaukee's votes and generally ran poorly in other larger cities.[30]

The Greenback Party never built an enduring constituency. Its electoral appeal varied from place to place and from election to election. Importantly, it never succeeded in cracking the resistance of most of Wisconsin's German Americans. There might have been some possibilities here since, as we know, Protestant German American areas in this period were not always loyal to either the Republican or Democratic parties. Thus, for example, as seen in my sample, they displayed no consistent support for either party in the 1871 or 1875 gubernatorial races. While this fact pleased neither party, the Greenbacks did not benefit from the situation. Support for the Greenback Party in German American areas was always very small. German American voters in Wisconsin had a well-deserved reputation for economic conservatism.[31]

On the one hand, the limited but not negligible flare-up of Greenbackism reminds us that at certain points, and with some voters, the ethnic-religious nature of Wisconsin voting behavior could be cracked. On the other hand, the German American example illustrates how tough this was to do. In the end, the fairly quick demise of the Greenback movement, modest in electoral terms in the first place, shows that the traditional ways in Wisconsin voting were too robust and enduring for this economic movement to overcome, for better or for worse.

THE LATER 1870S AND EARLY 1880S

The election of 1877 proved to be an important election because it was the moment when the Democratic Party slipped away from any reform Republican influence. Then it sank into old (and losing) patterns and was solidly controlled by conservative business elites. Quarrels between business elites and reformers of various sorts had been the story in the party from 1873 on, but by 1877 these disputes were over. Reformers were passed by in the fight against Allis for the sound dollar.[32]

State elections of 1879 and the presidential election of 1880 confirmed the weak Democratic situation. In 1879 Republican William E. Smith sailed to victory again. He garnered 53 percent of the vote while his Democratic opponent, James G. Jenkins, a Milwaukee lawyer, got only 40 percent. This decisive victory reduced the Democratic Party to deep minority status. The Greenback Party remained a proverbial fly in the ointment, though Allis was gone from the ballot. Its candidate for governor, Reuben May, picked up 6.9 percent of the three-party total vote. His total signaled that underground discontent continued in the Wisconsin electoral scene, though the presidential contest of 1880 offered scant evidence of it.[33] That contest produced a vote that was by then quite standard in Wisconsin: a victory for James Garfield, the Republican dark horse from Ohio. Garfield, with 54 percent, beat Winfield Hancock of New York, who trailed well behind with 43 percent while other party candidates won just 3 percent of the vote.[34]

This outcome was almost exactly duplicated in the 1880 Wisconsin vote for members of the House of Representatives and suggested that there was now a more definite Republican majority, one as large as at any time in the badger state's history. Key to this development was the continuing slow and uncertain drift of Protestant German Americans away from the Democratic Party. By this time about half were voting Republican. (German Roman Catholics, however, continued to cast heavily Democratic ballots.) Yet this reality was also something of an illusion for two reasons. First, serious third-partyism was about to reappear, and suddenly; second, the Democrats in Wisconsin were about to begin a steady movement forward that was to last until the depression of 1893.

The election for governor in 1881 was historic in terms of the growth of third partyism. The victor, Republican Jeremiah Rusk, known affectionately as "Uncle Jerry," was a fascinating character. He had a storybook life of pioneering, generalship in the Civil War, and service in political office at the local, state, and, after he was governor, federal levels, as secretary of agriculture under President Benjamin Harrison. His achievements were all the

Jeremiah Rusk, governor 1882–89
(Wisconsin Historical Society, WHi-48605)

more impressive because Rusk, though shrewd and experienced in life, was distinctly uneducated and notoriously uncouth in nineteenth-century drawing room terms. His record of electoral success, however, was impressive. He was elected governor not just in 1881 but also in 1884 and again in 1886; the popular governor from Viroqua served seven years.

What stood out in Wisconsin electoral history was not Rusk's election in 1881 but the picture of the vote, for Rusk, in winning, did not muster even 50 percent of the vote, and his Democratic opponent, N. D. Fratt, barely made 40 percent. This was the case not just because Allis was again running on the Greenback ticket, snaring 4 percent, but because for the first time there appeared a candidate for the newly formed Prohibition Party, T. D. Kanouse, who rolled up an impressive 8 percent of the total.[35]

THE PROHIBITION PARTY

Enduring multipartyism began in Wisconsin in 1881, and a player on that scene for the next several decades was the new Prohibition Party. The entire phenomenon of the Prohibition Party's existence in Wisconsin is highly paradoxical. It is no shock that the Party was never very successful; after all, the idea of prohibition was hardly popular in Wisconsin—at any time. Wisconsin was, and is, a drinking state with bars seemingly everywhere. Its drinking culture undoubtedly traces back to the large German and Irish populations that settled in the state in the first half of the nineteenth century and were accepting of alcohol consumption. And by the later nineteenth century the drinking culture had spread well beyond these groups. Yet there were plenty of critics. The pietistic were appalled that Wisconsin taverns were open on Sunday, that many served virtually any age male, and that some were busy locations for various forms of "vice" as well as dubious political associations and machinations. In this soil the Prohibition Party took root, since neither of the two major political parties was so electorally stupid as to promote prohibition in Wisconsin.

The national Prohibition Party was created in 1869 and at first was controlled by those whose focus was almost exclusively on prohibition, politicians known as "narrow gaugers." There was no doubt about their moral fervor at the time, nor was there any doubt when the party became a significant player in Wisconsin voting twelve years later. Critics then and since have complained that the Prohibition Party and the much larger prohibition movement it represented were a troubling example of moralism in Wisconsin politics. This is a somewhat strange complaint, however, because all politics involves people's moral judgments and opinions; it is either about proposing people do or pay for what others think is right or opposing such actions in the name of an alternative notion of what is right. So the issue was not really a question of the presence of morality in politics but of *which* morality ought to be in politics. To prohibition crusaders, their morality was justified, far more so than the morality of Wisconsin's drinking culture.[36]

After the Republicans learned in 1873 that trying to curb the drinking business was not a winning formula, prohibitionists in Wisconsin seemed to be without any hopeful political direction. The Democrats, so closely tied to German Americans and Irish Americans, offered no hope. And yet in Wisconsin and elsewhere in the United States, prohibitionist sentiment was growing, especially among many middle-class women in church groups and other organizations. The pressure was building. By 1881 in Wisconsin, a state that also, after all, did have a pietistic population and was a longtime reformist haven, there were enough men ready to join reformer women to make the commitment for the prohibition effort and willing to enter electoral politics.

The story of the Prohibition Party at the polls in Wisconsin is an interesting one. Its relative glory days were in the first decade. It got about 8 percent of the vote in its first gubernatorial race in 1881. In 1886 it still got 6 percent of the vote for governor, with John Olin as its candidate. Olin, a prominent businessman and great benefactor of the City of Madison, reflected the Prohibition Party's brief period in the 1880s when it attracted significant elite support. Some of these supporters were not insignificant figures, and they indicated real bases of strength. Thereafter, though, the party, failing to gain momentum, went downhill. By the 1890s the party was greatly diminished and pulled much less of the vote, usually well under 5 percent and often no more than 1–3 percent.

However, even doing this well year after year in Wisconsin is notable. In rural areas the party never was able to get anywhere close to the approximately 8 percent it got in 1881. That was inevitable given the tremendous proportion of the rural population that was German American. Among German Roman Catholics in rural areas and small towns in the sample the Prohibition Party rarely could get as much as 1 percent of the vote. Among Protestant German Americans the picture was not much better; the party had no appeal in these quarters. In Madison the Prohibition Party did better, often garnering 3–5 percent; but in German Milwaukee, apart from a 2 percent showing in the top year of 1881, the party could not muster even 1 percent. The party always ran better in villages than in rural areas. Its strongest base of support, until its decline late in the century and after, was in Swedish American areas, reflected a long tradition among pious Swedish Americans of opposition to drink. Another area of considerable strength, of course, was in the areas where many Yankees and people of British origin settled, the old "reform" region of southeastern Wisconsin especially. There a 6–9 percent vote for the party was standard until the turn of the century. Overall, the Prohibition Party's appeal was more robust in Wisconsin than it was nationally, where it got 2 percent in its top showing in 1892 and normally less than 2 percent. By 1920 the party's national showing was less than 1 percent.

From the first, the Republicans rightly feared that much of the Prohibitionist vote would come from potential Republican voters. Certainly it did in the 1880s. Yet the Republican Party leaders well remembered 1873 and were prepared to pay the price of lost votes to the Prohibition Party rather than take up that cause themselves and lose yet more votes. Robert La Follette, in his days as an orthodox Republican, illustrated the situation well. Like other Republican politicians, La Follette was disliked by prohibitionists, who noted that as a young district attorney of Dane County La Follette carefully avoided alienating most citizens and did not enforce Madison's Sunday no-drinking laws.

Over time the Prohibition Party changed, leaving behind the "narrow gauge" approach, exploring the possibilities of joining with the Populists in 1890 and more and more linking prohibition with other causes such as exploitation of women at home and in the workplace. At no time was the party's journey easy. The party always lacked money and organization to match the main parties. Organization did improve in some areas even as the party was simply out of commission in others, including Milwaukee. The party's views were quite rigid regarding drinking, of course, and that made for problems working with others who were interested in addressing in a somewhat less drastic fashion Wisconsin's longstanding problems with alcohol. Thus coalitions proved hard to form.[37]

The actual progress of prohibition in Wisconsin was another story. After all, as late as 1918 both major parties' platforms avoided discussion of prohibition. Still, by 1900 there began to be increased enforcement of the expanding number of local laws restricting or even eliminating the serving and/or selling of alcohol. By 1917, before the United States entered World War I, a substantial number—still less than half the population—of Wisconsinites lived in dry areas. Significantly, after a major battle Madison had voted to become dry. With the coming of the war, dry efforts soared and so did prohibition's success as it became simple to link Germans and the enemy Germany with drinking as associated evils. Finally, in 1919 the Eighteenth Amendment to the U.S. Constitution instituted prohibition nationally. Wisconsin's wartime legislature voted for prohibition over the objections of the minority Democratic and Socialist legislators. Very soon, however, this amendment and this decision were to prove hugely unpopular and be widely flouted in Wisconsin.[38]

THE 1880S CONTINUED

The picture of tight electoral competition in Wisconsin grew sharper as the 1880s proceeded. The 1882 elections saw Wisconsin consistently behaving within the national pattern, as Democrats made striking gains in congressional races. In Wisconsin Democrats received a large plurality of the congressional and state legislative vote, winning twenty-five seats in the Assembly (though remaining a minority). Wisconsin Democrats again obtained the plurality of votes for Congress in 1884, but they did not do so well in either the presidential or gubernatorial races. As usual, the Republicans won in the presidential contest in Wisconsin, with James G. Blaine edging out the national winner, Democrat and New York Governor Grover Cleveland.[39] Blaine managed only 50.4 percent of the vote in Wisconsin, showing a weakening of the Republican grip on the state's electorate. The non–major party vote went to the Greenback and Prohibition candidates, who together garnered 3.8 percent.

Nationally, Blaine was identified with the Stalwarts, the conservative wing of the Republican Party, and this fact alienated some Republicans and many independents. He was also dogged with unhappiness over the corruption that was now plaguing the long-time Republican rule in Washington. These problems did lead nationally to some defections of liberal Republicans and may have made a difference in Blaine's crucial loss of New York to Cleveland, who was admired in that state as an honest governor. Another factor that did not help was the unusual mobilization of Democrats in many parts of the country in response to the declaration by a Blaine partisan that the Democratic Party was the party of "rum, Romanism, and rebellion."[40]

In any case, in Wisconsin the vote for the governorship went about the same as it did for the presidency. Governor Rusk won reelection over Democrat N. D. Fratt, who got 45 percent, as well as over the Greenback and Prohibition candidates. Voting followed familiar party lines, and the consequence was that the Republicans continued to be narrow winners in the state. There was, however, nothing comfortable about their situation, and they knew it. Meanwhile, the Democrats remained a strong, but very frustrated, second party.

Rusk's course did not prove smooth. More and more of southeast Wisconsin was industrializing, and there, as in the nation as a whole, signs of

industrial unrest were increasing as workers began to resist their harsh working conditions and decry their low pay. In 1886 Rusk called out the state
militia to deal with a strike in Milwaukee of 15,000 largely Polish American
workers who sought an eight-hour work day. The nature of the situation that
led to this action is even today fiercely debated, but there is no question that
the violence that came from clashes between the National Guard and strikers
produced not only several deaths but lingering, terrible bitterness. Hard
feelings about the conflict lasted a long time, with many middle-class citizens
in Milwaukee and throughout Wisconsin lauding Rusk, even as he became
a hated figure in Polish American Milwaukee. It is no wonder that the 1886
election was unusually intense.

Another reason for that tension was the sudden emergence in Wisconsin
of the People's Party, organized in part by the Knights of Labor and Robert
Schilling, who would go on to become secretary of the national People's
Party. This new Wisconsin party was formed out of anger over Governor
Rusk and his use of the state militia, and it succeeded in capturing Milwaukee County in the elections (with 45 percent of the multiparty vote), marking the first time a third party did so without support from the two major
parties. A study of the insurgent party's voters in Milwaukee shows that the
People's Party drew great support from Polish Americans and picked up the
majority of German American voters as well as a good chunk of Irish Americans, a combination in Milwaukee that proved (for a moment) irresistible.[41]

Yet in 1886 the People's Party did not get as much support from the rest
of Wisconsin, which was unlike Milwaukee in so many ways. The People's
Party ended with 7.5 percent of the state's vote, though that combined with
an unusually strong 6 percent from the still-determined Prohibition Party
guaranteed that both main political parties would fall well below 50 percent.
The People's Party just could not establish a connection with the German
population of the state, getting less than 1 percent of the German Protestants
in my sample and not much more among German Catholics in rural areas
and small towns; nor was it able to do any better with other groups outside the bigger cities. Larger cities were its base, but Wisconsin was not an
urban state.[42]

This was far from the end of the story for the People's Party in Wisconsin.
And while its endeavors in 1886 complicated the results, the party did not
stop Uncle Jerry Rusk from gaining the governor's chair once again with
46.5 percent compared to an even weaker 40 percent for Democrat Gilbert
Woodward of La Crosse. So though the voters of Wisconsin appeared in 1886
to be splintering, when the ballots were counted the Republicans stayed on

top, a result affirmed in the voting for both the state legislature and for
Congress. Like the earlier Greenback Party, the People's Party showed that
temporary—and localized—economic issues and grievances could break down
the established patterns of Wisconsin voting, grounded as they were in traditional ethnic-religious loyalties. It also demonstrated, however, that it could
not do so for most of the state and could not do so for very long. The stark
truth is that the People's Party failed in Wisconsin.[43]

Also in 1886 the legislature put before the voters a measure to allow women
to vote on school matters. This event was partially the result of a rejuvenated
women's suffrage movement in the state. The remarkable Olympia Brown, a
Universalist minister, assumed the presidency of the organized movement in
the 1880s and undertook a much-needed revival. This followed a quiescent
period after the founding in 1869, after several failed attempts, of the organization that became the Wisconsin Woman Suffrage Association. While it
had begun grandly in 1869 with the presence of both Susan B. Anthony
and Elizabeth Cady Stanton, the enthusiasm and energy waned very quickly.
The 1870s were not productive for the cause in good part because so many
women activists turned to the struggle for temperance, some women serving
as officers in organizations for both causes.[44]

Before 1869 there had been a few stirrings about women suffrage in Wisconsin, though they were weak compared with those in many states both
east and west of Wisconsin. The oft-cited debate at the University of Wisconsin's Athenaeum Society in 1851 over women's estate included the topic of
suffrage, but that was an unusual public airing of the issue. The Civil War and
the politics around it ended any serious focus on the question until 1865.[45]

The vote on the question of school suffrage for women in 1886 resulted
in confusion in many parts of the state. Many places did not prepare for the
referendum and had no ballots. In the end only 29 percent of citizens who
voted for governor marked ballots on this referendum. Nonetheless, the
measure carried with 53 percent, quite surprising in light of the later 1912 vote
and the adamant opposition of many ethnic groups in Wisconsin to women
participating in politics. Perhaps the measure's success derived in part from
the confusion over this vote in parts of the state that resulted in a low vote.
Certainly it helped that this proposal called for a very limited suffrage only,
one that many men agreed was legitimately relevant for women.

Examination of the results, partial and fragmentary as they sometimes are,
found quite predictable voting. In my samples, German American precincts
of all kinds overwhelmingly voted no; German Protestant areas were 80 percent no, German Catholic areas 64 percent no. Thus the town of Jackson in

Washington County voted 94.6 percent no, Fredonia in Ozaukee 95.1 percent no, Leroy in Dodge County 89.5 percent no, Schleswig in Manitowoc County 95.5 percent no, and the City of Appleton 82.1 percent no. Some other ethnic groups were also equally uninterested. Belgian Brussels in Door County voted 90.9 percent no.

However, support came from Yankee and British-settled areas such as the cities of Beloit, which voted 80.7 percent yes, and Janesville, 93.2 percent yes, and from rural Linden in Iowa County, 92 percent yes. The "good government" center of Madison voted 84.5 percent yes. More often than not, on this vote cities proved more sympathetic to women's suffrage than did rural areas and villages; rural areas rejected the referendum, with only 39.9 percent in favor on average, while even small cities voted yes 62.2 percent of the time on average. Mostly sentiment followed predictable ethnic lines. Sometimes, however, no clear picture emerged. Scandinavian views, for example, were mixed. Some areas were sympathetic, such as the town of Stockholm in Pepin County, which voted 98.7 percent yes, but others, such as the village of Christiana in Vernon County, voted 93.7 percent no. Overall, though, Scandinavians' sentiments contrasted with Germans'. On average Norwegian towns and villages voted 54.4 percent in favor of women's suffrage on education issues, Swedish 45.2 percent.[46]

The irony was that even though the referendum passed, the law went nowhere in practice. Legal challenges soon arose—just as they so often do today with referenda—and implementation was blocked for fifteen years. The issue was over what "pertaining to school matters" meant and how, in practice, voting on such matters could be accomplished at a general election. The practical matter was that separate ballots for women for school issues would be necessary. Meanwhile, some suffragist activists chose to interpret the law as permitting them to vote a regular ballot for all candidates and referenda, arguing that everything was relevant to school matters in one sense or another. In some places in the state some women did proceed to vote without opposition; in others it was a different story.

The legal dimension came to the fore in 1887 when Olympia Brown sought to vote in the 1887 election in Racine. Officials there denied her a ballot, insisting that for her to vote in the general election went way beyond her right to vote "pertaining to school matters." She sued. Eventually the Wisconsin Supreme Court, in several cases in the 1887–88 period, held that women could vote "pertaining to school matters" only and that this could be done only with the use of separate ballots. This resolution was no resolution, however, because the state refused to arrange for separate ballots for women to vote on school issues and thus denied women even this limited right to vote. This situation continued until 1901, when the state legislature relented and passed a law allowing for separate ballots for men and women.

At last, in 1902, Wisconsin women had a limited right to vote. Statewide, though, it meant that they could vote only for the state superintendent of instruction. But at the local level in some places, for example in Madison, they were able to have a real impact on elections regarding schools. In an oft-cited example, many women voters participated in a controversial vote over whether to build a new high school in Madison in 1905. A narrow majority of male voters rejected the plan, but a strong majority of women cast their ballots for it and put the referendum over the top.[47]

What the election of 1886 showed, apart from the vote on women suffrage, was the familiar outline of this decade. On the one hand, it was further evidence of the unending reign of the Republicans at the ballot box in Wisconsin. On the other hand, it was another moment in the curious nature of that Republican rule, based as it was on approval of only a minority of voters. All this was reaffirmed in both presidential and gubernatorial elections of 1888, which, in fact, suggested how stable, if not identical, both parties' cohort of voters had been for decades. In my representative sample, the Republican and Democratic votes in 1888 correlate strongly with the 1868 and the 1872 results. The 1888 results are associated less well with the 1860 patterns, since in 1860 matters were not yet firmly settled.[48]

In 1888 Benjamin Harrison carried Wisconsin on his way to unseating President Grover Cleveland.[49] The Republican candidate for governor, William Dempster Hoard, defeated his Democratic opponent, James Morgan, by about the same margin, a modest 6 percent. Hoard as well as his Democratic opponents got less than 50 percent of the vote, the reason being, again, the continuing third-party activity in Wisconsin. The Prohibitionists were still campaigning, and they received about 4 percent of the vote. They were joined this time by a Union Labor ticket, which didn't match the intense response to the People's Party of 1886 coming out of the Milwaukee labor struggles but still appealed to organized labor and its causes. It garnered over 2 percent of the vote, though the party faded quickly thereafter when it was unable to unite with the emerging Socialists to protest the plight of the industrial workingman.

William Hoard proved to be a fateful choice for the Republicans' candidate for governor in 1888. Hoard came to Wisconsin as a young man, and after serving in the Civil War, he made his reputation as a newspaperman, focusing on dairy issues in the age when dairy farming and Wisconsin agriculture were synonymous. He eventually began publishing his famous and widely read *Hoard's Dairyman,* a publication that gave him tremendous name recognition and, in fact, broad and deserved respect among Wisconsin farmers. He seemed the perfect candidate for Wisconsin's business elites who ran the Republican Party. After all, he himself was successful, well-known in farming circles in still-rural Wisconsin, and a widely admired figure.

As usual, ethnic voting patterns in that 1888 gubernatorial election were what mattered, and the connections with well-established ethnic coalitions were firm. Scandinavian and Yankee voters mostly favored the Republicans, and Catholics of all sorts, and a still considerable number of German Protestants, lined up for the Democrats. A deep stability (or rigidity) existed in both parties' voter cohorts, party leadership, and ideological outlook, which reflected both parties' unwillingness to change, governed as both were by elite elements who feared change (and which was certainly part of the reason for the frequent appearance of third parties). These tight party lines are exemplified by the remarkable unity of party correlations on voting for governor and president of the same party in 1888. Republican voters correlated at .997 and Democrats even higher at .999. Everything seemed set. But this was not to last, for the Republicans had made an astonishing mistake in 1888 when they selected William Hoard to be their candidate for governor.[50]

ELEMENTS OF THE VOTE

During this era, 1861–88, ethnic identities remained the key to Wisconsin voting behavior, and German Americans were the crucial group. The slow drift of Protestant Germans toward the Republican Party was evident in the 1870s and 1880s, spurred in part by the active work of the leading German Protestant newspaper, *Die Germanie,* as well as the sense that Protestants belonged with Protestants. But the shift was modest, and connections between Democrats and ethnic German areas remained strong throughout the century. The typical German Protestant town or village still voted Democratic, though its vote was likely split, with the Democrats no longer getting more than 50 to 60 percent. This drift away from the Democrats, however, met its match in the slight countervailing move of Wisconsin voters in general toward the Democrats in the 1880s and early 1890s.[51]

Other factors were at play too. During this period several ethnic groups came into their own as vital elements in the overall electoral picture. Crucial was the emergence of Scandinavian voters, especially Norwegians.[52] Norwegian immigrants began appearing in Wisconsin well before the Civil War. The center of Norwegian Wisconsin, Westby in Trempealeau County, was settled in 1848, but the two largest periods of Norwegian immigration were 1866–73 and 1879–93. Estimates differ as to the overall number of Norwegians that came to the United States, but it may have been as many as a million. Except for Ireland, no country saw as great a percentage of its population migrate to the United States, driven by lack of economic opportunity at home. Most came from struggling inner fjord or central mountain districts of Norway. Another impetus for emigration, however, was the widely disliked, oppressive state-church relationship in Norway that bore down too hard on many families.[53]

Numerous, sometimes quite stirring, accounts of the Norwegian settlement in Wisconsin have been written. As with all pioneers far from home, and not unlike other Wisconsin settlers, theirs was a sometimes trying but often remarkable story. By about 1870 the basic pattern of Norwegian settlement in Wisconsin was established. Norwegians sought to have farms and overwhelmingly chose to live in rural Wisconsin. This group, in fact, proved to be the most rural of all immigrant groups that ventured to America in the nineteenth century. In Wisconsin the Norwegians settled particularly in west central Wisconsin, especially in Trempealeau and Vernon counties, though there were other large concentrations, such as in parts of Dane County.

In general, the land the Norwegians obtained was distinctly inferior to that on which earlier Yankees and then Germans had settled. The reason was quite simply that most came later and the best land in eastern and southern Wisconsin was already taken. Thus it is no surprise that Norwegians as a whole proved less successful economically as farmers than did many others in Wisconsin, a factor that was to play a significant role in Norwegian electoral behavior. And this was not a short-lived reality. The state's 1905 census showed that the average Norwegian farm was worth well below the state average.[54]

A major factor in Norwegian cultural life in the nineteenth century and beyond was religion. With few exceptions, Norwegians were devoted Lutherans, though hardly united. At least fourteen synods or formal groups of Norwegian Lutherans disagreed regarding doctrine, church structure, and the degree of personal piety that was appropriate. These divisions represented significant conflicts in the nineteenth century. Time softened them, however, and by 1917 the main branches of Norwegian Lutheranism united. While Norwegians moved toward unity within their own religious lives, they remained intensely hostile and deeply antagonistic toward Roman Catholics, a bitterness that lasted long after the end of the nineteenth century. Time and again many Norwegian clergy, in sermons and otherwise, abetted the anti-Catholicism that persisted in the Norwegian American culture.[55]

Given Wisconsin's ethnic-religious divides, one might expect that Norwegians in the nineteenth century and after would be pro-Republican. This was not the case among Norwegians who settled before the Civil War, who often voted Democratic. But that changed quickly. From the 1850s on the typical Norwegian American voter in farm areas, villages, and cities became and remained overwhelmingly Republican, embedding themselves in "a culture of Republicanism" and serving as an integral part of the party's coalition of the nineteenth century.[56] Virtually every Norwegian town and village was overwhelmingly Republican (at least 75–80 percent) throughout the post–Civil War period. Voters in Christiana in Vernon County, for example, usually voted less than 5 percent Democratic.[57] The line was drawn first on religious grounds; Democrats turned out to be mostly Catholics. Later, many Norwegians identified general social respectability with the Republican Party. Yet ideology also mattered; Norwegians did not approve of slavery and were commonly devoted to the cause of the Civil War.

At the same time, signs appeared early on that plenty of Norwegian Americans were not comfortable with the plutocratic leadership of the Republican Party. After all, many Norwegians, especially in rural areas, were hardly well-off and were often critical of the railroads and other big businesses. Moreover, many were in rural cooperatives and otherwise showed a strong community orientation. Such attitudes did not lead them toward a Democratic Party that was no more open to their economic concerns than the established Republican Party. It did, however, lead many to embrace a more radical or reform-minded version of Republicanism. This shift began in the 1880s and increased by the end of the century, becoming something of a movement eventually led by Robert La Follette.[58]

Many more Norwegians came to Wisconsin than did Swedes; indeed, almost 10 percent of Wisconsin's population in the 2000 census claimed Norwegian ancestry, and Wisconsin was the fourth-most-Norwegian state after the Dakotas and Minnesota. Yet plenty of Swedes also came. In the United States as a whole about 1.5 million people migrated from Sweden in the years 1850 to 1920.[59] Swedes never constituted 5 percent of Wisconsin's population, though, and they were never the major presence in Wisconsin that they were in Minnesota or Washington State. Nonetheless, in Wisconsin they still were a significant presence, and in the 2000 census about 3 percent of Wisconsin citizens claimed to be of Swedish descent.

Major Swedish immigration to Wisconsin began in the late 1860s. It had as its origin poor economic conditions in Sweden compounded by population growth. In Wisconsin Swedes settled on poorer land, often poorer than Norwegians had, in western and northern counties of Wisconsin. There they lived in closely knit communities and spoke Swedish. As a group, however, the Swedes assimilated to the general culture far faster than many other immigrants, a process pretty much completed by World War I, though some use of Swedish lingered after that.

Swedes were no more religiously united in their Lutheranism than Norwegians were. For Swedes too, Lutheranism meant a deep opposition to Catholicism and Catholics, but it did not mean freedom from often sharp divisions within their general Lutheran commitment.[60] From the beginning, however, there were few political divisions among Swedes. Most were devoted Republicans; their loyalty was rooted partly in an intense dislike of the Democratic Party and its Catholic supporters and partly in many Swedes' pietism, whose home was often the Republican Party. In election after election throughout the nineteenth century, Swedes voted Republican as Roger Wyman has pointed out and my sample confirms.[61]

The strong pietistic streak present in a many Swedes also explained Swedish support for the Prohibition Party. The current of support for the Prohibition Party in some Swedish towns and villages in the 1880s and beyond was real. My sample of largely Swedish places shows that the Prohibition Party drew some 16.5 percent of the vote for governor in 1881, 15 percent in 1886, and 18.8 percent in 1890, well more than the percentage the Democrats received.[62] Yet this attraction was, even at its height a minor one in the larger picture of Swedish American voting behavior, which always was overwhelmingly Republican.

Indeed, Scandinavian Americans, both Norwegians and Swedes, proved central to the continuing rule of the Republicans in Wisconsin in the second half of the nineteenth century. Without their huge support for Republican candidates in election after election, both parties' fates might have been very different in Wisconsin, demonstrating yet again the presence and importance of ethnic- and religious-based voting in this era.

This serves as further example of how divisions in Wisconsin could not be simply characterized as immigrants and their children versus others. What is crucial to know and understand is how each immigrant group and its descendents fit into the complex of interacting groups. For many Scandinavians, they were Luther's children, standing against the dangerous Catholic Church and its often culturally suspect adherents. Thus Scandinavians were consciously Republicans at first and then by tradition. Only with the upheavals of the 1930s and 1940s did this set pattern fade away and much of Scandinavian electoral distinctiveness recede into history.

The Democratic vote in Swedish places was very weak. According to my sample of Swedish areas in Wisconsin in this era, 1888 produced the highest average Democratic vote, a very small 15.3 percent of the total, while 1876's 6.4 percent was more characteristic. The town of Stockholm in Pepin County was 9.6 percent Democratic in 1888 but in the more typical 1880 was 2.6 percent, while the town of Trade Lake in Burnett County was 9.3 percent Democratic in 1888 but more usually in the 4–5 percent range. These percentages are very low and suggest how tight the group coherence was in Swedish areas.[63]

Another important element of the remarkable Wisconsin ethnic mix that appeared in the second half of the nineteenth century was the Polish community. Poles came in great numbers, especially in the later years of the century. In the 2000 census more than 9 percent of Wisconsinites identified themselves to be of Polish descent. Most Poles who came to Wisconsin settled in urban areas, most famously on the south side of Milwaukee. Yet they also went to many other cities, and after 1880 they went wherever hard labor was needed, especially in northern Wisconsin, where lumbering, among other tasks, drew them. Many Poles also settled in rural areas in order to farm. Portage County in the center of Wisconsin became the most Polish county in Wisconsin, and it remains so today. That was true of many of the county's agricultural areas and its main city, Stevens Point. The first Polish town chair was elected in Sharon in Portage County in 1870. In 1914 the first Polish American was elected sheriff of Portage County, and the first Polish American was elected mayor of Stevens Point.

The actual number of Poles who came to Wisconsin will never be accurately known, because most came when Poland was not an independent nation and therefore many were counted by the census as being Prussians, Russians, or Germans. (The country that is now Poland was ruled by Russia and Germany in the years before World War I; its brief interwar period of independence had not yet become a reality.) Many Poles who migrated to Wisconsin sought not only better economic lives but escape from political, cultural (such as forced learning of German), and sometimes religious oppression.

Most Poles were Roman Catholics and often committed to the church. This was without doubt a major part of the reason they quickly became an active part of the Democratic Party coalition in Wisconsin. The exceptions were those Poles who, against the vigorous sentiment of church leaders, showed support for socialism, a phenomenon restricted almost entirely to a portion of Milwaukee Poles. Elsewhere the Democratic allegiance emerged very rapidly. As soon as Poles settled an area, became citizens, and established the place as a legal unit, it became a Democratic stronghold. For example,

Bevent in Marathon County voted 93.3 percent Democratic in its first state election in 1888; Sharon in Portage County was the same at 96.2 percent; and Dodge in Trempealeau County at 84.1 percent.

In general, Poles in Wisconsin were also highly loyal to their group in political terms and as late as 1940 notably more inward-looking than other Wisconsin ethnic groups. Even today, as European ethnic party loyalties of the nineteenth century have been long abandoned, Polish Americans' loyalties to the Democrats have merely softened. It still holds that wherever in Wisconsin Polish Americans dominate, one will likely encounter a Democratic stronghold.[64]

Of course, the behavior of other ethnic groups during this period mattered. German Protestants, as we know, were gradually shifting toward the Republican Party, though the arrival of Polish Americans into the electorate as the century waned helped compensate for the decline of German Protestant Democratic votes.[65] A significant factor in the decline of German Protestant Democratic loyalties was the slow movement of German Americans toward assimilation into American culture. Assimilation was modest in the nineteenth century, however, except in neighborhoods, towns, or villages where German Americans did not predominate. The German language flourished throughout the nineteenth century, though the average German young person soon came to speak both English and German. Close-knit communities, usually built around common religious and/or place of origin, remained the rule outside of the few cites. Wisconsin was full of citizens with one or more parents who were foreign-born—still an astounding 62 percent in 1890, and half were German-born. And a full 31 percent of all white people in Wisconsin in 1890 were foreign-born, again many of them from Germany. Even so, Germans in Wisconsin in the nineteenth century never constituted 50 percent of the state's total population. They got close, but even so, to speak of German Americans in Wisconsin implies a unity that rarely existed and thus could not be brought to life politically.[66]

The complicated voting picture of German Americans in the second half of the nineteenth century is easy to confirm. The range could be remarkable. Take the 1884 election and observe the Democratic percentages in these sample German Protestant towns: Centerville in Manitowoc County 49.8 percent, Meeme in Manitowoc 73.2 percent, Hustisford in Dodge County 80.8 percent, and Auburn in Fond du Lac County 52.7 percent. German Roman Catholic areas were more Democratic but exhibited plenty of variation also: Woodville in Calumet County 86.1 percent, Leroy in Dodge County 56.1 percent, or Calumet in Fond du Lac County 92.3 percent.[67]

Overall the picture was a familiar one even as late as the 1888 gubernatorial election. Correlations showed people who were native-born of native parents correlated positively with the Republicans at .595 and negatively with the Democrats at .544; Scandinavians positively at .510 with the Republicans and negatively with the Democrats at .554; Germans negatively with the Republicans at .593 and positively with the Democrats at .628; Catholics negatively with the Republicans at .646 and positively with the Democrats at .681; Yankee Protestants positively with the Republicans at .344 and negatively with the Democrats at .425.[68]

Anyone interested in voting may wonder, with all the focus on ethnic-religious factors, whether there was evidence of class voting, whether income or wealth were somehow *the* factor or at least a major factor in Wisconsin voting. Student after student of Wisconsin voting has found that when one gets down to specific voting units, religious and ethnic factors were far and away the best predictors of voting in most places and in most years. As Paul Kleppner has stated, and as this study confirms, "Partisan affiliations were not rooted in economic class distinctions. They were political expressions of shared values from the voter's membership in and commitment to ethnic and religious groups."[69]

Still, the question of class lingers. There is no question that income and wealth inequality abounded in nineteenth-century Wisconsin, so there was opportunity for class-based voting. But few signs of it can be found. Thus, in using conventional understandings of our time, had class voting been present, German American areas, which had the best land and most successful farms, might have leaned strongly Republican, and Scandinavian farming areas might have been robustly Democratic. But this was not the case.

Moreover, one of the most important elements in Wisconsin voting as the century wore on was Milwaukee's shift from the Democratic to the Republican column even as the city grew into an industrialized, urban working-class center. Milwaukee had been a steadily Democratic city until the 1879 governor's race, but thereafter it turned Republican and remained so through the 1880s, with the exception of the 1886 election. This shift greatly helped the Republicans statewide, of course. What's more relevant here, however, is that this change confounds easy generalizations about class voting given the voting patterns in that largely German working-class city.[70]

The reason that class is no guide in this period is straightforward. There were no real economic or class issues that divided the parties, and the parties made no effort to distinguish themselves from each other on economic issues. Party cleavages were about ethnic-religious identification and loyalties, not economic matters. After all, both parties were controlled from the top by wealthy businessmen, so it was hardly likely they would promote many conflicts about economic issues. Nationally, divisions arose over tariff policy, and these came into state politics also occasionally, but there is no evidence they had a serious effect in Wisconsin. So since voters rarely experienced significant differences between the two parties on economic or class matters, why would we expect voting behavior to reflect such divisions? If anything, poorer rural voters—and keep in mind that Wisconsin was overwhelmingly rural throughout the nineteenth century—often saw the Republicans as more beneficial to them since they were more likely than the Democrats to favor internal improvements that helped them market their farm products. This was true not just in Wisconsin but throughout the northern United States.[71]

And there were moments, illustrated by the Greenback movement, when economic and class issues broke through established Wisconsin patterns. But few citizens were involved in these exceptions and the moments and movements did not last. One has to return to the start: cultural, ethnic, and religious divisions and the voting loyalties they nurtured were what counted—and counted powerfully—with most voters in the area. They were the keys to Wisconsin voting behavior.

3

The Decisive 1890s

WISCONSIN WAS STILL an overwhelmingly rural state in 1890. The large majority of residents did not live in any county with even a modest-sized city in it, and a majority of those who did live in counties with cities—such as Winnebago with Appleton, Dane with Madison, or Brown with Green Bay—were also rural residents. Only one-third of the state's citizens lived in places with 2,500 people or more, and the second largest city after Milwaukee was La Crosse, with only 25,000 people. Yet by this time the industrial revolution in Wisconsin was well under way. Milwaukee counted over 200,000 citizens, and the city and closely surrounding areas in southeast Wisconsin saw significant growth as industry rapidly expanded. The source of the expanding population was new immigrants as well as Wisconsinites seeking to escape the farming life. Industrial conditions, both in terms of factory work life as well as the general housing and other urban conditions, were often poor in Milwaukee and elsewhere in the industrializing southeast corridor of Wisconsin, but the jobs were there, and workers poured in to take them.

Farther north, lumbering also was thriving, providing employment for many workers at each stage of the process, from timber cutting to the production of paper and other lumber-based materials. Agriculture and activities related to it, however, remained the number-one occupation for Wisconsinites in the 1890s. The shift to dairying from wheat farming as the major form of agricultural production had been successful, and after the 1893 economic crisis agriculture grew strongly until the outbreak of the World War I. Overall, and viewed from the perspective of the time, Wisconsin's economy was vibrant in 1890 and diversifying in a healthy way.

That situation, however, came to a crashing halt when the depression of 1893 hit Wisconsin, as it did the entire nation. Industrial layoffs were widespread and painful in those days before government or union cushions. Farm prices in Wisconsin fell to an all-time low, and the situation became grim in much of rural Wisconsin. By 1900 matters had improved, though, and Wisconsin's economic growth, especially in the industrial sector, grew faster than it had before the depression. Meanwhile, the widespread conversion to dairying meant that Wisconsin was a more egalitarian farm state than many others; the quality of the land a farmer had mattered less than it did in wheat or other grain states. Prices were also more stable, leading to less economic volatility than in states whose farming focused on grain commodities.[1]

By 1890 the majority of citizens in Wisconsin had been born in the state, and another 10 percent or so were born in other parts of the United States. Still, 31 percent were foreign-born and 74 percent were foreign-born or born of foreign-born parents. The largest group of foreign-born and native born of foreign parents remained the Germans, who constituted 47 percent of the foreign-born and 39 percent of those born in the United States of foreign-born parents. Norwegians, at 11.9 percent of the foreign-born, were a distant second, with the Poles in third at 6.2 percent. Wisconsin remained very much a state with many people who had come from all over Europe for a chance to improve their lives and those of their children. It was a land of economic struggle for many in 1890, as it had been in 1848, but also a place of opportunity, and so immigrants—Poles, Czechs, and Germans—continued to pour in.[2]

The Finns also arrived in Wisconsin in the late 1880s and into the 1890s. While never a large proportion of the Wisconsin population, the Finns were nonetheless a distinctive component, especially electorally. They were the last of the many European groups to come to Wisconsin, though others, such as the Poles, continued to come to Wisconsin in great numbers after the brief Finnish influx. More than 300,000 Finns came to the United States, almost all of them nurturing dreams of a better economic life here on good farms. The good farmland, in Wisconsin, however, was all gone by the time they arrived, so logging and mining became the main occupations of the large majority of Finnish immigrants who ended up in northern Wisconsin. It was rough work best suited to tough, strong, young men, who many of the Finnish immigrants were. Many had been radicals at home, believing little in a capitalism from which they gained no benefit, and they carried that attitude to their new homeland and eventually to the ballot box.[3]

Much of the ethnic and cultural division in Wisconsin remained based in religion, which continued to be a determining factor in the Wisconsin of 1890 and beyond. The religious component of voting behavior was of great importance in this era in part because religious institutions had become thoroughly organized and established. This included the Roman Catholic Church, which had grown significantly since the church's first explorer priests had come two centuries before and even since the days of Father Samuel Mazzuchelli (1806–1864), the official founder of the Roman Catholic Church in Wisconsin. By 1890 Roman Catholics made up as much as 25 percent of the state's population. While the Diocese of Milwaukee was established as early as 1843, it took a long time before the church was thoroughly organized and spread throughout the state. And when it was, it manifested the reality of ethnicity in Wisconsin. Almost every individual Catholic church was an ethnic church. So in 1896 there were 172 German Catholic churches, 113 Irish, 41 French, 13 Bohemian, 29 Polish, and so on.[4]

Throughout this period no real changes occurred in the basic political loyalties of various religious and ethnic groups. Nor did the religious tensions that sometimes surfaced disappear, as the formation of a secret anti-Catholic group, the American Protective Association, in the 1890s illustrated. It remained the case that religious loyalties did not correlate with class positions of various groups. Catholics tended to be Democrats, more before the realignment of 1896, a little less afterward, but steadily so. Non-Catholics tended to be Republicans, a bit more so after 1896. But there were exceptions. For example, Belgian Americans were Catholic but mostly voted Republican, and just as many German Protestants voted Democratic, especially before 1896 and especially among the older generation. With every group and every religious outlook, variety could be found, just as each election produced its own variations on the theme.[5]

THE 1890 ELECTION

The election of 1890 ranks with that of 1920 and those of the early 1930s as being one of the most sweeping in Wisconsin history. What made it especially remarkable was that it was an overwhelming Democratic victory, something truly rare in previous Wisconsin electoral history. Equally amazing was that in just a few short years after 1890 the Democrats found themselves hurled into a permanent minority status for what appeared to them to be forever. Their moment of glory was followed by decades of deep minority status as Wisconsin realigned as a solidly Republican state, more so, in fact, than it had ever been.

But such events could not be foreseen in 1890. By the beginning of the last decade of the nineteenth century, the two parties in Wisconsin were true electoral competitors, the Republicans having a slight edge but with the Democrats close behind and getting closer. Everything changed dramatically in the 1890 election, however. Suddenly and overwhelmingly the Democrats scored a massive electoral victory in Wisconsin, shattering records and stunning both Democrats and Republicans.

Two reasons seem apparent. The year 1890 was a Democratic year across the country, and particularly so in the Midwest. The Democrats captured the U.S. House of Representatives, Republicans losing no fewer than seventy-eight seats. Probably the most important national factor was reaction against the high Republican tariff, which threatened foreign demand for Midwest agricultural products. High tariffs deliberately made it difficult for foreign countries to sell their goods in the United States. Democrats argued that if foreign countries had difficulty selling to the United States, those nations would retaliate by refusing to buy from American goods. Thus in Wisconsin the high Republican tariff policy drew sharp opposition—even from some normally Republican Scandinavian farmers, who feared the consequences for the sale of their farm products.[6]

One event in Wisconsin, however, was predictably more important for understanding the 1890 results: the passage of the Bennett Law in 1889 and all that followed in 1890.[7] The story begins with Republican Governor William Hoard. Widely admired and known all over the state for his publications, especially his *Hoard's Dairyman,* Hoard was a respected household name in Wisconsin. He was also known as a lively storyteller and speaker who had already given more than 300 speeches to farmers in Wisconsin before he ever ran for governor in 1888. While he was not a favorite of Republican kingmakers, they selected him to carry the Republican banner in a year of likely close contests, appreciating that his statewide name recognition and popularity made him a good candidate and a winner.

As matters developed, however, Hoard turned out to have a passionate interest in making sure that Wisconsin's immigrant children—and their children and their children's children—who could not read and write in English, learned how to do so. In particular he had in mind the many rural and small-town German Americans who lived in a largely German world of language and culture in Wisconsin and who were not, he argued, adapting to American ways and the English language. And so Hoard became involved in the passage and defense of the Bennett Law.[8]

The Bennett Law, passed in 1889, was mostly about mandating schools for all children seven to fourteen and was a fateful step toward requiring ever more schooling for youth in Wisconsin. The originators of the bill were especially concerned to eliminate fulltime child labor but also believed in the value of formal education. The eventual sponsor of what was assumed to be a noncontroversial bill was Michael Bennett, a Republican and Catholic, who was a member of the Assembly representing rural Iowa County. He was the logical person to sponsor the bill as he happened to head up the State Assembly's Education Committee. Bennett did not concern himself with the provision tucked into the bill that was to produce such a controversy in 1890. That provision held that basic subjects from reading to writing to math to history had to be taught in the English language. Schools that did not do so were in violation of state law.[9]

Passage of the Bennett Law prompted an almost immediate uproar from supporters of ethnic parochial schools all over the state, as they saw in the law a blatant and dangerous attack on their cultures. The reaction was fierce, especially among German Americans. Democrats denounced the law quickly and perceived at once that Governor Hoard and the Republican majority had made a serious mistake. And as the campaign of 1890 began, Democrats were determined to take maximum advantage of the huge Republican political error.[10]

The campaign was a deeply frustrating one from the point of view of many Republican leaders. They understood that Governor Hoard's approach meant defeat, if not disaster, unless he moderated his views and persuaded the legislature to repeal the Bennett Law. Some, such as folksy former Governor Jerry Rusk, warned Hoard to reverse course. Others simply despaired of Governor Hoard then and later as someone who had no political sense. Still others tried to finesse the issue, as was true of Congressman Robert M. La Follette. In the end, though, La Follette lined up behind his fellow Republican and endorsed the law, a decision that had its costs. For a time (but certainly not after he opposed entering World War I with Germany) La Follette faced occasional accusations from within the German American community that he was hostile to them. In fact, La Follette was no nativist and was never much interested in ethnic politics. Belle La Follette, his wife, was especially irritated by these complaints; she was part German in ancestry and both spoke and wrote German.[11]

Many Republicans, including Republican Wisconsin Senator John C. Spooner, understood that the consequences of doing nothing would be detrimental to the entire Republican ticket (and to his own reelection). But Hoard did not agree. He had no intention of backing down from his position. While his critics complained that he was too rigid and did not understand people or politics, he declared that the "little German boy" must learn English and move toward assimilation and that this would not happen unless English instruction was enforced in every school, public or private.[12]

Governor Hoard did not understand during the campaign of 1890 the extent of the opposition to his law, since he was confident that most Wisconsinites agreed that it was time everyone gave up speaking a foreign language as their primary language. Even later on Hoard did not waver from his claim that, when many German Americans and their religious leaders went after him, it was only due to a terrible "religious fanaticism that swept all before it" leaving so many kids in a kind of isolated darkness in America. He went so far as to believe that some Wisconsin German Americans planned to create a German State of Wisconsin united by the German language and culture.[13]

Plenty of Wisconsinites agreed with his stance on the Bennett Law. Some Democrats (largely Irish Americans) even organized the Democratic Bennett Law League. Though there was no significant swing toward the Republicans in Irish American areas in 1890, the Democrats did not expand their margins either, despite the intense hostility of Catholic Church toward the Bennett Law.[14] Defenders of the law again and again celebrated the common school and argued that it was the way to bring all children together in an English-speaking America. This sentiment saw something very precious threatened by separatist schools that often conducted classes in a foreign language. Such a perspective had special appeal, not surprisingly, among already Republican-leaning groups concerned to preserve "American" culture.[15]

Opposition did come from plenty of sources. The Democratic Party, delighted to have such a controversial issue on their side, insisted that being

William Hoard, governor 1889–91
(Wisconsin Historical Society, WHi-26649)

an American did not require every child to go to a school taught in English. Thus Democrat William F. Vilas, who was to win Spooner's Senate seat as the result of the 1890 election, proclaimed it did not matter how one said "2 plus 2 equaled 4"; what mattered was learning the sum itself. Meanwhile, ethnic leaders of all sorts protested the law. Polish Americans, Czech Americans, and others spoke up quickly and frequently. The Roman Catholic Church bishops also made clear their opposition.

But the most prominent opposition came from German Americans, which did not end until well after the election of 1890 and the subsequent repeal of the law. Since there was little confusion as to whom the Bennett Law targeted, the German American fusillade of criticism was predictable. Certainly there was strong opposition from German Catholics and their parochial school establishment, but it was at least matched by German Lutherans. All sorts of German American anti–Bennett Law organizations sprung up that were closely associated with various Lutheran churches, and many Scandinavian Lutherans also strongly protested. Some Republican Norwegians and Swedish religious and civic leaders went as far as to urge Hoard to alter his position. When he didn't, several endorsed his Democratic opponent, even though their religious schools operated only during the summers and there was little interest in building a separate Scandinavian culture.[16]

Governor Hoard's Democratic opponent in the 1890 election, George Peck, was the perfect person to exploit the Republican Bennett Law mess. Peck was a highly successful newspaperman, famous all over the state (and, indeed, the country) for his "Peck's Bad Boy" humor writing. Elected mayor of Milwaukee in 1890, he rapidly obtained a reputation there, as he had elsewhere, as a congenial and highly popular good fellow. Peck also posed no ideological threat to most Republican values. He was a conservative Democrat who favored a weak state. Indeed, when the 1893 depression hit Wisconsin, Peck favored having private charities rather than government deal with the situation. In short, in personality and in ideology there was nothing sharp-edged about him, nothing dangerous to Hoard's critics, nothing that made him seem like someone who would be a bad governor (except, of course, that he was a Democrat).[17]

The November results were hinted at in the Milwaukee municipal elections of April 1890, when the Democrats achieved a sweeping victory. With the November vote, Democrat George Peck emerged the victor with the majority of the votes cast, 51.9 percent. Incumbent Hoard was badly defeated, garnering only 42.7 percent of the vote. The Prohibitionists got a typical 3.6 percent and the upstart Socialists 1.8 percent. Moreover, since in this era voters tended to vote a straight party ticket, the consequence of the 1890 rebellion was felt all the way down the ballot. Democrats carried both houses of the state legislature (a first since before the Civil War), all state offices, and six of Wisconsin's congressional seats.

The key indicator to explain the vote was the unmistakable surge of support by German American voters for the Democrat Peck. The Bennett Law brought back German ethnic voting solidarity with a vengeance in many parts of the state at painful cost to the Republicans, especially in German Protestant areas, where the 1890 median Democratic support soared to about 70 percent and almost every single Protestant German voting unit went Democratic. German Roman Catholic areas were already Democratic and had been since statehood, but in 1890 they became even more so. The median vote in such units was 75 percent for Peck. More religiously mixed German American precincts saw a major shift toward the Democrats, giving Peck close to 75 percent of their votes.

DEMOCRATIC CANDIDATE FOR GOVERNOR
OF WISCONSIN.

George Peck, governor 1891–95
(Wisconsin Historical Society, WHi-48603)

But the main shift came from German Protestant voters, more and more of whom had drifted into Republican ranks in the later nineteenth century. Thus the town of Grant in Shawano County went from 61.6 percent Democratic in 1888 to 84.8 percent in 1890; Pine River in Lincoln County from 35.3 percent to 59.4 percent, the town of Herman in Dodge County from 68.1 percent to 86.9 percent, and Eldorado in Fond du Lac County from 41.8 percent to 57 percent. Milwaukee also shifted from 40 percent Democratic in 1888 to 55 percent in 1890.

In sampled Norwegian areas there were also Democratic gains in 1890 over 1888. The average Democratic vote in 1890 was 31.2 percent versus 24.9

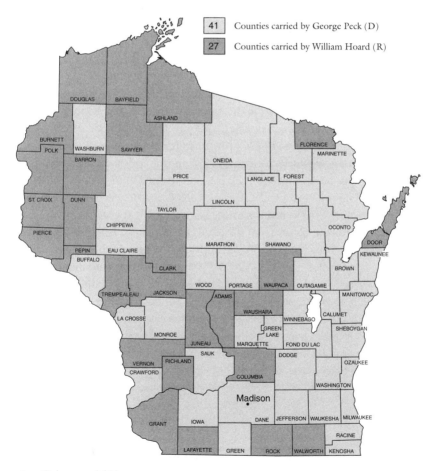

1890 Gubernatorial Vote

percent. In the Swedish sample the gains were modest, going from an average of 15.3 percent Democratic to 18 percent with a 3 percent advance for the Prohibition Party. Obviously, in neither instance did the Democrats do very well. This relative stability was characteristic of much of the rest of Wisconsin in 1890. It was only in some German Protestant areas that a really dramatic break occurred, and there was no general shift in Wisconsin's established partisan alignments. This is why if one compares the 1888 vote for governor with that of 1890 in my representative sample, the 1890 vote is much closer to the pattern in most places than one might suspect at first. Yet it was where it was different, given the close electoral system, that brought dramatic change.[18]

Another factor in the big Democratic win was turnout. While turnout dropped in Scandinavian areas, for example, as one would expect all over the state in a nonpresidential election year, in many German locations this was not the case, or was only slightly so. German American voters came to the polls in 1890 in high numbers to protest the Bennett Law. Their turnout, combined with their swing toward the Democrats, counted in heavily German Wisconsin and explains the dramatic shift from 1888 to 1890.[19]

In terms of government policies, the serious Republican defeat at the polls in 1890 did not mean much, apart from the almost instant repeal of the Bennett Law. The newly victorious Democrats did not have a change agenda and pursued none, exhibited in the election to the United States Senate of William F. Vilas by the new Democratic state legislature. Vilas was a kingpin of the conservative, so-called Bourbon, Democratic Party of his era. A highly successful Madison lawyer from a Democratic family—his father was a War Democrat who nonetheless opposed Lincoln—Vilas was known as a splendid orator and skilled politician, always a voice for small government and big business. Vilas was also deeply dedicated to civic life and public education in particular, above all to his beloved University of Wisconsin in Madison, to which he was a major benefactor. Upon his election to the Senate, Vilas returned to Washington, where he had already been postmaster general in the first Cleveland administration. He played a predictably conservative and effective role both in the Senate and in national Democratic politics.[20]

THE ELECTION OF 1892: THE DEMOCRATS' CONTINUING DAY

The election of 1892 was discouraging for Wisconsin Republicans in many ways. Their hope was that after their defeat in 1890, which then led to the repeal of the Bennett Law in 1891, the furor would die and with it the Democrats' success. Their hope was the Democrats' fear, and Edward C. Wall, the

Democrats' party leader, did everything he possibly could in the 1892 election to keep memories of the Bennett Law alive at the polls, especially among German Lutherans.[21]

This strategy was not the only factor that assisted Democrats in Wisconsin in 1892, but it helped. Memories were still alive. What also mattered was the popularity of Grover Cleveland's successful campaign for the presidency. What was different about this, the third of Cleveland's campaigns, however, was that the Democrat actually won the State of Wisconsin. It marked the first time a Democrat running for president had carried Wisconsin since 1852, forty years earlier. It was a historic event. Moreover, 1892 saw the Democrats capture the second U.S. Senate seat, reelect Governor Peck, and retain control of the state legislature. It was a glorious day for the Democrats, and no one could blame them for sensing that at last, after so many close elections and so many close defeats, they were on their way to being the ruling party in Wisconsin.

The vote for governor and president closely paralleled each other, which is not at all surprising in that day of straight party voting. What might seem surprising, given the earlier discussion, is that the vote was very close between the two parties.[22] Democrats were triumphant but by no great margin. The margin in both cases was no more than 2 percent of the vote, with the winning total less than 50 percent, given that third party totals added together came to 5 to 6 percent of the vote. The key to the Democratic success was the continuing high Democratic vote in Protestant German areas. Accounts differ, but even a conservative estimate from my sample has heavily German Protestant towns and villages going for the Democrats with 65 percent of the vote, well above their pre-1890 totals, though down some from 1890. Roman Catholic towns were, of course, more Democratic, though again a little below 1890 too. It was the continued movement of German Protestants to the Democratic Party that made the difference.[23]

THE POPULIST MOVEMENT IN WISCONSIN

The Populist Party (or People's Party) made its first serious appearance in the 1886 election in Wisconsin. It continued subsequently as a third party in the state, participating in a stronger form in Wisconsin in the election of 1892 and especially in 1894, after the onset of the depression. The party's life in the 1890s, as it had been in the 1880s, was based on economic protest, and with that theme it campaigned in every election. But a comparison of the Populist effort in 1892 to that of 1894 reveals significant differences. To be sure, in both elections a good many of the Populist voters were ex-Democrats who turned to the Populists in protest as they perceived that in Wisconsin the Democrats were twins of the Republicans, and neither party had anything to offer the economically distressed. But otherwise the base of the Populist vote in the two elections was different in several senses.

To begin, the party did much better in 1894, picking up a substantial 6.8 percent of the vote, while in 1892 it got less than 3 percent. More important, however, the Populist Party in 1892 drew its vote from protestors all over the state, especially in rural areas, and from some previous Prohibitionist voters, already radicals, who turned to it as the most available party of protest over economic and political conditions in the United States. Commodities prices fell in the period 1890–97, which is why in 1892 complaints over rural economic conditions were at the protest's heart. Thus it is no wonder that the Populist Party ran especially well among poorer farmers and Scandinavian, especially Swedish, rural voters (though, of course, the vast majority of Scandinavians voted Republican). And while some others were attracted by the Populists' pietist, moralist style, the party's main appeal related to economics.

But the Populist Party was tremendously limited in these very rural areas by the fact that Wisconsin's principal agricultural focus, dairying, never fell into a serious depression, unlike the situation in such grain states as Kansas or the Dakotas. By 1894, with the depression well under way and greatly affecting industrial regions, the Populist Party became much more of an urban worker's protest party, especially in big cities, where more than half of its 1894 votes originated. The Populists rolled up more than 20 percent of the vote in Milwaukee, Sheboygan, La Crosse, and Racine and ran best in working-class neighborhoods in those cities.[24]

After 1894 the People's Party essentially disappeared in Wisconsin. While it took some tentative steps to cooperate with the Socialists in 1893–94, tension existed in both camps, and cooperation did not last. In 1896 the Wisconsin party essentially collapsed into William Jennings Bryan's Democratic campaign for the presidency.[25]

Though Populism, like Greenbackism several decades earlier, did disappear after not making much of an impact in Wisconsin, each party had its moment in various Wisconsin localities. This fact reminds us that nineteenth-century voting behavior was not entirely a matter of ethnic-cultural divisions. There were economic factors at work sometimes too. This was obviously true in the successful struggles of economic elites to control not just the Republican Party but the Democratic Party as well. It was also true in the sudden burst of prominence of the economically aggrieved Greenback and Populist movements. But it is equally correct to note that these parties failed not just in the long run in most Wisconsin localities but even in their brief prime. The cultural hold over Wisconsin voting behavior did not break easily.[26]

THE BRIBE

The 1890s were also very important because they saw the emergence of Robert La Follette as a force in Wisconsin electoral politics. La Follette, born in 1855, had a tough childhood at times. His father died when he was very young, and he had a troubled relationship with his stepfather, who died when Bob was seventeen. La Follette was close to his mother and, for that matter, a number of other women all his life, especially his wife, Belle. He grew up in rural Dane County and attended the University of Wisconsin, from which he graduated in 1879. Though not a stellar student, he was well-known and admired for his oratorical and dramatic skills.

He began practicing law in 1880 and by 1881 was already district attorney of Dane County, clearly a young politician on the rise. He was known as a cautious prosecutor. In advancing his career in Dane County, La Follette and his allies did not always have an easy time. Political fights occurred regularly, especially with "Boss" Keyes, an influential local politico, but the fights were within Republican circles—"our Republican guys versus their Republican guys." They were often intense, but they had nothing to do with issues of "reform," though La Follette always equated issues surrounding his career advancement as major reform matters. In 1884 La Follette was elected to Congress, and he served there until the election of 1890, when the Bennett Law crisis sent him, and so many other Republicans, down to defeat.[27]

We know both political parties in this period were controlled by conservative business and financial interests, none of whom had any serious reform agendas about anything. La Follette was, by all appearances, and as evidenced by his votes in Congress, absolutely no different. He was a successful conservative, traditional Republican politician. However, all that began to change after U.S. Senator Philetus Sawyer apparently offered La Follette a bribe in September 1891. The bribe was to influence La Follette to get his brother-in-law, a local judge, to clear an associate of Sawyer's in a court case. As La Follette and his supporters told the story, La Follette indignantly refused this effort and in time emerged as a force for political reform in a boss-run state.[28]

The bribe story had two sides. Sawyer flatly denied any attempt to bribe La Follette and suggested that La Follette misunderstood a normal enough plea for help. La Follette did believe there was an effort to bribe him, and there probably was. Equally true is that over the next several years he engaged in more and more patronage fights with the elites of his Republican Party, became more and more disillusioned with the behind-the-scenes Wisconsin political and electoral system, and realized that the system was in fact blocking his own career advancement. While it is not exactly clear when La Follette began to get serious about political reform—the key issue being his proposal for primary elections to determine political nominations—it was not directly after the bribe attempt.

By 1896 La Follette was edging toward reform, bucking the established Republican state leadership and trying to get the Republican nomination for governor. He still had no developed reform agenda, but there was a growing perception on the part of the established Republican elites that La Follette could be, indeed already was, trouble. In 1898 he tried and failed again to obtain the Republican nomination for governor through the established convention system under the rule of the old bosses. In the process he began explicitly demanding political change, asking for a primary system and a general cleanup of what was a corrupt (what we now call a "pay-to-play") political order.[29]

At no time in this process did La Follette fail to back the Republican nominees in November. While his support was often muted, it was nonetheless there. And he made no effort to support Democratic nominees, who La Follette believed were not acceptable alternatives, or to start a third party. It is also important to note that in the 1890s La Follette was only one of several younger men seeking to replace the established Republican bosses. He did emerge as the leader over time, but in those earlier years it was something of a group effort.

For example, one of his compatriots was Nils P. Haugen, who was from Pierce County, a heavily Scandinavian area, and emerged early as an ally and coconspirator for change with La Follette. First elected to the State Assembly in 1878, Haugen was elected railroad commissioner as the ethnic Norwegian on the Republican ticket in 1880 and thereafter until he was elected to Congress in 1886. There he got to know La Follette as a fellow Wisconsin member of Congress in the late 1880s. Like La Follette, he eventually turned against the Republican bosses, in part for career reasons but also because he believed Wisconsin politics needed to shed boss rule and corporate dominance and shift toward more democratic practices. He ardently sought the Republican nomination for governor in 1894 with La Follette's support but got almost nowhere in his effort. Later, roles reversed, and he went on to serve La Follette, especially helping with the creation of the state income tax and drumming up Scandinavian enthusiasm for La Follette.[30]

THE GREAT REVOLUTION: THE ELECTIONS OF 1894 AND 1896

The election of 1896 has long been a benchmark in American electoral history. At the presidential level it was the year in which Republicans achieved a commanding position, which they did not relinquish until Democrat Woodrow Wilson broke through in 1912 after the split in the Republican majority coalition. The election of 1896 set a major realignment changing America's voting behavior (outside the South) from a close two-party competition to Republican rule. It happened nationally, and it also happened in Wisconsin.

In fact, the realignment began with major Democratic reverses in 1894 stemming directly from the acute depression of 1893. Though this depression was less painful in dairying Wisconsin than in some crop-oriented farm states, its impact was still severe. In 1893 alone, 119 Wisconsin banks failed, and as many as 40 percent of Milwaukee workers may have been out of work at the height of the depression.[31]

The election of 1894 was a disaster for the Democrats and a victory for the Republicans. In twenty-four states not a single Democrat was elected to the House of Representatives; in six others only one made it. The shift was greatest in the Midwest, where after the 1892 election forty-five Democrats and forty-four Republicans were elected to the House; but after 1894 the balance changed to three Democrats and eighty-six Republicans. Overall, the Democrats went from a massive majority after the 1892 election in the House of 219 to 127 to an even more pointed minority status as with the Republicans' 244 seats to the Democrats' 104. This is how staggering the Republican sweep was (outside the South).[32]

In Wisconsin the Democrats knew they were in trouble by the fall of 1894, and they tried to hold back the tide. Edward C. Wall, the Democratic party leader, did all he could, dredging up once again the old ethnic issues of Bennett Law days and warning of the anti-immigrant American Protective Association. Yet those issues were now dated. The Democratic nominee for governor was the incumbent, Peck, but he had no chance given the wave of economic discontent gripping both the state and the nation. On the one hand, the dire economic state swept the Republican William Upham into the governor's office, beating Peck by a decisive margin of 52 percent to 38 percent. On the other hand, it resulted in a sudden burst of Populist support on the left, to the tune of 6.8 percent of the vote with the remaining votes going to the Prohibition Party.

Upham was a good choice to break through the Democrats' brief time of success. A wealthy lumberman from Marshfield, Upham was also a distinguished Civil War veteran who had been captured and interned in the war.

He was chosen to run because he was not a politician, had money to spend, had been head of the state's Grand Army of the Republic, and had sounded vaguely reformist because he had supported Milwaukee's adoption of civil service. He seemed to be a fresh face for tough times, and in a way he was. Once he served one term as governor, however, he left politics, which he did not like, and returned to his business interests.[33]

While the general pattern of votes in 1894 was about the same as before, and so Republican and Democratic votes correlated closely with past results, across all categories the degree of support for the Democrats dropped way down. Indeed, the only place where Democrats held on to anything resembling earlier elections was in rural Polish precincts. In Milwaukee, where the depression was acutely felt, the Democrats, who had carried the city in both 1890 and 1892, crashed to about 30 percent of the vote as the Republicans won and the Populists surged to 19 percent of the total vote.[34]

While the issue of realignments continues to engage many scholars of electoral history, and although controversy continues over how to measure a realignment, few doubt that a realignment took place beginning in 1894, continuing in 1896, and stabilizing thereafter. In Wisconsin during this period a significant and lasting shift in voting behavior benefiting the Republicans occurred. It is especially the "lasting" aspect that establishes that 1894–96 constituted the crucial move toward a realignment in Wisconsin.[35]

In understanding Wisconsin voting in 1896, it is important to remember that in the 1880s, and then more strongly in the early 1890s, Wisconsin was a competitive two-party state, one actually edging toward becoming Democratic. The trend was clear and had been greatly facilitated by the Republican Bennett Law fiasco. All that, however, was moot in the 1894 elections and became just a distant memory after 1896.

The contest for president in 1896 was between Democratic nominee William Jennings Bryan and Republican candidate William McKinley. Bryan was badly beaten in Wisconsin, where McKinley received 60 percent of the vote to Bryan's less than 37 percent; the Prohibitionists received less than 2 percent; and the John Palmer supporters, dissident "Gold Democrats" who were unsympathetic to Bryan's inflationary monetary program, got 1 percent.

The whole story of Bryan's dramatic but quite futile 1896 campaign is a fascinating one. Yet this story translated in a decidedly negative fashion in Wisconsin when placed against that of the steady and traditional William McKinley of Ohio—and Wisconsin returns were hardly unusual. While Bryan carried the controlled Democratic South and some smaller Populist states in the West and farm belt, he did poorly nationally; he carried not a single

county in New England and only a few rural counties in places like Pennsylvania and did especially badly in major urban areas, even losing Democratic
New York City. Overall, the evangelistic Bryan did better in rural areas and
small towns, predictably perhaps, than in urban areas, but he was no winner
in either realm.[36]

In Wisconsin Bryan's opponents included prominent Democrats as well
as Republicans. The Democrats who opposed him did not usually go so far
as to endorse McKinley, but their unwillingness to endorse Bryan spoke
loud and clear, especially when it came from such figures as William Vilas,
U.S. senator and star of the Wisconsin Democratic Party. Such Democratic

67 Counties carried by William McKinley (R)

3 Counties carried by William Jennings Bryan (D)

1896 Presidential Vote

opposition to Bryan was predictable. Wisconsin's Democratic Party was controlled by business, and many of its supporters were German Americans, economic conservatives who had no sympathy for Bryan's inflationary monetary policy. It was all foreshadowed at the Democratic National Convention when a majority of the Wisconsin delegates refused to pledge to vote for Bryan in November. Just how many conservative, so-called "Gold Democrats," voted Republican in the end is not clear, but some did, though the Gold Democratic alternative ticket attracted few votes. In Wisconsin, hoping for a knockout blow, Republicans even had important Archbishop John Ireland come to the state to denounce Bryan as a dangerous radical in an effort to attract Catholic voters.[37]

The vote in 1896 showed a distinct rise in Republican strength, as had the 1894 returns, among most groups, but in varying degrees, though the majority of partisans of both parties remained loyal in Wisconsin as they did nationally. Those groups McKinley and the Republicans gained only modestly with were those already quite Republican or intensely Democratic. The Republicans included many native-born citizens who were children of native-born parents and Wisconsinites of Scandinavian descent. Implacable Democrats were often Polish and Irish Americans, though even among these loyalists there was a mild falling off of Democratic allegiance.

Among German Americans McKinley and the Republicans made significant gains, though it was not as if support for the Democrats disappeared here either. However, in German Protestant areas Bryan got only 39 percent of the vote, and in German Catholic places he got a relatively low 61 percent on average. Huge Republican advances occurred in Czech areas of Wisconsin and among the already Republican Belgian towns. There was variation among different groups, but in each case the movement was always in one direction: toward McKinley and increased Republican support.[38]

Bryan actually did better in 1896 on average in the larger cities in Wisconsin, including Milwaukee, than the Democrats did in their terrible year of 1894 and better than in the countryside, which was not his national pattern. But doing better than in 1894 was not doing well. McKinley carried Milwaukee easily with 56 percent of the vote and, in a rare triumph for the Republicans, won Madison as well. In Milwaukee Bryan lost every single German ward; the three wards out of twenty-one he managed to carry were south side Polish American wards. This meant that there was, in fact, little sign of class voting in Milwaukee. Similarly, in Sheboygan and Manitowoc there was no class basis in the patterns of shift to McKinley.[39]

Some scholars have contended that Bryan had real appeal in the country-side with some evangelical Protestants, that in Wisconsin, for instance, he did better than any Democrat since 1876 among rural Norwegians. It is possible to find a few exceptions, but overall there was no evidence of a pietist rallying toward Bryan. In fact, Bryan did much, much worse among rural and small-town Norwegians in Wisconsin than Democrats did in 1890 and 1892; he ran very poorly there, as all Democrats did in that era, getting an average of 18 percent of the vote. There just was no rural shift to Bryan in Wisconsin.[40]

Nor was there any sign of class voting in rural Wisconsin. Bryan did not appeal to poorer rural voters, and his enthusiasts' expectation that he would proved as illusory as their many other electoral dreams. One hope that had a bit more substance was Bryan's gain of some votes from the Prohibition Party, whose Wisconsin voters by this time were often radicals on a range of issues. It is true that even as turnout in Wisconsin soared in 1896 far above the 1892 turnout, the number of Prohibition Party voters fell by nearly one-half, though it is not clear how many of the defectors went to Bryan.[41]

Republicans gained ground significantly in 1896 at the state level, which confirmed their 1894 victories. Thus Republican Edward Scofield was easily elected governor, and his vote correlated well with that of McKinley's at .997 and with past Republican governor votes such as 1888 at .804. This confirmed not that whole groups of the electorate switched but that Republican strength grew generally across categories. It was impossible to guess then that Wisconsin would soon have in essence three parties, as two factions of the Republicans would struggle year after year but somehow manage to unite each November to defeat what became the distinctly third party—the Democrats.

In 1868, when he was in his twenties, Scofield came to Wisconsin from Pennsylvania with a distinguished record of service in the Civil War, including surviving incarceration in no less than twelve different Confederate prisons. After the war he became successful in the lumber business and, representing typical conservative Republican attitudes of the time, defeated a not-yet-reformist Robert La Follette for the 1896 Republican nomination for governor. Scofield then went on to receive 60 percent of the vote to Democrat Willis Silverthorn's 38 percent (the Prohibition candidate received 1.8 percent). That Scofield's huge victory paralleled the outcome of the presidential contest made sense, since Silverthorn, a Wausau lawyer, was a Bryan and inflation supporter.[42]

ELEMENTS OF THE VOTE

The shift to the Republicans after the depression of 1893 came in almost all categories, classes, ethnic groups, geographical areas. It may well have been generational, that is, particularly a shift among younger votes, though this is not clear. Study has demonstrated that there was no class dimension to the change. The Democrats lost ground among all classes and in roughly equal numbers. The shift was always marginal, but the marginals added up to firm Republican control, a realignment that lasted long after the elections of 1894 and 1896.[43]

In comparing the patterns of the early 1890s with the several decades beginning in 1894, we can see how serious the shifts were. Sampled Dutch areas already two-to-one Republican in the early 1890s became four-to-one; Norwegian regions moved in the same way. German Protestant areas that had recovered Democratic strength in the early 1890s fell sharply to less than 40 percent Democratic; German Catholic regions that were more than 70 percent Democratic fell just below 60 percent; Swiss areas that were less than 50 percent Republican became more than 60 percent; Belgian areas that were slightly more than 50 percent Republican turned to about four-to-one Republican. My samples also show that the average rural town, which was about 50–50 in the early 1890s, became almost two-thirds Republican. Villages were strongly Republican throughout this period but became four-to-one after the realignment. Democratic Milwaukee became Republican Milwaukee with a shift of about 10 percent of the electorate to the Republicans, and very Democratic Madison altered to become a contested city. A realignment had indeed taken place.[44]

4 The La Follette Progressive Era through 1914

THE PROGRESSIVE ERA BEGAN soberly enough as the realignment formed in 1894–96 played itself out, but it ended with the dramatic electoral events of 1912 and 1914. The Progressive movement itself was intensely complicated, and what distinguished various "progressives" in this period is fiercely debated among contemporary historians. For our purposes, both in Wisconsin and in the nation, progressives were united in seeking to promote the "common good" and to tame the excesses of capitalism to bring greater protection and care to workers, consumers, and farmers and to the nation as a whole. The movement also addressed government reform and supported creating a more honest, open, and democratic political system through such changes as primary elections, direct election of U.S. senators, and, often, women's suffrage. Almost always progressives had a confidence in government action as a primary (though far from the only) means of change—if it was influenced by "experts" and guided by the "facts" of social science.[1]

The voting behavior of the time was complicated. Fortunately, however, the Progressive Era has attracted more serious and valuable scholarship than any other period in Wisconsin voting history.[2] The central dynamic was Republican rule, which was never fundamentally threatened even by renewed Democratic strength from 1910 on, given how weak the Democratic Party was as the result of the post-1893 realignment. At the same time there was fierce in-fighting within the Republican Party between two factions, the Progressives, eventually led by Robert M. La Follette, and the conservative Stalwarts. At points the real electoral struggle for rule in Wisconsin took place in the Republican primary, and there is a case to be made for the proposition that Wisconsin in those years was somewhat like a state in the old Democratic Solid South, where the primary election was the real election. Yet another dimension in the picture was the active and determined Socialist Party, which consistently drew plenty of votes, especially in Milwaukee.

People in Wisconsin during the Progressive Era lived in a time of general, if not universal, prosperity. By the turn of the century, the Depression of 1893 was history and Wisconsin was doing well economically. Its industrial sector was rapidly expanding, especially so along Lake Michigan in cities such as Racine, Kenosha, Sheboygan, Manitowoc, and of course Milwaukee. And these were also excellent years for Wisconsin's farm economy. Although dairying remained the main pursuit, there were other profitable farm enterprises, including the production of tobacco and various fruits and even some livestock. Agriculture flourished best in the lower third of the state; farming, and even life itself, was often a struggle in the northern parts of the state.

Very early in the twentieth century, about 25 percent of Wisconsin's residents were born outside the United States and more than 25 percent were born of foreign-born parents. Germans made up about half of the foreign-born population, but Norwegians at 12 percent and significant groups of Swiss and Poles were also part of the ethnic mix that constituted Wisconsin's immigrant population.

By now, about 38 percent of the population was urban, though the standard definition of "urban" as places with more than 2,500 people suggests something about just how urban Wisconsin was. Milwaukee was truly urban with 14 percent of the state's 2,069,000 population. Overall population was growing rapidly in Wisconsin, having increased by more than 20 percent after 1890 as people poured into the state, principally into its urban and industrial sectors. At the same time, the older ethnic enclaves in the state were slowly lowering their walls and interethnic marriages were on the rise.[3]

ROBERT M. LA FOLLETTE

To explore Wisconsin voting behavior in the Progressive Era, it is important to turn early to an examination of Robert M. La Follette, whose presence loomed over elections and politics from the turn of the century until his death in 1925. La Follette was elected governor of Wisconsin in 1900 and served from 1901 to 1905, when he was elected to the U.S. Senate, where he served until 1925. But whatever his office, so much of what happened at the polls in those years revolved around La Follette that discussion of him must come at the beginning. Consideration of La Follette must necessarily draw on his own writings as well as the many reflections on him by others, most of which were, until recently, more essays in hagiography than anything else. Each, however, is illuminating in its own way.[4]

The previous chapter told the story of La Follette's break with the established Republican machine, and his version of why that happened. It is well to recall that La Follette began as just another Republican politician on the make within the established party system. In his time in Congress in the 1880s, La Follette was certainly an orthodox conservative Republican. In the 1896 election, he supported the conservative Republican nominees all the way, even though in that year he lost his first bid to become the Republican candidate for governor. There was little hint then that the contest for the gubernatorial nomination was about principles so much as about two rivals struggling for (personal) power. In 1898 he tried again and lost again, though by that time he was unmistakably seeking and attracting reformist support.[5]

While La Follette moved rapidly toward adopting his famous reform program after 1897, it was not until he was first elected governor in 1900 that he articulated it boldly or was able to make a practical difference toward accomplishing it. Even then his agenda and actions occasioned a tremendous amount of surprise—and in some circles shock—because he had run a quite conventional campaign in 1900 that gave little hint of the extent of his reform aspirations. To be sure, in 1900 as before, La Follette was no darling of the machine bosses, but he was able to get the nomination for governor that year due to the death and distraction of key Stalwarts, his relentless campaigning and organization, and his canny (and misleading) interactions with significant railroad and industrial leaders in the state.

Robert La Follette Sr.,
governor 1901–5
(Wisconsin Historical Society, WHi-10900)

However, conflicts soon enough broke out as La Follette pursued his reform agenda vigorously, alienating him from his Republican opposition, the Stalwarts. By 1902 the Republican Party was completely polarized, and La Follette and Stalwart leader Senator Spooner openly opposed each other. This situation did not end when La Follette moved to the Senate in 1905. Tough battles took place over patronage as well as more substantive issues, but the two did manage to maintain a surface civility.[6]

La Follette's reform policies that defined the terms of Wisconsin electoral debate in the years leading up to 1914 were not thought of as policies by La Follette and his admirers. Rather, they were holy causes to be advanced against evil enemies. Those policies were different from those promoted by the famous Mugwumps of an earlier era, activists who were also Republicans in many cases but very different from La Follette. Many of the Mugwumps' middle-class campaigns addressed personal lifestyle moral issues, including, for example, alcohol use and abuse, issues La Follette was not interested in.

As governor and then as U.S. senator, La Follette focused his attention on political reform and economic change. In terms of political reform, La Follette made central the creation of the direct primary so that political candidates would be selected by the voters, not by political bosses; also important was the direct election of U.S. senators. In terms of economic reform, as governor La Follette concentrated on regulating railroads, creating a progressive income tax system, and generally addressing the tremendous economic inequities in the state and their attendant undemocratic political consequences.

His reform program, including attention to economic regulation, did not draw Milwaukee's energetic Socialist movement into a warm alliance. The Socialists saw La Follette as a tepid reformer not at all serious about sweeping economic change. Thus as the Socialists gained strength, they became a distinct impediment for La Follette in his efforts as they drained off reform votes for his crusades.[7]

Early in his remarkable political and electoral career, certain characteristics of La Follette's public persona and campaign style appeared that would become defining and sometimes controversial features of his work. There was his firm recognition that political organization was essential. Scholars recognize now that the La Follette who spent so much time denouncing the conservative Republican "machine" was himself an expert in machine politics. He fashioned "grassroots organization within the Republican Party that reached into every nook and cranny within the state and not just to the usual leaders in the county seats."[8] He also employed patronage freely in doing so; for example, he used state game wardens to promote him and his allies at the polls. La Follette was a reform boss who knew how to play effective and tough machine politics; he was a realist who knew strong organization was essential for political success. But La Follette did not see himself as a hypocrite in the slightest; rather, he saw himself as the leader of an organized crusade, and he believed that only cynics would confuse that with an evil machine.[9]

La Follette had a wonderful talent for inspiring followers to work for him and his causes. Much of that stemmed from his ordinary public face. An extrovert, La Follette was a warm, entertaining, and interesting person who had unusual powers of persuasion and who attracted men and women in equal numbers. He was known for his powerful handshake, his willingness to look voters directly in the eye, and his uncanny memory for names—priceless assets of a successful politician. His platform and oratorical skills, first honed when he was a University of Wisconsin student, were legendary and thrilled many a crowd. He was famous for being able to highlight a few and always highly moralized issues, illustrated with a few carefully selected points and presented with what his wife, Belle, recognized as his superb "dramatic instinct."[10]

Contrary to the romantic image of the La Follette movement, key personnel in his organization were often paid, but the bulk of his many volunteers, year after year, election after election, were not. They were devoted to La Follette, and he did indeed inspire them. These volunteers cannot be ignored in discussion of the fabled La Follette organization; their vital role did not change, though the cast of characters changed as the years went by. The one constant among this cast was Belle Case La Follette. Her central roles were both public and private, as loving wife and adviser as well as public advocate, and she was enormously helpful to her husband. Belle La Follette is at last beginning to get the recognition and discussion she merits, not only for her influence with and care for her spouse but also for her own activities, especially her active suffrage work.[11]

Perhaps the most famous and important La Follette follower was Irvine Lenroot, a Swedish American lawyer who was first elected to the State Assembly in 1900. He quickly rose to its leadership and by 1901 already was a part of La Follette's inner circle. It was Lenroot who arranged La Follette's appointment to the U.S. Senate in 1905, pushing away a host of very determined competitors and preserving the public image La Follette wanted, the charade that La Follette (who eagerly wanted the job) was accepting it only because he was asked to do so. Lenroot later fell from grace, a not uncommon fate of La Follette political intimates as the years and then decades went by. What did not change, however, was the existence of a small inner circle on whom La Follette depended and from whom he expected absolute loyalty.[12]

However, there was constant fighting within his camp that led to many bitter divisions. Well before the crisis of 1917 and certainly thereafter, La Follette's movement divided into factions that at best could barely tolerate each other and that often undercut each other. One was led by La Follette himself, and the other came to be composed, often in uneasy alliance, of those disenchanted with him, such as James Davidson, Isaac Stephenson, and Francis McGovern. Some of these conflicts were inevitable given particular issues and personalities or geographical loyalties, but they were never helped by La Follette's disastrous tendency to obsess about those who proved "disloyal" and to plot vengeance on them.

Not to be ignored either is the consistent pattern of personal illness La Follette experienced. Life for him involved great stress, and his uncompromising moralism and relentless ambition exacted costs as well. The recurring bouts of illness were, at times, useful, since they forced the hyperactive La Follette to take desperately needed rest. He also used ill health as an excuse when he did not want to take a stand or even, too, as in the 1908 governor's contest, as a way of silently expressing his anger at developments.[13]

Of course even in his own time many things about La Follette struck some commentators and his numerous enemies as disturbing. As the endless celebrations of La Follette continue to this day, and as politicians from every point of view invoke him for their pet political reforms, it is important to recall that his programs generated opponents, as did his practices. To his critics he was a near-despot, a phony actor, a person who cared about personal loyalty above all else. They were not entranced by the tendency of La Follette and others in his camp to see themselves as an embattled group of idealists fighting terribly evil enemies, since La Follette and his allies so often employed hardball organizational tactics.[14] Critics also portrayed La Follette as a poor senator—arrogant, moralistic, and frequently unrepresentative of the majority of his constituents, as in his stand against World War I. They saw him as embarrassingly, even pathetically, motivated by personal ambition and given to misjudgment deriving from his passion for the presidency. They noted his serious runs both in 1912 (for the Republican/Progressive nomination) and 1924 (as a third-party candidate) as well as his desire for the nomination in other years.[15]

A more balanced image of La Follette is now emerging, one that recognizes the unmistakable fact that La Follette was indeed a driven moralistic prophet who had great impact for good and who was also just as unmistakably an "effective professional politician," an unusual and successful combination.[16] It acknowledges that while there were many elements in La Follette's success, his personal charisma and his machinelike organization were both essential to his success. He was a remarkable force for change and a splendid politician. There can be no doubt of it, and there should be no doubt of it. At the same time, even those who gush that La Follette was "a ceaseless battler for the underprivileged in an age of special privilege, a courageous independent in an era of conformity who fought memorably for the social and economic reforms which ultimately proved essential to American progress" now also understand that La Follette was "frequently ruthless, partisan, vindictive, and egotistical."[17] Perhaps La Follette's greatest limitation was his demand for excessive loyalty and his concomitant inability to share power with others.[18]

THE STALWARTS

Wisconsin in this period had a three-party system, and much of the time the struggle that mattered most occurred in the Republican primary. The focus on La Follette throughout much of the historical writing on Wisconsin electoral politics has inevitably led to neglect of the La Follette Progressives' opponents, the so-called Stalwarts. The fact is the Stalwarts represented a huge portion of the Wisconsin electorate, one that cannot be correlated with any income level. In election after election, Republican primary voters (once La Follette got the primary established) had a choice between Stalwarts and Progressives, and they voted accordingly. From 1908 to 1914, for example, Stalwart candidates' votes correlated with each other, and so did the votes of Progressive candidates. In short, citizens picked sides and voted for their candidates with consistency, suggesting a good deal of awareness among Republican voters over time.[19]

During the time when La Follette and his fellow Progressives (who were first known as "Half-Breeds") were active in politics, the three most famous Stalwarts were Philetus Sawyer, John C. Spooner, and Emanuel Philipp. They were all proponents of business and economic development, convinced that giving business free rein was the way to prosperity and freedom for all. They were for minimal government and low taxation and against democratizing the political process through primary elections, popular election of senators, and the like. Indeed, the bitter fight over the creation of the primary in Wisconsin was one of the most decisive events in hardening the Stalwart-Progressive split.[20]

Philetus Sawyer became famous in Wisconsin history for his apparent attempt to bribe La Follette, as discussed in the previous chapter. Sawyer was a highly successful lumber magnate who was important in developing the U.S. lumber industry. He was also an able politician. When he first went to Congress after the Civil War, Sawyer was quite the radical Republican, reflecting the hostile attitudes of most Wisconsinites toward the South. Elected first to the U.S. House of Representatives, Sawyer allied with the Republican faction that was determined to punish the South. Later he was elected to the U.S. Senate by the Wisconsin state legislature, and he served from 1881 until 1893. In that office he was renowned for his defense of business interests, his ability to bring federal appropriations to Wisconsin, and his skill and influence within the halls of the Senate as a respected member of the club.[21]

John C. Spooner was a longtime effective participant in Wisconsin Stalwart politics. He, too, was a highly successful Wisconsin businessman, active in both the railroad and the lumber industries. He served one term in the U.S. Senate, from 1885 until the Democratic landslide of 1890 ensured his defeat. Spooner was later reelected due to the Republican landslide of 1896 and served until 1907. While Sawyer was known as a very practical, bring-home-the-bacon Stalwart, Spooner cut quite another figure. Highly educated and sophisticated, he was a lawyer who concentrated on legal issues in the Senate and contributed a presence that was often impressive and widely admired.[22]

A third key figure was Emanuel Philipp. The child of immigrant Swiss farmers from Sauk County, he represented a second generation of Stalwart or conservative Republican politicians. He was a steady opponent of the La Follette Progressives after 1900 and served as governor of Wisconsin from 1915 to 1921. He blocked the progressives at the state level during the war years, though he was never a jingoistic zealot.[23]

The Stalwarts' supporters within the Republican world tended to be found in Wisconsin's cities, big and small, and villages, as distinct from the rural areas of the state. Stalwarts also tended to be most popular, predictably, among ethnic groups who had well-established reputations as being reluctant to change and opposed to public spending. These included Dutch Americans and, especially, many Republican German Americans.[24]

THE ELECTORAL STORY

The first election after the famous landslide year of 1896 came two years later in 1898, and it confirmed that a realignment had indeed taken place. Republicans now ruled without question in Wisconsin. What that meant in particular was that Edward Scofield was reelected governor in a landslide in 1898, defeating Hiram Sawyer, the Democratic candidate, 53 percent to 41 percent, with third parties getting the rest of the vote. Scofield's totals correlated with the 1896 returns at almost .9, suggesting how stable the realignment pattern was. Thus it is no surprise that all the usual groups and places repeated the voting behavior adopted during the tumultuous 1894–96 period. In that sense the 1898 election was merely a maintaining election of the classic—and uninteresting—sort.[25]

The year 1900 was no different, except that it was a presidential election year. Republicans won without much challenge at all levels. William McKinley won Wisconsin in a blowout defeating Democrat William Jennings Bryan 60 percent to 36 percent, while the Socialist and Prohibition parties together got less than 4 percent. The Republican candidate for governor won almost as overwhelmingly. A major difference, however, was that the Republican candidate was not just anyone; it was Robert M. La Follette. At last, after three attempts at becoming the Republican nominee for governor, La Follette got his long sought chance in 1900. He ran as an orthodox Republican, dutifully addressing and endorsing national party concerns and the entire Republican ticket. There was one exception, however: La Follette insisted that it was time to have primary elections to select party nominees and move away from selection being made at the often-corrupt and undemocratic party conventions.[26]

All that the election of 1900 showed was that the realignment had passed another test, that it had become solid and was lasting. Results in 1900 correlated highly with those of 1898 and even 1896. By every measure, Republicans ruled; and while Democrats ran a bit better in Milwaukee and in urban areas generally than they now did in rural areas and small Wisconsin towns, they were not the majority party in urban areas either. As usual, there did not appear to be signs of class division outside the cities. Indicators of class allegiances in cities faded away when controlled for ethnic origin. This is not surprising since by that point class and ethnicity were still quite closely connected. Thus those of Yankee background tended to make up the bulk of the upper and much of the middle classes in many cities. Only in very German and Roman Catholic cities, such as Sheboygan, was the Republican orientation reversed, and then only narrowly. Only among Irish, Polish, and German Catholic voters were the Democrats now favored. The party had visibly subsided into a weak minority status.[27]

One enterprising and informed estimate of the shift due to the realignment put the Republican state gain at about 12 percent. This estimate works for 1888 but not for the more robust Democratic years of 1890 and 1892 and thus may underestimate the degree of realignment to the Republicans. What would be fascinating to learn is whether or not this movement was largely generational or was age-random. One might speculate that it was generational given what we know about how firm party loyalties were in this era, but we lack the poll data to confirm it.[28]

AFTER 1900: FROM 1902 TO 1910

The years after 1900 were pretty straightforward for the Republicans in their relationship with the Democrats and the emerging Socialists. Briefly, it was one (virtually) automatic Republican victory after another. The Democrats proved hapless and absolutely not an electoral threat. The Socialists were noisy but also not threatening, and they had the additional advantage, for Republicans, of dividing potential anti-Republican voters. Neither was the Prohibition Party a threat; this party that had once seemed a possible threat to the Republicans had become nothing more than a minor diversion for voters who were not needed by the Republicans. As time went on, though, the unending fights within the Republican Party between the Progressives and the Stalwarts, as well as conflict among Progressives, proved every bit as intense as the two-party contests had been before 1894.

The 1902 gubernatorial election closely paralleled the results of both 1900 and 1904. La Follette won reelection as governor, comfortably defeating David Rose, a well-known lawyer and Milwaukee's mayor. Rose tried hard to go after La Follette from a conservative perspective, attacking him for his advocacy of an income tax and stressing that La Follette had his own political machine. But it was all to no avail. La Follette got 53 percent of the vote and Rose a mere 40 percent, while Emil Seidel won 4.4 percent on the Socialist ticket and the Prohibitionists got the remaining 2.6 percent.

The results were nothing new, even though rumors did abound that some Stalwarts did not vote for La Follette and some more liberal Democrats did. La Follette even carried Milwaukee over Rose, but with far less than 50 percent of the vote as Seidel garnered 19 percent there. La Follette's strongest support continued to be in rural and small-town Scandinavian parts of the state. But with him the variations were always just a matter of degree, because La Follette and the Republicans showed robust strength virtually everywhere except in German Catholic or Polish Catholic precincts.[29]

La Follette won less convincingly in the Republican year of 1904 and got barely more than 50 percent of the vote. For president, Theodore Roosevelt won in a landslide over the conservative Democrat Alton Parker in Wisconsin, 63 to 28 percent, while Eugene Debs got over 6 percent on the Socialist ticket and the Prohibitionists received 2 percent.[30] La Follette's weaker showing did not mean that his principal opponent, Democrat and former governor George Peck, came close. Peck got only 39 percent. But if it was unreasonable to predict that La Follette, facing a well-known and respected Democrat, would run as well as Theodore Roosevelt did against a weak Democrat, it is also true that La Follette ran behind the whole state Republican ticket by about 5 percent. He was hurt by the third-party protest candidacy of Stalwart former governor Scofield. Socialist candidate William Arnold got more than 5 percent, and the Prohibition ticket got roughly 2 percent.

The point here is that while La Follette won without any serious challenge, not everybody loved La Follette in his time in Wisconsin. He had, in fact, a good deal of opposition from Democrats, Socialists, Prohibitionists, and, not least, fellow Republicans. He was, for example, notably weak in Milwaukee, where, even though he carried the city in 1904, it was with only 39 percent of the vote, while his Democratic opponent received 34 percent and the Socialist candidate 27 percent. How much Stalwart dissent there was at the polls, however, is debatable. There was much talk of it, especially in 1904, and a study of La Follette's vote in the more affluent areas of such cities as Milwaukee and Oshkosh shows that it was there and that he ran behind the general Republican ticket.

Yet former governor Scofield's small 3 percent in 1904 suggests there was more talk than action among conservatives about abandoning La Follette. La Follette was a controversial figure whom many people of good will did not support. His campaigns, certainly that of 1904, were intense affairs not just for his remarkably able campaigning but for the determined opposition he attracted. Yet he certainly had many fervent supporters, self-identified Progressives and, outside urban Wisconsin, Scandinavians, people of British ancestry, and native-born offspring of native-born Americans. There is no mistaking that La Follette had the majority with him when it came election time in 1904 and in every election thereafter.[31]

But 1904 was not just about La Follette winning reelection. It was a clean sweep for the La Follette Progressives, who gained control of the legislature and the other state offices, completely defeating the Stalwarts. Even more, it was also about the final step toward success of La Follette's most important reform proposal, the direct primary, the process by which voters rather than party conventioneers would decide who should run for office. Nothing was dearer to La Follette's heart than this reform, which was aimed at bringing democracy (or at least, as it has turned out, a party's most committed voters) to party and state government.

The primary bill went through many stages on its tortuous path toward becoming a law. After much complex political jockeying over a period of years, but especially in 1903, the state legislature passed the bill and Governor La Follette signed it. The law provided for a wide-open primary, even allowing crossover voting, permitting citizens loyal to one party to vote in the primary of another (an established feature of Wisconsin primary elections today), despite Governor La Follette's initial opposition. But, for it to take effect, the law required approval by the voters in the November 1904 election. This duly happened; the law passed, receiving 62 percent of the vote. This victory brought La Follette and his entire movement tremendous personal satisfaction. Indeed, it was a historic triumph for La Follette, and it was finally achieved in the way he wanted—by vote of the electorate.[32]

The election of 1906, however, brought out the worst of La Follette's political gamesmanship. In 1905 a seat had opened up in the U.S. Senate, and La Follette arranged for the state legislature, which he then controlled, to elect him to fill the vacancy. The move enabled him to fulfill a longtime dream, and he was to hold the seat with distinction for more than twenty turbulent years, until his death in 1925. When La Follette went to Washington, his lieutenant governor and Progressive ally, James O. Davidson (known as "Yim" Davidson), moved into the governor's chair. Davidson, born in Norway, was the first prominent Norwegian to gain serious power in the Wisconsin political process. He was a prosperous merchant, long active and successful in local and state politics, and quite popular with fellow Norwegians, as was his leader.

La Follette, however, was much more enthusiastic about a closer ally, sometime Assembly majority leader Irvine Lenroot, and preferred him for governor in 1906. Davidson had other ideas and was quite shocked that La Follette planned to push him aside. La Follette then discovered, and not for the last time, that he could not rule every fellow Progressive. Davidson refused to back down, and he and Lenroot conducted an embarrassing and bitter primary, with La Follette backing Lenroot all the way.

Lenroot lost to the popular Davidson in the first Republican governor's primary, a defeat for La Follette that was not without irony. Indeed, Lenroot and La Follette lost big as Davidson rolled up 64 percent of the vote and carried sixty-eight of seventy-one counties then in the state. Davidson had the support of many Progressives, especially in Norwegian areas, where he was a favorite son and where there was plenty of hostility to Sweden and Swedes like Lenroot (Norway declared independence from Sweden in 1905), a vivid reminder that ethnic politics was very much alive in the Progressive

Era. Davidson also got solid and enthusiastic support from Republican Stalwarts, who were only too happy to use La Follette's own primary to cut La Follette and his perceived toady, Lenroot, down to size.

Davidson, who was negatively described in La Follette family circles as little more than a rural grocer, got the last laugh, but the movement as a whole suffered because of La Follette's poor judgment. Even though Davidson never abandoned his commitment to the Progressive movement, his break with La Follette was permanent. He went on to win the governorship in a landslide in 1906 brushing aside Irish Roman Catholic Democrat John Aylward and the Socialist and Prohibition candidates, getting 57 percent of the vote, 25 percent more than Aylward, his nearest opponent. Republicans again ruled.[33]

The next election, in 1908, was relatively routine, with little of interest to report at the gubernatorial or presidential level in Wisconsin. William Howard Taft had no problem winning the presidency.[34] He carried Wisconsin in a landslide over William Jennings Bryan, 54.5 percent to 37 percent. Eugene Debs, running on the Socialist ticket, got 6 percent, and the Prohibition Party won 2.5 percent. The La Follette movement had accepted Davidson as governor by that point, and there was no contest as he rolled over the Democratic, Socialist, and Prohibition candidates. It was all quite straightforward in a state that was now one-sidedly Republican.

Within the La Follette Progressive world, however, things were never simple, as illustrated in 1908 as a primary developed for the other U.S. Senate seat. La Follette designated Wisconsin state senator William Hattan as the individual whom he wanted as his Senate colleague. Even as he did so, Francis McGovern, leader of the Progressive movement in Milwaukee, which was at best in an uneasy alliance with La Follette, decided he wanted to run, and he did. Yet a third candidate associated with the movement was Isaac Stephenson, who had actually been elected to the seat in 1907 after the resignation of Senator Spooner. Stephenson, a lumber magnate and sometime-officeholder, had been a big-time contributor to the La Follette political efforts over the years, giving as much as $500,000, an extraordinary amount worth millions in current dollars. La Follette intended that Stephenson would just fill in until the election for the full term in 1908, but Stephenson had other ideas. Not surprisingly, after La Follette proposed to drop him, Stephenson became sharply critical of La Follette. According to his autobiography, Stephenson believed that La Follette had used him as a money man only to finance La Follette campaigns, as just another cog in what Stephenson argued was a machine politics operation.

So another nasty primary fight took place within the La Follette movement, and Stephenson emerged as the victor while La Follette lost, with
plenty of bitterness and bad feelings all around. But there was also good
news for the La Follette movement in 1908. In a historic vote the electorate
supported another longtime goal of La Follette's: a state income tax. The
vote was never in doubt, since both parties endorsed a state income tax, and
it won with just shy of 70 percent of the statewide vote. When the legislature
then passed an income tax law, La Follette could and did take personal satisfaction that yet another plank in his reform platform was in place. La Follette
knew that his victory came only because of his efforts to sell the once-radical
idea and because he created a political movement that made its accomplish-
ment irresistible in the end.[35]

Two years later, 1910 was again business as usual from one angle. The
Republicans won as they always did, this time with Francis McGovern,
who sailed into the governorship defeating Adolph Schmitz, the Democrat,
161,619 to 110,442. But there were some signs of turmoil. McGovern got
only 50.6 percent of the total vote for governor; Socialist candidate William
Jacobs, by rolling up 39,547, gained 12 percent of the vote, and the Prohibition candidate received his usual 2 percent. Moreover, McGovern won only

Francis McGovern, governor 1911–15
(Wisconsin Historical Society, WHi-2802)

after a bruising fight in the Republican primary, a three-way fight among one Stalwart and two Progressives. The Stalwart was Edward Fairchild, a state senator from Milwaukee (a different Milwaukee than Socialist Milwaukee), and the other Progressive was William Lewis, who addressed the increasingly controversial drinking issue by proposing a county option solution.

Francis McGovern was an impressive figure, a lawyer who served as a hard-hitting Milwaukee County district attorney from 1905 to 1909. In that role McGovern built his reputation while fighting corruption in Milwaukee city government. As leader of a busy and determined team, he was often successful in bringing down corrupt prominent city politicos, generally Democrats. He first entered our story when he dared run against the approved La Follette candidate for Senate in 1908 and lost, but then won the governorship in 1910 and was reelected in 1912. An Irish American whose parents were born in Ireland, McGovern was noted for his interest in what may be called urban progressivism. He was interested in economic and social programs for workers and the urban poor, favoring the progressive income tax, workers' compensation for industrial accidents, and a minimum wage and other protections for working women, and he did what he could to advance that agenda.

La Follette was never enthusiastic about McGovern, but he did not oppose his bid for the governorship, and meanwhile McGovern carefully kept his distance from La Follette. They were warily cooperative Progressives, though frequent conflicts occurred among La Follette and McGovern Progressives in primaries and in the state legislature over, among other things, who should be the Republican nominee for president. There was little that McGovern favored that La Follette opposed in terms of policy, and vice versa, but a difference in emphasis was sometimes present. La Follette was more oriented toward political reform and McGovern toward urban, industrial reform. The modest policy differences between McGovern and La Follette reflected their backgrounds and their bases of support more than anything philosophical. La Follette's base was rural and small-town Wisconsin; McGovern's was the bigger, industrial cities, especially Milwaukee. It is probably fair to say that most of the tensions between La Follette and McGovern camps had their deepest roots in the clash of two ambitious and competitive personalities, each eager to direct Wisconsin Progressivism.[36]

THE 1912 ELECTION

All the serenity and stability of the Wisconsin electoral system collapsed in 1912, paralleling what happened in the country at large. Theodore Roosevelt's split with his hand-picked successor, William Howard Taft, led Roosevelt to run as a third-party candidate, just as the governor of New Jersey, Woodrow Wilson, emerged as a formidable Democratic presidential candidate. The results in Wisconsin were startling; Woodrow Wilson won the state as a Democrat, the first time a Democratic presidential candidate had carried the state since Grover Cleveland in 1892. Wilson obtained only a distinct minority of the popular vote, 41.1 percent, though it was 4.5 percent over Bryan's last showing in 1908. Taft came in second with 32.7 percent, while Roosevelt won just 15.6 percent. The Socialists were a significant factor in this wild presidential election: their ticket headed by Eugene Debs pulled in 8.4 percent of the vote.[37]

An electorate divided among four major parties was what ensured Wilson his victory, especially the Republican split between Taft and Roosevelt. What was surprising was that Roosevelt did not do as well in Wisconsin as he did in other states with an equally vibrant reform tradition. The best explanation is the falling-out between Roosevelt and La Follette over who should be the Progressive candidate for president in 1912. Never shy, La Follette felt he deserved that honor and was bitter that the 1912 Progressive Party convention did not agree. La Follette had run in and won the Wisconsin presidential primary with 73 percent of the vote over Taft's 26 percent, but the Progressive Party did not choose him as their nominee, in part for very practical reasons. Roosevelt was enormously popular in the country, and no one could match his energy and charisma in American politics.

La Follette did not get on board when Roosevelt was nominated. Instead he sulked and cast a blank ballot for president. Outside his inner circle his characteristic egocentric stance drew mixed reviews, but it was widely agreed that some votes that might have gone to Roosevelt if La Follette had campaigned for him went to Wilson instead. Moreover, some among La Follette's supposed allies, such as Irvine Lenroot, fell afoul of La Follette in his struggle to win the Progressive Party nomination, and they quickly fell out of favor.[38]

Roosevelt ran well, according to my Wisconsin sample, especially among Swedish Americans, who were long linked to liberal causes. (In fact, he carried most Swedish areas in the nation, not just those in Wisconsin.) He ran well among German Protestants in rural and small-town Wisconsin but less well among Catholics, whether they were German, Polish, or Irish. He was stronger in farm areas than villages, and he was also a force in smaller cities throughout the state. Yet Roosevelt's campaign failed in both Milwaukee and Madison, where he drew considerably less than 10 percent of the vote, and that seriously hurt his overall totals. Milwaukee Socialists did not vote for Roosevelt, and Madison Democrats were happy to support Wilson.[39]

In the contest for governor, Republican Francis McGovern won reelection, though he faced an unexpectedly close contest, beating Democrat John Karel by a slim 4 percent. The Socialist candidate, Carl Thompson, ran ahead of Debs's presidential showing, garnering 8.8 percent. Karel, known as "Ikey," was a serious opponent, well known as an experienced Milwaukee judge and a famous football player at the University of Wisconsin in the 1890s. He picked up some Stalwart support from voters fed up with the liberal McGovern and seeing that they were completely out of the picture in Wisconsin Republican politics. They recognized that Karel was a conservative Democrat.

Meanwhile, La Follette offered only tepid support for McGovern, remembering McGovern endorsing Roosevelt in the fight over who should be the Progressive Party nominee for president. Meanwhile, the regular Republican organization was upset when McGovern, their nominee for governor, endorsed Roosevelt's Progressive Party candidacy.[40]

THE WOMEN'S SUFFRAGE MOVEMENT, THE CAMPAIGN OF 1912, AND ULTIMATE VICTORY

On one issue 1912 was not a good time for Progressivism in Wisconsin, and that was evident as the negative results rolled in on the statewide referendum on women's suffrage. By the late 1880s the movement was in poor shape. There were few members, fewer local branches, little money, and much debt and a real sense that nothing good was happening for the cause, a situation that lingered until well after the turn of the century. The one positive development in this period was the founding in 1887 of the movement's periodical, *The Wisconsin Citizen,* which continued publication until 1917.[41]

Despite the limited viability of the Wisconsin Woman Suffrage Association and its efforts to achieve women's suffrage into the first years of the twentieth century—including failed efforts in 1903, 1907, and 1909, among other years, to get the state legislature to cooperate—1911 proved to be year of beckoning opportunity. That year the state legislature, responding to pleas of suffragists, approved giving the vote to women, subject to the electorate ratifying this judgment at the ballot box in 1912. Governor McGovern signed the bill and suddenly the campaign was on, one that had an electrifying effect on women's suffrage supporters. A tremendous energy was injected into the movement as it swung into action to win the 1912 referendum. The story of that effort is an interesting one of politics in action. But in the end it was defeated, 63 percent to 37 percent.[42]

While there was only modest organized political opposition to women's suffrage in the 1912 campaign, there was plenty of evidence of opposition in the media and elsewhere. Certainly there was argument and debate all over the state. Advocates advanced their cause in the two-fold appeal that characterized not just Wisconsin supporters but was standard nationally as well. They spoke of women as equal beings who deserved all the natural and legal rights of men. They also argued that giving women the suffrage could have excellent public policy benefits for the social good, from improving politics to combating evils in industrial and family life. Opponents insisted that giving women the vote would hurt women and men by destroying traditional, valuable gender roles, undermine the family, and even offend God.[43]

The campaign by the women suffragists involved several key dimensions. One concerned the organizations that carried on the fight. The Wisconsin Woman Suffrage Association (WWSA) had long dominated the flagging women's suffrage movement. It tried to reorganize and rejuvenate in 1909 and actually did so in 1911 as it came alive with the suffrage campaign. A second organization also entered the fight, the Political Equality League (PEL), formed in 1911 by those who were dissatisfied with the WWSA as the vehicle to organize and carry out a campaign, especially one that was aggressive. The leader of the PEL was Ada James, formerly active in the WWSA, whose state senator father shared his daughter's passion.[44] The suffrage movement in 1911–12 this time had considerable success in making local contacts and building local organizations, more than it had ever before. This mattered, as the movement tried hard to run a popular and "less elitist campaign" than in the past.[45]

Leadership in the campaign was crucial and sometimes problematic. Olympia Brown had been head of the WWSA since 1885. Her story as a pioneering Universalist minister and campaigner for women's rights in Wisconsin and all over the country is a compelling one. However, by the time the 1912 referendum was announced, a restless second generation of suffragists in Wisconsin wanted change they thought could only be achieved by a more militant leadership. Ada James and her dissatisfaction with Olympia Brown and the WWSA led to the creation of the PEL in 1911, which she led during the campaign. She was assisted by a dedicated corps of leaders and many volunteers at all levels, among whom Belle La Follette was the most prominent.[46]

Getting the word out was the essential task of the suffragists in the 1912 campaign. There were many approaches. There were innumerable appearances at county fairs, public debates, formal addresses, out-of-state speakers—Jane Addams was the biggest draw—even a movie, *Votes for Women*. They tried "stunts," including dropping leaflets from the air, many car parades, street meetings—whatever might lead to "grabbing the masses' attention."[47] The press campaign was vital, too, in getting the word out, and the work of journalist Theodora Youmans then and later was significant. Great effort was made to garner favorable coverage in both the regular and the foreign-language newspapers, while suffrage activists created their own press by advertising where they could and printing leaflets celebrating their cause, and, as election day approached, reminding the faithful (men) to vote.[48]

One area of notable success was in building a coalition of groups to back the referendum and the larger cause. Between 1910 and 1915 close relations with pro-suffrage socialists were established, and the Socialist Party gave their unqualified endorsement to the referendum. Meta Berger, spouse of Milwaukee Socialist leader Victor Berger, even became an officer of the WWSA. While this connection eventually fell apart in tactical disputes and then over Socialist Party dissent from World War I, in 1912 it was important. Other groups joined the WWSA in 1912 for the referendum, including the Grange, the Woman's Christian Temperance Union, the State Federation of Labor, and the state teachers union—and the WWSA and PEL welcomed them all. No endorsement mattered more, however, than that of the Wisconsin Federation of Women's Clubs, hard-won by Theodora Youmans, since so many suffrage activists had first learned their leadership and organizational skills in the extensive club movement in Wisconsin.[49]

Ada James, Wisconsin
suffragist leader
(Wisconsin Historical Society, WHi-9334)

Two sets of problems in particular beset the 1912 campaign for women's suffrage. One was internal. There were innumerable conflicts and tensions—as there are in all movements—based on alternative conceptions of tactics and strategy as well as clashing personalities. Before, during, and after, the movement was bled by "perpetual schisms" and various figures "parting company," not always peacefully.[50] Moreover, having two organizations, sometimes cooperating but often in conflict, was a serious problem. Another was the chronic shortage of money during the whole history of the movement, very much including the 1912 campaign. Then, as now, money mattered in elections, and the suffrage campaign lacked rich angels who could fund it sufficiently. And the national movement, which was dealing with six other states with referenda that year, was not able to help much. Meanwhile, outside the movement there were other problems. The disappointing lack of interest and even support of many Wisconsin women was a frustration, of course. There was also the intense opposition of the state's brewing industry, which had a lot of money and used it against the movement, fearing that with women suffrage would come prohibition.[51]

It was in addressing the ethnic makeup of the state that the proponents had their greatest challenge. Indeed, it was understood from the start that German Americans in particular and their widely shared patriarchal cultural attitudes posed a huge threat to women's suffrage. After all, it was one thing to talk about equal rights and about women as needed social reformers and it was another thing to confront and overcome the ethnic resistance to their suffrage. This was true not least because few leaders of the movement were part of the self-conscious ethnic groups in Wisconsin. The leaders were generally Yankees of long ancestry in the United States and were frequently of upper- or upper-middle-class background. Moreover, like the leaders of the National American Woman's Suffrage Association, they were at best ambivalent about various "foreigners" who sometimes could not speak English and knew little of the political system *but* who could vote while the highly educated women suffrage activists in most states still could not. Some suffragists spoke of the possibilities of "education" and "advancement," for immigrant women and men, but there was also plenty of fear—and hostility—not far below the surface.[52]

In any case, it was quite a stretch for most women's suffrage leaders to address German American farmers in Shawano County or Polish Americans in south Milwaukee. They made efforts to get their message out by sending ethnic speakers into the various communities, publishing pamphlets in various languages, and attempting to get their word into the many ethnic newspapers that still existed. But the problem remained: many Wisconsin ethnics (and not just males) suspected—correctly—that too many of the ardent proponents of women's suffrage were distinctly uneasy about various ethnic groups. This uneasiness they perceived even extended to wondering whether such people should be part of the American democratic experiment at all.[53]

Rallying the vote for women's suffrage was in vain, however, as there was no way this idea was going to carry Wisconsin in 1912. Wisconsin was a state composed in good part of Americans from traditions that flatly disapproved of a public role for women. Among German Americans vote for the proposition was clearly below 20 percent, and among Protestant Germans it was

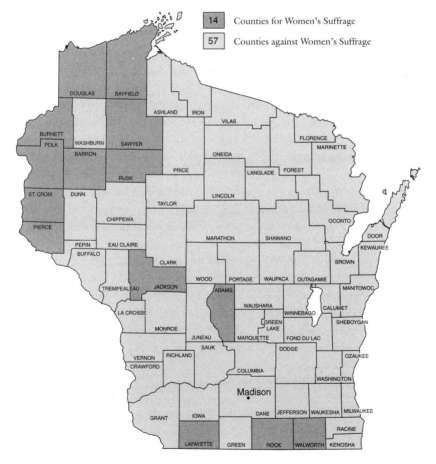

1912 Women's Suffrage Vote

even lower. Thus the town of Brillion in Calumet County was 14 percent in favor of women's suffrage, Lowell in Dodge County was 20 percent, Auburn in Fond du Lac County was 17.7 percent, and Hamburg in Marathon County was 9.2 percent.

In this context it was predictable that the vote for women's suffrage was similar to the later 1926 vote against prohibition. Much of German American Wisconsin, for example, detested liberal reformers who seemed bent on invading their home or interfering with their right to have a beer. But this was hardly a sentiment restricted to this group. Women's suffrage did poorly with voters in one ethnic group after another. There was no interest in Polish American areas in my sample (less than 25 percent support); the town of Dewey in Portage County was 15.2 percent in favor and Dodge in Trempealeau County was 9 percent in favor, and it was the same with Belgian Americans (less than 20 percent support), Dutch Americans, and Catholics in general. The suffrage vote was yet another example in Wisconsin history of ethnic voting, one that was not likely to produce any positive results for pro-suffrage ideas.[54]

Suffrage got nowhere in heavily German and Polish American Milwaukee, either, and it lost in Milwaukee Socialist wards by 2 to 1. Nor did it carry Madison and Dane County. It did carry in the wards around the university, but Madison, then as now, was more than the university. In the more German and Irish American sections of the city, the measure failed.

Where was the liberal vote? After all, Belle La Follette was a leading suffragist and Robert La Follette definitely supported women's suffrage. The answer is that there were some areas of reform sentiment that supported women's suffrage. This was most notably true among Swedish areas in my sample (62 percent) and even more so for the much smaller Finnish areas (72 percent). Norwegian areas were close to 50 percent in favor also. This relative support was predictable since rural and small-town Scandinavians were the most loyal part of the Progressive movement in every dimension. It is also important to note that their home countries had by this time already extended the right to vote to women. These ethnic votes allowed the measure to carry a few counties in western Wisconsin and come close in others that had a heavy concentration of Scandinavians.[55]

One other constituency also showed support for women's suffrage. At least some places heavily Yankee rallied in favor of the proposition, such as the village of Rewey in Iowa County (57 percent) and the town of Forest in Richland County (50 percent) or the prime Yankee county, Walworth, one of the few counties in Wisconsin to vote for women's suffrage. This support was not necessarily a matter of class, though there was an aspect of that in some cities. Rather, again, it was a matter of ethnic background. Here in the strongholds (relatively speaking) of prohibition and, much earlier, antislavery, there arose a firm belief that women should be able to vote. Much of this sentiment was rooted in the belief that enfranchised women would eradicate such evils as drinking and other perceived moral imperfections so often associated with "foreigners." The conclusion we can draw is that liberal Scandinavian and socially conservative Yankee voters came together for women's suffrage as strange allies, and quite unsuccessful ones.[56]

Of course this was not the end of the story. Women's suffrage did come to Wisconsin, but it came from the national level. After the 1912 defeat, the movement in Wisconsin suffered from understandable disappointment and exhaustion. Yet while so much of the organized movement, especially at the local level, faded away, at the state level Theodora Youmans, the new leader, worked hard to keep the cause alive. She turned out to be just the kind of efficient manager the Wisconsin movement needed to see it through to the hour of victory. Youmans got the movement reorganized, if not exactly reenergized. In 1913 she facilitated the delicate task of reuniting the two suffrage organizations. She became president and writer Zona Gale vice president, Ada James executive secretary, and Olympia Brown honorary president. Youmans also undertook a series of attempts to get the state government to schedule another referendum, all of which failed at one point or another.[57]

What finally mattered most in the victory was World War I, as the Wisconsin women's suffrage leaders understood themselves. The tremendous involvement and service of so many women across the state and nation in the war effort stimulated a widespread sense of appreciation and moved Congress to approve a woman suffrage amendment to the Constitution, the Nineteenth. It did so in 1919, triggering the next step, the requirement that three-fourths of the states had to ratify the amendment. Soon after, the Wisconsin legislature approved the amendment. State senator David James, long an advocate of women's suffrage and father of suffrage leader Ada James, raced to Washington by June 13 and made Wisconsin the first state to file its approval.[58]

But it was not until 1920, and after a hard struggle, that sufficient states ratified the Nineteenth Amendment. When they did, the battle was suddenly over. Women had the vote—in Wisconsin and everywhere in America. There was a certain bittersweetness to the Wisconsin story since victory did not really come from within the state, despite all the effort by the movement over so many years. This fact was perhaps ironic given the state's famous reputation at this time as being a center of "progressivism." The truth is that while

Theodora Youmans, Wisconsin suffragist leader (Wisconsin Historical Society, WHi-1927)

women's suffrage was never a major item on Wisconsin's male Progressives' agenda, its eventual adoption was arguably the most important reform of the Progressive Era.

1914 AND BEYOND

If 1912 did not provide enough turbulence in Wisconsin voting behavior, 1914 was at least as spectacular. Once again at the center was the bitter feuding within the Republican Party, the three-way struggle between the La Follette, McGovern, and Stalwart factions. In the Republican primary "brawl" might be the best word to describe the behavior. La Follette sought to promote his associate, John Blaine, to the nomination for governor, the office McGovern was leaving. But in the multicandidate primary, Emanuel Philipp defeated Blaine. Philipp had earlier been associated with La Follette, but like others he had long since moved on and had become the candidate of the Stalwarts. A successful businessman of Swiss descent, Philipp had been active in politics as well as business. He saw himself as someone who could bring stability and calm to Wisconsin politics, as distinguished from the La Follette "haters," with whom he had and was to have many more conflicts. Philipp went on to win the governorship with only 43 percent, defeating the familiar Democratic candidate, John Karel, who got 37 percent, while the Socialist Oscar Ameringer received 8 percent.[59]

In the process he also defeated a third candidate, John Blaine. The most intriguing aspect of the November 1914 election for governor was Blaine's insistence on running as an independent. La Follette and Blaine agreed that they could not possibly support the official Republican candidate, Philipp, since he had defeated Blaine and was an agent of their enemies; nor could they support the Democratic or Socialist candidates. As a result, Blaine decided to run himself, with La Follette's hearty approval. But Blaine was able to muster only 10 percent of the total vote, which resulted in La Follette and his allies losing control of the state Republican Party. In a way, this election defeat and loss of party control marked a kind of end of the first Progressive Era in Wisconsin. It was compounded by the simultaneous defeat of ten referenda that the Progressives had promoted, principally to reform state government and politics. Suddenly it did seem as if the Progressive movement just "fell apart."[60]

Meanwhile, although La Follette lost these races, he "won" (if winning is defined, as he too often did define it, as taking revenge) another, the election for the vacant U.S. Senate seat. Governor McGovern very much wanted to go on to the Senate, but the La Follette who never forgot grievances did not want McGovern to be his colleague there. So La Follette arranged to have McGovern challenged in the Republican primary by Lieutenant Governor Tom Morris. However, as seemed to be happening regularly, La Follette's candidate lost in the primary. It has been suggested that Morris was hurt because he was a Catholic, and there is no doubt that he faced criticism in some Protestant Scandinavian circles because he was a Catholic. However, more to the point was the fact that he was running against a well-established Progressive governor who could count on Stalwart sympathy whenever he faced a primary contest with a La Follette candidate.[61]

McGovern had every reason to assume that, as winner of the Republican primary, he would be elected to the Senate in November. La Follette, however, had other ideas. The Democratic nominee was Paul Husting, a well-respected politician and state senator. He was not a conservative Democrat. With Husting as the Democrats' challenge to the disliked McGovern, the La Follette camp quietly passed the word that Husting would make a good senator, and in a truly stunning surprise he emerged as the winner by 956 votes. Husting was the first Democrat elected to the Senate from Wisconsin since 1892. Although some ticket-splitting had to occur, since Husting could not otherwise have won in a Republican state, the areas he carried were the dependably Democratic ones, aided above all by German Americans returning to the Democratic fold. Although the Democratic Party was temporarily strengthened in the early Wilson years, La Follette undoubtedly had an effect, as margins for McGovern in Republican areas dropped allowing Husting to slip through.[62]

WISCONSIN SOCIALISM

It is not possible to write about Wisconsin electoral politics without considering at some length the phenomenon of Wisconsin socialism and its role in elections. At one time, especially from about 1900 through 1920, the Socialists were major players in Wisconsin electoral dynamics. In fact, the energy for socialism was a significant factor then, an interesting historical note for those who would understand the complexities of Wisconsin's frequently unconventional electoral behavior.

The center of socialism in Wisconsin was always Milwaukee, with its huge German American population and its extensive industrial workforce. By 1900 Milwaukee had become a large industrial city with a population of 285,000. The organized labor movement there had a long uneven history, but socialist efforts before the formation of the Social Democratic (Socialist) Party, always heavily composed of German Americans, had gone nowhere. After

1897 the movement galvanized much of organized labor in Milwaukee, and it was that that allowed for electoral success over time. Without the complex, often troubled but strong relationship between the unions and socialism in Milwaukee, the socialist story would have been different indeed. Equally central, though, was the presence of so many immigrants who had the example of the vibrancy of German socialism as a model. And Milwaukee was extraordinarily German as American cities went—the most German, in fact. It was also the city in the United States with the most foreign-born residents, 39 percent in 1890. They were mostly German, but a large proportion was Polish.[63]

The Social Democratic Party was born July 9, 1897, in Milwaukee, with the national party leader Eugene Debs delivering the main address. That event came about only after a highly complicated and lengthy effort by an array of would-be midwives seeking to birth a serious socialist party in the United States. For example, many of a socialist inclination had tried to work with the Populist Party and movement and even did so in the early 1890s. But that effort eventually failed when the Populists opted for the cause of free silver and its spokesperson, William Jennings Bryan, and chose the Democrats as their vehicle in the campaign of 1896.[64]

The first Socialist Party campaigns did not have much impact on city elections in Milwaukee. But in 1898 the party began running a full slate of candidates both in Milwaukee's municipal elections and statewide. In the process organizers started learning how to build an electoral machine. Slowly but determinedly the party eventually operated on a block-by-block basis in German and later Polish workingmen's areas of Milwaukee, often led by paid organizers. They created a local press, a process party leader Victor Berger played an important role in, and every campaign also saw an intensive use of leaflets and other literature. A Milwaukee Central Committee was in charge, whose members were elected in sometimes spirited elections, and applicants for party membership were screened and expected to sign an oath of commitment.[65]

By 1904 progress was obvious as the party elected its first batch of alders and county supervisors. Throughout this period, one factor that helped the party was the corruption that was rife in the controlling city party, usually the Democratic Party. The Socialists offered an alternative, stressing their clean government credentials and their separation from the traditional parties while downplaying any real socialist ideas. This approach did not work with everyone. The Roman Catholic Church opposed the party intensely, recognizing as it did the atheistic beliefs of orthodox socialists. Meanwhile, however, the party advanced in organization and in popularity.[66]

The best year for the Socialist Party in Milwaukee was 1910. After all the careful and hardworking preparation, victory was theirs. They captured the mayor's office and control of the city council. The new mayor, Emil Seidel, won with an impressive 46.5 percent of the three-party vote. A native of the United States, Seidel had moved to Milwaukee when he was five years old, but later in life he spent six years in Germany, where he converted to socialism. He assisted in the founding the Social Democratic Party and played a major role in the Milwaukee branch right from the start. He was a Socialist alder both before and after his term as mayor and even ran as the party's candidate for vice president of the United States with Eugene Debs in 1912.[67]

Seidel's victory was a significant first step toward the long mayoral rule of Milwaukee by the Socialists, dominance that over the years produced a remarkably successful city administration, though it was not a full realization of the socialist ideology. In fact, little in Milwaukee was ever socialized by the Socialist governments of the city. The 1910 victory, and later ones as well, built on the carefully nurtured Socialist image of honest municipal government that focused on successful delivery and workings of ordinary services, especially sewers and streetcars.[68]

It was Victor Berger who was the dominant force in Milwaukee socialism. Berger was born in 1860 in Austria-Hungary and came to the United States as a teenager and to Milwaukee when he was twenty-one. Tall with a solid build, Berger taught German in high school for a number of years before becoming a full-time Socialist Party organizer and publisher in 1892. He was a Jewish agnostic who married into a family of Lutherans and was skillful at avoiding fights and smoothing divisions. He loved the life of Socialist Party politics, the tactics, the practical maneuvers, the development of long-term strategies. He was an effective speaker and tireless campaigner. He lived a middle-class life with a happy family and even owned a second home in the countryside.[69]

Berger's commitment to his form of reform-oriented socialism never wavered, even in the face of serious persecution. He was committed to nonviolence as the means of change in the United States and sought reconciliation between classes on the path to socialism. Solidarity with the working classes was always essential, though, and he was a determined supporter of the trade union movement, one that often disappointed him by its conservatism and frequent antisocialism. Thus, for example, much as he disapproved of the world of drinking, he always fought prohibition, standing with the Milwaukee-based brewers union. For him, socialism had to acquire an American face, deal with American issues and situations, and proceed gradually forward toward popular democratic control of the main means of production.

Victor Berger, Socialist Party leader (Wisconsin Historical Society, WHi-1901)

Berger's central role in the formation and organization of the Socialist Party in Milwaukee (and elsewhere) included taking an active part in electoral politics. The most famous side of that was his election to Congress from Milwaukee in 1918. When he was expelled from Congress in November 1919, he sought and obtained reelection in a special election the following month. The House of Representatives expelled him a second time. He lost in the Harding Republican landslide of 1920 but was elected again in 1922. He continued to be reelected through the 1920s, even as socialism was in steep decline in Milwaukee and the country as a whole. In 1924 Berger supported La Follette's third-party run for the presidency but with a notable lack of enthusiasm for the man he viewed as a mild reformer.

Berger's troubles with Congress derived from his 1919 conviction for conspiracy to hurt the World War I effort, a conviction that the Supreme Court eventually overturned on a technicality. His repeated reelections were tributes to him personally and reflected disgust over his poor treatment during the war, but they were also a part of Wisconsin (in his case, Milwaukee) German payback for those who had turned on them during the war. Like La Follette, when the tide turned after the war, the memories of German Americans in Wisconsin proved long, and Berger was one of the beneficiaries. At the same time, however, Berger feared (correctly) that he was so integral to Wisconsin socialism, despite all the efforts to build a party that transcended any leader, that the party might not endure as a viable organization after he left the scene. That proved to be true, though his death in 1929 was far from the only reason his prediction panned out.[70]

Later Socialist Party figures in Milwaukee were unabashed "municipal" socialists, whose connection with the historic party, much less real left-wing politics, was highly tenuous. These included Daniel Hoan, Socialist Party mayor of Milwaukee from 1916 to 1940, who later became part of the effort to rebuild the Democratic Party during the World War II era. He resigned from the Socialist Party the day after Pearl Harbor in 1941, and in 1944 and again in 1946 he was the Democratic candidate for governor of Wisconsin. Still later, before his death in 1961, he tried unsuccessfully for the House of Representatives, the State Senate, the U.S. Senate, and even the mayoralty of Milwaukee.

Hoan's long and distinguished service as the Socialist mayor of Milwaukee began with his election in 1916. His first victory came more from his reputation as one who would fight the private electric company, its pricing, and its practices than anything else. And his later triumphs were on the basis of his "sewer socialism," taking care of basic services in an efficient and honest way that appealed to people quite apart from abstract socialist doctrines or party pronouncements from New York or, for that matter, Milwaukee.

He was born in 1881 to a working-class family in Waukesha. His parents divorced early in his life, and Hoan went to work full time when he was thirteen years old. He became a committed socialist early on, and from the start of his career he stressed what he saw as being "practical socialism." At the University of Wisconsin, where he was noted for his effective oratory, he formed the Socialist Club and became the first socialist class president. In 1908 he began working as a labor lawyer in Milwaukee.

Hoan came into the mayor's office in 1916 from his service as the popular city attorney, and in his first race for mayor he ran far ahead of the rest of the municipal Socialist ticket. He ran on such issues as garbage collection and city planning and avoided grandiose Socialist Party rhetoric. His most diffi-cult challenges came during World War I, when he was caught between the opposition to the war by the Socialist Party and the huge backlash that stand temporarily caused. He also had to deal with federal and local efforts to sup-press civil liberties while at the same time facilitating the army draft in Mil-waukee and avoiding giving aid and comfort to those advocating revolution. He did manage the diverse elements of turbulent Milwaukee well enough so that even though he alienated the most hard-edged ideologues on all sides, he gained reelection in both 1918 and 1920. It was not easy given both the attack on him and all Socialists as traitors or near-traitors, or at least obvi-ously anti-American, as well as the active antiwar campaigns of Victor Berger and other Socialists.[71]

Hoan's eventual loss as mayor in 1940 to Carl Zeidler was not a repudia-tion of a socialism that was long since dead in Milwaukee in all but name. The time had come for a change. In fact both Carl Zeidler and his brother Frank Zeidler, who was mayor from 1948 to 1962, were also self-declared socialists. When Frank Zeidler's time as mayor also came to the end in 1960, there was no more pretense. Socialism had come to an end in Milwaukee.[72]

There are valuable studies of the phenomenon of the Socialist Party in Mil-waukee and elsewhere in Wisconsin. It is no secret that the core and the sub-stance of Socialist Party support lay among German Americans, especially skilled workers (who were more likely to be union members) but also many unskilled workers. In fact it is reasonable to argue that the most truly ethni-cally based party in Wisconsin history was the Socialist Party, though that is not its image.

However, class issues were relevant as well. The Socialist Party in Milwau-kee was consistently a working-class party and was opposed by the middle and upper classes in election after election. Closely connected to this scenario was the considerable Socialist Party influence over Milwaukee's unions and, for some years in fact, control of those unions. In many cases union support of Socialist candidates was decisive.

Over time, support among Polish American workers in the city also expanded considerably, though it varied from election to election. It sometimes made up 15 percent or more of the Socialist vote in the later years after 1910, though with the arrival of World War I Polish American enthusiasm for the Socialist Party in Milwaukee declined in light of Socialist opposition to a war many Poles saw as a means to a free Poland.

How well the Socialist Party did in any given election from 1898 through 1920 depended entirely on how well it did with German, and to some extent Polish, working-class voters in Milwaukee. This revolved around all sorts of issues in the larger political environment, the quality of Socialist candidates and their level of organization, and the efforts of their opponents. It was rare, for example, for the party to command a majority of the electorate in Milwaukee. Socialist candidates obviously profited from the usual three-or-more-party elections in Milwaukee. In its first great victory for mayor in 1910, no particular element swung to the Socialist Party, but support among its target groups did increase. When the party lost ground, as it did in 1912, it suffered from a temporary perception that it was just another political party and it faced a unity ticket from the Republican and Democratic parties. No consistency could be seen, only dynamic change.[73]

Despite continued success in winning the mayor's office, Socialist Party control of the city's Common Council continually proved elusive after 1910. Year after year, far into the 1920s and beyond, some Socialists were able to win election to the council, but control of it was something else again. That kind of triumph did not happen again after 1910, and from that perspective 1910 was the high point for the Socialist Party of Milwaukee.[74]

The actual amount of support for Socialist tickets statewide varied greatly but was a significant aspect of the Wisconsin electoral system from 1908 through 1920. Milwaukee was the center, and it could be counted on to deliver many Socialist votes in November, quite apart from its varying but often real success in the spring municipal elections. Rarely did its November totals fall below 25 percent of the city vote by 1908 and after, and it reached a high in 1918 of 42 percent as Socialist voting became a vehicle for protesting an unpopular war and an unpopular insistence on militant patriotism. The situation in Wisconsin as a whole was different, but even the Socialist

Party generated more than 5 percent of the state vote regularly and 17 percent in 1918 and a still-impressive 11.5 percent in 1920. Of course the 1918 and 1920 votes were misleading as indicators of authentic Socialist strength, but votes they were, and Socialists welcomed them.

Socialist Party strength in its heyday in major cities ran from 5 to 10 percent depending on the city, with industrial German Sheboygan proving again and again to be the most Socialist city outside Milwaukee. Similarly, the Socialist vote in industrial Kenosha was greatest among skilled workers, many of German extraction. Socialist voting in Wisconsin was consistently an urban affair. Rural and village support was thin, usually in the 1–2 percent category, even in German areas, never exceeding that proportion in Polish rural areas and small towns and falling well below that in other locations.

The prime exception, however, was the explosive and bitter election of 1918, when German rural areas turned sharply toward the Socialists, yielding an average vote for the Socialists' ticket in German Lutheran rural areas of an astonishing 61 percent and an even more astounding 53 percent in German Roman Catholic towns. For example, the German Lutheran town of Hamburg in Marathon County went Socialist in 1918 with 90 percent of the vote and even Day, a German Roman Catholic town in Marathon County, did so with 52.5 percent. This revolt was still present in a much-reduced form in 1920 as the bitterness against a war directed by Democrats and fully supported by Republicans caused mass defection of German American Wisconsinites from the two "mainstream" parties.

Other ethnic groups in Wisconsin, such as the Norwegians and the Swedes, showed little interest in voting Socialist, though at times their support inched toward 5 percent. Similarly, outside Milwaukee almost no Polish Americans voted for the Socialists, though a few more did in Polish areas of Marathon County in the antiwar years of 1918 and 1920. Only the Finns, the most leftist of all Wisconsin ethnic groups, showed a different face, regularly giving more than 20 percent of their far northern mining and lumbering votes to Socialist Party candidates.[75]

After 1920 Socialist support died away slowly in Milwaukee and throughout Wisconsin, except in the city elections of Milwaukee, where we know it hung on in name only for many decades. Even there, except for Mayors Hoan and Zeidler, who maintained little more than the name, socialism as an ideal as well as a party faded away. A brief moment in the 1930s raised the possibility that this situation might reverse, but hints of such a reversal did not last. Franklin Roosevelt killed socialism in Milwaukee, as elsewhere, in the 1930s.

Among the factors that hurt the movement prior to Roosevelt and the New Deal was the antiradical mood of the 1920s that certainly affected both the state and the national Socialist Party cause. With the Roosevelt alternative available in the 1930s, socialism struck citizens as foolish or dangerous radicalism. Even Mayor Daniel Hoan, who seemed to be the exception to everything, had to face this challenge. Thus in 1936, when the sheriff of Milwaukee County, Joseph Shivers, ran against Hoan for mayor, Shivers argued that, as a socialist, Hoan was a far leftist and was no longer relevant. Hoan survived, but the rest of his ticket was crushed.

Another important part of the story of the decline of the Socialist Party was the shift away from the socialist cause by the Milwaukee union movement. As the twentieth century wore on, the old alliance deteriorated, which hurt the Socialist Party tremendously. The last time that the Wisconsin Federation of Labor suggested voting Socialist in any race was in 1934. By then the unions were in league with Wisconsin's Progressive Party, not the Socialist Party. By the 1940s unions had shifted firmly into their present role as allies of the Wisconsin Democratic Party. Another factor that contributed to the failed relationship with the Socialist Party in the 1930s was the considerable influence that the Communist Party began developing in the Milwaukee CIO unions and in the union at Allis-Chalmers in particular. It meant that the radical wing of the labor movement no longer needed Milwaukee socialism, which it considered too conservative and staid and not at all likely to be sympathetic to the Soviet Union. The feeling was mutual and came to light most sharply as early as 1940 when Mayor Daniel Hoan and the widow of Victor Berger engaged in a spat over the legitimacy of Communism and the Communist Party in the union movement.[76]

In looking at the national picture, scholars suggest several factors that rendered socialism a relative failure in the United States as a whole. The sense of foreignness that originally attracted immigrants and their children (as in some German Americans in Milwaukee) did not help in the long run as assimilation inevitably took its toll and doctrines and dogmas without much American tradition no longer held appeal. Particular events hurt as well. This was true of World War I especially, though, again, Milwaukee socialism did get a temporary boost from that war. But overall the war hurt socialism in America and its reputation, as did the reaction to the war and to radicalism of any sort in the 1920s. This did matter in Wisconsin. The plethora of splits, especially between Socialists and those to the Left, including the Communists, also hurt. Neither group could match the appearance of a more "American" alternative in FDR and the New Deal, the final blow.[77]

ELEMENTS OF THE VOTE

Considerable and valuable attention has been paid to the question of class voting in the Progressive Era. On balance, class voting was modest at best, assuming a distinctly secondary place in the overall picture. Thus efforts to discern some class aspect to rural voting, which was so important in early-twentieth-century America, do not get far. Part of the explanation may be that from the 1870s through World War I, rural Wisconsin did not experience any serious, enduring economic crisis. Patterns of farm income did not correlate with any party, and this was true even with controls for type of agriculture. The exception is the mild evidence that poorer land values did correlate with a greater-than-average vote for La Follette Progressives in the Republican primaries, but the relationship was soft and reflects Scandinavian affection for the La Follette cause more than anything else. Among German American towns in rural Wisconsin, relative income did not predict voting behavior.[78]

The urban picture is a bit different. Although ethnic variables continued to be a far better predictor of voting behavior in the Progressive Era than anything else, there was also a class aspect at work. This was especially true in urban German American voting, but there was also some evidence of class voting overall with, all other things being equal, Republicans tending to do better among more affluent voters. Work on ethnic and occupational measures for class in Kenosha, Oshkosh, and Sheboygan shows that class elements were present though weak.[79]

By 1900 there was a distinct movement of cities toward the Democrats and Socialists and, among the Republicans, toward the Stalwarts, the more conservative wing of the party. This latter fact, of course, seems to clash with the classic thesis of Richard Hofstadter that it was in the urban centers that "progressive" politics made its impact in the Republican Party. But it is not so clear that the two theses clash. Hofstadter's argument is about where the Progressive movement's leadership came from, which he found was distinctly urban. With this in mind it is true enough that "Wisconsin progressivism derived its vitality from the political radicalism of city dwellers."[80]

But that is quite another thing than finding that the typical Republican voter in cities was drawn to the progressive cause. Hofstadter does not really address this issue; but if he had, perhaps he would have discovered that the average Republican in urban areas, at least in Wisconsin, was not an enthusiast for La Follette's brand of progressivism. True, La Follette and other Wisconsin Progressives did better among working-class Republicans than did Stalwart Republicans, but the urban working class and working-class

Republicans were never at the heart of the Progressive voting bloc. They were a part, and they counted, but most of the movement's strength lay elsewhere, in rural and small-town Wisconsin.[81]

Certainly an examination of the ethnic variable during the Progressive Era is needed. To what extent was ethnic solidarity still evident? Based on this study, and even more so on Roger Wyman's impressive work, the results are quite clear: ethnic voting remained present and was indeed more important than any other variable as a guide to voting behavior in the era. After the shock of the 1896 realignment, the old ethnic divisions reappeared and held sway, if in a milder form. The exception was a major decline of Democratic support among German Protestants, a phenomenon that had been occurring gradually over a twenty-five-year period.[82]

Nonetheless, a correlation between German Americans and Democratic voting, especially among German American Catholics, remained, if at a much lower level than before 1893. German Catholic areas consistently voted Democratic in the low 60 percent range throughout the period. A similar level of support occurred in Polish American rural areas and small towns. On Milwaukee's south side, populated by Polish Americans, Democrats also ran well, and the situation was the same among many Irish and Czech Americans. In general, the majority of Roman Catholics remained Democrat.

Republican support also often followed ethnic lines. Belgian areas were overwhelmingly Republican (though anti–La Follette after he attacked Door County's Belgian American congressman in 1904), casting only between 15 and 35 percent of their votes for Democrats from election to election. Scandinavian regions and areas settled by those of British descent were heavily Republican, with Norwegian areas as high as 91 percent Republican in 1906. This was also true, as before, of much of the hodgepodge of native-born of native parents mix that made up a large part of rural Wisconsin. So it went.

The entire subject of German American voting behavior in this period has rightly been described as complex. One good guide to any German American community's behavior at the polls is through its tradition and culture, which varied tremendously from place to place. Another factor in their voting was generational; that is, as time passed more and more younger German American Protestants passed out of the old (usually) Democratic fold. Thus in this period in rural areas and small towns where residents were of German Protestant background, Republicans regularly won, but always in closely contested elections; Democrats won in the 1912 presidential election with a minority of the vote in the four-way contest. Division remained a reality, however.[83]

Equally relevant to this discussion are the ethnic dimensions of the divisions within the Republican primary electorate. La Follette and his allies were popular in many rural areas and small towns in Wisconsin, especially in those settled most thickly by people of Scandinavian origin. Indeed, there was "virtual unanimity" in their combination of Republicanism and allegiance to the La Follette Progressive cause. A good case to be made is that, from an ethnic perspective, Wisconsin Progressivism was about the rise of Scandinavian ethnic groups, which had long been outsiders in the state's Republican politics. Yet Stalwarts had plenty of rural support, especially among German Protestant Republicans. So while ethnic solidarity did not seem as intense in the Republican primary (Democratic ones rarely mattered), ethnic voting was very much present.[84]

The reflections of Jørn Brøndal on the subject of ethnic dynamics in Wisconsin voting in the Progressive Era provide especially valuable perspective. Brøndal argues that Robert La Follette and his movement generally were not sympathetic and indeed not very interested in Wisconsin's traditional, often ethnic politics. Their agenda was oriented in very different directions. Certainly "from an ethnic perspective the movement represented nothing less than a benign attempt to de-ethnicize politics, to rechannel political argument . . . by confronting . . . social problems and . . . economic issues."[85]

Brøndal also notes that this situation presented a paradox. After all, the Progressive Republicans and La Follette were very much allied with specific ethnic groups—especially Scandinavian Americans, who supported them virtually as an entire ethnic group.[86] And as this chapter has suggested, the ethnic factor otherwise hardly disappeared in Progressive Era Wisconsin—though its sway did diminish, as Progressives had hoped.

5
Turbulent Years
WISCONSIN IN THE TEENS AND TWENTIES

THE ELECTORAL CHAOS OF 1912 in Wisconsin, followed by the surprising victory of Democrat Paul Husting as U.S. Senator in 1914, seemed to leave observers unclear what direction state voting behavior would now take. It wasn't long, however, until that question was answered when events of national and international scope brought state Democrats to their knees and ushered in a new Republican era, a result few would have predicted in 1912 or 1914. The pivotal event was World War I. The war and its aftermath determined Wisconsin's voting behavior from 1916 through the 1920s.

In the early decades of the century Wisconsin was a growing state. By 1920 more than 2.6 million people lived within its borders, up almost 13 percent from 1910. It was also a prosperous state. Manufacturing continued to grow and by 1920 was generating 34 percent of the state's income (up from 23 percent in 1890). Milwaukee and the rest of the southeast industrial region were booming and employed well over a third of the state's workforce. By 1920 Milwaukee had 17 percent of the state's population, a figure that rose to 20 percent in 1930. Nearly half of the citizens of the state lived in jurisdictions with more than 2,500 inhabitants, a figure that advanced to more than half by 1930. Meanwhile, the rural farm population steadily fell, to 35 percent in 1920 and 30 percent in 1930. Agriculture had its ups and downs in Wisconsin during these years, but even still it was more economically stable than most other industries because of its focus on dairying. To be sure, there were differences among farmers, as in any other occupation; those with the best land, often German Americans, tended to do better than many Scandinavian farmers, who came to Wisconsin later and often had poorer land and less successful husbandry practices.[1]

While the First World War greatly slowed the tremendous European migration to the United States that took place from 1890 on, immigration legislation and government actions of the early 1920s largely ended it. In the instance of Wisconsin, however, the rise and fall of the numbers of migrants to the state from the 1890s to the 1920s did not matter as much as it did in some other places. Wisconsin was no longer a prime destination for immigrants, and thus its population steadily became more native-born. By 1920 less than 20 percent of Wisconsin's population was foreign-born, a new low for the state. Of these about one-third were born in Germany, 11 percent in Poland, and 10 percent in Norway. Although religious census data are not the most reliable, of those who claimed church membership in the 1926 religious census 45 percent were Catholic, 33 percent Lutheran, and 2.2 percent Jewish; non-Lutheran Protestants made up the other 19.8 percent in Wisconsin.[2]

THE APPROACH OF WAR

As the result of the Progressive Era, the electoral setting in Wisconsin was unusual for that time. Wisconsin laws now made political parties and their bosses relatively weak, unable to dominate even their explicit adherents. Citizens did not have to register to vote; party primaries decided who party nominees were, not party conventions; and voters could vote in any party's primary. In this way 1916 was just another year in Wisconsin electoral politics. Feuding Progressive factions battled it out within the Republican primary allowing the sole Stalwart candidate, Emanuel Philipp, to win the Republican nomination. He was elected with 53 percent, overwhelming his Democratic opponent, Burt Williams, who received an embarrassingly low 38 percent, while the determinedly antiwar Socialists gained more than 7 percent of the state vote and the Prohibitionists received their usual 2 percent or so.

In the Senate race matters favored the Republican Progressives, since Robert La Follette was the Republican nominee, and he went on to an expected victory. There were, however, some signs even in that contest of a different future. La Follette's Democratic opponent, William F. Wolfe, a La Crosse lawyer, attacked La Follette as being less neutral regarding the war than distinctly pro-German. Wolfe was the son of parents born in Germany and spoke German, but he was an ardent supporter of the supposedly neutralist Wilson and suspected La Follette of having other sympathies.[3]

The year 1916 saw a tumultuous presidential election. Woodrow Wilson had achieved victory in 1912 in Wisconsin, as in the nation, even though he received a distinct minority of the vote. There was no Theodore Roosevelt in 1916 to split the Republican cause, but Wilson and the Democrats made a hard-charging effort to win Wisconsin in 1916 anyway. Wilson was assisted in this effort by Senator La Follette. La Follette sympathized with President Wilson, mistakenly believing Wilson to be a committed noninterventionist peace president and because domestically Wilson had proven to be a fellow progressive.[4]

This Democratic effort to carry Wisconsin was not realistic, however, in the face of the normal Republican majority of Wisconsin. It was not just a matter of the disappearance of a Roosevelt third-party ticket. As much a problem, or more, for Wilson was the well-founded fear among many German Americans that Wilson was not to be trusted and would soon take the United States into war with Germany. Even though the abject hatred of Wilson that World War I produced, especially among many Wisconsin German Americans, which damaged and haunted the Democratic Party in Wisconsin in the 1920s, was not yet a reality, by 1916 many German Americans already sensed that Wilson was sympathetic to the Allies and hostile to Germany. Nor was their confidence boosted by Wilson's too frequent disparaging references to ethnic Americans, which many Wisconsin German Americans took personally.[5]

To be sure, the Republican candidate, Charles Evans Hughes, was no ideal antiwar candidate for Wisconsinites fearing war with Germany. He waffled a great deal and proved too friendly with the bellicose Theodore Roosevelt for many German Americans and Norwegian Americans, among other communities, who were opposed to a war. But he was not Woodrow Wilson. For those in a more intense protest mood there was the Socialist Party, which by 1916 was beginning to pick up plenty of German American votes statewide.[6]

The November results for president were clear even as they reflected Wisconsin's characteristic splits. Hughes carried the state with 49.4 percent, Wilson was second with 42.8 percent, Socialist Allan Benson picked up 6.2 percent, and the Prohibition Party the rest. Overall Wilson gained very little over 1912, but the voting pattern had altered sharply. His biggest losses came in German American areas of the state. For example, in German Catholic rural towns and villages Wilson skidded down from 65 percent in 1912 to an all-time low for a Democrat of 47 percent in 1916; in German Protestant areas he dropped even more, from 44.9 percent in 1912 to 26.8 percent in 1916. In both cases the drop was much greater than it appears because Roosevelt's third-party vote in 1912 also held down the "normal" Republican vote. This vote was back with the Republicans in 1916, helping to create sometimes huge margins in German American areas for Hughes. The result was that more than one-third of Wisconsin's counties switched out of the Wilson column in 1916.

Wilson's gains came in the cities of Wisconsin, including Milwaukee (though even there his margin was held down by the 22 percent Socialist

Benson received), and among non-German rural areas and villages. Evident in my samples is how his advances added up, compensating for some of the dramatic German American losses. In a few cases the gains were dramatic. In Wisconsin's Belgian areas, solidly Republican up until that time, Wilson won big margins; the same thing happened in Czech areas. A very sharp increase in his support in already-Democratic Polish areas occurred as well, each of these results reflecting intense ethnic hostility toward Germany.[7]

In the long run, however, Wilson's poor showing among Wisconsin's German Americans, even including the Roman Catholics, was a sign of approaching disaster for the Democratic Party, which was hardly dominant as it was. Wilson scared the German base of his party in 1916, and when Wilson took the United States into World War I, he destroyed that base and badly injured the party in Wisconsin. He gave the Republican Party the most unexpected and wonderful gift imaginable at the time: the vast majority of German American votes in a hugely German American state.

THE WAR

The decision to enter World War I was a wrenching and divisive one in many parts of the United States—but nowhere more so than in Wisconsin. Wisconsin's star politician, Senator Bob La Follette, opposed the decision to go to war, a decision that dramatically affected him and the electoral politics of Wisconsin until his death in 1925. The wartime hysteria that swept much of Wisconsin, including its local elites, such as those at the University of Wisconsin, while brief, was intense and often directed against La Follette. The entire La Follette family felt it deeply and personally.

The hostility was especially difficult for Belle Case La Follette, Bob's loyal and devoted wife. Though an accomplished woman in her own right and, in 1885, the first woman graduate of the University of Wisconsin Law School, she was shy and did not like being in the public glare, and certainly she did not appreciate bitter vituperation and controversy. While she gave many addresses in and between campaigns, Belle preferred to make her points through her writings in La Follette publications. She wrote hundreds of essays in which she advocated all sorts of reforms, but she especially advanced the case for women's suffrage and later other aids for women's estate. It was no easy task being the wife of "Fighting Bob," the mother of four children, political companion, and a reformer activist in her own right, and the 1917–18 attacks on her husband were very hard on her.[8]

The behavior of some Wisconsin citizens in those war years was shameful, even as the state's young men in great numbers served honorably in the war and many other citizens contributed to the effort at home. Reprehensible behavior included the persecution of German Americans and all things German, especially in areas of the state where German Americans did not predominate. There was plenty of ugly "coercive patriotism," such as forced war bond sales or forced public renunciation of German ancestry and culture, often led by the Wisconsin Loyalty Legion. Many German-ancestry Americans experienced frightening pressures that were a denial of their rights as American citizens, and much of Wisconsin's rich cultural heritage was abandoned in the face of "the massive campaign against everything German."[9]

Two electoral contests took place in 1918 in the midst of the deep tensions and cross-pressures. The first, a special spring election, concerned who would succeed Democratic U.S. Senator Paul Husting, who had died in 1917 in a hunting accident. The contest became a tremendous fight. Indeed, there probably has never been such a senatorial contest in Wisconsin since. The eventual winner was Republican Irvine Lenroot, former speaker of the Assembly, then member of Congress, and longtime La Follette ally. But in 1918 Lenroot had not rallied to support an embattled Senator La Follette, so in the Republican primary La Follette set out to punish Lenroot and backed the candidacy of ally James Thompson. The fight was ugly and bitter, but Lenroot won, in part because he held the loyalty of many traditional Scandinavian La Follette voters who were not willing to abandon Lenroot and who often did not agree with La Follette on the war. Lenroot also had the support of other Progressives who were not of the La Follette camp. It is easy to forget that when the Progressive movement got under way in the late 1890s and early 1900s, La Follette was not the only major voice. There were other Progressives, such as John Esch, who served in Congress for the cause, who were ignored as La Follette rose to prominence, and, as with Esch, they proved to have long memories when the great fight over who would join La Follette in the Senate came to the fore in 1918.[10]

Thompson lost by fewer than 3,000 votes, doing well even in a time of great hostility toward La Follette. Old Bob still had his loyalists, but Thompson fared well also because of a huge wave of German American voters for whom La Follette and any La Follette candidate were now true heroes. Thus Thompson swept the Republican primary vote in heavily German American counties; for example, he received 87.9 percent in Washington, 86 percent in Calumet, 87.4 in Ozaukee, and 73.3 percent in Dodge counties, with an overall correlation between Thompson and German Americans in the Republican primary of .74.[11]

Meanwhile, the Wilson administration was actively involved in the Democratic primary to fill Husting's seat. Naturally eager to retain the seat in the Senate for the Democrats, and especially determined to hold this Senate seat as a rebuke to La Follette, whom they viewed at best as just short of a traitor, the White House promoted the candidacy of distinguished diplomat Joseph E. Davies. He emerged victorious only after a hard contest in the Democratic primary against Charles McCarthy, longtime hero of Wisconsin progressivism because of his work organizing and reorganizing Wisconsin state government. As the winner, Davies undertook an intense campaign against Lenroot. He had the help of both President Wilson and Vice President Marshall, who made it very clear that they viewed Davies as a marvelous alternative to Lenroot, whom they explicitly characterized as of dubious loyalty demonstrated by his shameless bidding for German American votes.

Meanwhile, the two-party contest in 1918 was shadowed by the third-party Socialist effort of Victor Berger. Though he was attacked from all sides as being antiwar and a virtual traitor, he did remarkably well at the polls. Lenroot won the election with 39 percent of the vote; Davies was second with 35 percent, but Berger got a record-breaking 26 percent as the result of a massive shift of German Americans protesting both the war abroad and their treatment at home. The vote marked the high point of Socialist representation in the Wisconsin legislature, with four senators and sixteen members of the Assembly elected.

In his Senate race Berger captured 42 percent of the Milwaukee vote, carrying the city, and got astonishing margins in one German Lutheran community after another—93 percent in the town of Berlin in Marathon County, 93 percent in the town of Mosel in Sheboygan County, 86 percent in the town of Teresa in Dodge County, 92 percent in the town of Hamburg in Marathon County, and 85 percent in the town of Lincoln in Buffalo County. So it went in many German areas as German Americans, especially Protestant ones, voted Socialist in unprecedented numbers. When faced with two pro-war candidates for the Senate, they rebelled and voted for the Socialist, whom they knew hated the war as much as they did.[12]

The second contest was the race for governor, and the victor once again was Governor Emanuel Philipp, Republican, though he managed to obtain only 47 percent of the vote. The Democrat, Henry A. Moehlenpah, a banker, aggressively promoted himself as a loyal American ardently behind the war effort, but he received a quite modest 34 percent of the vote. Meanwhile, Emil Seidel, the first Socialist mayor of Milwaukee, elected in 1910, reappeared as the Socialist candidate and received a stunning 17 percent.

Philipp's reelection as governor was no sure thing, in part because the Democrats tried every way they could to suggest that he was less than 100 percent behind the war effort. While this was not true, he did try with some success to control the patriotic extremists across the state who persecuted those they suspected or knew were not enthusiastic about the war. This moderating effort condemned Philipp in some eyes, but not enough to defeat him in the general election. It did, however, almost defeat him in the Republican primary of 1918, where the same charges forced him to struggle hard and squeak through with a slight margin and the nomination.[13]

THE 1920S

The years 1918 through 1930 marked a period of overwhelmingly Republican dominance in Wisconsin. Although some elections, including the 1924 and 1928 presidential elections, were unusual, they did not alter in the slightest the Republicans' rule of Wisconsin. The Democratic Party was a mere shell in the 1920s. Already seriously damaged in the years after the 1893 depression, it suffered far worse from the reaction—above all from German Americans— to World War I and Wilson. Every Democratic gubernatorial candidate in the five races in the 1920s was decisively defeated. Even worse, scarcely any Democratic opposition could be found in the state legislature; indeed, there were often more Socialist representatives from Milwaukee than there were Democratic representatives from the whole state. At their nadir, in the 1923 and 1925 legislatures, the Democrats had only one member of the Assembly, and between 1923 and 1930 they had no members of the State Senate.[14]

The situation was very different for the Republicans. The party's great founding year for the decade was 1920, the year they had the pleasure of watching the Democrats suffer for Wisconsinites' deep war-weariness and feeling that the peace was lost. This situation was drastically compounded by the lingering bitterness of so many of the state's German Americans over the war. For many of them there was no doubt that the Democrats should be punished—and they made sure of it at the polls.

The presidential election of 1920 was an election in name only in Wisconsin. The most interesting aspect of this contest for Wisconsin was the serious consideration given by Republican kingmakers to making Senator Lenroot the party's vice presidential nominee. The convention resisted this idea, however, and was attracted more by the certain orthodoxy of Calvin Coolidge than the dubious orthodoxy of the former La Follette disciple Lenroot. The actual vote for president in Wisconsin was a huge landslide for Republican Warren Harding, who garnered an astonishing 71 percent of the total. Democrat James Cox got a very low 16 percent; Debs received 11.5 percent, and the still-existent (but about to die electorally) Prohibition Party got 1 percent. The vote pattern for Congress was similar. It is not an exaggeration to say that almost no one in Wisconsin was willing to vote for a Democrat, so deep was the disillusionment and anger.[15]

The actual pattern of the vote, insofar as it was not totally Republican, showed that German support for the Democrats had all but evaporated, falling well below 20 percent even among German Catholics. Closely paralleling this pattern, sometimes even exceeding it, were other neo-German areas, Swiss- and Austrian-based precincts, where, again, memories proved fresh to the detriment of the hapless Democrats. Everywhere, though, the scene was terrible for the Democrats by any measure, often tumbling to well below 10 percent, as was the case in Norwegian, Belgian, and Dutch Protestant areas. The only discernable areas of above-average support came in Polish American areas, rural and urban, though they were also far beneath their previous levels of support. It was a true electoral slaughter, and the Democrats could blame Woodrow Wilson for it.[16]

The level of Socialist support, while declining from 1918, was still substantial, with Eugene Debs receiving 11.5 percent in his run for president. Debs was in jail at the time for his antiwar efforts, but that did not hurt him at the polls with many voters. Indeed, while there he was a symbol for many Wisconsinites of the oppressive wartime federal government. He got 31 percent of Milwaukee's vote, faring best in Polish wards and German working-class wards. He also did well in many other non-Catholic German American areas in the state. In some cities, such as Sheboygan, Manitowoc, and Wausau, he ran strongly, but he also ran well in plenty of German towns, often ones far from the prosperous German areas of south central Wisconsin. To be sure, most of the Socialist vote was a protest vote striking out against the conservative established parties that had so tightly tied themselves to World War I and to the persecution of dissenters in Wisconsin.[17]

The gubernatorial situation was different in that the Democrats did better, getting 36 percent of the vote for their nominee, Robert McCoy. The Socialists managed to get 10 percent for their candidate, William Coleman, a longtime Socialist alderman and later a state assemblyman from Milwaukee, roughly what Debs received in the presidential race. But the election was business as usual for the Republicans, whose candidate, John Blaine, won easily. True, Blaine's portion of the total was only 53 percent, far less than Harding's, but his margin over Democrat McCoy was a significant 17 percent.

Blaine did lose a fair number of Harding voters, running into objections from all sides. His opponent was a war hero who looked very attractive to those who admired war service, something Blaine lacked. Yet, ironically, Blaine's support of the war alienated the rising number of antiwar citizens. Blaine got the nomination only after a bitter fight in the Republican primary. The story is complicated but familiar: Blaine had long been a La Follette acolyte. He had run for governor as an independent in 1914 in hopeless service of a La Follette vendetta against the Republican nominee. Elected attorney general in 1918, Blaine was the logical candidate for the Republican nomination for governor in 1920, but by that time La Follette had split with him. The issue was not Blaine's general commitment to La Follette's Progressive agenda but his support for World War I—a make-or-break issue for La Follette. La Follette failed to endorse Blaine in the primary, as six Republicans fought hard for the nomination, and Blaine only narrowly squeaked by to victory with a distinct minority of the total vote. Undoubtedly Blaine was helped by the fact that La Follette put much more energy into trying to defeat Lenroot's effort to obtain the Republican nomination for senator than in trying to knock off Blaine. La Follette saw Lenroot as a much greater traitor to the La Follette cause, though for the same reason that he broke with Blaine.[18]

John Blaine, governor 1921–27
(Wisconsin Historical Society, WHi-41344)

While La Follette's candidates for both governor and senator lost in the Republican primary, for the Senate race La Follette did not give up, running an ally in November as an independent candidate. Lenroot, however, coasted to victory, riding in on the Harding landslide. Blaine did as well, despite La Follette's lack of support. His war hero opponent could not overcome the anti-Democratic sentiments of 1920. By 1922 Blaine had returned to professional, if hardly warm, relations with La Follette, and he served as governor through 1926. In 1926 Blaine won a seat in the U.S. Senate, where he served one term before he was unseated in the 1932 Republican primary, bringing his political career to an end.[19]

Another reading of the 1920 results, one that steps back from the typically nasty La Follette camp fights, notes that the La Follette movement was still very much alive in Wisconsin. After all, Blaine and Lenroot were unquestionably Progressives, and their victories were certainly not flukes. Moreover, Old Bob won a smashing victory in the state's 1920 Republican presidential primary. And though it had absolutely no influence on the selection of the eventual Republican nominee for president, it did mark an amazing recovery by La Follette in a party and a state that so totally repudiated him only three years earlier.[20]

But the picture was mixed for the Progressive wing of the Republican Party. In fact, much of the energy drained out of the liberal wing of the Wisconsin party in the 1920s, turning it into what historian Robert Nesbit called "a tired, middle-aged movement which supported in office a number of spent political volcanoes."[21] It did, however, still have some political potency at the polls. Indeed, Stalwarts knew how frustratingly true that was. They complained over and over that the La Follette Progressives continued to win because they had an effective machine. What had changed with the Progressives in the 1920s was less the appearance of a machine (the La Follettes ran one almost from the beginning) and more the nature of its constituency. That change made the movement often little more than a continuing protest over World War I and a lost peace, not a source of social dynamism or energy for change.[22]

THE GREAT LA FOLLETTE VINDICATION I: THE ELECTION OF 1922

The year 1922 was a glorious one for Robert La Follette. It was the year of his first great vindication, which is exactly how La Follette himself interpreted it. He was up for reelection to his Senate seat in 1922, and as incredible as it seems, the man so vilified during World War I now had become a great hero in Wisconsin. He swept the Republican primary against William Ganfield, president of Carroll College, with 72 percent of the vote, and then he won in November with about 80 percent of the total vote. To be sure, La Follette's victory in November came against a liberal woman, Jessie J. Hooper, not perceived as a serious alternative by the Wisconsin electorate. But the fact that he did not have a more serious opponent was a significant message in itself. There is no doubt that La Follette's sweeping victory was personal: it was both an apology to La Follette by some voters and a profoundly meant thank-you for his brave opposition to the war by others.

He won by massive margins among Wisconsin's German Americans, who before the war were hardly known as leading La Follette enthusiasts. But in 1922 they took revenge on those who supported the war (and by whom they were sometimes persecuted). German Lutheran areas in rural Wisconsin lined up for Fighting Bob with 93 percent of their vote on average; German Roman Catholics in rural areas supported him with 95 percent on average, and German areas in cities at 87 percent and Milwaukee at 74 percent. It was a tidal wave of German sentiment for La Follette, not for the Progressive on domestic policy but for the great man who stood against the war that so angered and alienated them.[23]

While La Follette's triumphant reelection to the Senate overshadowed everything else, John Blaine won reelection as governor. It was a strange election, because the pathetically weak Democratic Party could not field an official candidate to oppose him since too few Democrats had voted in their primary. The situation for the Republicans could not have been more wonderful, and that of the Democrats more absurd. As an independent Democrat, Arthur Bentley did run against Blaine and got a mere 11 percent of the vote. The Socialists received 8 percent and Blaine a record-breaking 76 percent.[24]

THE GREAT LA FOLLETTE VINDICATION II: THE 1924 PRESIDENTIAL ELECTION AND BEYOND

Senator Bob La Follette's third-party run for president in 1924 is an amazing story. La Follette faced major problems, not least of which was the fact that the United States was at peace and quite prosperous (except in some agricultural areas, though even here conditions were improving). He also encountered all the challenges any third-party candidate without a sophisticated national organization faces, even more so in those more party-oriented times. He had little money and scant local organization. He had problems with supposed allies such as the railroad unions and the American Federation of Labor, and he believed there was intimidation of working-class voters in some places. Moreover, the press was overwhelmingly hostile to him, repeatedly portraying him as a coward or near-Communist or both. On one level, though, none of this mattered to La Follette, who campaigned vigorously all over the country, often under the most difficult conditions, frequently with his family at his side.

La Follette was aided in his efforts by the Democrats' nomination of John Davis, a West Virginia corporate lawyer who hardly offered a challenge to President Calvin Coolidge. Davis received 29 percent of the vote to Coolidge's 54 percent, and La Follette captured 16.5 percent. The disparity between Davis and Coolidge's vote looked more impressive than it actually was because of the way Davis and La Follette split the Coolidge opposition. What was more noteworthy than Coolidge's margin over Davis was La Follette's third-party support. It reached a level that would not be exceeded by a third-party candidate for president until Ross Perot's bid in 1992. La Follette did well overall but especially well in some places. He ran second in a number of states, mostly in the West—including California, Idaho, Montana, Nevada, Oregon, Washington, Wyoming, as well as the Dakotas and Iowa—where he was aided by his vice presidential candidate, Democratic Senator Burton Wheeler of Montana, and he swept Wisconsin. Things went much worse for him in the East, however, and he was predictably completely shut out in the one-party South. While La Follette carried only one county east of the Mississippi, he did run nicely in a number of eastern cities, such as Cleveland and Pittsburgh.[25]

Of course the campaign in Wisconsin was different from anywhere else. La Follette won handily, fashioning what Karl E. Meyer rightly called a "coalition of incompatibles."[26] He got 54 percent of the three-party vote; Coolidge received 37 percent, while Davis lagged far behind with 8 percent and minor parties won the remainder. As with Coolidge's national vote, there was no doubt in Wisconsin of La Follette's big victory over his nearest competitor. But it is also true that he was hardly a unanimous choice in Wisconsin.

His victory coalition consisted of liberal voters and German Americans wanting to support him for his stand against entering the war, two groups that at the time, and certainly later, had little else in common. But they constituted the basis for a "progressivism" in postwar Wisconsin that was larger but more divided than the prewar movement. La Follette's greatest strength in the prewar years had been among Norwegian, Belgian, Swedish, and Finnish voters, in rural areas and villages especially but in cities as well, people who were often quite liberal on economic issues. In reduced numbers

they stayed with him after the war. They were attracted by his 1924 platform attacking the railroads and monopolistic capitalists as well as his political proposals for extensive referenda on issues and curbs on the Supreme
Court. As James Weinstein suggests, radicals were plentiful in that of age
of "normalcy."[27]

Yet in 1924 La Follette had added tremendous support also from Wisconsin's German American voters, including the German Catholics, who had a
score to settle and an affirmation to make. Sampled German support for La
Follette soared above the 80 percent range, especially in rural German American towns, and German support for La Follette in villages was well over
70 percent, often exceeding La Follette's numbers in Scandinavian localities.
In such German Protestant areas as the town of Herman in Dodge County,
La Follette polled 92.3 percent of the vote for president; in Lebanon in
Dodge County 98 percent; in Manchester in Green Lake County 84.8 per-
cent; in Centerville in Manitowoc County 83.5 percent; in Union in Waupaca
County 81.7 percent; and in Grant in Shawano County 89.5 percent. Even in
German Catholic areas the vote was one-sided: Brothertown in Calumet
County 83.1 percent; Day in Marathon County 81.4 percent; St. Cloud in
Fond du Lac County 66.7 percent.[28]

With such loyal German American support, it came as no surprise that La
Follette easily carried Milwaukee and did well in other cities with a high proportion of German Americans, though he did not run as well among urban
German Americans as he did in the countryside. Indeed, La Follette was no
electoral powerhouse in urban Wisconsin apart from Milwaukee and selected
cities densely settled by citizens of German ancestry.

In some areas La Follette did not have support. He had numerous enemies and faced competing parties in 1924, and they tried to defeat him.
His enthusiastic approval from many German Americans was a negative to
many other Wisconsinites, a reminder of his despised antiwar radicalism.
Critics complained that La Follette's 1924 campaign was controlled by socialists and other far leftists. Many Republicans saw his break with the party
as rank disloyalty. Anti–La Follette sentiment was serious among citizens
of British ancestry and many highly assimilated Wisconsinites (native-born
of native-born). Where these Wisconsinites were numerous, so were Republicans and World War I patriots. Thus Beloit, Richland Center, Kenosha,
Mineral Point, Sturgeon Bay, and similar cities proved unswayed by La
Follette. They went for Coolidge, as did numerous towns and villages of
similar ethnic background. Once again, the ethnic cast to the election was
unmistakable.[29]

Study of La Follette's vote in class terms, however, leads nowhere. In the first place, La Follette's appeal was so widespread that he carried the day quite consistently across all classes. Nor do there appear to be any common class characteristics where he did not run well. Rather, the dimensions that mattered were ethnic-cultural, and they mattered a lot.[30] Coupled with La Follette's legendary appeal, they were what brought him his Wisconsin triumph that for him was a vindication and as such a deeply personal victory. But La Follette saw it also as a victory for progressivism, and he was pleased that John Blaine, with whom he had by now reconciled, gained reelection as governor. It was an easy victory for Blaine, even though his opponent, Democratic judge Martin Lueck, did get 40 percent of the vote, an excellent showing for a Democrat in that era.[31]

Of course, for Robert M. La Follette, defeat in 1924 in his national presidential race was still a defeat for a man who liked to win. Sweet as his Wisconsin tribute was, 1924 was also his last hurrah. In 1925 La Follette died.[32] After his death, his son Robert La Follette Jr., known as "Young Bob," was first appointed and then elected to fill the rest of his father's term in the Senate. This event might have pleased Fighting Bob, but it was always a mixed blessing for Bob Jr. He was a hardworking and serious senator, but he was neither a natural politician nor a great public speaker. Nor did he like the campaigning that his father and his brother, Phil, mastered. Nonetheless, Bob had a remarkable career as a senator, winning reelection in 1928, 1934, and 1940 until he lost the 1946 Republican primary to Joseph McCarthy.[33]

THE CONTINUING REPUBLICAN STRUGGLES: THE ELECTION OF 1926

One might expect that in a nonpresidential election year in a state fully reclaimed by La Follette and his brand of Republicanism all would be quiet. But that was never the case in the years of the 1920s in Wisconsin, despite the total Republican dominance. While by 1926 Fighting Bob was dead and his son Bob Jr. was installed as his successor, that did not mean that conflict within the Republican Party was over. Far from it. This fact was starkly brought home in the Republican primaries for both governor and senator in 1926.

In the Republican primary for governor, there were several candidates. The La Follette forces rallied to Herman Ekern, a longtime Progressive and close personal ally of Old Bob. The Stalwarts sought to defeat him with their own candidate, W. Stanley Smith. But when it was all over neither candidate emerged victorious. Instead, the winner was Fred Zimmerman, a moderate

Progressive who had began his long elected career in Wisconsin politics as secretary of state in 1922. Well-known and well-liked, he went on to be elected governor in a predictably overwhelming fashion in Republican times. He received 63 percent of the vote, while his Democratic opponent, Virgil Cady, got 13 percent. An independent, Charles Perry, outpolled the Democrat with 14 percent; smaller parties, including the Socialists, got the rest.

Zimmerman figured in Wisconsin electoral politics for a long time. He was defeated in 1928 in the Republican primary for governor by Stalwart Walter J. Kohler, and he lost in another effort in 1934 before being elected secretary of state again in 1938. As secretary of state Zimmerman proved an enduringly popular politician. He was successful election after election until he died in 1954.

Herman Ekern, whom Zimmerman defeated in the 1926 governor's primary, was in a number of ways a more interesting character than Zimmerman, but he traveled a much less successful electoral path. From Trempealeau County in western Wisconsin, the most Norwegian county in the state, Ekern emerged early as a devoted follower of the La Follette Progressive cause. After a political career in the county, Ekern was elected to the Assembly in 1902 and eventually became speaker, always loyal to La Follette. Innumerable conflicts followed over the years that affected his service in a number of roles both in the Assembly and as elected insurance commissioner, conflicts in which he won and lost elections and other contests. He emerged in 1922 as part of the La Follette state revenge victory and was elected attorney general, a post he won again in 1924.

In 1926 Ekern suffered his shattering defeat to Zimmerman in the gubernatorial primary while carrying the La Follette banner. Two years later when he sought to run for governor again, Phil La Follette wanted the spot and Ekern proved his loyalty by joining in the younger La Follette's campaign. He continued working actively with Phil La Follette in the years following and enthusiastically joined the La Follettes' Wisconsin Progressive Party in the early 1930s and the national party in 1938. He even briefly served as lieutenant governor under Phil La Follette when the incumbent resigned in 1938. At last he was rewarded for all his dedication when he received the official Progressive Party backing for the U.S. Senate in 1938, running alongside Phil La Follette, who was seeking reelection as governor. This honor, however, proved to be just another disappointment for loyalist Ekern. In part this was because to get the Progressive nomination he had to win a messy and contentious Progressive primary. He had to and did defeat a fellow Progressive, Congressman Thomas Amlie, whom the La Follettes at that time deemed too radical and too independent. It was also a disappointment because 1938 was hardly a good year for the already badly fading Progressives. In November Republican Alexander Wiley defeated Ekern to become the first Republican-elected senator from Wisconsin not in the La Follette camp since Joseph Quarles in 1898. Neither was it a good year for the Democrats, as incumbent Senator F. Ryan Duffy not only lost to Wiley but came in even behind Ekern.[34]

Intense as the gubernatorial primary was in 1926, the contest for the U.S. Senate nomination was even more so. Senator Lenroot, whom La Follette never forgave for his abandonment during World War I, sought renomination. But the La Follette forces were determined to unseat him and settled on Governor Blaine to carry the pennant of the movement. By that point Blaine had his own organization, and the campaign ended with him defeating Senator Lenroot in the Republican primary 53 percent to 47 percent. In German American areas especially the vote went overwhelmingly against Lenroot. Memories lingered, and Lenroot's defeat was the last punishment delivered as part of the La Follette movement's revenge. It was the most stunning as it brought down a respected U.S. senator.[35]

The elections of 1926 were notable not just for the internecine battles within the Republican Party. It was also the year that Wisconsin voters had a chance to vote on Prohibition, specifically whether or not they thought the U.S. Congress should repeal (technically, amend) the Volstead Act to allow for weak beer. Predictably, in a state that remains well-known for its drinking culture, there was no enthusiasm for Prohibition. The vote to repeal swept to victory with almost 72 percent.

Prohibition had been adopted as an amendment to the U.S. Constitution by a nation in a wartime mood, and the Wisconsin state legislature did ratify that amendment. But Prohibition within the state had not advanced before the amendment at a pace that matched the nation's. After the turn of the twentieth century only 11 percent of the state was officially dry, and by 1919 only 45 percent of the state was. But the war brought little sympathy for German Americans and beer drinking, and so Wisconsin went along with Prohibition at first. This sentiment did not last long, however. Opinions soon shifted, and in Wisconsin, with its huge German American population and its deep cultural engagement with beer, Prohibition became highly unpopular.

As early as 1923 Governor Blaine was attacking Prohibition publicly, and by 1929 there was not even a pretense that it was being enforced in Wisconsin. Yet the situation was complicated politically throughout the 1920s. The

Anti-Saloon League and its allies in the Republican Party did all they could to
support Prohibition and its enforcement. Governor Blaine constantly bobbed
and weaved over the issue and the various related controversies though over
time showed his "wet" leanings. A major part of the repeal movement came
from the Socialist Party and its voices inside and outside the state legislature
and Milwaukee. After passage of the 1926 referendum, the legislature passed
in 1927 a bill legalizing weak beer. Governor Zimmerman vetoed it since it
was clearly an unconstitutional nullification of the federal Constitution. In
1928 yet another referendum was held on whether to repeal any state enforcement. This was agreed to (64.1 percent yes), and all state enforcement of Prohibition ended. The day of repeal nationally was April 7, 1933, and more than
100,000 people celebrated in the streets of Milwaukee.[36]

The picture of the classic 1926 repeal vote revealed how real ethnic, rather
than class, divisions were in Wisconsin voting. Most German Americans were
united in favor of repeal. In villages and rural areas the German American
vote topped 80 percent for repeal, and support was also heavy in cities populated by German Americans. Those of many other ethnic backgrounds agreed.
Belgian rural areas and villages voted 86 percent for repeal; Swiss 77 percent;
Polish 84 percent. Cities voted heavily for repeal in the 70–85 percent range.
The more German American the city, such as Mayville in Dodge County, the
stronger the vote for repeal (85 percent in this instance); and where there
were more residents that were Yankees or of British descent, such as Platteville, the smaller the support was (37 percent in this case). Thus while Milwaukee voted overwhelmingly for repeal, Madison at 57 percent was considerably
more cautious. And there were areas where support was not just below the
72 percent statewide figure but even below 50 percent. These areas reflected
longtime support for Prohibition, especially rural and village areas with many
citizens of British, Swedish, and Norwegian descent, frequently places where
pietistic churches were especially active.[37]

The vote demonstrated that "reform" is a subjective concept. For the
overwhelming number of Wisconsin voters in 1926, reform meant getting rid
of Prohibition. Its defenders saw the vote as a loss for reform. Yet this 1926
"reform" vote to quash Prohibition and the 1912 "reform" vote for women's
suffrage do not correlate positively with each other. "Reform" clearly meant
different things to different voters, as it so often does. In fact, the 1912 and
the 1926 votes are associated negatively in my representative sample: they
were related but to some real extent as opposite appeals. Many areas where
support for women's suffrage had been strong led the way in opposing weakening Prohibition, and vice versa.[38]

1928 AND THE END OF THE ERA

The dramatic and unprecedented nomination by the Democrats of Catholic Al Smith for president in 1928 had immediate but quite temporary effects on the Wisconsin electorate. Data show that the Wisconsin electorate split sharply according to religious lines in the 1928 presidential vote. Smith received 44 percent of the vote, Herbert Hoover 54 percent. It was a robust Hoover victory in Wisconsin as in the nation, but Smith's showing was by far the best Democratic percentage in Wisconsin in the 1920s at this level because Smith attracted the votes of many Catholics who had left the Democratic Party in the 1920s. Every measure supports the high association of Smith's votes with Roman Catholics in Wisconsin. His vote also was somewhat associated with the vote for beer in 1926, though it was not higher because so many German Protestants supported repeal while opposing Catholic Smith. Even after almost twenty years of inevitable changes, Smith's vote later was more associated with the 1946 state referendum over whether to permit government to pay for transportation to parochial schools, a largely though not quite entirely Catholic versus non-Catholic issue. Smith, it should be noted, did get some votes from non-Catholic voters who had supported La Follette in 1924, were Progressives, and/or were dissatisfied with the agricultural economy. For example, Progressive Republican Senator Blaine backed Smith.[39]

Within specific groups and precincts, the nature of the religious divide—and its continuing power in Wisconsin when the issue was directly raised, as in 1928—becomes manifest. According to my data, German American Roman Catholic towns and villages swung dramatically to Smith, going on average 74 percent for Smith. Some units were virtually unanimous for him as in Marshfield in Fond du Lac County, which voted 97.7 percent for Smith; and many others were almost as one-sided. Sample precincts with a large Belgian population were for Smith at 87.6 percent, Polish towns and villages at 77 percent, sample Czech areas at 62.9 percent. The City of Milwaukee, with its large Catholic population, also swung to Smith with 55 percent of the vote, with especially heavy Polish Catholic support (86 percent).

In fact, virtually every single voting unit in Wisconsin in which Roman Catholics were a serious majority went heavily for Smith in 1928. In almost every case their shift to the Democrats was dramatic. Equally important, these shifts were not matched in non-Catholic areas. This was especially obvious in German Protestant areas of rural and small-town Wisconsin, but it was also apparent in cities that were not especially Catholic, such as La Crosse, Beloit, and Janesville. And all the traditional non-Catholic areas, the

Scandinavian places, the Dutch areas, and the locations with many British descendents voted decisively against Smith.[40]

While the presidential election received the most attention in Wisconsin in 1928, other important elections also took place, especially earlier in the Republican primary. Bob La Follette Jr., running for reelection to the U.S. Senate, faced Stalwart Roy Wilcox, whom he brushed aside successfully. The governor's race in the Republican primary was another classic. It was an important contest whose outcome sent one candidate down to a defeat that he would very soon avenge at the hands of the winner, Republican Walter Kohler.

An industrialist in the bathroom fixtures business, Walter Kohler narrowly won the 1928 Republican primary in a multicandidate field, defeating the

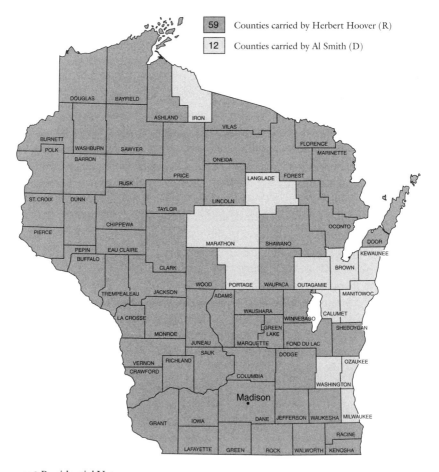

59   Counties carried by Herbert Hoover (R)

12   Counties carried by Al Smith (D)

1928 Presidential Vote

"official" Progressive candidate, Joseph Beck, a farmer who was in equal need of both charisma and campaign money. Also losing was another Progressive, and the resulting split enabled Kohler to win. Although he was a minority choice among Republican primary voters, in November Kohler handily defeated his Democratic opponent, Madison mayor Albert Schmedeman, 55 percent to 40 percent, with the rest going to other candidates. But Kohler's easy victory in November, similar to his triumph in the September Republican primary, did not mean the Progressive wing of the Republican Party had changed its mind about him. It remained determined to get rid of Kohler.

As governor, he proved to be a steady, moderate governor in the inactive style of Wisconsin Republican governors of the 1920s, not so busy that he was unable to continue to direct the Kohler Company at the same time.[41]

The dynamic Phil La Follette, with the support of a united Progressive wing of the Republican Party, defeated Kohler in the 1930 primary and went on to be elected governor. Phil began his political career by being elected Dane County district attorney in 1924. As district attorney from 1925 to 1927, he was noted for his vigorous, determined campaign against crime and lawlessness associated with the illegal liquor business and other activities in the Greenbush section of Madison. After serving only two years as district attorney, he moved on to seek other political goals, his run for governor in 1930 being the most immediate. Growing up in the household of Belle Case

Walter Kohler Sr., governor 1929–31
(Wisconsin Historical Society, WHi-24259)

and Robert M. La Follette had prepared him to become a successful politician. He proved to have the skills and ambition of his father, but at no time in his political career did everything go smoothly.[42]

The year 1930 was the end of an era, as the Great Depression was now underway and gaining momentum by voting time in November 1930. Yet there was nothing in the November 1930 election results to suggest the upcoming revolt against Republican rule in the nation and in Wisconsin. Phil La Follette swept to a smashing victory in his governor's contest, receiving some 65 percent of the vote while his opponent, Democrat Charles Hammersley, managed a mere 28 percent (other parties got 7 percent). Indeed, Republican congressional candidates garnered 75 percent of the state vote. It was Republican business as usual in Wisconsin, it seemed, though all that was to end very soon.[43]

ELEMENTS OF THE VOTE

Over the dramatic period 1916 through 1930, plenty of electoral change occurred in Wisconsin voting. Yet there were also consistencies in this era. For example, rural Wisconsin, represented by its towns, was on balance dependably Republican and produced so many Republican state victories. Yet this steadiness hid variation in Wisconsin town voting. A tremendous

Philip La Follette,
governor 1931–33, 1935–39
(Wisconsin Historical Society,
WHi-19822)

difference existed between a 6.3 percent Democratic vote for governor in 1922 and the 44 percent Democrat Al Smith garnered for president in 1928. And of course La Follette's average 63.5 percent vote in towns in 1924 broke both parties' patterns in rural Wisconsin.

Villages in Wisconsin were both less volatile and more Republican than towns were, though for them, too, 1924 was an exception in supporting La Follette, albeit with a much more modest margin. Why villages tended to be more stably conservative in their voting behavior than rural areas, given that they were usually deeply intertwined with them, is an intriguing subject. A favorite hypothesis concentrates on the idea that they often had a larger component of older voters, often retired farmers, who were conservative in their temperament, set in their political ways, and less moved by shifts in the health of the rural economy.

In urban Wisconsin the picture was distinctly Republican in that period too, but not to the degree that was true in the countryside. This was partly because of the sometime-presence of a Socialist Party vote, and, weak as they were, Democrats also ran a bit stronger in urban Wisconsin than in rural areas. In 1928 there was an urban swell of support for Smith, but he did not carry many cities. In Milwaukee he received 55 percent of the vote (La Follette got 49.9 percent in 1924).

According to my samples, during the 1920s Republicans overwhelmingly commanded the votes in Dutch Protestant areas, often getting 90 percent or more; even La Follette, in his third-party run in 1924, could not garner 25 percent. The same was true in Czech areas, except for a strong showing for Wilson in 1916, a vote of hope, and a big swing toward Smith (63 percent) in 1928, reflecting Catholic loyalties. Belgian town voters reflected the same patterns as the Czechs. Voters in Swiss localities were strongly Republican and loved La Follette in 1924 to the scale of 79 percent, since most shared close ties with Germany. All the Scandinavian groups remained monolithically Republican throughout the period, in many precincts casting less than 10 percent for the Democrats. The Finns were the most interesting example, as they also had a large subset of radicals among their number who often voted for Socialist and Communist Party candidates. As for the ethnic group that mattered far more than any other in Wisconsin—the German Americans— they self-consciously gave huge margins to Republicans. Protestant or Catholic, it did not matter (except in 1928). Few German Americans could bring themselves to vote for the Democrats who brought so much grief to their community during the First World War. Wisconsin's German Americans had long memories.[44]

6 The New Deal and War

TRANSFORMATIONS

T HE PERIOD BETWEEN 1932 AND 1946 was as turbulent in Wisconsin's electoral history as it was in the rest of the nation's. It was the period of the Great Depression, World War II, and generally remarkable politics, electoral and otherwise.[1] Agriculture remained important to the state economy, with more than half the state's counties still rural. Even so, manufacturing had moved to the forefront. Wisconsin had become an industrial state by the 1930s, a process accelerated during the mobilization effort for World War II. After the war, manufacturing employed the greatest share of workers in Wisconsin and generated the single biggest share of personal income. By the end of this period, in 1947, 44 percent of nonfarm employees were in industry. Manufacturing was centered in Milwaukee and southeast regions but took place all over the state in big and small cities. Wisconsin was especially noted as a producer of heavy industrial goods and electrical machinery in particular.[2]

By 1940 the effect of immigration restrictions and the virtual end of German and Scandinavian migration to the United States meant that the percentage of foreign-born residents in Wisconsin fell to 13 percent of the population. About 40 percent of the population was offspring of one or both foreign-born parents. Estimates placed between 25 percent and 33 percent of the citizenry of German extraction, but later figures, based on actual census data, suggest that this figure was probably too low. Norwegian Americans were estimated to comprise 10 percent, while estimates for the significant Irish, Polish, and Swedish Americans vary. Although a serious urban sector of the population lay beyond the City of Milwaukee, Milwaukee proper was home to about 19 percent of the state's population, actually slightly down from 1930, with the next fifteen largest cities together making up nearly 20 percent of the population. When all the citizens who lived in places larger than 2,500 or so were combined, they constituted 55 percent of the state's people. Less

142

than 30 percent of Wisconsin's citizens were farm families, though that was still a large number in a manufacturing state.[3]

While the Depression occurring under a Republican president, Herbert Hoover, turned out to be a great gift to the national Democratic Party, the Wisconsin Democratic Party did not much capitalize on it. Perhaps this was no surprise for a political party that in Wisconsin had elected no governor since 1892, no U.S. senator or member of the House of Representatives since 1918, and sometimes had not a single member in the State Senate. Instead, Wisconsin electoral politics in the 1930s developed into a three-party system as the liberal politics generated by the Depression found a new party outlet when neither the Republican nor the Democratic parties met expectations.

Even in Wisconsin, however, the Democrats improved in the 1930s from being a virtually nonexistent party to a player at the polls. However, the banner of liberalism in Wisconsin throughout the 1930s was carried by a new entity in the age, the Progressive Party, created in 1934. This party had no direct or immediate historical lineage with the Progressive movement of the late nineteenth century and early twentieth century, the old Progressive Republicans under the leadership of Robert M. La Follette, or the 1912 Progressive Party campaign for president by Theodore Roosevelt. But its founders saw themselves very much in the spirit of this history, one they embraced with enthusiasm. Its rise temporarily retarded the transformation of the Democratic Party into a liberal party with ballot box clout. The eventual collapse of the Progressive Party, followed by the defeat of its hero, Senator Bob La Follette Jr. in the Republican primary of 1946, finally provided space for the liberal transformation of Wisconsin's Democratic Party in the 1940s. Realignment then proceeded, the result being a conservative Republican Party and a liberal Democratic Party, the situation that remains the reality today.[4]

In Wisconsin the discussion of the 1930s and early 1940s begins with the Progressive Party, which often had the approval of Franklin Roosevelt (and got some of his patronage in the state) and other liberals from both traditional mainstream parties. It loomed over all else in the state's electoral history in these years and made a huge impact. Its demise in 1946 marked the end of the era.

THE PROGRESSIVE PARTY

From the 1934 to 1946 Wisconsin was a multiparty state, as it had often been in the past. The existence of the La Follette–backed Progressive Party, along with the Democratic and Republican parties, made Wisconsin elections interesting, competitive, and often volatile.

The Progressive Party's creation in 1934 came about for several reasons. By the early 1930s Phil La Follette had no use for the Republicans at the national level (and often at the state level, too) who so often rejected his liberal causes and frustrated his personal goals. He had no more use for the frequently reactionary Wisconsin Democrats either. But he knew by the early 1930s that he had the support of many Depression-wracked farmers, members of the emerging organized labor movement in the state, and many others for whom the La Follettes were always the embodiment of progressive politics. Always crucial, also, was La Follette's desire to have a party he and his brother, Senator Bob La Follette, could control and one that would serve Phil's enormous political ambitions.[5]

Like his father, Phil had succeeded in his quest for the governorship in 1930 by first defeating the candidate of Republican conservatives and then winning an easy victory in the general election over the nearly dead Democratic Party in Wisconsin. Yet everything was not quite so rosy for Phil La Follette with the Republican Party. The struggle in the Republican primary between La Follette and Walter Kohler in 1930 for the nomination for governor continued in 1932 when Kohler got his revenge on La Follette and defeated him in the Republican primary, only to be defeated in turn in the general election by Democrat Alfred Schmedeman. Thus by the end of 1932 Phil was no longer governor, and he came to realize that he and his values and allies were just not in line with the Republican Party. This realization led directly to his 1934 formation of the Progressive Party with his brother, Senator Bob La Follette, thus allowing the La Follettes to pursue their liberal agenda in Madison and Washington. The new party also allowed them to endorse much of Franklin Roosevelt's New Deal and, at first, to work in a warm mutual association with FDR.

Phil La Follette's leadership was essential. He had a personal commitment to the cause and devoted great energy to building a party. He possessed strong oratorical skills (much like his father, Phil La Follette was sometimes an electric speaker) and a willingness to campaign tirelessly. Setting up a third party was a huge gamble, but Phil La Follette and his allies were gamblers and were willing to take the risk given the unsatisfactory state of the Republican and Democratic parties in Wisconsin. They made their assessment at the height of the Depression, when people were demanding change. At that time in Wisconsin a third party of the Left looked like a great idea, and for a time it proved to be so.

Nineteen thirty-four was a banner year for the new party, which succeeded in bringing Phil La Follette back into the governor's office. This was repeated much more decisively in the 1936 election. Indeed, for Phil the outcome of the 1936 election, in which the La Follettes endorsed Franklin Roosevelt's reelection, was the best ever. The Wisconsin legislature was nearly completely in the hands of Progressive Party legislators and their friends, so La Follette was able to get a good deal of his "little New Deal" legislation passed. For example, he pushed through a Wisconsin version of the organized labor–friendly Wagner Act. At first, La Follette worked well with this legislature despite plenty of tension, not all of which was ideological and political. La Follette was sometimes headstrong and authoritarian, and he was handicapped when Tom Duncan, his effective key aide, died in a car accident.

La Follette experienced so much success at the ballot box that he was emboldened to make the mistake of his career and launch the national third party he had long yearned to lead. His decision to form the National Progressives of America (NPA) Party in 1938 grew out of his own ambition as well as deeply felt policy concerns that had been simmering for some time.

Both his ambition and his policy goals by 1937–38 were frustrated in Wisconsin. A briefly friendly legislature turned truculent. Both the Republicans and the Democrats in the legislature united in their hostility to La Follette and his Progressive allies in the legislature, and they did much to harass La Follette. The 1937 session of the legislature ended with Republican and Democratic legislators marching out with arms up in a Nazi-style salute shouting "Heil!" in mockery of their Progressive opponents.

Another factor in La Follette's move toward a national third party was his sense that he could do a good deal better than Roosevelt. La Follette became increasingly alienated from FDR and his performance in the White House. La Follette saw that by 1938 FDR had definitely not licked the Depression and that suddenly the progress La Follette sought had collapsed in the face of the sharp recession that year. He thought Roosevelt had lost his way.

La Follette went ahead with forming his national party despite his brother's lack of enthusiasm and the intense opposition of some other Progressives, such as influential William T. Evjue and his Madison *Capital Times*. Famously, the effort ended as a huge flop. The NPA's notorious flag and salute, with their uncomfortable similarity to those of the Nazis, was one factor in the failure, as were its fuzzy ideology, poor organization, and lack of grassroots leadership. Moreover, the recession of 1938 led the American electorate away from the Left, not toward it, an important factor. Timing proved fatal to the NPA and to Phil La Follette's dreams.

A national party of Phil's design might have succeeded in 1932 or 1934 or 1936, but 1938 was not a propitious year. The New Deal wave was receding in the face of recession, and the La Follette movement proved to be a fish far out of the water. Phil blamed the forces of the established political Right and Left who feared him and political competition. He was right about having lots of enemies who did all they could to destroy the party on the ground, but Phil's choices—and the times—made it easy for his enemies.

As the party went down, and as Democrats nationally and in Wisconsin also went down in great numbers in the election of 1938, so too did Phil La Follette. This result was misleading given the Democrats' good long-run prospects in Wisconsin. But for Phil La Follette his 1938 defeat for the governorship was fatal for his political life; suddenly and permanently his electoral political career ended. He did continue to have an active life, to say the least, after electoral politics. He worked as a prominent lawyer in Madison from 1939 until his death in 1965, except for almost three years' service in World War II, during which time he fashioned another distinguished record. Phil La Follette's story is as memorable as any in the annals of Wisconsin electoral history.[6]

But there were many among the cast of players in the Progressive Party. Thus even after La Follette's defeat the Progressive Party in Wisconsin staggered on until 1946, enjoying an occasional victory. That larger cast deserves some attention. Three figures in the Progressive Party's heyday were Thomas Amlie, Gerald J. Boileau, and Sol Levitan, each of whom represented different party impulses.[7]

Amlie was a political activist and early Progressive Party enthusiast who was first elected to Congress under that party label in 1934. He came from a poor rural background and had been involved in the radical Nonpartisan League decades before. Eventually Amlie became a lawyer and settled in Beloit, Wisconsin, and it was from that southeastern part of the state that he was elected to Congress. Amlie always wanted to push the Progressive Party to the Left, associated as he was with the leftist Farmer-Labor Political Federation, and make it committed to much more government direction and control of the economy. Reelected to Congress in 1936, Amlie continued to try to get La Follette as well as the Roosevelt administration to favor more government intervention in the economy, to support what was essentially a socialist approach, though this was not Amlie's term. As a member of the House of Representatives, he found the process increasingly frustrating and decided to run for the Senate in 1938 in the Progressive Party primary. His decision did not meet with Progressive Party leadership approval and such party voices as the Madison *Capital Times*. He lost, though he did garner more than 45 percent of the primary vote, suggesting that there was a considerable element of the party that was prepared to move in a more radical direction than La Follette and his fellow Progressive Party leaders.[8]

Even if Amlie had won the Progressive Party nomination for Senate in 1938, it would not have been worth much, since he would have joined La Follette in going down to a resounding defeat. That this fate awaited all Progressive Party figures in 1938 was well-illustrated by what befell Gerald Boileau. A Wausau Progressive, Boileau was a self-consciously practical Progressive who accepted La Follette's leadership and shared what they both thought were the limits that liberal reform could accomplish in their time. Boileau, like most Progressive Party activists, was of a Republican background. In fact, he was first elected to Congress in 1930 as a liberal Republican. In 1932 he was reelected as a liberal Republican who openly endorsed FDR rather than the incumbent, Republican Herbert Hoover. By 1934 Boileau followed the La Follettes and committed to the new Progressive Party. Under that banner he won election to Congress in 1934 and 1936. For him, as for Amlie and La Follette, 1938 brought defeat, and though Boileau ran again in 1940, it was to no avail. His political career was also over.[9]

Finally, consider Sol Levitan, a fascinating figure who, while not part of the La Follette inner circle, was deeply involved in the movement. Levitan came to United States fleeing the hideous anti-Jewish pogroms of Russia and became involved with Fighting Bob La Follette's campaigns, supporting him in the difficult days of the First World War. In 1922 he won the Progressive Republican nomination for state treasurer, after losing two previous campaigns, and was elected in the La Follette triumph of that year. He continued as state treasurer in Wisconsin, regularly winning reelection every two years until 1932, when he, like Phil La Follette and the rest of the Progressive Republicans, was defeated in the Republican primaries of that year. By 1936 he was back in office as state treasurer, this time in Phil La Follette's Progressive Party, ever a loyalist. Problems developed, however, as he, like so many others in the movement, could not seem to work with the volatile Phil La Follette. It did not matter much though, because in 1938 Levitan went down to defeat with La Follette and all the rest, a defeat that marked the end of a political career for the aging Levitan. He died in 1940 at almost eighty years old.[10]

THE ELECTION OF 1932

The Great Depression did not have any significant impact on Wisconsin voting behavior until 1932, by which time the Depression's effects were deep and widespread. Between 1928 and 1932 the index of Wisconsin farm prices fell by half, marking an astounding collapse. It was, in fact, in the country-side where the Depression was felt most severely in this first period. But the Depression soon enough hit everywhere, including in Milwaukee and other industrial areas of the state.[11]

In Wisconsin in 1932 there occurred an unprecedented earthquakelike elec-toral shake-up that crushed long-ruling Republicans and yielded a historic Democratic Party victory in 1932. Roosevelt received a stunning 63 percent of the major party presidential vote, President Hoover a hapless 31 percent, and Socialist Norman Thomas 5 percent.[12]

Remarkable as this was, there was much more to the extent of the revolt that so benefited the Democrats. Albert Schmedeman, who was nearly sev-enty, suddenly found himself the governor of Wisconsin in what was an easy victory over Walter Kohler: 52 percent to 42 percent, with 5 percent for Socialist Frank Metcalfe. Schmedeman, who ran for governor and lost in 1928, was a native of Madison, the son of immigrant German Protestants. His father was a tailor, but Schmedeman became a clothing store merchant. He was a popular Madison figure, easy to get along with and devoted to working cooperatively with others. He had long been active in Madison pol-itics — on the school board and the police and fire commission, and he served as mayor.[13]

No doubt Schmedeman was helped by Kohler's defeat of Phil La Follette in the Republican primary of 1932, a defeat that led many La Follette sup-porters to vote for Schmedeman in November 1932. What mattered more was a down-the-line rejection of Republicans by a majority of Wisconsin voters in the face of the Great Depression. Indeed, this mood explained in good part why La Follette lost the Republican primary. Any statewide incumbent was doomed in 1932. La Follette explained his defeat in part by the costs of relief to Depression victims that forced him, as governor, to raise taxes and cancel tax exemptions. Such measures had angered voters. But he also appreciated that behind those specific explanations lay the broader one, a voter revolt caused by the Depression.[14]

As astounding, or maybe even more so, was the election in 1932 of a Dem-ocratic senator from Wisconsin, F. Ryan Duffy. On the one hand, once again, Senator Duffy's surprise victory benefited from fights within the Republican primary. In this instance it resulted from the defeat of John Blaine, longtime Progressive Republican darling, by John Chapple, who campaigned aggres-sively attacking Republican liberals and generally warning of the danger of Communists in America. His campaign against "the Reds" proved popular enough to give him success in the Republican primary, in part because many more liberal Republicans entered the Democratic primary disillusioned with the national Republican administration of Herbert Hoover.

But once Chapple won the primary, the Progressive wing of the Republican Party openly disavowed him. Thus the Progressive organ of the day, the *Capital Times,* endorsed Duffy, and so did John Blaine. In this race, as in the presidential and gubernatorial contests, Progressive Republican support for the Democratic candidates mattered. Yet at the same time there is no denying that regardless of internal Republican Party disputes, it was a remarkably Democratic year in Wisconsin in 1932, and Duffy benefited enormously from the fact that he was not a Republican of any stripe.[15]

Roosevelt's overwhelming victory in Wisconsin in 1932 was based above all on his huge sweep of the rural towns and villages. This is one reason my representative sample showed a very low association between FDR's showing in 1932 and his more urban showing in 1940.[16] In the sample the average town swung to the Democrats by a huge margin, with Roosevelt obtaining a smashing 72.5 percent of the vote; four years earlier the sample showed only 21 percent Democratic. The villages' mean for Roosevelt was 60.8 percent, up from 39.7 percent. German Protestant rural areas and villages went for Roosevelt at 79.2 percent, rising from 39.1 percent in 1928; Belgian areas voted 94.7 percent for FDR, Polish areas 90.2 percent. Even Swedish and Norwegian rural areas and villages fell in line. Places with a high degree of descendents of British immigrants also voted for Roosevelt, though narrowly, up 30 percentage points from 1928 and achieving a margin of victory that was not to be repeated for a Democrat running for president until 2004. The rural and village revolt was amazing and total. There were few exceptions in a state where 63 percent of the voters selected Roosevelt.[17]

A few rural areas and villages did not get on board, however, especially the Dutch ones. And there was some sign of different economic responses in the degree of support for FDR, with the more affluent farming areas stronger for FDR than less affluent ones. This was a reflection of the higher vote for Roosevelt from the relatively well-off German areas than from the often poorer Scandinavian locations that were always more Republican. Still, the basic picture was that percentages for Roosevelt in rural areas far exceeded his overall state percentage, high as that was.

The urban picture was more mixed, though not that of Milwaukee. Roosevelt swept that city with an overwhelming 67 percent of the vote. In the other cities of Wisconsin, big and small, Roosevelt mostly won, and in doing so he achieved substantial gains over Democratic performance in the 1920s. Still, there is no doubt that at first, in 1932, the Democratic surge in

Wisconsin did not come primarily from the urban sector of the electorate, Milwaukee excepted. The Depression was felt less acutely in Wisconsin cities in 1932, at least in comparison to the near-desperation that swept over much of rural Wisconsin by November 1932 and propelled the Democrats to victory across the board (even winning the State Assembly for the first time in forty years) under the banner of FDR.[18]

High Tide of the New Deal and Progressivism: The Elections of 1934 and 1936

The results in Wisconsin of the 1932 election presented a great opportunity for the state's Democrats, and Governor Schmedeman in particular, to act in the spirit of the times and respond to popular demand for government action, perhaps creating a New Deal realignment in Wisconsin, something that took place in many other states. But it did not happen in Wisconsin. Schmedeman, like many other leaders of the state Democratic Party, had different, conservative principles in mind. They stood by their "Jeffersonian values" affirming a weak state and resisting the idea that the government ought to be active in citizen affairs no matter what issues or conditions arose.[19]

The 1934 campaign was a strange one for the national Democratic administration and Franklin Roosevelt in particular. His visit that year to Wisconsin was necessarily awkward. He was caught between conservative Democratic Governor Schmedeman, who was running for reelection, and the liberal Philip La Follette, the newly minted Progressive Party's candidate for governor. Roosevelt was not sympathetic to Governor Schmedeman's Democratic Party, but neither did he get along particularly well with the prickly La Follette, who was to Roosevelt's Left as Schmedeman was to his Right. Schmedeman received only a very tepid endorsement from FDR. And it was no secret that it was the other La Follette, Senator Robert Jr., running for reelection, who engaged FDR's affections and sympathies. He received a virtual, but not explicit, endorsement from the president, much to the chagrin of Bob La Follette's Democratic opponent. FDR had hoped Bob Jr. would follow his advice and become a Democrat, in which case Roosevelt could have formally supported him. But Bob Jr. did not then or ever take that step.[20]

Governor Schmedeman carried a great burden into the 1934 campaign. He had run into plenty of problems as governor. During his brief tenure the full impact of the Depression finally hit Wisconsin, and discontent naturally fell on him in part since he was the incumbent governor, one guided by his belief that government should not do a lot to help. While this was a view typical of traditional Wisconsin Democrats, many citizens of all parties resented it intensely at that time. The Depression also produced huge turmoil in the dairy industry, generating milk strikes in 1933. The governor's response was to call out the National Guard. He followed the same approach during a bitter strike at Kohler Corporation in 1934. Neither action won him much sympathy from those suffering the effects of the Depression.

The launching of the La Follettes' Progressive Party in 1934 was followed by the defection of many of Schmedeman's more liberal 1932 supporters to the Progressive Party. The governor had no way to stem those defections, since FDR and the national Democratic Party showed no particular interest in helping the conservative Madison Democrat. Governor Schmedeman did have a special relationship with many Progressive-inclined Norwegian voters—he served as ambassador to Norway under Woodrow Wilson—but in the end he got few votes among Norwegian Americans. Moreover, rumors flew that Schmedeman, who had had his leg amputated while in office, was dying or at least unable to continue serving as governor effectively. And the list went on, one event and situation after another piling on and sinking Schmedeman's 1934 reelection efforts. As well, the personal appeal of Schmedeman on the campaign trail just could not begin to match that of the dynamic Phil La Follette. This cannot be dismissed, because while Schmedeman lost the governorship, the Democrats won most of the other state races, including lieutenant governor, attorney general, and state treasurer.[21]

In November 1934 Governor Schmedeman managed to win only 38 percent of the vote. Phil La Follette received only 39 percent of the vote, just squeaking by to victory by a few more than 13,000 votes. Howard Greene got a historic low percentage for a Republican candidate for governor at 18 percent, and Socialist George Nelson got 5 percent. From one perspective these results suggested that Phil La Follette had no great mandate. Yet from another angle his victory, combined with his brother's smashing reelection as U.S. Senator in 1934, was remarkable. After all, both La Follettes ran as candidates in a brand-new third party. At that moment, Wisconsin politics and voting behavior were transformed, and, at least to enthusiasts of the Progressive Party, the state was on its way to becoming a new and better place.

The 1936 election was the high point for presidential Democratic Party fortunes in Wisconsin as well as for the Progressive Party in state elections. Both relied on new voters and younger voters for the age cohort shift that brought change to the electoral scene in Wisconsin and in the nation. FDR received an overwhelming 64 percent of the vote in Wisconsin to his Republican opponent Alfred Landon's 30 percent. William Lemke of the Union Party did the best of the third parties by picking up 4.8 percent.[22]

FDR's Wisconsin vote in 1936 was no carbon copy of his vote in 1932. This fact might seem curious since his total percent of the state vote was equally overwhelming in both elections. Still, there was a shift in FDR's support between the two elections. On the one hand, although he was a strong winner virtually everywhere in 1936, his strength in rural areas declined compared to what it was in 1932, as it did across the rural Midwest. The reason in Wisconsin in part was that New Deal relief for Wisconsin's farm problems was modest. The famous Agricultural Adjustment Act designed to aid farmers did not include the dairy industry. There was also dissatisfaction in Wisconsin with tariff-lowering measures that brought in cheap Canadian cheese. Yet robust support for Roosevelt endured in rural areas in 1936, if softening from 1932. My samples show the average town vote for FDR was 65 percent (in 1932 72.5 percent), the average German Protestant town and village for FDR was 63.5 percent (1932 79.2 percent). Support was heavy in Norwegian and Swedish rural areas and villages, and overwhelmingly so in Polish ones, and dramatically weaker in British- and Dutch-ancestry rural areas and small towns.[23]

On the other hand, Roosevelt ran better in urban Wisconsin in 1936 compared even with his huge success in 1932. The smaller the city the weaker Roosevelt ran in 1932; but matters sharply improved for him in 1936 in small cities. In 1932 in cities of well under 50,000, FDR received 53.8 percent, but in 1936 this jumped to 63 percent. In Milwaukee Roosevelt did even better in 1936 than in 1932, when he had received 67 percent of the vote. He scored a record-setting 78 percent of the city's vote in 1936, the largest FDR victory in any big city except in the then-Democratic South. There was the first sign of what was later to become true in Wisconsin as elsewhere: the Democratic Party as the party of the city.[24]

A sidelight to the 1936 campaign, and in its way an indicator of the disenchantment with FDR that was to come so swiftly to electoral politics in Wisconsin, was the campaign of William Lemke, who received about 5 percent of the 1936 presidential vote in Wisconsin. Lemke was a North Dakota politician with a long record of radical political activism there through the Non-Partisan League. He served in state office in North Dakota in the early 1920s and then was in Congress all but one term from 1932 to 1950. Although he was formally a Republican, he was in fact a quasi-socialist. He was in favor of state banks, state grain elevators, and the like in North Dakota and was committed to the goal of implementing monetary policies to encourage debt-avoidance inflation. He started out as a supporter of Roosevelt (he backed La Follette in 1924 and Smith in 1928), but he soon broke with FDR, believing, along with his allies Francis Townsend, G. L. K. Smith, and Father Coughlin (all of whom backed his presidential campaign), that Roosevelt was not serious about radical economic change, especially regarding help for farmers.

When he ran for president in 1936, Lemke found that his greatest appeal was to some Catholics (though he was not Catholic or even religious). Lemke possessed a mix of radical economic and anti-Communist isolationist views, and in 1936 this combination attracted some Catholic and German midwesterners, among others. It was the basis of his appeal in Wisconsin, insofar as he had one. Thus he got his votes from German Catholics in Wisconsin in particular, people who in most cases had voted for FDR in 1932 and were to leave the Democratic Party (the "war party") permanently in 1940. He got fully 13.4 percent of the total vote of German towns and villages, far more than anywhere else in Wisconsin.[25]

At the state level Governor Phil La Follette and many of his legislative and state office Progressive Party allies were elected or reelected in 1936. There was no hint of the disaster that would soon befall them. A close reading of the election returns suggested how fractured the Wisconsin electorate really was. Governor La Follette did well in 1936 by corralling 46 percent of the total. His Republican opponent, Alexander Wiley, got 29 percent, with Democrat Arthur Lueck at 22 percent and minor candidates the rest.

THE END OF LIBERAL RULE AND INTIMATIONS OF A NEW ELECTORAL ORDER: 1938 AND BEYOND

The 1938 congressional election resulted in major gains for the Republican Party nationally, though the Democrats remained in solid control of Congress. These Republican gains were closely tied to the sharp recession of 1938. In Wisconsin the Republicans also advanced, indeed more than nationally, but it was the Progressives, not the weak Democrats, who suffered as the Republicans surged. And surge they did, winning the state legislature, taking back the governorship, and electing Alexander Wiley to the U.S. Senate. The winner of the governor's race, Julius Heil, collected a convincing 55 percent of the vote on the way to beating Phil La Follette's 36 percent, ousting him convincingly. Even with Phil's defeat, Progressive Party state victories did not come to an end, but things were never the same again. Indeed, La Follette's loss signaled the beginning of the end of the Progressive Party in Wisconsin; it finally acknowledged reality and surrendered in 1946.

The Democratic nominee for governor in 1938, Harry Bolens, received 8 percent of the vote. His sad showing was no accident: there was an implicit agreement in 1938 between the Republicans and Democrats across the state to "get" Phil La Follette. This was an unusual occurrence, because even while most Democrats and Republicans at that time detested the Progressives, they assiduously maintained their separate and competitive identities. Indeed, Bolens was on the ballot mostly so the Democrats could maintain their position as a major party under Wisconsin laws.

In 1938 the Republican Party leaders, especially with the energy and direction of William Campbell, who had begun working on this cause in the 1920s, were determined to take advantage of anti–La Follette sentiment. Out to crush the liberal and disloyal former Republicans who were so key to the Progressive Party and bring back what they considered sane government to Wisconsin, they were eager to form a coalition with the Democrats, splitting between the two parties the nominations for significant state offices. Democrats shut out of state influence by the Progressives readily embraced this arrangement.[26]

The 1938 outcome did stem from a widespread reaction against La Follette personally, the whole La Follette regime, and the proposed new national Progressive Party, but the painful 1938 recession, which many voters took out on La Follette, also mattered. Dairy farmers, who were not major beneficiaries of the New Deal, had gone into a serious economic freefall. And, too, many citizens were resentful of the labor unrest sweeping through Wisconsin urban centers.

Democratic nominee Bolens had no real objections to the coalition to defeat Phil La Follette. He was an old-line conservative Democrat of a breed about to disappear. He detested the La Follettes and eagerly sought their demise even at the expense of his candidacy. The issue was Phil La Follette, and so the real energy of the 1938 gubernatorial campaign went into unseating him. Bolens's electoral campaign was at best a sideshow, and the success of the main show, the action on center stage, came as good news to him and so many others in both parties.

The Republican winner, Julius Heil, was an effective campaigner. He was a gregarious and colorful character who related well with the Wisconsin people, and he was loved by the press. Born in Germany and poor at the start of his life, he became a highly successful Milwaukee businessman. At times positively flamboyant, and not particularly intellectual, Heil received mixed reviews as governor. But as a candidate he was often underestimated by his opponents, to their regret. His victory in 1938 was historic in that it marked the end of the reign of liberal politics in Wisconsin in the 1930s.[27]

Two years later, 1940 confirmed that the climate had indeed changed in the state, though it also showed that reelected FDR and Senator Robert La

Follette Jr. represented a politics not yet dead in Wisconsin or in the nation
as a whole. FDR continued his equivocal relations with the Progressives,
tacitly supporting Senator La Follette's reelection to the annoyance of the
state Democrats. Thus when Democratic vice presidential candidate Henry
Wallace campaigned in Madison, his praise of Young Bob prompted the state
Democratic candidates to get up and walk out.[28]

Yet there was a spectacular drop in FDR's strength in 1940, as evident in
comparing his overwhelming vote of 1936 to his 1940 "squeaker" victory in
Wisconsin, where he won by a mere 25,000 votes over Republican Wendell
Willkie, getting a bare 50 percent of the vote. The major reason for the Republican surge was quite clear: among most voters FDR's support softened only
a little but a dramatic drop in support came from a massive and stunning
abandonment of Roosevelt by German Americans in rural towns, villages,
and small cities in Wisconsin. German Protestant areas that voted 64 percent
for FDR in 1936 voted 24 percent for him in 1940, and German Catholic
votes that, on average, were more than 67 percent for FDR in 1936 shrunk to
an average of 29 percent for him four years later. In contrast, Polish areas
voted 85 percent for FDR in 1936 and were still 80 percent for him in 1940.[29]

German-ancestry voters in Wisconsin revolted in 1940, which made a
huge difference. Some of the sample German American towns and villages
illuminate the big shift: Rantoul in Calumet County went from 50 percent
in 1936 to 12 percent in 1940; Lebanon in Dodge County, 87 percent to
17 percent; Leroy in Dodge County, 82 percent to 22 percent; the village of
Bondural in Shawano County, 71 percent to 19 percent; Union in Waupaca
County, 40 percent to 14 percent; Calumet in Fond du Lac County, 75 percent to 19 percent; and so on.[30]

The reason for the massive switch of so many German Americans was
obvious enough. It came from a tremendous (and well-placed) fear among
many in that community that under FDR the United States was heading
toward another war with Germany. It was not that German American voters
were of one mind or, certainly, that they harbored sympathy for Nazi Germany. But they had not forgotten World War I, and the resulting antiwar
and isolationist attitudes were much in evidence among them—and they
brought them to the polls in 1940. These attitudes were also present among
some Wisconsin liberals. The consequence, the election's outcome, reminded
observers that ethnic voting was still far from dead in a Wisconsin whose
population in 1940 was still almost half bilingual and bicultural.[31]

Roosevelt's weak standing in rural and small-town Wisconsin overall was
real. The farm revolt was over, or at least the disposition to vote Democratic

had waned. The Republican capture of the majority among rural and small-town German American voters in particular was to endure, making that group a "red" mainstay of Republican voting even to this day. Similarly, FDR's 1940 showing in Wisconsin's two biggest cities, Milwaukee and Madison, endures; and even as it has increased since 1940, it is checked by the suburbs of Milwaukee that were Republican in 1940 but were so much smaller then and cast many fewer votes than they do today.[32]

The national election of 1940 has long had the reputation for being the most class-based vote in United States history.[33] There was considerable evidence

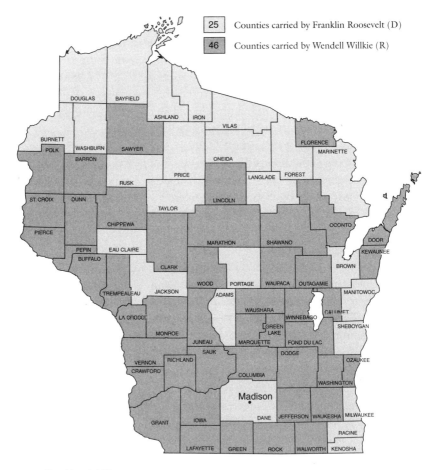

25	Counties carried by Franklin Roosevelt (D)
46	Counties carried by Wendell Willkie (R)

1940 Presidential Vote

of class voting inside the cities in 1940 in Wisconsin and after. Moreover, that year the areas of northwest Wisconsin that had been Republican but were quite poor stayed Democratic—and have remained so. On the other hand, the shift of many relatively affluent German areas to the Republicans in 1940 had less to do with class-sensitivity than foreign policy concerns. Still, the overall pattern of the 1940 Wisconsin presidential vote looks much more class-sensitive than did previous elections, though how to confirm this in any tight empirical fashion is not clear.[34]

The confused and divided Wisconsin electorate in 1940 was best revealed by the three-candidate race for governor. Incumbent Republican Julius Heil won reelection with 41 percent of the vote, inching just 12,000 votes ahead of Progressive Party candidate Orlando Loomis, who had 40 percent and whose appeal seemed to eclipse temporarily declining Progressive Party fortunes. Francis McGovern, the distinguished longtime Progressive Republican, running now as a Democrat, was third with 19 percent. McGovern's candidacy as a Democrat was the most significant element in the race. It marked a trend already under way toward many urban Progressives capturing and transforming the weak Democratic Party into a liberal party in line with the national party, a phenomenon that would be fully completed after World War II.[35]

THE EARLY FORTIES: REPUBLICAN HOPES RISE FURTHER

The election of 1942 was a good one for Republicans all across the nation, including Wisconsin, where Republicans gained complete control of both houses of the state legislature as well as the U.S. congressional delegation. But they almost faced a setback at the governor's office when the popular Orlando S. Loomis, known as "Spike," who had become head of the Progressive Party, unaccountably won election as governor in 1942. He received almost 50 percent of the total vote, while the now unpopular Republican governor, Julius Heil, slid way down to 36 percent; the weak Democratic candidate, William Sullivan, got 12 percent and Socialist Frank Zeidler 1 percent.

Loomis was from Mauston, and he, like most Progressives, was of Republican lineage. He was first elected to the Assembly in 1928 as a Republican and in 1930 moved up to the State Senate. In 1936 he was elected attorney general as a Progressive but lost in the 1938 Republican landslide and then narrowly lost as the Progressive candidate for governor in 1940. His defeat of Heil in 1942 was sweet revenge for him, and largely a personal victory, since he was the only Progressive who won that year—or ever again—statewide. But that ray of light for the Progressives was quickly blotted out when Loomis died in December 1942 even before taking office.

Elected lieutenant governor, Walter Goodland was duly sworn in as governor on January 4, 1943, capping an interesting career for this Republican
who was a decided maverick. Goodland, who was reelected governor in 1944
and 1946, started out in politics as a classic nineteenth-century Democrat
(he was born in 1862). He later joined with the La Follette movement and
became a Progressive Republican and was elected a state senator in the 1920s.
Goodland clashed with Governor Phil La Follette and the Progressive Party
in the 1930s. Yet while he was elected lieutenant governor in 1938, 1940, and
1942 as a Republican, his nominations often came against the wishes of the
regular party. Goodland proved to be just another example in Wisconsin of
an individual who could and did thumb his nose at a party establishment and
get away with it. Thus it was no surprise that Goodland and the Republican
legislature frequently disagreed during his governorship or that he remained
popular in the state until his death in 1947.[36]

The elections of 1944 confirmed that things were definitely going the
Republicans' way. The presidential election was close again in Wisconsin, but
it went Republican with Thomas Dewey, governor of New York, edging out
FDR by 24,000 votes, 50 percent to 49 percent. Walter Goodland cruised
into the governor's office again, winning over Dan Hoan 53 percent to 41
percent, while the Progressive Party candidate, Alexander Benz, garnered less
than 6 percent of the total. The Progressives were failing, and their future
was obviously grim.

The very fact that Dan Hoan was the Democrats' candidate for governor,
however, had considerable significance for the future. Hoan, after all, had
been longtime Socialist Party mayor of Milwaukee, but now he had finished
walking that path. Hoan ran well, all things considered, against the popular
Goodland. That fact and the frankly liberal orientation his campaign took was
yet another foreshadowing of what was to come for the Democratic Party
after World War II as former Progressives and other liberals refashioned it in
the image of FDR.[37]

THE END OF THE OLD NEW ORDER: THE ELECTION OF 1946

The 1946 national elections were a disaster for the Democrats as they yielded
a huge majority in Congress for the Republicans. A response to continual
shortages and infuriating inflation after the war, the elections were but a
brief moment of Republican command. By 1948 the Democrats were back in
control of Congress and 1946 was just a wistful memory for the Republicans.
But though this was the national story, it was not Wisconsin's. In Wisconsin
1946 was a chapter of great significance in the state's electoral and political

history, one that cemented a Republican control that lasted. The 1946 elections were followed by a long string of Republican electoral victories that, with the exception of the presidential election of 1948, did not end until the election of Democratic Senator William Proxmire in 1957. For Republicans, 1946 marked the beginning of another golden electoral age.

The 1946 election in Wisconsin was important for another reason. That was the year of the election that ended the presence of Robert La Follette Jr. in Wisconsin electoral politics and substituted that of Republican Senator Joseph R. McCarthy, who defeated Bob Jr. in the 1946 Republican primary.[38]

When 1946 rolled around, Senator La Follette knew he was tired of electoral politics, an activity about which he had long been ambivalent. He was a serious senator, well regarded in Washington, but not a willing politician. At the behest of liberals both in Wisconsin and in Washington he agreed with scant enthusiasm to run once again in 1946 for the Senate seat he had held since his father died in 1925. The Progressive Party was now dead. At its convention in 1946 it had voted—far from unanimously—to disband, some of its remaining leaders joining the Democrats, others the Republicans. In this context La Follette had to choose whether to run as a Republican or Democrat. He rejected bids by liberal Democrats and some former Progressives to run under the Democratic label, correctly perceiving that the Democratic Party in 1946 was still weak and in a state of some confusion. It did not seem to be a vehicle for victory, a judgment most other more or less neutral observers shared at that time.

Thus La Follette opted to run as a Republican. He knew that he would receive no support from the establishment of the Republican Party, which was now firmly in the hands of the former Stalwarts, whose czar, Tom Coleman, detested La Follette and all that he stood for and very much wanted to see his political demise. At the same time, however, Coleman and other old guard Republicans did not have any particular brief for the upstart McCarthy, who was decidedly not their choice to take on La Follette in the Republican primary. But circumstances conspired otherwise. McCarthy built up considerable momentum with many rank-and-file Republicans, and Coleman bowed to the inevitable and joined in endorsing McCarthy's candidacy.[39]

Meanwhile, La Follette's decision to enter the Republican primary cost him dearly among many liberal Democrats, who were more and more central to the emerging postwar Democratic Party and who had no intention of entering the Republican primary in order to vote for him, not least because he had spurned the idea of running as a Democrat. Most prominent of these would-have-been supporters was longtime Progressive William Evjue of the Madison *Capital Times,* who blasted La Follette on this very score.[40]

In the spectacular 1946 Republican primary campaign for the Senate nomination, La Follette faced the already-well-known McCarthy. While a Marine, McCarthy had run well, if unsuccessfully, in the Republican Senate wartime primary of 1944 against incumbent Senator Alexander Wiley. In 1946 McCarthy campaigned as a Marine veteran who was still something of a fresh face, dynamic and clean-cut in contrast to the aging and weary La Follette. This image was only enhanced when La Follette proved reluctant to campaign for the nomination in Wisconsin, no longer home to him in much of any sense, citing Senate business. Despite the pleadings of his supporters, day after day La Follette stayed in Washington, and each day he remained there only hurt him. When he did eventually appear in-state before the primary in September, he had little time to campaign effectively, as his brother Phil observed in retrospect. Voters were left with the unfortunate impression that he was not that interested in Wisconsin. In addition, La Follette's campaign concentrated on his past record, which added to the sense that he was out of date.

Moreover, matters became badly complicated for La Follette by the campaign of Howard McMurray in the Democratic primary. McMurray, the clear leader, was a University of Wisconsin political science teacher, and he spent much of his effort running against La Follette. His articulate critiques definitely added to the generally negative din about La Follette. His strategic conclusion, perhaps a correct one, was that in the general election McCarthy would be easier to beat than La Follette, and McMurray characterized La Follette as old news when Wisconsin was entering a new era. In fact, McMurray and some liberal Democrats, unlike others of their Democratic compatriots, had been delighted when La Follette chose to enter the Republican Party primary. They felt they could not build a new liberal Democratic Party until the La Follettes were off the scene, and, in any case, they were not sympathetic with the isolationism that was increasingly the fare that Bob Jr. offered.[41]

La Follette had many other troubles in his campaign. The most famous was the issue of his poor relationship with organized labor. This was especially evident in Milwaukee, but the state American Federation of Labor (AFL) refused to endorse him (or McCarthy) as well. In part it was because organized labor on the whole was moving confidently into the Democratic Party. Roosevelt had done his work, and the result was a lack of enthusiasm for Republicans, even for La Follette. And the AFL was not inclined to urge its voters to enter the Republican primary and vote for La Follette.

In Milwaukee, specifically, there was a nasty quarrel within organized labor that ensnared La Follette. That issue swirled around the question of Communists in the CIO of Milwaukee. No one doubts that there were some Communists within the union organization, even highly placed in the organization. The same was true of the union at Allis-Chalmers, then a big company in Milwaukee. They had vehemently opposed La Follette ever since he had begun warning about the danger of Communist aggression abroad, and their literature portrayed him as a warmonger who did not care for working people. They also worked to have their loyalists in Milwaukee enter the Democratic primary, not the Republican one, because they wanted to get Edmund Bobrowicz, a favored union official, nominated for Congress. Bobrowicz, who attacked his opponents for their criticism of the Soviet Union, won that primary, though he lost in November once it was discovered that he was actually a member of the Communist Party.

Unfortunately for La Follette, he also did not have enough sense to stay out of quarrels in the Republican camp in 1946. Despite the fact that his credentials as a Republican were suspect, he just could not resist pleas to leap into the Republican primary for governor with his own endorsement, a move guaranteed to make enemies. Moreover, he endorsed the gubernatorial candidate, Ralph Immell, who was running against the very popular (if aging) incumbent, Walter Goodland. Goodland was himself no conservative, and many of his supporters were also La Follette backers, so La Follette's move was without political sense. There was no chance Immell would win, and La Follette could absolutely expect that some disgruntled Goodland supporters would seek to punish him for his intervention.

The results of the Republican senatorial primary in 1946 gave McCarthy 47 percent, La Follette 46 percent, and a third candidate around 7 percent. It was close, and it is reasonable to say that La Follette lost the election in Milwaukee County. McCarthy carried it by 10,000 votes in an election he won by a little more than 5,000 votes statewide. The standard analysis at the time was that in labor- and liberal-oriented Milwaukee County, La Follette should have done better than McCarthy. But perhaps this analysis needs to be turned around. Perhaps what is surprising is how well La Follette did in Milwaukee and overall given the problems he faced. The truth is McCarthy won because more Republicans saw him as one of their own, which after all he was. La Follette had not run as a Republican since 1928.

Another part of the explanation for McCarthy's win has less to do with Milwaukee than with McCarthy's strength in German American areas all over the state, especially in rural areas, small towns, and villages. For many

German Americans sick of war, isolationist, and concerned about the spread of Communism, McCarthy struck the right notes, despite La Follette's own public concern with international Communism. Yet this analysis must be put in perspective. The fact is that among rural and small-town voters in the Republican primary, including in German American areas, La Follette won narrowly. After all, he came to the Milwaukee County line ahead of his opponent. But everywhere, not just in Milwaukee, urban areas were least supportive of him, while memories of old allegiances and battles probably helped him in rural Wisconsin, most obviously in Scandinavian areas, especially Norwegian ones, strongholds of the dead Progressive Party. One problem, however, was that turnout was low in these areas. So if it was the past that brought voters out for La Follette, postwar Wisconsin's memory was too faint to pull him through one last time.[42]

McCarthy's victory path continued in November 1946. He defeated Democrat Howard McMurray in an ugly campaign that had the two impassioned candidates sparing few words in denouncing each other. McCarthy was re-elected in 1952, and he continued in the Senate until alcoholism eventually caught up with him in 1957. Always a remarkable campaigner, he had a phenomenal memory and a jovial backslapping style, and for a long time he had a great many admirers in the state to more than match his detractors. Whatever role McCarthy played nationally, a role still bitterly debated, his most significant lasting legacy in Wisconsin was to aid the creation of the postwar liberal Democratic Party. By knocking out La Follette as a Republican, McCarthy ensured that postwar liberals would definitely turn to the Democrats.[43]

The 1946 Republican landslide also brought Walter Goodland back into the governor's office with a strong (60 percent) victory over Dan Hoan, who was trying once again on the Democratic ticket (and who received only 39 percent of the vote). Oscar Rennebohm, a Republican from Madison, was reelected lieutenant governor (he had first been elected in 1944), and he became governor in 1947 when Goodland died.[44]

This 1946 Republican victory was typical of the national results, which saw a major shift from 1944 to 1946, one that made Wisconsin even more Republican. Thus in 1944 the average rural town was 55.9 percent Republican and in 1946 61.6 percent Republican. The average village went from 56.6 percent to 64.9 percent Republican. Milwaukee went from 60.5 percent Democratic to a little less than 50 percent Democratic, and Madison fell even more, from 61.7 percent to 43.4 percent Democratic. In fact, the 1946 Republican swing was especially urban in nature, which was reflected in smaller cites also, the average there going from 51.4 percent Democratic to 35.6 percent.

Thus Neenah went from 39.8 percent to 32 percent, Stevens Point 63.9 percent to 43.5, and Chippewa Falls from 50.3 percent to 37.8 percent.

In 1946, there was also a fight over a controversial referendum proposal that would, in effect, allow state payment to private (i.e., parochial) schools for busing their kids to school. The issue became engaged as many Protestant, Jewish, and secular voices fought to block what they argued was a referendum to aid the Catholic schools (which was mostly true, though in Wisconsin there were, and still are, many Lutheran schools as well). Catholic voices insisted that it was only fair that as taxpayers they got the benefit of having their kids bused to school just as public schoolchildren were. Charges of bigotry and more flew through the air. The Wisconsin Council of Churches, which represented mainline Protestants, was extremely active in trying to defeat the referendum, and it and its many allies proved successful when 55.5 percent of the voters said no.[45]

Predictably, heavily Roman Catholic areas rallied to the referendum. In German Catholic towns and villages the average vote was more than 75 percent in favor, as it was in Polish American places, and it reached almost 90 percent in Belgian areas. In Milwaukee, however, the referendum passed with only 52 percent, which was unexpectedly low given the city's large Catholic population and the support the referendum had from both major newspapers. The referendum did not get more than 35 percent of the vote in Madison, and it ran only at a little over 44 percent in the state's smaller cities. But where it really lost was in areas with few Catholics, underscoring how much this was a religious vote and how close to the surface the old tensions lived. In Norwegian towns and villages the average yes vote was about 8 percent, in German Protestant ones 26 percent. The correlation between the busing referendum and the 1928 vote for Catholic Democrat Al Smith for president was .524.[46]

ELEMENTS OF THE VOTE

At times it is hard to discern what the constants, if any, were in this turbulent period of Wisconsin voting. One clear factor was the association of economic issues and economic class with voting. Economic issues and concerns underlay the New Deal realignment toward the Progressives and the urban movement toward the Democrats. How tightly class voting can be shown is another matter. The claim that Progressivism in the 1930s was class-based is not self-evident, and at present there are no data to establish this thesis firmly. But there is evidence for the view that by the 1940s there was some economic-condition sensitive voting in Wisconsin. The union factor deserves emphasis. In Wisconsin, as elsewhere, the Democratic Party was immeasurably aided by the union movement and its growth in the 1930s and 1940s. The Democrats were helped at first at the presidential level but over time, as the Wisconsin party began to become more liberal in the 1940s, in state races as well. This was most apparent in southeast Wisconsin—in Milwaukee, Racine, and Kenosha, among other cities. It was not as widespread as one might suspect, however. Wisconsin has small industrial cities all over the state, and many were not unionized (or, if they were, they were not militant), which hurt the emerging liberal Democratic Party.

All these factors are demonstrated by looking closely at cities by size in this period. The bigger the city the more likely it was to be Democratic, as was most obviously demonstrated by Milwaukee and Madison. Most other larger cities, with the exception of very Republican years like 1946, were quite Democratic in the 1930s and through the war. Midsize cities, however, were not too far off the pattern of the state as a whole, and the raft of small cities in Wisconsin were, like the countryside, distinctly more Republican than the state generally after 1936.[47]

The distinction between villages and towns in Wisconsin is another interesting feature of the voting behavior in this period. Again and again, as my sample demonstrates, villages as a whole proved to be much more Republican than did the state's rural areas. They were also much less volatile than the towns. Consider that in 1932 the vote for FDR in towns averaged almost 73 percent, but by 1944 the number had sunk below the state average to 44 percent. FDR won Wisconsin villages in 1932 by 61 percent, a far smaller margin, and by 1944 got the same 44 percent as rural areas, a figure reached much sooner in villages in the declension process of FDR's vote than in rural areas. For towns and villages the steadily rising Republican strength revealed how much Wisconsin Republicanism in the period was grounded in villages and agricultural areas, just as a good portion of its strength today is. Alternatively, we can see just how much the Democrats relied on big city votes, as they do today.

The ethnic factor cannot be ignored any more than the economic one can be. Detailed study of voting in rural areas and small towns in the Roosevelt pre-1940 period establishes opposition to FDR in Dutch Reformed and Yankee areas (regardless of economic position). More mixed support would be found in German Lutheran areas (the more wealthy the more supportive) and German Catholic places (with a similar result by income). The most supportive ethnic areas were Polish, Swiss, Belgian, and Finnish places (with Swiss and Belgian areas relatively affluent and Polish and Finnish distinctly less so).

Shifts were the order of the day in the 1930s and 1940s. The most spectacular, of course, was the massive abandonment of the Democratic Party by German Americans outside the big cites in 1940 (though it actually began in 1938). Many had supported the New Deal because of the economic depression, but they had become Republicans and returned to the party by 1940. They were then joined by many Catholic German Americans in the massive switch prompted, above all, by the sense that FDR was moving toward an interventionist (and anti-German) war policy. This was the end of the old rural and small-town base of the conservative Democratic Party. Such areas today remain determinedly Republican, as they have been since 1940.[48]

The elements of the vote in this period report the story of two great turnarounds in Wisconsin voting. From a tightly Republican state, Wisconsin became a strikingly Democratic and Progressive Party state in its voting behavior in the New Deal years of the early and mid-1930s. Then it became a Republican state, firmly so by 1946. The key variable in this situation was the shift of the German American electorate, at least a third of the state's voters, especially those in rural and small-town areas. For that moment in Wisconsin electoral history they were decisive. And this state of affairs remained for a decade and more—a period that seemed like forever to Wisconsin's Democrats.[49]

7

The Emergence of the Modern Democratic Party and Modern Voting Patterns
1948–1964

AFTER WORLD WAR II, Wisconsin underwent an electoral realignment as the political parties became distinctly divided along ideological and policy issue lines. The Democratic Party became a party supportive of economic and social liberalism, while the Republican Party became united on conservatism. The echoes of the Progressive Party faded, and it became clear that that third-party movement had merely delayed the realignment that made Wisconsin's electoral politics similar to the rest of the nation's. The Roosevelt revolution finally came home to Wisconsin and altered its politics and voting.

The 1940 presidential Democratic vote correlated highly with the 1950 Democratic gubernatorial vote at .795, and the 1940 La Follette Senate vote correlated with the 1950 Democratic vote at .750. The postwar era brought together the Roosevelt Democrats and most former Progressives to form the new Democratic Party even as the Republican Party freed itself of the La Follette liberals, welcoming so many of the German Americans who left the Democrats in 1940 never to return. Realignment had taken place.[1]

At first, and for almost a decade, the realignment did not seem to have any particular effect at the polls, because after World War II the Republican Party was securely in control of Wisconsin and Wisconsin voting. The margins were nothing like what they had been after World War I, but the overall picture of steady Republican dominance repeated itself election after election. This picture was misleading as a guide to the future, however, just as the 1920s were a bad guide to the 1930s. The fact was the Democratic Party after the war was infused by new energy, and its leaders were determined to alter its subservient role and were waiting for the right moment. That moment came suddenly in 1957 and was followed by others in startlingly quick succession in the later 1950s and 1960s.[2]

The story of the Republican Party in this period was, at first, one of victories. It does not require any special treatment because it did not undergo any great postwar revolution. It became a party controlled by conservatives the minute the La Follettes began running as Progressives in 1934. After the war it only became more so, known above all as resistant to expanding the government and state taxation. Within the party plenty of fights and disputes occurred, sometimes rather costly ones. Such disputes are normal fare for parties and they did not diminish in the late 1950s and early 1960s. Yet throughout those two decades the Republicans consistently maintained a good statewide organization. The outstanding leader during those years was Tom Coleman, longtime head of the Kipp Corporation in Madison and a shrewd conservative strategist.[3]

The party had plenty of bases of devoted support, as well as, for a long time, strong national and state candidates, such as President Dwight D. Eisenhower, who was tremendously popular in Wisconsin, Governor Walter Kohler Jr., and Senator Joseph McCarthy. While McCarthy unintentionally helped mobilize Democrats in Wisconsin, it needs to be remembered that McCarthy was no loser at the Wisconsin polls, despite strenuous Democratic efforts. He never lost any statewide general election.[4]

The New Democratic Party

The Democratic Party, however, underwent a dramatic change after World War II. The story of the emergence of a liberal Democratic Party in Wisconsin is a long and fascinating one,[5] and the construction of the new party was

Joseph McCarthy, U.S. senator 1947–57 (Wisconsin Historical Society, WHi-8006)

integral to the emergence of modern, and indeed contemporary, voting patterns in the state. When the Progressive Party voted itself out of existence in 1946, and Robert La Follette Jr. met defeat in the 1946 Republican primary, there was no more thought that there might continue to be a viable "progressive" third party in Wisconsin or that the Republican Party might be home to the "progressive" forces in Wisconsin politics.[6]

While some La Follette supporters and Progressive Party loyalists drifted back to the Republican Party, many instead entered the Democratic Party. These citizens were more often from urban areas and were often younger people, a newer generation.[7] This is why it is perfectly accurate to claim that many of "the ancestors of the modern liberal Democrats of Wisconsin were the La Follette progressives, not the party which called itself Democratic in the pre-war period."[8]

Yet former Progressives becoming Democrats also melded with a new breed of activists who were of Democratic lineage, the James Doyle family being a famous and influential example. Many were young World War II veterans, often urban in orientation, liberal in economics as well as politics, and quite determined to transform the conservative and ineffective state Democratic Party into a vehicle of political liberalism. They joined with the union leadership and many rank-and-file labor union members in the state, which, despite the moment of Communist influence in Milwaukee unionism for a few years during and just after the war, also aligned with the national Democratic Party. They, too, were committed to shifting Wisconsin in a very different direction.[9]

A major energizing force in building a new party was the Democratic Organizing Committee set up in 1948. It was composed of young activists, former Progressives, and liberal Democrats and included some who would become famous, such as Gaylord Nelson (governor and senator), John Reynolds (governor and federal judge), James Doyle (federal judge and father of Wisconsin Governor Jim Doyle), Carl Thompson (gubernatorial candidate), and Thomas Fairchild (state official, candidate against Senator McCarthy, federal judge). Some of these people had met each other while undergraduate students at the University of Wisconsin before the war or after, through the American Veterans Committee or at the University of Wisconsin Law School. Also key was a group of women activists, mainly from Dane County, including Ruth Doyle, Gretchen Pfankuchen, Julia Boegholt, and Virginia Hart.

Their earnest and determined work to build a vibrant party bore fruit. Working county by county, these liberal Democrats were able to remake the party ideologically. A major part of this transformation, perhaps the decisive step, was their capture of the state Democratic Party apparatus, a move led by liberal Dane County Democrats. To be sure, once the old Democratic Party was defeated, the result was not always perfect peace in the postwar years. Other conflicts inevitably arose (for example between Madison and Milwaukee Democrats), but intraparty dispute was not the important story. What mattered was the emergence of a new and energized Democratic Party after the war.[10]

Another important step in the process, especially as the Democrats sought to become a liberal party that won, was the service of Patrick Lucey as party chair in the later 1950s and early 1960s. A former member of the Wisconsin State Assembly from Crawford County on the Mississippi River, Lucey had moved to Madison and achieved financial success as a realtor. Able to devote time and resources to the state party job, he led the way to a more organized, centralized, efficient, and financially sound state party in the 1950s. He fostered much county, local, and even precinct organization and encouraged Democrats to run for office at all levels, constantly working to establish the party everywhere, often in places where there was no party presence at all and had not been for a long time.[11]

ELECTIONS: 1948–1957

In this period Republicans ruled at the polls in Wisconsin. This was true even in a year such as 1948, when President Harry Truman, the Democratic incumbent, carried Wisconsin. Indeed, Truman won, but Republicans won the races for governor and most other state constitutional offices and the state legislature.

Truman's vote quite closely paralleled the established pattern of the new Democratic Party in part because he ran well in the cities, especially the big ones, as expected. But the key to his unusual victory was the fact that he narrowly carried the majority of rural farm towns in Wisconsin, a phenomenon that most certainly did not happen for other Democrats in the 1940s or much of the 1950s. As Samuel Lubell famously noted, Truman did well in rural areas due to a temporary fear that a Republican president might hurt farm prices. He did well even in some German rural areas where the death of FDR made voting Democratic a little less troubling.

Truman was not hurt in Wisconsin by Henry Wallace's third-party campaign for president. Wallace, FDR's third-term vice president, ran as a peace-and-justice leftist candidate in an effort influenced by Communists and sympathetic fellow travelers. Wallace did get more than 2 percent of the three major parties' Wisconsin vote, but that did not stop Truman from winning comfortably with 51.2 percent to Dewey's 46.8 percent.[12]

The race for governor reflected the more typical situation in postwar electoral Wisconsin. The winner was Republican Oscar Rennebohm, a wealthy drugstore chain businessman, who defeated Democrat Carl Thompson, who came from a background in the old Progressive Party. Besides being a Republican in a then-Republican state, Rennebohm had the additional advantage of serving as governor during the campaign. He had succeeded to the governorship when Governor Goodland died in 1947, and Rennebohm had delineated his moderate views to considerable favorable approval. Yet he had a disadvantage in that he and his fellow successful state candidates had to run well ahead of their Republican presidential candidate, Thomas Dewey, in order to win. That proved no problem, and Rennebohm's victory was easy, as he outpolled Thompson by 10 percent.

There were two other important elections in Wisconsin in 1948. One was earlier in the September Democratic gubernatorial primary when Thompson defeated William Carroll. State Senator Carroll was an old-time, anti–La Follette Democrat, and his defeat symbolically closed a chapter in the state's Democratic Party. New Democrats had not just won the Democratic Party apparatus; they had gained the support of the majority of the party's loyalists. The other key contest was part of the regular November election and took place in Dane County, home of the University of Wisconsin and the capital city. There the Democrats (new Democrats all) won control of Dane County, ending Republican rule and beginning a remarkable unbroken reign of Democratic dominance that continues still. The liberals had captured the state capital.[13]

In 1950 Republicans ruled in Wisconsin. Walter Kohler Jr., of the Kohler bathroom fixtures industry family, was elected governor, a post he was to hold for three terms. Kohler's father was the principal developer of the Kohler business and of the village of Kohler, and he was governor of Wisconsin from 1929 to 1931. Walter Jr. did not serve as an executive of the business, however, and he divested all holdings relative to it during the bitter Kohler strike that began in 1956.

A recent excellent and detailed biography of Walter Kohler Jr. has raised him considerably from the obscurity into which he had sunk in Wisconsin electoral history. While its author not entirely unfairly complains that too many "historians had been so intent on celebrating the Progressives and their liberal successors that they had largely ignored their conservative opponents" in the Wisconsin story, this account does not picture a particularly remarkable Kohler.[14] A child of substantial privilege, Kohler was educated in the fanciest private schools in the East, including Yale, and gave little evidence of being anything but a somewhat aimless member of the wealthy classes until the onset of World War II. Then, though old for service, he volunteered and compiled an impressive war record in the Navy in the Pacific.

After the war, Kohler got involved in both business and politics and eventually succeeded in obtaining the Republican nomination for governor after contentious struggles for the party's endorsement and victory in the Republican primary. Kohler's victory in November 1950 came when he defeated Democrat Carl Thompson, running again, 54 to 46 percent, overcoming Thompson's pointed jibes regarding Kohler's life of wealth and his meager political experience.

While no landslide, Kohler's victory followed what had become well-established postwar voting patterns. Carrying Milwaukee, which comprised about 25 percent of the state's vote in that era, and running respectably in other cities, Thompson simply could not overcome the substantial resistance to the Democrats. Small towns and villages in Wisconsin, especially those made up of German-ancestry voters, remained satisfied with conservative Republicanism.[15]

Republicans enjoyed the year 1952, both nationally and in Wisconsin. Dwight Eisenhower's election as president broke the Democrats' hold on the presidency since the election of 1932. Ike proved immensely popular in Wisconsin, overwhelming Adlai Stevenson, the Democratic governor of neighboring Illinois, by a smashing 61 percent to 39 percent. The more interesting and more significant Wisconsin elections, however, lay down the ballot line. Walter Kohler swept his governor's race by an even greater margin than did Ike, winning with more than 62 percent of the vote. His opponent was a little-known Democrat by the name of William Proxmire, who saw what others took to be a hopeless situation as an opportunity for him to begin building future success. It was a wise move from a man who was to make electoral history in Wisconsin.[16]

Much more attention on all sides went to the race for the U.S. Senate. Republican Senator Joseph McCarthy was up for reelection, and some Republicans, many Democrats, and Madison's *Capital Times* were absolutely determined to defeat him. Anti-McCarthy Republicans and others (mostly others) tried to get Governor Kohler to run against McCarthy in the Republican primary. Kohler, whose relationship with McCarthy had deteriorated over time, eventually decided he was not interested. A Republican lawyer from northern Wisconsin, Len Schmitt, was interested, and he took on McCarthy in that primary, attacking McCarthy over and over as an irresponsible specialist in smear tactics who dishonored the Republican Party and the country.

McCarthy brushed him aside easily, picking up 72 percent of the vote in the Republican primary, but his Democratic opponent in November, Thomas Fairchild, proved harder to dismiss. Fairchild, a former Progressive and a new Democrat, was a straightforward and dignified liberal. From Verona, near Madison, he had served as attorney general of Wisconsin from 1949 to 1951. He became McCarthy's November opponent only after his own Democratic Party primary battle, which undoubtedly hurt his efforts to ultimately win the Senate race. In his primary he defeated another liberal, Henry Reuss of Milwaukee, in a contest that reflected the tensions between liberal Democrats in Milwaukee and Madison. It was a close battle, with Fairchild winning with 50.4 percent. Although Reuss enthusiastically backed Fairchild, the cost to Fairchild was the fact that the contest kept Democrats voting in the Democratic primary; without Wisconsin's open primary system, more Democrats might have entered the Republican primary to vote McCarthy down.

Fairchild ran a vigorous, hard-hitting campaign and received much press support. But McCarthy, who also knew how to fight hard and, according to his critics, how to fight dirty, beat Fairchild 54 percent to 46 percent, with a margin of 139,000 votes. Anti-McCarthy writers like to note, and correctly so, that McCarthy ran far, far behind Governor Kohler and President Eisenhower on the Republican ticket. But McCarthy did win, which was all that mattered to him. He was obviously no favorite either in Democratic Madison and Dane County (38.5 percent) or in Milwaukee County (where Fairchild led by 97,000 votes), but he otherwise ran very well. Indeed, he ran noticeably well in the areas of traditional La Follette strength, in the Scandinavian areas that served as progressivism's homeland before World War I and during the New Deal years. He also ran well in the post–World War I areas of greatest progressive support: German American rural villages and towns.

This reality about McCarthy's bases of support cannot be ignored. The truth is that McCarthy, like the La Follettes, did appeal to a certain portion of the electorate who liked hard-hitting protestors, which is exactly how McCarthy presented himself. The protests of McCarthy and the La Follettes differed to be sure, though less than one might suppose. In 1952 in particular McCarthy campaigned on a program stressing dissatisfaction with a war (the Korean War) and opposition to evil forces entrenched in government who flagrantly ignored the will of the people (Communists and the Democrats as coddlers of Communists). Of course much of McCarthy's support came from people outside the bigger cities who were never in favor of any kind of serious social or economic change, including a substantial portion of the German American population. This group supported Fighting Bob for a brief period before his death, not because he was a reformer but for his antiwar stance and in order to get revenge on the Democrats, whom they saw as warmongers and persecutors. Thus while McCarthy got some of what one might consider a radical vote, it was not a leftist or liberal radical vote. But what elected McCarthy in the end was that he was a Republican in a then-Republican state in what was a tremendous Republican state landslide. His vote correlated with Ike's at a very high .93.[17]

It has been argued, and plausibly so, that the defeat of Fairchild and the reelection of McCarthy proved a benefit for the Democrats in the long run. No doubt McCarthy was already something of a burden for Wisconsin's Republican Party by 1952. He became steadily more so as his alienation from his fellow senators grew until he was censured by the Senate and fell deeper and deeper into alcoholism. But the Democrats' failure to defeat McCarthy in 1952 had the additional benefit that it forced them away from what had become an obsessive, and losing, cause. To be sure, that focus had helped build the liberal, new Democratic Party, but at some point it also became limiting. With McCarthy reelected, the Democrats began turning to other issues, principally economic ones, which became a vital next step in building their party.[18]

THE MIDDLE 1950s

After 1952 the scene was quite stable in Wisconsin in terms of voting behavior. Republicans were in complete command, and there seemed to be no reason to think their control would ever end. However, in 1954 in Wisconsin, as in the country at large, there was something of a mild reaction to the Eisenhower landslide of 1952, and the Democrats improved their situation, even recapturing a majority in the U.S. Senate. In Wisconsin this was reflected by a much closer gubernatorial election, one in which Governor Kohler won by only 3 percent (about 35,000 votes). His opponent, once again William Proxmire, capitalized on rural discontent both in Wisconsin and across the nation that year and got more cooperation from the organized labor movement, making the race a contest. Yet Proxmire lost anyway, and the assumption was made in some Democratic Party circles, as it had been before, that this defeat would (at last) get rid of him. This goal was greatly accentuated by the earlier 1954 Democratic primary for governor in which Proxmire dared to stand in the way of James Doyle, one of the founders of the reborn Democratic Party and hero to many of his fellow Democratic liberals. But in beating Doyle and outraging the liberal leaders, Proxmire forced the Democratic Party's leadership to acknowledge him. Though disliked by many party activists because he paid scant attention to party politics, and even less to the party regulars themselves, Proxmire proved he was a favorite of Democratic voters, and his vote-gathering ability could not be ignored.[19]

Proxmire tried for governor again in 1956. Again he lost, and, in fact, by a slightly larger margin than in 1954, 48 to 52 percent. This time he lost to a new Republican figure, Vernon Thomson, a lawyer from Richland County who was a well-established political activist and politician and who had long served in the State Assembly (1935–50). Thomson was elected attorney general of Wisconsin in 1950 and served in that prominent role until he became governor. His time came and he was duly selected.

There was reason for Republican concern over the 1956 state results. Governor Kohler had tired of conflicts with the Republican Speaker of the Assembly, Mark Catlin, as well as the McCarthy wing of the Republican Party and their threats to defeat him in the Republican primary. He happily chose retirement. While Eisenhower again won a huge victory at the polls in Wisconsin—gaining some 62 percent of the vote and proving quite unstoppable for the hapless Democratic nominee, Adlai Stevenson, making his second try for the presidency—the state Republicans had run far behind Ike's margin and those of most of the earlier postwar races. Still, there was not much concern in the Republican Party; after all, they were still firmly in control of every branch of state government. As events unfolded, however, they were not sufficiently concerned. Meanwhile, Democratic Party state leadership was experiencing an increased optimism. By their analysis, Ike had pulled Thomson through, and the state Republicans were looking vulnerable.

In fairness, it was hard to read the results. One could speculate about possible Democratic gains, but one could also look at the presidential race and the Republican Party control of the state legislature and state offices. Eisenhower won so overwhelmingly that Republican optimists could read it as a sign of final realignment of the state to the Republicans, at least at the presidential level. Yet the evidence was genuinely mixed. After all, the Republican primary vote as a percentage of the total primary vote had dropped to 59 percent in 1954 and stayed at 60 percent in 1956, after being in the 70s and 80s in the earlier postwar era. Clearly, more citizens were considering themselves Democrats. They did not constitute a majority, but there was a more and more substantial and loyal Democratic Party constituency emerging in Wisconsin.[20]

1957

The first breakthrough for the Democrats and the first real postwar defeat for the long-ruling Republicans came in a special election in 1957 after the death of Joseph McCarthy, when William Proxmire was elected to the U.S. Senate.[21]

To be sure, Proxmire had become a familiar face in Wisconsin electoral politics. His campaigns for governor had raised his name recognition level as high as it could realistically get. Yet his name was also associated with defeat after defeat. Moreover, once again in 1957 Proxmire was embroiled in conflict with state Democratic Party leaders who did not want him as their senatorial candidate. To them his nomination seemed to guarantee only another loss by a candidate they did not much favor anyway. They instead backed Milwaukee congressman Clement Zablocki, whom Proxmire easily defeated in the primary. Zablocki and the Democratic establishment, however, did rally behind Proxmire after the primary, which was not a bitter fight, in good part because they wanted victory.

Proxmire's November opponent, former Republican governor Walter Kohler, did not come to the race in a good situation. He had won his primary, defeating Congressman Glenn Davis, a neo-McCarthyite, in a tense struggle, and many Davis supporters refused to support Kohler, which hardly helped him. Yet Kohler remained foolishly overconfident; after all, he had beaten Proxmire twice before in races for governor, and this overconfidence cost him as too little effort went into getting Republicans to the polls. Legendary campaigner Proxmire, meanwhile, campaigned harder than ever, and he was aided in his efforts by widespread discontent over the poor agricultural situation of the moment.

When it was all over, Proxmire had swept in with almost 57 percent of the vote, while Kohler was left far behind with less than 41 percent (an independent got about 3 percent). It was a stunning upset, which came primarily because of Proxmire's ability to cut deeply into the Republican vote in rural towns in Wisconsin. In Lima in Grant County, for example, his vote increased from his last governor's race from 40 to 50 percent, in Clyde in Iowa County from 71.1 to 81.3 percent, and in Johnson in Marathon County from 39.8 to 52.5 percent. Indeed, he even snared almost half of the very Republican German American town and village vote. Proxmire's crisscrossing of the state to appear in small villages and towns with his basic message and outstretched hand had truly paid off.[22]

Proxmire came from Lake Forest, Illinois, an affluent suburb of Chicago, a place that accurately reflected his well-to-do family background. He attended a prep school in the East and then Yale. In both settings his sport was boxing, a sport suitable for the endlessly determined. In fact, Proxmire was always noted for his focus on his chosen goals and for his recognition that they could be achieved only after a determined struggle. After more education and assorted adventures, Proxmire got a job at the Madison *Capital Times,* a

first step toward the goal he had decided on when he was in his twenties: he
would succeed as a politician in Wisconsin.

Proxmire first won election to the Wisconsin State Assembly in 1950,
when he was thirty-three, after a typical (for him) all-out personal campaign.
He had already recognized that he could break into the relatively open fledg-
ing Democratic Party and get far—he hoped for higher office—as long as he
kept at it and showed patience. Although Proxmire was not a favorite among
those who led the new Democratic Party, there were those who were grateful that he was willing to run hopeless races for governor in the 1950s. They
appreciated his uncanny ability to garner support from the endless stream of

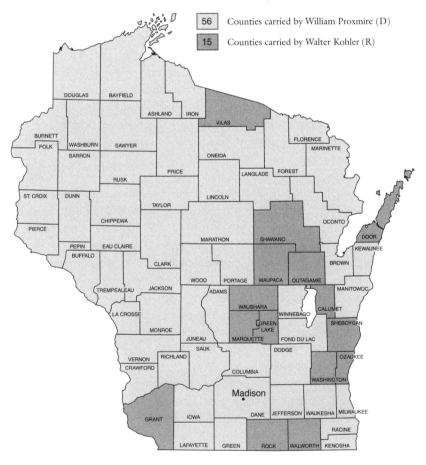

56   Counties carried by William Proxmire (D)

15   Counties carried by Walter Kohler (R)

1957 Senatorial Vote

citizens he met as he shook the hands of the electorate everywhere. What proved certain was Proxmire's popularity once he was in office. He was unbeatable and served as U.S. senator from Wisconsin from 1957 until he retired in 1989. He spent almost no money campaigning for his reelections in 1958, 1964, 1970, 1976, and 1982—an impressive record of electoral success.[23]

THE DEMOCRATIC ERA

By the 1958 elections Republicans were still as much in shock at the upset victory of William Proxmire in the special senatorial election of 1957 as Democrats were jubilant. Riding on a national sweep that Wisconsin voting reflected, 1958 proved to be a splendid year for Wisconsin Democrats. The economic downturn of that year sharpened divisions and benefited Democrats, both in Wisconsin and nationally. Surveys of the period found Wisconsin voters quite issue-oriented, and, under the economic circumstances, Democrats benefited from this. Suddenly Wisconsin had become an authentic, and competitive, two-party state.

William Proxmire on his election to the U.S. Senate, 1957.
(Wisconsin Historical Society, photo by Milwaukee Journal Sentinel, WHi-30142)

In 1958 Gaylord Nelson was elected governor, the first Democratic governor of Wisconsin since the one term served by Alfred Schmedeman in 1933–35. Nelson's victory with almost 54 percent of the vote was even more impressive because he unseated the incumbent, Vernon Thomson. Nelson tirelessly campaigned in the Proxmire mode, visiting small towns all over Wisconsin, going to all but two counties, and traveling 30,000 miles in his successful effort. Meanwhile, Proxmire was reelected to the U.S. Senate, and the Democrats captured the State Assembly, four of the five other state offices, and half of the state's congressional seats. It seemed like a miracle to many Democrats and brought satisfaction to the determined organizational efforts of Patrick Lucey. Lucey had managed Proxmire's 1957 victory and shortly thereafter began his successful service as state party chair, which lasted until 1963.[24]

With his victory, Nelson emerged as a significant figure in Wisconsin electoral politics and was to remain so until his defeat for reelection to the Senate in 1980 in the Ronald Reagan landslide. Nelson was of largely Norwegian descent, from Clear Lake in rural Polk County, the son of a country doctor who, along with his wife, was a long-time local Progressive. Nelson, known as "Happy" in his youth, proved to be a natural politician. He was a friendly, warm, genial, and at times hard-drinking man. Nelson actually ran for office first in 1946 as a Republican in a legislative primary and lost. After that he headed to Madison to practice law. In 1948 he ran as a Democrat for the State Senate in Madison and won, beginning his career as a capitol officeholder. He was to lose again in 1954 when he ran for Congress in a district that in those days Madison did not dominate.[25]

THE ELECTION OF 1960

The presidential election of 1960 is a most famous contest.[26] It might seem that in Wisconsin that year's presidential election was somehow a break in the resurgent Democratic era that began in 1957. But that is not so obvious. True, Republican Richard Nixon narrowly defeated Democrat John Kennedy in Wisconsin 52 percent to 48 percent. Yet Gaylord Nelson won reelection as Wisconsin's Democratic governor, defeating Republican Philip Kuehn 51.6 percent to 48.4 percent, maintaining Democratic control in the key office in Madison.

The entire electoral season in Wisconsin in 1960 was an amazing one, and most of the action and controversy took place among Democrats and about Kennedy. The contest for the Democratic nomination in the nation was an intense one between Kennedy and Senator Hubert Humphrey of Minnesota. Kennedy made winning the Wisconsin April primary part of his task to convince Democratic bosses that he could win outside of majority-Catholic states. Kennedy did win the primary with 56.3 percent of the vote, but he did not convince any of the skeptics with this win, unlike his later victory in very Protestant West Virginia. The reason was that Kennedy's vote in Wisconsin was highly associated with Roman Catholics. They comprised a huge proportion of the Democratic primary voters but were then and now still a minority among voters in the state as a whole. Many Catholic Democrats turned out enthusiastically for fellow Catholic Kennedy in the primary (and general election). It is also true, however, that Humphrey was far too liberal for many Catholic Democrats, so religious solidarity was often reinforced by political ideology in leading toward a vote for Kennedy.[27]

Skepticism about Kennedy's appeal in Wisconsin was confirmed in November. While Kennedy did pick up some Republican Roman Catholic voters, he lost many weak Democrats who were Protestants. Moreover, Kennedy was unable to gain as many Republican Catholics as he might have wished because of the intermixing of class and ideological factors. The widespread perception that Kennedy was quite liberal turned off many German Catholics and alienated many middle- and upper-income Republican-leaning Catholics. Still, he did well with Catholics if we hold all economic and educational variables constant. Everywhere in Catholic areas of Wisconsin Kennedy ran far ahead of Adlai Stevenson's 1956 race for president. In heavily Protestant areas Kennedy held his own or did just a bit better than Stevenson had. Overall, there can be no doubt that Kennedy's vote intersected with the religious patterns of Wisconsin. Every effort to test this thesis has confirmed it.[28]

And yet matters are complicated, as always, in election analysis. In my samples JFK's vote did not closely replicate his fellow Catholic Al Smith's in 1928. The most obvious reason, of course, is that thirty-two years had gone by and many places had seen demographic changes, sometimes drastic ones. But this was not the whole story. Also important was JFK's inability to attract nearly as many affluent German Catholics as Al Smith had. Compare their votes in German Catholic areas that had not much altered in their religious composition: Woodville in Calumet County, Smith 74.4 percent to Kennedy 53.6 percent; Leroy in Dodge County, 78.7 to 47 percent; Addison in Washington County, 82.6 percent to 60 percent; Plain in Sauk County, 96 percent to 74 percent; Franklin in Sauk County, 90.2 percent to 72 percent; St Cloud in Fond du Lac County, 91.6 to 46.2 percent; and Calumet in Fond du Lac, 84.7 percent to 48.1 percent.[29]

As always, party identification was the best single guide to how people voted in 1960, and that is revealed well enough in the high correlation (.92)

between Governor Nelson's vote and Kennedy's. But the key difference was
that while Nelson ran very well in Kennedy's Catholic areas of strength,
Kennedy did not do as well in Nelson's. This was apparent in the old Progressive and quite Scandinavian western Wisconsin counties. There Nelson
ran as much as 8 percent ahead of Kennedy, and he won, while JFK lost.
Nelson's victory was no sure thing, and it was fortunate for him that the
Democratic Party was able to come together in November given the assertive
efforts earlier by various Wisconsin Democrats for Adlai Stevenson, Hubert
Humphrey, of course, and Kennedy. The fact is that relations between and
among the different camps during the primary campaign and after were
far from harmonious, as highlighted in the intense irritation that cropped up
between ardent Kennedy advocate Patrick Lucey and Humphrey supporter
Governor Nelson. Conflicts over who was running the party had occurred
between these two able and ambitious men beginning in 1958, and they continued right through Nelson's tenure as governor.[30]

While Nelson did win in 1960, his narrow margin of victory margin disappointed him. His governorship had its ups and downs, like any other, but the
issue that brought him the most trouble related to how to raise state revenue.
His reluctant openness to a sales tax brought him much more criticism from
fellow Democrats than from Republicans. Otherwise, there is no real evidence that anything that happened during his governorship hurt or helped
him particularly in his reelection race. What is true is that 1958 was an arti-
ficially robust Democratic year in Wisconsin, and 1960, with Kennedy as the
Democratic standard-bearer, was a much weaker year. Nelson's showing in
1960 compared to 1958 simply reflected this.[31]

AFTER 1960

The closeness of Wisconsin's elections continued after 1960. In 1962 Governor Nelson defeated incumbent Republican Alexander Wiley in his bid for
the Senate. Wiley, who at seventy-eight was aging and was rarely seen in
Wisconsin, no longer generated much enthusiasm from his own party, which
failed to endorse him for the Republican primary. In the governor's race
the Democrats again prevailed, as John Reynolds, a lawyer and one of the
builders of the new Democratic Party, defeated Republican Philip Kuehn
50 percent to 49 percent, with a margin of 12,000 votes. While Reynolds's
victory was tight, it was accomplished boldly; he campaigned in favor of
using increased income taxes to deal with budget needs, explicitly opposing
Kuehn's solution, which was staying with a sales tax. Governor Nelson had
signed a sales tax into law, but Reynolds refused to rest with it. Instead, he

insisted that the more progressive income tax was a fairer means of raising revenue. He escaped defeat in what was now a marginally Democratic state.[32]

The Democratic Party should have seen 1964 as the glory days in Wisconsin, as they were for their party in the nation as a whole. In some ways they were. How could they not be given the utterly crushing blow that Lyndon Johnson, the Democratic candidate for president, delivered to his Republican opponent, Barry Goldwater, in Wisconsin. By rolling up some 62 percent of the vote in Wisconsin, Johnson created a huge plurality that was bound to have some consequences down the ballot line, and it did. The Democrats captured the State Assembly and narrowed the Republican margin in the State Senate. They also gained in the congressional delegation from Wisconsin. And, meanwhile, Senator William Proxmire won a massive reelection victory. But this was not the whole story, because despite the huge Johnson win, 1964 also saw Democratic governor John Reynolds lose to moderate Republican Warren Knowles, who got 50.6 percent of the vote.[33]

The tale of 1964 in Wisconsin is a complicated one. It really began in the campaign for the April Democratic presidential preference primary. When George Wallace of Alabama entered the presidential race, he campaigned hard in Wisconsin. He believed that because there was plenty of racial turmoil in Milwaukee and because Wisconsin was in so many ways a working-class state, his populist message would be well received. In Wisconsin as elsewhere he campaigned against Lyndon Johnson and other liberal Democrats as "pointy-headed" elitists who cared more about busing and open housing for poor blacks than they did about average (white) folks. In the process Wallace definitely hit emotional chords with some voters, evoking deep hopes and fears and winning some voters but also drawing intense hostility from many others. Everywhere he went, rallies tended to be raucous and sometimes outright confrontational. Wallace did not mind, and even welcomed, the opportunity to engage his attackers.[34]

Wallace received 34 percent of the vote in the Democratic presidential primary against Governor Reynolds as the Johnson stand-in. While Reynolds won the primary by almost 2 to 1, his margin was far lower than the leaders of the Democratic Party expected. This result, which came as a shock to party leaders, received fiercely disputed scrutiny, perfectly matching the mood of Wallace's campaign. Some analyses emanated from more or less neutral sources while others were derived from distinctly ideological origins; all claimed to be based on data.

One view was that Wallace's vote was in good part a protest against Governor Reynolds, who was widely perceived as a bumbler on issues of taxation

and race relations, and thus had little to do with Wallace himself. Some protestors were Democrats, to be sure, but many were Republicans. Wisconsin
had (and still has) an open primary in which people of one political persuasion can vote in another party's primary; so as a means of protesting Reynolds
(and Johnson, for that matter), many Republicans took that route.

The evidence for this view is plentiful. Wallace ran best in conservative and
Republican counties, especially in some Republican suburbs around Milwaukee and in Republican German American counties, which suggests Republican
crossovers (and/or considerable appeal to conservative Democrats). Yet some
analyses stressed that Wallace did too well in Milwaukee and in some other
Democratic southeastern industrial areas to be ignored. Thus he was not just
the protesting agent of crossover Republicans, as some observers claimed a
bit too eagerly in order to suggest that Wallace had no appeal to the working-
class voters and Democrats in particular. These observers noted that in the
Fourth Congressional District—then white, working class, Democratic south
side Milwaukee—Wallace ran well over his state average, as he did in some
Democratic satellite cities around Milwaukee.[35]

In November Johnson's appeal overwhelmed all else. He presented himself as the candidate of peace and prosperity, despite the building crisis in
Vietnam and the tremendous racial tensions at home. He was the conservative candidate in the sense of supporting the basic social contract of American life in his time, and voters chose him with this in mind. Wallace was
forgotten, and Johnson's opponent, Barry Goldwater, was unable to get more
than strong Republican voters, particularly college-educated Republicans and
those concerned about defeating Communism. His appeal to independents
and weak Republicans, not to speak of Democrats of any variety, was nil.
Johnson's Wisconsin victory was overwhelming and in this entire period
Johnson was the only Democrat to carry the majority of the vote in Wisconsin's villages and small cities. He was also the only Democratic candidate for
president who carried the Protestant German areas of Wisconsin in the period
1948–64. And so it went as he marshaled record-setting margins in Democratic constituencies and breakthrough percentages in Republican ones. It was
quite a victory.[36]

None of this, however, saved Reynolds, the unpopular Democratic incumbent governor saddled with the reputation of being a taxer. His Republican opponent, Warren Knowles, had a reputation as a moderate, thoughtful
Republican. He ran as a fresh voice against a governor whose critics, unfairly
so, labeled him a taxing extremist, and Knowles won despite the Johnson
landslide.[37]

ELEMENTS OF THE VOTE

In the postwar period the question arises as to whether ethnic and religious divisions still mattered. The suggestion that "religious and ethnic political divisions, which were unrelated to twentieth-century issues and problems, had little influence on the 1962 two-party division" is accurate. There was little, if any, self-conscious ethnic voting. Yet ethnicity did often remain a good predictor of voting preference in this period, especially in rural areas, villages, and small cities where the majority of the Wisconsin electorate lived. It was simply a fact that German Americans usually voted Republican, Poles leaned Democratic, British-ancestry and mixed and diverse areas supported Republicans, and most Norwegians voted Democratic.[38]

One feature that has been extensively studied is the issue of "size of place" in this era and whether size was at all a guide to voting behavior. Political scientist Leon Epstein found that the answer was yes. What was true in the postwar years was that smaller villages and cities were much more Republican than were big cities, especially Madison and Milwaukee. In Milwaukee, however, Democratic though the city had become, there was no neat correlation between the industrial working population and the Democrats.

In contemporary terms, Wisconsin was then, as it is once again, more red in the countryside than in the larger urban areas. To be sure, the differences by size of place, for example from 1948 to 1954, were modest, but the differences were there. What did not fit in the picture was the vote in rural farm areas. At that time this vote was sometimes volatile, at some points swinging toward the Democrats, other times toward the Republicans, at all times quite sensitive to perceptions of the health of the farm economies. At any time, however, the more profitable agricultural areas tended to be more Republican, the less flourishing more Democratic. But was this a sign of class or economic voting? Perhaps not entirely, since, after all, German American rural areas tended to constitute much of the most affluent farming regions, and their Republicanism preceded postwar years.[39]

One might argue that the relative Republicanism of small towns, villages, and the smaller cities reflected the homogeneity predictable in small places. But this explanation does not work; it does not explain the much more Democratic vote in the big cities in Wisconsin. One might ask, as proponents of the small-town homogeneity thesis definitely do not, whether the one-sided vote in Wisconsin's big cities is merely an expression of "big-town homogeneity." The answer may be yes, but this does not explain why small towns and villages were decidedly more Republican in this age and big cities decidedly more Democratic. That reality had nothing to do with size of place but a lot to do with such things as the role of pro-Democratic unions in the bigger cities and hostility among the rural and small-town German Americans toward the Democrats as the party of the war and big spending.

Public opinion polls from that era indicate that Wisconsin voters were relatively issue oriented compared with many other areas of the country, and they were divided along familiar liberal-conservative lines, as that division was defined in that era. Also true was that Wisconsin voters were relatively more informed about issues and, importantly, able to make the link between candidates and parties and their own issue orientations. While class was an uncertain guide, and although ethnicity was often still a good predictor, ideology was a real factor that crossed but did not necessarily eliminate traditional ethnic, religious, or class electoral boundaries. More and more Wisconsin postwar voting was ideological, and voters' roles in that scene were well understood.[40]

Again, however, the patterns of vote across demographic variables were hardly irrelevant. This fact, along with the changes in the two parties' constituencies over their traditional nineteenth- and early-twentieth-century counterparts, may be illustrated by comparing selected elements of the vote in 1910 with the vote in 1950. What such a comparison shows is that ethnic realities were not to be ignored in the postwar period, whatever the degree of self-consciousness operating in the process. For example, while in 1910 German Lutherans were divided in their sentiments in rural areas and villages in Wisconsin and German Catholics still leaned toward the Democrats, in the post–World War II period all German areas were Republican. Polish areas, however, whether urban or rural, were unchanged. They remained as robustly Democratic in 1950 as they had been in 1910. Dutch areas were also just as Republican forty years later. The most dramatic changes were in Norwegian and, to a lesser extent, Swedish areas of Wisconsin, which in 1910 were overwhelmingly Republican. Norwegians in the postwar period leaned Democratic, and Swedish areas were divided. Consensus was gone. Another area that saw change was Milwaukee, which had become a Democratic stronghold.[41]

There was also variability within the post–World War II era when the Republicans tended to be (but not always) in electoral control. Milwaukee, for example, was firmly Democratic in the 1950s, but by the 1960s it was becoming more so with Democratic vote moving into the sixtieth percentile. According to my samples, most villages were solidly Republican, but in the 1964 Johnson-Goldwater race that was dramatically reversed. Norwegian areas tended to vote Democratic; but in the 1960 presidential race, the

Catholic, Kennedy, could barely get 40 percent of the vote in such places. German Catholic precincts were usually Republican, but in 1960 they narrowly swung behind Kennedy and in 1964 more decisively for Johnson. Rural voters confirmed their oscillating behavior when, although they usually voted Republican, they went Democratic in the 1948 and 1964 presidential races and in the 1954, 1960, and 1962 governors' elections and when they opted for Democrat William Proxmire in the Senate race of 1957.[42]

The electoral picture was complicated during the years 1948 to 1964. Wisconsin had evolved from a solidly one-party Republican state to one in which both parties in any given year had a chance to win, where some old electoral guideposts remained firm while others changed. It was something of a new age after World War II, and Wisconsin had become a competitive political environment.

8

Electoral Stability in a Two-Party Politics

1965–1998

ACCORDING TO THE 1970 CENSUS, Wisconsin had a little more than 4.4 million citizens, close to a 12 percent gain over 1960. It was an overwhelmingly white population (96.4 percent), with most of the rest African American. American Indians were a distant third. The state had a well-balanced economy of agriculture, industry, and white-collar and service businesses. Wisconsin was no longer a rural state by any means. About two-thirds of the population lived in jurisdictions of 2,500 or more. Milwaukee was the state's big city, of course, with more than 700,000 citizens, and Madison was a remote second at about 172,000; no other city in the state had as many as 100,000 citizens. Wisconsin had become urban, but with much of that population living in small cities and suburbs scattered all across the state.

Twenty years later, in 1990, Wisconsin's population growth had slowed noticeably, then just shy of 4.9 million people, and it grew by only 4 percent over 1980, far behind the national average. Wisconsin's economy had taken some serious blows, especially its manufacturing sector, which was clearly in decline. But the increase of the tech and educational sectors showed signs of promise. The state remained overwhelmingly white, at 92 percent; the black population stood at 5 percent and the Asian at about 1 percent. Wisconsin was no more urban than it had been in 1970, no cities except Milwaukee and Madison had more than 100,000 people, and while Madison had grown since 1970, Milwaukee had begun its steep decline in population, already tumbling to 628,000 citizens. Of residents with a religious affiliation, 45 percent were Roman Catholic, about 30 percent Lutheran, 8 percent Methodist, and most of the rest other Protestants.[1]

By the late 1960s the new Democratic Party was strongly established and had shown a stable pattern of often close electoral competition with the Republicans. The two parties seemed quite equal in appeal, though perhaps the Democrats were narrowly the majority party in Wisconsin from 1970 to about 1990. Either way this situation was not to last as the 1990s unfolded.[2] Studies demonstrated that Wisconsin had a great many self-described independent voters by the middle 1960s and thereafter. At that time party identification pointedly declined in Wisconsin as in the nation as a whole. The points of conflict between the two parties were ideological, with Democrats promoting policies described as liberal and state oriented and Republicans conservative and anti-state. What those terms meant varied greatly in practical and policy terms in the thirty-plus years between the middle 1960s and near-dawn of the twenty-first century. That there were policy and ideological lines of division was certain.[3]

How these divisions worked out did not erase all the old ethnic lines of the past in Wisconsin politics, even as a self-consciousness of the origins of these old splits was frequently completely lost. New ethnic and racial divisions emerged as significant factors in Wisconsin voting, as did such phenomena as the rising power of suburban voters and the appearance of "new liberal centers," such as Madison. They muddied any notion that Wisconsin politics since the New Deal was largely class-based, the affluent supporting the Republicans and the less-well-off the Democrats. The new situation was stable, but it was different in a number of ways, even as such factors as candidate image remained or became even more significant, exemplified above all by the tremendous political success of Republican Tommy Thompson, the most successful figure in Wisconsin electoral politics in the later twentieth century.

These patterns of voting behavior were complex, but they also operated out of a general "cultural matrix" that was, as Daniel Elazar formulated it, deeply "moralistic." That is, Wisconsin political culture was permeated by a dislike of political maneuverings and party regularity, an affection for independent voting and independent candidates, a hostility toward corruption, a support for citizen involvement—including voting—and a sympathy for competing visions of the common good as distinct from the raw pursuit of self-interest in politics. For Elazar such a moralistic culture was particularly connected with Yankee and Scandinavian ethnic political traditions. German traditions, he argued, were more associated with an individualistic culture less oriented toward the government and more focused on the individual. But neither culture had much use for conventional political parties or politicians.[4]

Elazar's analysis was not unique to him; other scholars report similar findings regarding Wisconsin political culture, attitudes, and orientations.[5] Such analyses got a major reaffirmation in practice in early 2007 when the Wisconsin legislature and governor established by overwhelming bipartisan support a new and independent agency, the Government Accountability Board, possessed of sweeping powers to watch over elected and other governmental officials who might violate Wisconsin's already unusually strict governmental ethics law. Wisconsin is not New Jersey.

To the End of the 1960s

Warren Knowles won reelection in 1966 as Wisconsin's governor with 53 percent over Patrick Lucey, longtime Democratic Party organizer. As governor, Knowles had established himself as a successful moderate who was widely seen as a thoughtful and genial figure. His popularity helped bring the Republicans back into play in Wisconsin, as did the important organizing work of Ody Fish, Republican state chair in the middle and late 1960s. The Knowles era of the middle 1960s was often a less sharply contested ideological age than was to be the case forty years later. To be sure, the differences between the two parties regarding the size of both government and taxes were real, and elections were hard fought. Yet as Jacob Stampen has skillfully shown in neatly contrasting the Wisconsin legislature of 1965–66 and that of 2005–6, the mood of legislative politics four decades ago was more open and congenial, and less strident, divisive, and tightly partisan.[6] Certainly this description fits the mood and spirit of Knowles Republicanism, though it is important to note that this approach is not a self-evident ideal for a political party. It certainly was not to the Republican critics of Knowles who thought he was far too "open" to Democrats and their ideas.

In his 1966 reelection campaign Knowles was helped by the contentious fight for the nomination for governor in the 1966 Democratic primary between Lucey and David Carley, another real estate magnate. There were overtones of the history of the Democratic Party as many of the original party revivalists, such as Senator Nelson, backed Carley while Lucey received the support of many more old-line Democrats. Whether Lucey's active Catholicism was an underground issue is hotly disputed. What is certain is that the primary was a bruising and at times ugly fight between two determined personalities.

That Knowles did not win more easily may seem a surprise, since he had the support of every major newspaper in the state except Madison's *Capital Times,* which, staunchly Democratic as it was and is, actually chose to be neutral. But the closeness of the November election between Knowles and Lucey merely underlined the competitive character of the two parties in postwar Wisconsin.[7]

The year 1968 was an important one in U.S. political and electoral history—the Vietnam War and the ensuing protests, the assassinations of Robert Kennedy and Martin Luther King Jr., the riots in black urban America,

Warren Knowles, governor 1965–71 (Wisconsin Historical Society, WHi-25352)

Lyndon Johnson's decision not to run for president again, the dramatic campaign for the Democratic nomination for president, the second George Wallace run for president, and the election of Richard Nixon as president in November 1968. All of this had its effects on Wisconsin electoral politics. The greatest drama came from the Wallace presidential campaign as he chose to run as an independent. Wallace believed he could have a real impact as a candidate in Wisconsin. He deliberately based his campaign to capitalize on anger over social disorder and his sense that a tough crackdown was needed. With this orientation in mind, he believed that Wisconsin looked like a place where he could gain traction. Tremendous racial turmoil shook Milwaukee in 1968, and that same year serious campus unrest and disorder hit the University of Wisconsin campus at Madison. Wallace did all he could to exploit the unrest, talking and acting tough while, perhaps ironically, arguing for the need for smaller government so that people could be left alone. As studies show, his greatest appeal was among young men of the lower-middle and working classes who were angry over their unpromising situation in life and furious that those they saw as favored in society—blacks and rich college kids—were acting up and getting away with it.

Wallace did very well nationally in 1968, getting 13.5 percent of the total vote. Of course he ran best in the Deep South, but in many urban areas in the North he ran well, especially in white areas near African American communities. There is no doubt that Wallace appealed to many young white males concerned about race and the increase in government that was a feature of the 1960s. But even though Wallace received 7.6 percent of the presidential vote in Wisconsin, he ran less well there than he had hoped. Part of his problem was that his vice presidential candidate, Curtis LeMay ("Bombs away LeMay"), scared people with his highly aggressive military views. More serious for Wallace was the charge that Wallace was a racist, which became a perception that stuck with him and hurt him.[8]

Thus in the end, despite his considerable efforts, Wallace got only 9.4 percent of the vote in working-class Milwaukee, where he had placed his greatest hopes. After Milwaukee, Wallace did best in German ethnic rural towns and villages and in German Catholic (9.1 percent) and German Protestant (8.2 percent) areas, suggesting that much of Wallace's appeal lay with conservative voters who ordinarily voted Republican. Wallace's vote had its effects, however, since in 1968 both the Republican and Democratic candidates for president, Richard Nixon and Hubert Humphrey, fell far short of 50 percent of the vote nationally. In Wisconsin Nixon got 48 percent, Humphrey 44 percent, and Wallace most of the rest. In the race for governor, unbeatable

Republican incumbent Warren Knowles defeated Democrat Bronson La Follette, son of Robert La Follette Jr., 53 percent to 47 percent.[9]

An earlier election story in 1968 Wisconsin received some attention also. To some, Eugene McCarthy's appeal to antiwar students and activists in the run-up to the April Democratic presidential primary in Wisconsin was of great significance, suggesting mounting antiwar sentiment in the Midwest. But as things turned out, the Wisconsin primary did not matter. It did not become the showdown between antiwar and pro-Johnson forces some had expected, since President Johnson announced his decision not to run for reelection before the primary took place.

THE 1970S

The election of 1970 brought Patrick J. Lucey to the governor's chair, another Democratic victory in the pendulum of electoral political swings of the 1960s and 1970s. Lucey had managed Senator Proxmire's breakthrough election to the Senate in 1957 and served as state Democratic Party chair into the 1960s, superbly organizing the Democrats into a party of equal competitiveness with the long-dominant Republicans.

Lucey's election as governor did not come without a good deal of internal Democratic Party conflict. Lucey was never a favorite of Madison's liberal Democrats. From Lucey's perspective, they were too interested in ideological purity while he felt compromise was necessary in order to win. From his critics' perspective, Lucey was a politician of dubious convictions dedicated only to his own success. Moreover, tensions remained from the 1960 Democratic presidential primary and Lucey's ardent support of his fellow Catholic, John Kennedy, over Hubert Humphrey. Nonetheless, Lucey won the Democratic nomination, and he rode to victory in November 1970, defeating Lieutenant Governor Jack Olson, who did not have a major state reputation. Lucey may well have been aided by the easy victory of the popular Senator Proxmire, who rolled up 71 percent of the state vote, but Lucey's victory was too hard-fought to be dismissed in an age in which voting coattails was on the wane. Lucey received 54 percent and Olson 45 percent.[10]

Gary Wekkin aptly describes the role Lucey occupied in Wisconsin political life in this era: "Gov. Patrick J. Lucey was easily the dominant figure in Wisconsin politics during the 1970s. . . . He was a consummate politician who had few peers in organizational skill and enjoyed exceptional national connections and prestige . . . the strongest Wisconsin governor since the elder La Follette. . . . Lucey had a knack for prevailing even when his actions were unpopular."[11]

The 1970 election was the first in which Wisconsin governors were elected to four-year terms. That was probably a good thing for Democratic Governor Lucey, since 1972 was not a Democratic year in Wisconsin or the nation. Like the rest of the country, Wisconsin was caught in the turmoil and division over the Vietnam War. Moreover, racial conflicts continued to be quite real in Milwaukee, which was in a continual uproar over issues of public school busing. George Wallace appeared again, still trying to run for president and hoping Wisconsin could be of special help. This time he was back competing as he had in 1964 in the Democratic presidential primaries. He ran well in the Democratic presidential primary, coming in second, using the busing issue to his advantage. But his campaign, though not his life, came to an effective end at the hand of a would-be assassin's bullet in May 1972. While, in fact, Wallace did try for a fourth time in the 1976 Democratic presidential primaries, his defeat in the Florida primary by fellow southerner Jimmy Carter ended his quest for the presidency before he got to campaign again in Wisconsin.

The shooting of Wallace, which left him permanently disabled, helped the dovish senator from South Dakota, George McGovern, capture the Democratic presidential nomination and run against Republican candidate Richard M. Nixon. McGovern was badly defeated in the general election, however, both nationally and in Wisconsin. The Wisconsin vote was Nixon

Patrick Lucey, governor 1971–77
(Wisconsin Historical Society, WHi-48604)

53 percent, McGovern 44 percent, and rightist American Independence candidate John Schmitz (Wallace's successor) 2.6 percent. Survey data from Wisconsin revealed that McGovern was perceived to be too radical for many, even among those who identified themselves as Democrats. Strong Democratic identifiers were notably more for him than anyone else, as one would predict.[12]

McGovern was just too far off for even Wisconsin's liberal and, by then, vibrant Democratic Party, but his defeat in Wisconsin did not change anything in terms of the state's general electoral picture. The next election, in 1974, came in a very good Democratic year. President Nixon had resigned following his cover-up of the Watergate scandal. In Wisconsin the Democrats carried every race—all the constitutional offices as well as a majority of the Assembly seats, and they reelected Gaylord Nelson to the U.S. Senate. Lucey, though ever controversial, ran the least one-sided race, but it did not matter. The controversial and hard-driving Lucey garnered 53 percent in defeating William Dyke, former mayor of Madison. Dyke was the last Republican up to this day to occupy the "nonpartisan" Madison mayor's office.[13]

The mid-1970s was a time of some electoral volatility in terms of those who voted Democratic or Republican. According to my representative samples, there was no tight association between the vote for any party in one election to another; they were associated but not at high levels. This was true, for example, of the Nixon election in 1972 and the Dyke for governor vote in 1974 and the McGovern and Lucey votes that same year. It was also true of the vote pattern in the 1976 presidential race between Jimmy Carter and Gerald Ford when compared with that of the 1974 governor's race. To be sure, each party had a large body of loyalists, but neither could depend on a committed majority. Independent voting in Wisconsin was now commonplace.[14]

One of the more intriguing aspects of the electoral picture in this period was the time it took for the state Democrats to advance to parity and eventual control of the state legislature, despite many statewide election victories after 1957. The Democrats were able to capture the Assembly for brief stints as part of national Democratic landslides in 1958 and then again in 1964. Yet it was not until the era of Democratic Governor Lucey in the 1970s that the Democrats won the Assembly and then held onto it for more than twenty years. This success was a result for which Lucey and his Democratic organization deserve credit in the first place. Yet it also reflects the fact that change at the state level, in this case Democrats having achieved statewide parity with the Republicans by the late 1950s, often comes much sooner than it does at more local levels. Assembly contests were and are often very much about local politics and local political loyalties. Eventually, the appeal of Republican Governor Tommy Thompson in the 1990s helped end the Democrats' Assembly dominance. Beginning with the 1994 elections, the Republicans won the Assembly back and they have held onto it well into the twenty-first century.

For the Democrats, progress toward equity in the Senate in the postwar era was a bit slower than in the Assembly, but eventually the result was similar. In 1974 the Democrats captured the Senate, again a success that was an artifact of the flush Democratic times in Lucey years. Yet once they had control, they did not lose it even in leaner times until the 1990s. Again during the age of Governor Thompson, the Republicans made their comeback in the Senate. From 1992 through 1997, who was actually in control of the Senate sometimes varied, even within a given legislative session. After the 1998 election the Democrats were narrowly back in power only to see the Republicans succeed them after the 2002 election. The year 2006 proved to be a big one for the Democrats and they resumed rule in the Senate.

Overall, since 1972, the Democrats, while beginning slowly in terms of their postwar revival, have done better marginally in terms of rule in the Wisconsin legislature. Only the Thompson phenomenon interfered. Mostly, but not always, the margins of control in either body and by either party have been close. They have inexactly mirrored the state's close voting patterns.[15]

Lucey's reelection victory in 1974 was followed in 1976 by Jimmy Carter's triumph in the state (as in the nation) in his presidential race against Republican Gerald Ford. While Ford was the incumbent president, he was an unelected one, president due to Nixon's resignation. The 1976 election was an especially sweet victory for Wisconsin Democrats because it suggested that their renewed strength was not just attributable to Lucey or because of in-state races but that it was spreading to national elections. Although Carter barely won with 50 percent, Ford getting 48 percent, and Eugene McCarthy 1.7 percent of the major candidate vote in Wisconsin, a Carter victory it nonetheless was. And since it so closely paralleled the national results, this outcome substantiated the claim that Wisconsin had become a competitive and even slightly Democratic-leaning state.[16]

By rolling up an average of 56.2 percent in rural towns, Carter did better with this portion of the Wisconsin electorate than any Democrat since 1932 (except Johnson in 1964) and better than any Democratic presidential candidate has done since. In Garfield in Polk County Carter got 62 percent (McGovern 45.8 percent in 1972); in Glendale in Monroe County 53.9 percent (versus 33 percent); in Eastman in Crawford County 48.5 percent (versus 40 percent); 59.3 percent in Clyde in Iowa County (versus 47.9 percent). Carter also did extraordinarily well as a Democrat in Wisconsin villages, carrying them with an average of 51.1 percent, the best vote for a Democratic candidate for president (except in 1964) since 1936.[17]

Why Carter did so relatively well in rural towns and villages in Wisconsin is an interesting question. This phenomenon was repeated in many places across the nation and was not at all unique to Wisconsin. The best explanation focuses on candidate image. Carter, among other things, was a farmer and sometimes effectively projected a country or small town image that resonated in places far from Plains, Georgia.

Carter's relative appeal for a Democrat in many less-than-affluent rural areas and villages contrasted with his (again, relative) weakness in the biggest cities of Wisconsin, confounding the usual picture a bit. Yet despite the unusual pattern of the 1976 presidential vote and the evidence of widespread independent voting in Wisconsin, Carter's vote was hardly distinct from McGovern's 1972 vote, and the same was true of Ford's 1976 vote when compared with Nixon's in 1972.[18]

This brief period of Democratic ascendancy in Wisconsin came to a stop in 1978 when the red-vested Lee Sherman Dreyfus, chancellor of the University of Wisconsin–Stevens Point, a flamboyant moderate Republican known for his high energy levels and outspoken wife, rose to take political office. Dreyfus's opportunity came when Governor Lucey left to become ambassador to Mexico. (Lucey later ran for vice president on John Anderson's ill-fated Independent ticket in 1980.) He left the governorship to his lieutenant governor, Martin Schreiber of Milwaukee. In what has become a common experience in Wisconsin politics, Schreiber's effort to keep his new office failed at the polls. He came across as colorless and uninspiring in comparison with the dynamic Dreyfus, a difference that helped get Dreyfus elected governor with 54 percent while Schreiber limped in with 45 percent (less than 1 percent of the vote going to other candidates).

The major issue of the campaign was taxation and how to deal with a state budget surplus. Dreyfus took a characteristic Republican position and insisted Wisconsin taxes were too high. He argued that the budget surplus should be returned to Wisconsin citizens as a rebate. This goal he subsequently accomplished when he became governor. Schreiber temporized on the issue, wisely or not, waiting for a task force recommendation on what to do, thus undermining a popular sense that he was a decisive leader. In the end, the Dreyfus triumph was mostly a personal victory of a popular Republican against a perceived lackluster Democrat. It did not change the Democrats' overall marginal control in the state, reflected in their continuing control of a state legislature that had fallen into their hands in 1974 and remained firmly so in 1978.

THE 1980s

Ronald Reagan, the Republican nominee for president in 1980, won a decisive victory in the nation by unseating President Jimmy Carter. The outcome in Wisconsin was considerably closer than Reagan's 10 percent margin in the nation as a whole. Reagan did carry Wisconsin, but he did so with only 47.9 percent of the vote. John Anderson ran a strong third-party race with 7.1 percent. Ed Clark, with 1.3 percent, received a historic high for a Libertarian Party candidate in Wisconsin.[19]

Reagan's triumph as a Republican was not the only noteworthy one in Wisconsin in 1980. That year brought the end to Democratic Senator Gaylord Nelson's long career of political successes in the state. By 1980 Nelson had been a senator since 1962. He was now very much a part of the world of Washington politics and seemed successful in that world. But he was less and less in touch with Wisconsin, especially with a whole generation of younger voters. In 1980, a Republican year, Nelson proved vulnerable as his opponent, Robert Kasten Jr., capitalized on the out-of-touch sentiment by noting that Nelson neither owned nor rented a residence in Wisconsin—and had not for years.[20]

The Anderson protest race was an interesting one. That he held on to 7.1 percent in Wisconsin, despite plenty of late defections, was impressive. Anderson's vote came from those who were uneasy about Reagan and at the same time dissatisfied with Carter's performance. Perhaps predictably, Anderson did best in Madison, rolling up 13.8 percent of the three-party vote, and ran above his average in the suburbs of the state, including the all-important suburbs of Milwaukee. He even received an average of 5 percent of the vote in the towns and villages of Wisconsin.[21]

There were no other especially interesting features to the Anderson vote. The idea that he drew mostly from Democrats and that his vote would come mostly from areas of Democratic voting strength was erroneous. So was any presumption that he would draw mostly from fellow Republicans. His appeal was general and broad, and he turned out not to be the special child of dissidents from one party versus another.

Study of the Anderson vote in connection with income analysis also does not reveal much. Anderson's vote came from all over the state—rich, poor, and middle-class places. This is no wonder, since Anderson was a candidate who did not focus on economic issues, and he attracted voters because of the widespread dissatisfaction with the two mainstream candidates. Clark, the Libertarian candidate, did not turn out to be most attractive in affluent areas of Wisconsin, despite what one might expect. He did best, in fact, in some poorer rural areas and small towns of Wisconsin, just as Ed Thompson, the Libertarian candidate for governor, was to do in 2002.

Still, Democratic high hopes for the 1980s in Wisconsin, despite Reagan's election, expanded greatly when Anthony Earl achieved election as governor in 1982. Earl, who had spent much of his life in Wausau and had been a legislator from there before becoming secretary of the Department of Administration and then head of the Department of Natural Resources, seemed to be exactly what those in control of the Democratic Party sought. He was committed to liberal economic and social values yet seemed to be a regular Wisconsinite, one who enjoyed hunting, a beer at a tavern, and other comfortable Wisconsin ways. His victory over Terry Kohler, whom the media portrayed as far to the right of Earl, was a convincing one, as Earl picked up 57 percent of the vote. There were no particular dramatic swings in one area or group or another to the new governor. Earl just ran well ahead of the usual Democratic vote virtually everywhere and among all identifiable categories of the electorate on the way to rolling up his impressive victory. Things seemed to be going very well for the Democrats.[22]

But this proved not to be the case. First, in the 1984 presidential election President Ronald Reagan carried Wisconsin with 54 percent to Walter Mondale's 45 percent. Mondale did well in Wisconsin compared with his national showing (where he got a very weak 41 percent). What may have helped him was a friends-and-neighbors vote. After all, Mondale was a familiar and well-regarded figure from next-door Minnesota. Nonetheless, he decisively lost in Wisconsin.[23]

With greater long-run significance for Wisconsin, Anthony Earl was defeated in his reelection bid in 1986, which stunned the Democratic camp. Earl was popular in Madison and with Democratic liberals. He was a true son, so to speak, of the postwar makers of the liberal Democratic Party. Yet Earl seemed to have something of a tin ear politically. He understood and sympathized with what was popular in Madison, but what is popular in culturally liberal Madison is not necessarily perceived so favorably in much of the rest of the state. He eventually acquired the fatal reputation as "the governor of Madison."

Even so, it was reasonable to expect him to be able to beat the Republican Assembly leader from Elroy, Tommy Thompson. Thompson was widely regarded in Madison political circles as a country oaf, to use one of the nicer descriptions. But Earl did not beat him. Instead, he was the one beaten 53 to 47 percent. The Democrats increased their margins in the state legislature, though, leaving Thompson with a hostile legislative branch as he began his governorship. Earl's defeat was a crucial one for the Democrats. For as things developed over the next ten years, Thompson was to be the major figure of Wisconsin state politics. Thompson, as events proved, was a master politician, campaigner, and electoral wizard.

Earl's defeat was curious. Both Earl and Thompson obtained votes in recognizable party patterns, only Earl just did a little worse than victorious Democrats do and Thompson a little better than defeated Republicans do.[24] But there is more to be explored. Detailed examination of the results shows that one common explanation for Earl's defeat and Thompson's victory does not work. That explanation is that Earl so offended rural and small village Wisconsin that this decided the election. There is little doubt that much of outstate Wisconsin voted for Thompson, but a lot of it was, and is, hardly Democratic territory anyway, and outstaters had not been enthusiastic about Earl in 1982. In fact, the largest changes in Earl's support from 1982 to 1986 came quite clearly in urban and suburban Wisconsin. My samples of suburbs show that the average vote for Earl fell from an impressive 50.8 percent in 1982 to 40.9 percent in 1986; the Madison vote went from 75.5 percent to 64.5 percent; in large second-class cities it went from 63.2 to 52.2 percent and in medium-range cities from 60.1 to 45.2 percent. The contrast with the drop in town vote, the heart of rural Wisconsin, where Earl slid from 50.1 percent to 44.2 percent, is clear. Earl was hardly loved in the countryside, but it was his failure to hold the urban and suburban vote percentages of 1982 that explained his defeat.

Earl's loss looked more and more like a missed opportunity for the Democrats in light of the 1988 presidential election, when Michael Dukakis was able to squeak by to win Wisconsin by defeating George H. W. Bush 51 percent to 48 percent, even as Bush won the presidency with little trouble by dominating in other areas of the country. The Dukakis state margin was 79,000 votes out of a total of well over 2 million. In terms of national politics, Wisconsin narrowly remained a Democratic state, but this fact did not translate to the governorship. That was abundantly clear by 1990 when Tommy Thompson ran for reelection and badly defeated well-known Tom Loftus, who had been the State Assembly's majority leader from a Madison suburb while Thompson had slogged away as minority leader from Elroy, a small town well northwest of Madison. The vote was 58 percent to 42 percent, a landslide that shocked Democrats while it pleased Republicans. The able Loftus was a predictably determined liberal Democrat, because, as he observed, "the soil in Dane County usually produced only one kind."[25] But Thompson as governor had become popular as a celebrator of Wisconsin, a Harley-riding man of the people who ran as a big-government Republican. The Democrats retained their majority in both houses of the state legislature, which only underlined Thompson's personal popularity.[26]

The 1992 election was a crazy, chaotic one in the nation as well as in Wisconsin. Dissatisfaction with the Bush administration was extensive. It was most famously articulated by J. Ross Perot, a Texas billionaire who attacked Bush for his dubious financial policies. He gathered a favorable response from voters who were disgusted by both parties and all politicians and who felt quite estranged from a president portrayed as out of touch with grocery store prices. Bill Clinton, governor of Arkansas, was the Democratic candidate.

Tommy Thompson, governor 1987–2001 (Wisconsin Historical Society, WHi-27077)

Clinton did not do well in Wisconsin, getting only 41 percent of the three-way vote, but it was enough because Perot proved popular in the state—as mavericks usually do. Perot got an astounding total of just under 22 percent. Bush limped in with 37 percent, a major repudiation.[27]

Perot hurt Bush everywhere he ran. But as has happened with third-party protest votes in recent decades, his most robust showing did not always come in places that some predicted, such as Madison (12.3 percent) or sub-urbia (17.6 percent on average), but in outstate Wisconsin. There, it is quite clear, a substantial vote can be won by candidates who fall outside the regular party confines. Thus Perot's median vote in villages was 25.5 percent and in the towns an even greater 27.6 percent. In the smallest cities (fewer than 10,000 people) he got 23 percent. Perot hurt Clinton in Madison and Dane County, but he hurt Bush more by his appeal outstate in what we now call red areas, normally dependably Republican. Still, the bottom line was that Clinton, the Democrat, won, and the Democrats continued to win Wisconsin at the presidential level.[28]

Clinton did much better in 1996, winning reelection quite easily and carrying Wisconsin with no trouble, though once again he did not get 50 percent of the vote. But in 1996 it was a four-person race, with Perot still getting over 10 percent of the vote, reflecting the continuing love of mavericks, and Ralph Nader of the Green Party running on the Left and getting 1.3 percent less. It was all standard stuff, with the Republicans reminded again that they were an ever-so-narrow but constant minority parity at the presidential level in Wisconsin.[29]

Meanwhile, at the state level the Tommy Thompson phenomenon continued apace. Thompson's upset of Anthony Earl was surprising, but perhaps even more surprising to both Democrats and Republicans was Thompson's ensuing popularity as governor and his effective management as a big government Republican, which won wide plaudits everywhere but in liberal Madison and Dane County. Unfortunately for the Democrats, their party leadership's Madison perspective led them to make a serious error in 1994 and nominate for governor State Senator Chuck Chvala, who represented parts of Madison and Dane County. Chvala was simple for the Republicans to parody as a stereotypical Madison liberal out of touch with the rest of Wisconsin.

The 1994 election result was a devastating defeat for Chvala and a stunning triumph for Governor Thompson as Thompson swept back into office with almost 67 percent of the total vote. While 1994 was decidedly a Republican year in the nation, Thompson's victory went way beyond that fact. It marked the lowest point for a Democratic Party candidate for governor in Wisconsin since 1946.[30]

Thompson's vote was associated with George Bush's presidential race in 1988 and with his own gubernatorial vote in 1990, but not as closely as one might think at first.[31] Thompson had such an overwhelming appeal to many working-class Wisconsinites, while at the same time he was even more popular than a Republican usually is in suburban Milwaukee, that his past performances, not to speak of Bush's in 1988, were hardly comparable with his huge victory in 1994. Most remarkably, although he did not carry the African American vote in Milwaukee, he was able to break out of the less-than-10

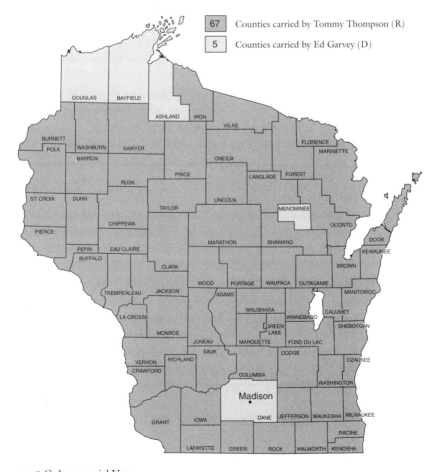

| 67 | Counties carried by Tommy Thompson (R) |
| 5 | Counties carried by Ed Garvey (D) |

1998 Gubernatorial Vote

percent figure that has long been routine for statewide Republican candidates among this constituency. He received a modern record-setting 27 percent.[32]

The election of 1998 was pretty much more of the same. Another favorite of Madison and Dane County liberals, Ed Garvey, ran as the Democratic candidate. A well-to-do former lawyer for pro football players, Garvey ran as a kind of Left populist and was badly beaten by Thompson, 60 percent to 39 percent in the total vote. Thompson ran well virtually everywhere except in the cities of Madison and Milwaukee. Again, as had proven true in 1994, there was only a very modest association between rising income levels and the Thompson vote.[33] Perhaps by this point Thompson was unbeatable because he had effectively bonded with the majority of the Wisconsin electorate. At the least it seemed obvious that he was unbeatable by Madison-area liberals.

While Thompson was cruising to another landslide victory in 1998, the major contest in Wisconsin that year was between Democratic Senator Russ Feingold, first elected in 1992, and his opponent, Congressman Mark Newman from southeast Wisconsin. The contest revealed once again, Thompson elections aside, the basic closeness of the division in the Wisconsin electorate. Much of the bitter and expensive campaign turned around social issues, especially the issue of abortion, with the two candidates each taking firm and contrasting stances. Feingold won a tight reelection with 51 percent of the vote, impressive since he was running the same year as the popular Thompson, who ran far ahead of Newman.

The voting patterns of the Feingold-Newman race have been extensively studied. There was no overall income or size-of-place correlation with either candidate, but there were a few interesting variations from the usual voting behavior in late-twentieth-century Wisconsin. On the one hand, Feingold lost support in middle-sized and small cities compared to the usual Democratic totals. Indeed, he lost the majority of smaller (third- and fourth-class) cities. On the other hand, Newman ran behind the normal Republican vote in the suburbs of Milwaukee, though he carried most of them. It is likely that in both cases the very public abortion issue had an effect.[34]

ELEMENTS OF THE VOTE

We know that there were many ups and downs in Wisconsin voting over the period of 1965 through 1988. On balance, though, it was a time in which the Democrats recovered from their post–World War II slump and were often victors in repeatedly close elections. Essential to the Democrats' state numbers were Milwaukee and Madison. Though Milwaukee had begun its decline, the growth of Madison and Dane County *and* the increasingly Democratic nature of Milwaukee and Madison served as vital compensation.

The old New Deal pattern continued to hold in the other cities of Wisconsin, granting, as always, variation for particular elections. That is, in the larger cities beyond Milwaukee and Madison, the Democrats normally continued to win, but in middle-sized and small cities their victories were far less common. Republicans were the urban majority in many small Wisconsin cities. Suburbia tipped no scales as yet because it was still a small part of the electorate. True, by the end of this period suburban Milwaukee was expanding significantly. Elsewhere, however, and even in Milwaukee County, suburbia was modest and far from monolithically Republican because it included a number of working-class areas.

Towns and villages presented a different scenario. Though Republicans benefited within their borders more often than not, when Democrats were perceived to be more oriented toward these worlds, as Jimmy Carter was as a Democrat in 1976, the overall town vote went Democratic. It also did so when towns rejected George Herbert Walker Bush, who just did not connect (comparatively speaking) with country voters in Wisconsin.

The state's villages were robustly Republican during most of this era, though over time this tendency faded. By 1988, villages were either reflective of the state vote as a whole or even a bit more Democratic than the state. This lack of enduring Republican strength in the towns and especially the villages as time went on explains why Republicans had trouble carrying the state, especially at the presidential level. The countryside (and suburbia) simply was not producing enough Republican votes to overcome Milwaukee and Madison.

Meanwhile, some of the old ethnic voting pictures no longer had focus. Once strongly Democratic, Norwegian areas were not so Democratic anymore and often closely paralleled the state results or were a bit more Democratic, as in the town of Northfield in Jackson County or the village of Ettrick in the heart of Norwegian Trempealeau County. Swedish areas were rarely distinguishable from the state results; nor were Belgian ones.

Yet plenty of constants could be seen in rural and small-town Wisconsin. Areas thick with citizens of British ancestry continued to be noticeably Republican. So were Dutch areas, such as the village of Oostburg in Sheboygan County, where Democratic candidates often did not get even 15 percent of the vote. Swiss areas in Green County were usually very Republican in this period. And, above all, with tremendous significance, German towns and villages were devotedly Republican. This was true of almost every heavily

German area outside of the cities, whatever its religious tradition. In smaller cities, the more German American they were the more Republican they voted. Thus the traditionally Protestant town of Herman in Dodge County rarely gave Democrats more than 30 percent of its vote; the traditionally Catholic town of Marshfield in Fond du Lac County rarely gave more than 40 percent of its vote to the Democrats, and usually much less; the more religiously diverse town of Hull in Marathon County rarely gave more than one-third of its votes to the Democrats.[35]

Some other areas were consistent in their commitment to the Democrats. Those with a relatively high proportion of Finns were very much so; for example, Marengo in Ashland County was solidly Democratic in this period. So was the town of Sharon in (relatively) heavily Polish Portage County. Major Republican statewide candidates just could not carry it, and it usually went to the Democrats by 60 to more than 70 percent, though it and other Polish areas tended to cool off a bit in their Democratic ardor as the era waned.

The area of "ethnic" population that came to be a factor in this era was the African American population, which grew rapidly in Milwaukee. By 1972 and thereafter African American sectors of Milwaukee were more than 90 percent Democratic and could not be ignored any longer in Wisconsin voting. Democrats also did very well in the largely American Indian areas in Wisconsin, such as Menominee County or the town of Russell in Bayfield County.[36]

Tests to measure for class factors in voting in this era have come up largely empty. Median household income data of sampled voting units yield no significant correlation one way or another with either party. Wisconsin voting behavior was so linked with various areas and groups and at the same time was so built on cultural and ideological divisions, as well as candidate image appeals, that this measure of class did not work to predict the voting behavior of particular jurisdictions. For example, for random Republican strongholds in this era, Chilton (Calumet County) had a median household income of $22,391, Mineral Point $12,945, suburban Brookfield $32,159, Viroqua $11,000. Among random Democratic bases the same range occurred with West Allis at $18,686, Black Earth (Dane County) $17,250, Weigor (Sawyer County) $8,897. The range and mix was amazing and confounding.[37]

The overall situation tells a tale of a closely competitive state with no obvious advantage for the future for either party from demographic trends. Into the late 1990s Wisconsin presented an exciting, closely contested electoral system, perhaps the very ideal of electoral democracy in action.

9 *The Current Scene*

2000 AND BEYOND

V OTING BEHAVIOR IN WISCONSIN in the twenty-first century is an ongoing chapter in a fascinating story. Continuity and change are both still evident in Wisconsin elections. While Wisconsin is a state that most of its life has featured one-party electoral dominance (or three-party battles), it is now one of the closest two-party states in the country. No party can count on victory. And often, as in the 2000 and 2004 presidential votes, the results are incredibly close.

The 2000 census put Wisconsin's population close to 5.4 million. By the middle of the decade (2006), it reached about 5.6 million. Wisconsin is not considered a big state anymore, but it has seen growth, more than 9 percent from 1990 to 2000. Its weather, the absence of a fashionable big city, its tax structure, and other constraints limit its potential for dramatic economic growth even as a brain drain of many of its best educated young people continues to worry state officials. Yet Wisconsin is still a strong state economically, not at all skating on the margins of economic existence as are such states as North Dakota or West Virginia.

Wisconsin remains notable for its ethnic character, above all for its German American population. Forty-three percent of the state's people list their ancestry as German, making Wisconsin the second-most German state in the country (North Dakota is about 1 percent more so). The second-most named country of origin by Wisconsinites is Ireland at 11 percent, and third is Poland at more than 9 percent. Somewhat below that range comes a variety of other groups, the largest being those of Norwegian ancestry. Wisconsin is a very white state, with almost 90 percent of the population white, less than 6 percent African American, and about 1 percent American Indian; the Asian American population is less than 2 percent and the Hispanic less than 4 percent. The state's population is distributed in a quite clear pattern. Milwaukee County now has well less than one-fifth of the state's population, about one-quarter of which are in the city's suburbs. Milwaukee County's proportion of the state's population is falling rapidly as the city declines (at its high point in 1960, Milwaukee accounted for more than one-fourth of the state's population). This fact was obvious by the 2000 census when the county was the only one in the state to see a decline (almost 2 percent). Meanwhile, suburban counties around Milwaukee now represent more than 10 percent of the state's population, their highest total so far and one that is bound to grow.

Dane County accounts for almost 10 percent, and it too is growing. As of 2007 it is the fastest growing county in the state. The rest of the industrial southeast of Wisconsin has now fallen below 10 percent of the state population and will likely continue to fall. Other large cities take in about 15 percent, leaving aside the Fox River Valley, which now has reached about 10 percent of the state, its largest percentage of the population, one that will also continue to grow. Less than one-third of the population lives in the rest of the state, which is most of the state geographically, and that proportion is declining as Wisconsin becomes more and more an urban and suburban state.

The most rapidly growing areas of the state are Dane County (Madison and its suburbs), suburban Milwaukee counties, and the entire area of central west Wisconsin, especially St. Croix County, home to a substantial Minneapolis–St. Paul exurbia. A number of very small populated counties were among the leaders in percentage growth by 2000, Marquette being the top at a growth rate of 28.5 percent. This gives a misleading picture, however, in that their population base is so small that any growth gives a false impression of the actual number of people who move there.

The state's population is divided by a huge complex of governmental units. There are the 72 counties, 192 cities and 402 villages, and 1,259 towns plus assorted other local government units in the state totaling more than 3,000 jurisdictions. While in some cases units are disappearing, in others new jurisdictions are being created. Whether this is a crazy-quilt situation that is out of step with the contemporary world or not, there is no sign whatsoever that this governmental, and thus political, diversity is about to die.[1]

The major unit remains the county. Menominee County, largely American Indian, is the poorest, but it is followed fairly closely by a number of other counties in the northern part of the state where farming is poor to impossible and the climate has proven unattractive to industry. Poverty rates for a few of these northern Wisconsin counties, such as Menominee, Florence,

Langlade, and Ashland, are high, some edging toward 50 percent and others exceeding 50 percent. Suburban Milwaukee counties have the largest per capita incomes, along with Dane County and the growing St. Croix County. The exact same pattern applies to where the most highly educated Wisconsinites live.[2]

THE PRESIDENTIAL ELECTIONS OF 2000 AND 2004

That voting in Wisconsin can be as close as any state in the Union in this era was underlined in the virtually identical presidential elections of 2000 and 2004.[3] In both cases the Democratic presidential candidate won by the narrowest of margins, Al Gore defeating George W. Bush in 2000 by just over 6,000 votes out of almost 2.6 million cast. Gore's percent was 47.8, Bush's 47.6, Ralph Nader's 3.6, and minor candidates the rest. In 2004, John Kerry edged Bush out by 11,000 votes, far less than 1 percent out of almost 3 million votes case. Moreover, the pattern of the vote in the two presidential elections was similar. The vote for Gore and Kerry correlated very closely, as did the vote for Bush in 2000 and 2004.[4]

Nader's vote faded to well less than 1 percent in 2004 in the face of a tremendous Democratic Party effort to get Nader voters to oppose Bush by voting for Kerry. His support in 2000 at 3.6 percent was substantial but not outstanding for a third-party candidate given the Wisconsin tradition. It was largely a protest vote, fueled in a few instances by poor northern rural counties but especially and predictably by Madison voters who gave Nader 7.6 percent of their votes, twice his state average.[5]

In the broadest outline, as table 1 suggests, the areas of each party's strength were quite clear in the 2000 and 2004 presidential contests. The most Democratic areas were Milwaukee and Madison (and its suburbs), but most larger cities were also Democratic, though often narrowly. The Milwaukee suburbs were Republican, especially the more distant from Milwaukee, with the exception of the north shore suburbs. African American, Hispanic, American Indian, Polish- and Norwegian-ancestry areas in Wisconsin were Democratic, while German-, Dutch-, and Belgian-ancestry areas were Republican. This is the picture that has characterized all really contested and close races statewide so far in the twenty-first century.

The surprise, if there was any, between the two presidential elections of 2000 and 2004 was that Kerry did not pull away a bit more from Bush in 2004 given the considerable Nader 2000 vote that went overwhelmingly for Kerry in 2004. The mystery of Kerry's relative weakness in victory deepens a little as one examines some categories of Wisconsin voters in the two elections, observing both similarities and some variations between the two elections. In most instances the similarities are predictable. Thus among Wisconsin cities little variation occurred between the two elections and indeed between size categories, with Kerry generally winning overall by size category a little more than 50 percent. Similarly, there was little variation among towns and villages in Wisconsin, with Kerry gaining just a bit in towns and Bush in the villages compared with the presidential vote in 2000.

It is no surprise that Bush was the winner overall in Wisconsin towns, 53.1 percent, and villages, 50.3 percent. But the variation over 2000 was small. The picture was the same with many villages and towns with heavy ethnic

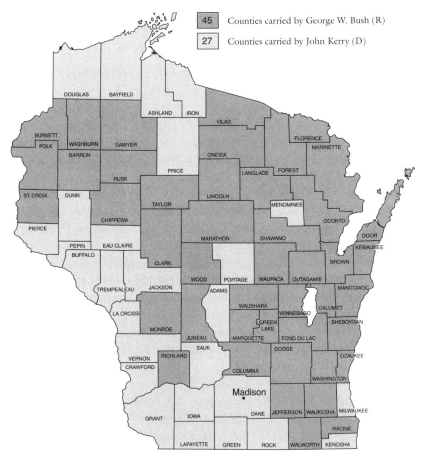

2004 Presidential Vote

TABLE 1. Change in Presidential Two-Party Voting in Wisconsin from
2000 to 2004*

Category	Percent Vote in 2004		Dem. Gain/Loss	Number Voting Units
	Democrat	Republican		
State	50.2	49.8		
Milwaukee	72.5	27.5	5.4	all
Madison	75.0	25.0	9.2	all
Towns	46.9	53.1	1.5	33
Villages	49.7	50.3	−1.5	31
2d-class cities (40,000–150,000)	53.3	46.7	2.5	14
3d-class cities (10,000–39,999)	50.3	49.7	0.0	12
4th-class cities (<10,000)	51.4	48.6	1.5	28
Milwaukee suburbs	35.9	64.1	.7	45
North Shore and northwest	55.8	44.2	4.2	5
New Deal suburbs	52.4	47.6	−2.7	4
Rest of Milwaukee Co.	40.8	59.2	.3	4
Waukesha Co.	31.3	68.7	−.7	13
Ozaukee Co.	33.6	66.4	1.3	7
Washington Co.	29.9	70.1	−.7	8
4 highly affluent suburbs	32.8	67.2	11.7	4
African American	95.6	4.4	−1.6	17
Latino	79.8	20.2	—	6
American Indian: Menominee Co.	83.1	16.9	2.9	1
German Protestant	35.5	64.5	−3.2	26
German Catholic	38.1	61.9	−2.3	30
Polish	59.4	40.6	−1.1	14
Norwegian	57.5	42.5	<1.0	27
Swedish	45.0	55.0	3.9	11
Dutch Protestant	19.9	80.1	<1.0	7
Belgian	44.2	55.8	−4.6	5

* See Appendix B for detailed descriptions of elements in table.

components from the past. Norwegian areas went 57.5 percent for Kerry and Polish areas 59.4 percent, while Dutch Protestant areas followed their tradition and voted over 80 percent for Bush. Slight variations did occur among others, for example, among Belgian areas, going for Bush at 56 percent, a 4.6 percent gain. Yet such shifts reflect very small numbers of voters and thus were of scant significance to the overall picture. More interesting was the solid 5 percent movement in the areas of southwestern Wisconsin.

There were no significant changes in the pattern of African American voting, with African American precincts in Milwaukee showing 95.6 percent for Kerry and in Racine 92.7 percent. The Menominee County, largely American Indian, results were typically one-sided also, more than 83 percent for Kerry. There was no sign in Wisconsin of any major shift to the Republican Bush among Hispanics, at least in the City of Milwaukee, where Kerry obtained close to 80 percent of their (small) vote.

Unlike the suburbs surrounding many big cities in the East, Republicans are doing very well in most Wisconsin suburbs, especially in hugely important suburban Milwaukee, where Republican margins now frequently cancel the Democratic margin in the City of Milwaukee. This was true, for example, in 2004. Exceptions occur in some suburbs in the state, especially around Madison, but the Republican suburban success was significant in the presidential elections of 2000 and 2004.

Yet Kerry should have done better in Wisconsin given that he made major gains in both Milwaukee and Madison over Gore, gains that matter tremendously in terms of the total vote in the state. Thus Kerry ran 5.4 percent better than Gore in Milwaukee and 9.2 percent better in Madison, two areas of the state that, taken together, represent about 20 percent of the total state vote. This showing reflected an absorption of the Nader vote in 2000 and even more gains to the Democratic nominee.

Thus the question remains: Why didn't Kerry do better? There had to be someplace where Kerry ran behind Gore, perhaps a sector of the state or its electorate that was already strongly Republican and not influenced by the messages pouring out from Madison and Milwaukee. And there was. Once again, the answer lies in the fact that, according to the 2000 census, 42.6 percent of Wisconsinites claimed German ancestry. To be sure, a great many of the citizens of German ancestry live in cities and suburbs, large and small, and there is no evidence that any of them recall their increasingly remote German ancestry when voting. Yet of the 25 percent of Wisconsin residents who still live in small towns and villages, the majority is of German heritage. In such settings there is a stability rooted in tradition, a voting tradition among others, and that tradition is overwhelmingly Republican today, as it has been since 1940. Along with suburbia, these worlds are the major parts of Wisconsin Republicanism.

It was here, in German American towns and villages, that Kerry did worse than usual for a Democrat, and definitely worse than Gore. It did not matter whether these areas were primarily Catholic or Protestant or of mixed Christian background. This was not the relevant variable. Rather, if they were areas inhabited by citizens of German ancestry, the vote was sharply Republican as usual and more so in 2004 than in 2000, between 2 percent and 4 percent more, a crucial difference that slowly but surely ate away at Kerry's margin elsewhere.

This was not exclusively a phenomenon of the countryside. Political scientist David Canon proposed exploring to see if the same connection between percentage of German ancestry and Republican voting existed in the cities of Wisconsin in 2004. The results are enlightening. In most cities with populations of more than 10,000 there was very little or no correlation, but in fourth-class cities, the small cities that dot the Wisconsin countryside, there was an association between the percentage of German-ancestry residents and the Republican vote. It was not dramatically high, but it was there and predictable, since such cities take on the color of the environment around them.[6]

It is appropriate to wonder why this particular, already-very-Republican sector of the Wisconsin electorate voted even more Republican in 2004. These are not areas, to say the least, known historically for their enthusiasm for wars, nor are they centers of enthusiasm for free-spending Republicans such as George W. Bush. Yet they are centers of cultural conservatism, places where marriage, religion, and similar values reign strong and where urban, socially liberal values are often viewed with suspicion. This showed in the presidential election of 2004, as it did with many Midwest voters in 2004, as John Green and Mark Silk have recently argued in their parsing of poll results.[7] And it is interesting to note that the same places voted for the 2006 marriage amendment on average by an overwhelming 75 percent.

Exploring whether there was a class dimension to 2004 or 2000 voting for president in Wisconsin is important. Median household income is our best means, given the available data.[8] Analysis of this data suggests that there was only very modest association between income and voting in Wisconsin places in either 2000 or 2004. In 2000 and 2004 there was a quite soft positive association with ascending median household income and the Bush Republican vote. The figures were about the same for the Democratic presidential candidates, except that the Democratic correlations were with declining income.[9]

The weak correlations should not be unexpected. Consider that, on the one hand, almost all the affluent suburbs of Madison voted Democratic while numerous poor northern towns voted Republican, while, on the other hand, poor areas of Milwaukee voted Democratic and affluent German American farming towns cast Republican votes. In short, the real-world picture is quite mixed. Interestingly, in 2000 Nader's vote did not correlate with high household income, despite what some of his critics, who view him as a darling of "limousine liberals," have suspected. On the contrary, his vote was not associated with household income in any significant direction.[10] Study of his vote shows why. For example, while he did well in the affluent Madison area, he did poorly in the well-to-do Milwaukee suburbs. Moreover, he ran quite well in many poor, rural areas of northern Wisconsin where he was viewed as a protest candidate but got almost no votes in the poor inner-city areas of Milwaukee.

Another hypothesis for why Kerry did not do better in Wisconsin focuses on turnout. Perhaps Kerry constituencies just did not turn out in quite as large numbers as did Bush areas or constituencies and that made the difference.[11] One can measure the difference between the number of voters in selected categories between 2000 and 2004, though this is far from foolproof as a measure of turnout since increases and decreases in voting numbers can reflect population shifts more than anything else. Nonetheless, if we do compare turnout in 2004 with turnout in 2000, we learn little. About 15 percent more voters appeared at the polls in Wisconsin in 2004 than did four years earlier. There was, however, no distinct increase in turnout in areas more favorable to Bush or Kerry. It looks like both parties were quite successful in generating new voters. It is true enough that in German American towns and villages the turnout was above the statewide average of 15 percent by a few percentage points. It is also true that in Milwaukee it was below the state average by a few points, though the explanation is principally declining city population. However, the turnout in populous Dane County and in Madison was well above the state average, while in the suburban units elsewhere in my sample it fell below by some distance (11.4 percent), despite the presence of a number of growth areas. In short, the picture is not clear, and it is not obvious that turnout benefited one party over another.

It is perhaps of some value to consider the media consortium's exit poll for Wisconsin in 2004 to see if that held any clues regarding the results. True, the 2004 exit poll and all exit polling is under a cloud due to questions about the accuracy of the 2004 poll. But when we look at the 2004 exit poll for Wisconsin there are few surprises. It reports what we know, that there was little evidence of sharp class division in the voting. Only at income extremes, 15 percent of the voter population, does it indicate class division. The clearest came in the 3 percent of the voters who claimed to make $200,000 or more. They were for Bush with 70 percent of the vote, reflecting both the findings regarding wealthy Milwaukee suburbs factored by liberal well-to-do Madison suburbs. On the lowest end, the 10 percent of the voters making the least, the outcome was reversed between the candidates.

Among the rest of the population's voting there was only modest, if any, connection between income and voting behavior. Exactly the same pattern repeated itself with education as a class measure, though here the differences were even softer. The well-known postgraduate (14 percent in Wisconsin's case) bulge for the Democrats partly reflected the fact that highly unionized teachers, many of whom have master's degrees, were and are tightly connected with the Democratic Party.

While the Wisconsin exit poll mildly exaggerates the support for the Republicans (at 14 percent) among African American voters (a figure that my detailed analysis shows is in error), it is particularly suspect in its claim that 47 percent of the Hispanic vote in Wisconsin (2 percent of the total) went for Bush. There is no other sign of that, certainly not in precinct analysis in Milwaukee. Otherwise, there is little to report from the exit poll, except the obvious: people against the Iraq War favored Kerry while people concerned about "morality" tended to favor Bush; people concerned about the economy were more likely to vote Kerry while people who worried about security to vote Bush. [12]

THE DOYLE YEARS

In 2008 Wisconsin is marginally a Democratic state. While the Republicans control the State Assembly, the Democrats rule the State Senate, carried the state in the last two presidential elections, have both U.S. Senate seats and the majority of the state's House of Representatives seats, and hold almost all the state-level constitutional offices. Supporting the claim that Wisconsin is a marginally Democratic state are Democrat James Doyle's victories in the governor's contests of 2002 and 2006, though both elections also reveal how divided between the two parties Wisconsin voters are and remain.

Doyle, son of two of the principal creators of the "new" post–World War II Democratic Party, was a successful lawyer in Madison who eventually became state attorney general and the most prominent Democrat in state politics in Wisconsin. He was in the perfect position to obtain the Democratic nomination for governor in 2002, and he did so by winning the Democratic primary.

No doubt his success was speeded by the good fortune he has had in his Republican opponents. In 2002 it was Scott McCallum, who became governor when Thompson left in 2001 to serve in the cabinet of George W. Bush.[13] McCallum had been the longtime lieutenant governor under Thompson and had unfortunately developed a less than impressive reputation, a reputation that, fairly or not, his brief sojourn as governor did not erase. At the same time, wonderfully complicating matters, two other candidates leaped into the 2002 governor's race. Jim Young, representing the Green Party, ran an aggressive campaign that threatened Doyle, while Ed Thompson, Tommy Thompson's free-spirited, tavern-owning brother, ran as a Libertarian, threatening McCallum.

It was an exciting fall campaign in 2002, and the four major candidates tore into each other vigorously. When it was over Doyle was the winner among them with 45.2 percent of the vote, McCallum had 41.5 percent, Ed Thompson got 10.4 percent, and Jim Young 2.5 percent. Doyle had his victory to relish, though his total was well below 50 percent, which seemed to pose a serious challenge for him when he looked toward a reelection campaign in 2006. The appeal of Ed Thompson turned out to be real. In Dane County and Madison and in some of the counties near his home in west central Wisconsin, Thompson's vote reduced *Democratic* margins. Elsewhere, however, Thompson drew down the normal Republican vote by a percentage that often equaled his own. Thompson really hurt McCallum in an election year where nationally there were no strong trends.[14]

Thompson ran especially well in rural and small town areas near his Tomah home in west central Wisconsin, but otherwise he did best where Republicans ran well *except* for suburban areas outside Milwaukee and elsewhere. Thompson did not appeal to suburban Republicans, for whom his self-conscious country boy persona was a nonstarter.

Jim Young, the Green candidate, did not generate much enthusiasm in suburban Milwaukee either. His vote was small everywhere. He did have his draw in liberal Madison but also in many places in rural Wisconsin where a small minority is determinedly green—or, perhaps deeply alienated from the regular political process, or both. McCallum's vote, however, was very mildly associated with rising household income and Doyle's slightly with the opposite. Overall, it is clear, there was no particular sign of much class-sensitive voting.[15]

The election of 2006 was a major success story for Doyle and for Democrats in general in Wisconsin as in the nation. In Wisconsin Democrats swept all state offices except the attorney general's post. They recaptured the State

Senate and came close to winning the Assembly. Herb Kohl was reelected to the U.S. Senate in a landslide, and Democrats gained a fifth of the eight seats in the Wisconsin House of Representatives delegation. The most important win for the state Democrats was the reelection of their leader, Governor Jim Doyle. He defeated Fox Valley Republican Congressman Mark Green. Doyle received 52.7 percent of the vote, Green 45.3 percent, and Green Party candidate Nelson Eisman 1.9 percent. In a vote total of more than 2.1 million, Doyle beat Green by 160,000 votes.

In a year highly favorable to the Democrats, Governor Doyle, who was at one time considered to be highly vulnerable, successfully positioned himself as a safe and satisfactory moderate Democrat. That he had not been an unusually controversial—or inspiring—incumbent was all to his advantage. His opponent ran a somewhat underfinanced campaign as a conventional Republican and, as a member of Congress, had the albatross of President Bush's unpopularity and unpopular war to bear. His persona as a candidate was no more exciting than Doyle's, and he was unable to find any issue with which to incite fires of opposition to Doyle.

James Doyle, governor 2003–
(Wisconsin Historical Society,
WHi-27076)

The 2006 outcome did not involve major voter shifts of one sort or another, or in one place or another toward Democrat Doyle. His secret, rather, was a modest enhancing of the Democratic percentage of the vote (over Kerry in 2004) with most groups and in most places. Doyle changed the landscape of voting partisanship not at all, but he increased the Democratic vote marginally almost everywhere. The accompanying table makes clear that except in the biggest cities of Wisconsin and among African Americans and Hispanics, Doyle's vote moved Democratic percentages ahead modestly over the 2004 presidential ones. Where he did not do so the difference was slight, and in one or two cases, perhaps among African American and Hispanic voters, his

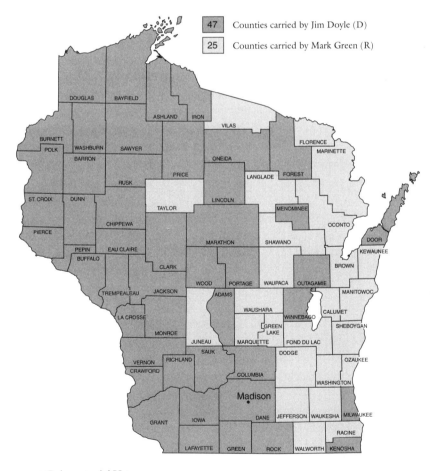

2006 Gubernatorial Vote

TABLE 2. Change in Party Voting in Wisconsin, 2004 (Presidential) to 2006 (Gubernatorial), and "Marriage Amendment" Results*

	Percent Vote in 2006				
Category	Democrat	Republican	Dem. Gain/Loss	Amendment Yes	Number Voting Units
State	52.7	45.3†	2.5	59.0	
Milwaukee	70.9	27.5	−1.6	53.1	
Madison	77.3	19.6	2.3	23.7	
Towns	48.5	49.2	1.6	68.1	33
Villages	54.9	43.4	5.2	66.5	31
2d-class cities	55.4	42.7	2.1	55.4	14
3d-class cities	54.3	43.6	4.0	59.6	12
4th-class cities	56.3	42.0	4.9	64.3	19
4 southwest counties	58.2	40.0	4.6	57.4	4
Marathon Co.	52.6	45.1	6.7	65.0	59
Milwaukee suburbs					
North Shore and northwest	60.2	38.7	4.6	40.3	5
New Deal suburbs	52.3	45.9	−1.7	63.0	4
Rest of Milwaukee Co.	44.8	53.9	4.0	62.0	4
Waukesha Co.	33.5	65.2	2.2	67.7	13
Ozaukee Co.	36.9	61.7	3.3	65.7	7
Washington Co.	32.8	65.1	2.9	72.8	8
4 highly affluent suburbs	25.8	73.0	−7.0	63.4	4
Twin Cities suburbs	49.9	48.6	5.2	62.6	12
African American	92.0+	7.0	−3.5	61.0	17
Latino	73.0	24.8	−6.8	55.5	6
American Indian: Menominee County‡	82.6	16.9	−.5	53.1	1
German Protestant	40.7	57.3	5.2	77.4	26
German Catholic	43.1	55.1	5.0	73.2	30
Polish	59.4	40.6	1.6	67.6	14
Norwegian	60.7	37.5	3.2	62.4	27
Swedish	48.4	50.2	3.4	70.3	11
Dutch Protestant	24.0	74.8	4.1	87.3	7
Belgian	48.4	49.8	4.2	75.5	5

* The percentage of Democratic gain/loss column compares Doyle (D) to Kerry (D) in 2004. "Marriage Amendment" was officially titled "In the Defense of Marriage Amendment."

† Republican and Democratic percentages do not equal 100 percent. The Green Party candidate received 1.9 percent of the vote.

‡ The small towns of Russell in Bayfield County and Sanborn in Ashland County are heavily composed of Chippewa and no other towns nor any county besides Menominee County is as populated by American Indians. In recent elections Russell and Sanborn have voted mostly in the same 80-plus percent range for Democrats. They divided on the marriage amendment, however, Russell voting no and Sanborn approving it.

position on the marriage amendment may have hurt a bit, though Doyle still won overwhelming victories with both these populations.

By the raw vote numbers Governor Doyle amassed about an 80,000-vote margin in Milwaukee County, which was offset by a similar Green margin in the surrounding three suburban counties of Waukesha, Ozaukee, and Washington. His margin was even greater in Dane County than in Milwaukee County at 91,000 votes. But Doyle did not need a single vote of his margin in Dane County to win reelection. He carried the rest of the state by enough votes to make his victory no Milwaukee/Madison artifact.

Since Doyle did not rearrange any of the basic features of Wisconsin voting behavior, it is only to be expected that his vote in my representative sample was as highly associated with Kerry's as Green's was with Bush's. Interestingly, neither Green's vote nor Doyle's was associated at all substantially with Thompson's Libertarian effort in 2002, suggesting that Green was not obviously successful at becoming the heir to Thompson's votes, which he needed to win in 2006.[16]

Exploring class dimensions of the 2006 results produces nothing remarkable either. Democratic and Republican votes for governor were only mildly associated with places that had different median household incomes. As has been argued, the association of income and voting behavior is just too soft in Wisconsin to expect anything different.[17]

The story of the governor's race in 2006 is that of an impressive win by Democratic Governor James Doyle. Nothing fundamental may have changed in the divisions in the state in the election, but from the perspective of the victorious Democrats, it was their big victory that mattered. Wisconsin may be a close, competitive, two-party state, but in 2006 things looked very good for the Democratic side.

The 2006 election was also notable for two referenda on the ballot. One was an advisory referendum on whether or not to establish the death penalty in Wisconsin. It passed with 55.5 percent voting yes with only four counties rejecting the idea: Dane, Eau Claire, Iowa, and Portage. This vote had no impact and will have none, at least to the foreseeable future. Instituting the death penalty lacks support from the governor, the Democratic State Senate, and a number of members of both parties in the Assembly.

The more controversial and much more significant referendum addressed a proposed constitutional amendment to define marriage as only between a man and a woman and to prohibit marriage and civil unions otherwise defined. This act was highly controversial among many citizens in Wisconsin. It was intensely opposed by some Wisconsinites, especially within the gay community as well as by many academic and business groups, the media (almost every single newspaper in Wisconsin opposed it), liberal church groups, and the leaders of the Democratic Party. Others, especially many evangelicals, fundamentalists, and the Roman Catholic Church as well as some Republican Party leaders, supported the measure. Opponents outspent proponents by almost 7 to 1, putting $4.3 million into the effort. But the majority of the electorate endorsed the amendment: 59 percent of the voters approved it, and it carried seventy-one out of the seventy-two counties in the state. Dane County overwhelmingly defeated it.

The pattern of the vote is fascinating, less predictable and more intriguing than the vote for governor and the state legislature in 2006. How much this referendum affected voter turnout is debatable. The Republican legislature, which put the referendum on the ballot, expected it to help the Republicans in 2006. As matters turned out, however, it helped the Democrats. In a number of college precincts all over the state, there was a sharp increase in voter turnout compared to recent off-year elections, leading to heavy votes against the referendum and upset victories for Democratic legislative candidates. The result helped switch the Senate to the Democrats and make the Assembly much closer.

It is tempting to analyze the vote on the referendum as another classic center-periphery or urban versus rural contest between liberal, urban Wisconsin and conservative, small-town Wisconsin. After all, the yes vote swept through my sample of towns with an average of 68.1 percent and villages with 66.5 percent, and its support was far lower in Milwaukee at 53.1 percent and in the largest or second-class cities of the state at 55.1 percent.

Moreover, the character of the city mattered. If the city was home to many social liberals and many citizens with advanced degrees, especially a college town, then the marriage amendment ran into serious trouble. In Madison some 73.6 percent of the voters rejected the amendment, and in Dane County overall some 57.3 percent did so. The amendment also failed in such smaller cities as Eau Claire, La Crosse, and Stevens Points as well as in small cities such as Platteville and River Falls. All are college towns, and most (but not all) lean Democratic. The result showed that in socially liberal urban settings support for the marriage amendment was weak and opposition was sometimes strong. Moreover, as the table indicates, the smaller the city, the more support there was for the amendment, suggesting some strength for the urban versus rural interpretation of the vote.

This view is further reinforced when one looks at the other side of the situation, areas of great support for the amendment besides towns and villages in general. In ethnic areas in countryside long known to be strongholds of social conservatism, the yes vote was overwhelming. In my samples Dutch Protestant places were 87.3 percent yes, German Protestant 77.4 percent, Belgian Catholic 75.5 percent, and German and Polish Roman Catholic 73.2 and 67.6 percent, respectively.

But there are problems with this center-periphery analysis, three especially noteworthy. One is the support that the amendment received in older, more working-class cities, such as those around Milwaukee, places where Doyle was simultaneously winning big. Another is the amendment's appeal for urban minorities. Sample African American precincts voted for the amendment at 61 percent and the Hispanic areas did so at 55.5 percent, while casting an overwhelming vote for Governor Doyle and other Democrats. A third problem, one that indisputably challenges the big city versus small town thesis, is the nature of the suburban vote except around Madison. The one-sided vote for the amendment from suburban Milwaukee, an area of high education and high income, is hard to ignore. Washington County gave 72.8 percent yes, Waukesha 67.7 percent, and Ozaukee 65.7 percent. The Twin City suburban area in St. Croix County voted for the amendment also at 62.6 percent.

That a few socially liberal north shore suburban enclaves defeated the amendment helps us refine any interpretation. Education or income level was not necessarily the issue. Social liberalism in Wisconsin, at least as measured by the vote on this amendment, cannot be automatically associated with education level. Nor can supporters of a change in the definition of marriage in Wisconsin take necessary comfort in the hope that rising education levels and increasing urbanization of the state will lead to success. The real challenge for them will be convincing already well-educated husbands and wives, especially in suburban Milwaukee.

The most popular hypothesis about the referendum vote contends that the vote had a generational character, as evidenced by strong college student rejection of the amendment and following the well-established national polls demonstrating more support for gay rights and gay marriage among younger people than among their elders.[18] According to this view, it will be just a matter of time before the vote is reversed and a different policy is in effect regarding gay marriage or at least civil unions. This analysis is convincing, but it does assume, somewhat paradoxically, that the sentiments of one generation of Wisconsin voters will be shared by the generation that follows it in turn and that the perspectives of any generation will not change as its members age and move into different life situations.

SOME BROADER REFLECTIONS

The presidential elections of 2000 and 2004 and the gubernatorial contests of 2002 and 2006 comprise the best guide to the current scene of Wisconsin voting, its patterns, and its close balance. Given this fact and what we know about the history of Wisconsin voting, we might ask where the best connections with the past are and to what extent the present picture is a copy of the past.

Has much really changed over time? In comparing the 2004 Republican and Democratic vote patterns with that of their counterparts a century ago, say in 1900, it is evident that there is no association. Nor is there for the presidential vote in 2000 or the governor's vote in 2006.[19] Too much has changed since then, and the parties' constituencies simply are not the same today as they were then.

A more plausible hypothesis is that the modern Republican and Democratic voting patterns derive from about 1940, when it was clear that industrial and big-city voters were moving permanently into the Democratic Party and that the state's large countryside German electorate was moving—again, permanently to this point, as it has turned out—toward the Republicans. Testing this hypothesis about 1940, however, does not confirm it. As chapter 7 observes, there is evidence of a connection between 1940 and 1950, but from the perspective of 2006, 1950 proved to be a long time ago. In representative sample associations with 2000, 2004, and 2006, the voting patterns of 1940 are nonexistent or very low.[20] And neither does the 1942 election confirm it. Then the Progressives made their last serious run in the governorship contest of 1942, but correlating their vote with contemporary Democratic votes, or their vote plus the 1942 Democratic vote with the present-day Democratic vote and the Republican vote in 1942 with the Republican vote of today doesn't get anywhere. Again, clearly much has changed in Wisconsin over the past three-quarters of a century.[21]

Among the reasons that the 1940s hypothesis does not work today is that once very Democratic industrial cities around Milwaukee are no longer the Democratic strongholds they were. Yet Madison and its suburbs are far, far more Democratic than they were in 1940. And there are many other changes in the rest of the state, such as the great growth of suburbia, that make the 1940s a chapter of electoral history and not a great deal more in understanding the origins of current electoral behavior.

Another hypothesis might be that contemporary voting behavior is best understood as a reflection of the major post–World War II development of the modern liberal Democratic Party and its modern conservative Republican Party counterpart. By this view, the ideological division hypothesis, Wisconsin politics—and voting behavior—by the 1960s had become a politics of ideological and policy division, and it has remained so since. Perhaps, therefore, looking at a typical election in the 1960s might reveal an association between Republican and Democratic voting then and now.

Testing this view with perhaps the best 1960s choice available, the race for governor in 1962, this thesis does not work either. Specifically, comparing 1962 with 2004 and 2006 does not yield impressive results.[22] That the current Wisconsin electoral scene is sometimes ideologically driven is not in dispute; but nothing follows in terms of the similarities between a "normal" election in the 1960s and today. Again, a lot has changed in the past forty to fifty years, and it just doesn't work to see either the Democratic or the Republican voting coalitions of the present era as a copy of this (or any) particular past.[23]

What has changed? Much of the countryside that was sympathetic to the Democrats in 1962 is far less so today, especially in Scandinavian areas of the state. But in southern and southwestern Wisconsin, once quite Republican, there is much more support for the Democrats. And this is just a start. Another dimension of the matter is that the nature of the relevant ideological issues has changed in part. Insofar as cultural issues have joined those focused on tax and spending matters as integral to Wisconsin divisions, the definitions of "progressive" versus "conservative" in Wisconsin from the 1960s have faded in importance.[24] And, indeed, it is serious exploration of current ideological divisions and their connections with contemporary voting behavior that is most urgently needed to understand present-day voting behavior in Wisconsin.

Crucial to such an analysis will be the all but impossible generation of sophisticated and detailed data on the faith and "values" identifications of Wisconsin voters in specific locales. Attitudes on these matters continue to be significant in understanding contemporary voting behavior in the nation as a whole and were significant even as recently as the 2006 elections.[25]

PARTICULAR PLACES AND GROUPS

The following specific geographic areas and populations merit additional discussion in light of their contemporary voting patterns.

Milwaukee

Milwaukee's electoral story has been interesting from when the city began as Kilbourn, the creation of entrepreneur Byron Kilbourn. Almost from the start, Milwaukee was the largest city in the state, a standing it retains today. But it was not until 1875 that Milwaukee's population exceeded 100,000, when it began its rapid expansion as a vibrant part of America's later-nineteenth-century industrial revolution. The top year for Milwaukee County electoral influence was 1960. In that year fully one-quarter of the voters in Wisconsin lived in Milwaukee County, the vast majority in the City of Milwaukee itself. Today the figure is about half that for two reasons. One is the city's ongoing population loss. In the 2000 census it had 597,000 residents, down 5 percent from 1990 and down dramatically (and steadily) from its high of 741,000 in the 1960 census. Second, the city is slowly becoming a diminishing proportion of Milwaukee County, whose population was 940,000 by the 2000 census, and this is exacerbated by the modest growth of some areas in the county outside the city.

The population figures measure the unmistakable decline in this city. German, and later Polish, immigrants and their children and grandchildren filled the many jobs in a city that by the late nineteenth century was a vital heavy industry center. Even by 1910 almost half the 57.5 percent of Milwaukee's population that was German was foreign-born and 86 percent had foreign parentage. Yet by this era most Milwaukee workers—German, Polish, and otherwise—could boast that they were literate, often highly skilled, and lived in their own wood-frame single-family houses in tidy neighborhoods, Germans settled mostly in north and west Milwaukee, Poles in south Milwaukee. Indeed, the physical size of Milwaukee continued expanding even as late as the 1920s, reaching 43,000 square miles.[26]

Those days seem far away, but 12–15 percent of the total Wisconsin vote, which is roughly what Milwaukee casts today, is still significant. That vote is overwhelmingly Democratic, increasingly so. The 2006 governor's vote was about 71 percent Democratic. The 2004 presidential vote was 72.5 percent for Kerry and a mere 28.5 percent for Bush; the 2000 vote was 68 percent for Gore, 3.7 percent for Nader, and 28.4 percent for Bush. The last Republican presidential candidate to carry Milwaukee was Dwight Eisenhower in 1956, and the one before that was Warren Harding in 1920, a situation that replicates Milwaukee's early voting history. From 1848 up to 1880 it was a Democratic stronghold, full of Democratic-voting Germans. However, by 1880 more and more Germans Protestants had begun to vote Republican, and for a decade and a half Milwaukee saw close elections. After the 1893 depression, Milwaukee split sharply in two directions, both inimical to the Democrats. Republicans gained ground and the Socialists appeared on the scene, sometimes outpolling the Democrats. After 1920 the Socialists faded and the Republicans advanced—until 1924, when Milwaukee swung behind La Follette's independent candidacy, and in 1928, when its substantial Catholic population rallied to carry the city for Al Smith. Then with the coming of the New Deal, Roosevelt proved immensely popular in Milwaukee and transformed it into a strongly Democratic city, though not quite as much so as it is today.

A major but distant part of the Milwaukee voting story is the history of its Socialist Party, which gained control of the city at the mayoral level with the election of Emil Seidel as mayor in 1910 and maintained at least nominal control there until 1960. The relative success of socialism there in the early twentieth century marked a crucial boundary in the city's electoral history. A city that was often Democratic on the local level until 1910, long after its vote for Democratic presidential candidates had receded, had become corrupt under the rule of Democratic mayor David S. Rose (1898–1910). Rose was a dashing leader who, while perhaps not personally corrupt, was certainly tolerant of a political order that was increasingly for sale. To be sure, Republicans after 1870 did sometimes gain control of the city, but they never were able to hold it for long. Party control see-sawed, but graft-free government was rare.[27]

This world is distant from today's Milwaukee, where Republican control of the mayor's office or the city council or a Republican victory for national or state candidates in the city is inconceivable. In fact, Milwaukee's margin for president for Kerry in 2004 (72.5 percent) was the largest ever with the sole exception of the vote for Roosevelt at the height of the New Deal in 1936 (78 percent). Governor Doyle's 71 percent with a lead in votes of about 80,000 was also very impressive. How long even these incredibly one-sided votes will stand as modern records is a legitimate question. Fairly rapidly changing demographics in the city suggest they may not last long. Milwaukee's increasingly Democratic voting behavior is inextricably linked to its growing African American population. Milwaukee's black voters are overwhelmingly Democratic in a city that is increasingly African American. In the 2000 census 37 percent of the residents described themselves as African American; 12 percent of the city described itself as Hispanic, and some in this group characterized themselves as partly African American. Both these numbers will be considerably higher in the 2010 census.

The steadily growing numbers of African Americans in Milwaukee guarantee Milwaukee's increasing devotion to the Democrats unless something radically changes in the relationship of African Americans to the Democratic Party or the Republican Party. Milwaukee is no longer the white New Deal unionized Democratic city of fifty and more years ago. Rather, it is a newer, often poorer, and much more racially diverse city, but its role in determining Democratic fortunes in Wisconsin remains significant.

The mayor in 2007, former Democratic congressman Tom Barrett, clearly has his hands full. The social and educational problems he and the city must grapple with are enormous. Yet Milwaukee has vibrant sides even if its industrial base continues to erode. Its traditions of good government, nurtured for long periods under Socialist mayors Dan Hoan, Carl Zeidler, and Frank Zeidler, and then Democrat Henry Maier, have served it well. But it faces no soft challenge, especially with a serious crime problem, a stressed public school system, and an expanding poor population.[28]

African American and Hispanic Voting Behavior

African Americans have been voting in Wisconsin a long time. Struggles to obtain the vote for (male) free blacks in Wisconsin were a part of the Wisconsin politics from statehood (and before). While success was not achieved until after the Civil War, from then on blacks had the opportunity to participate in Wisconsin elections and often did.

Few black Americans, however, actually lived in Wisconsin until after the Second World War. Those who resided in Wisconsin lived in a very few places. In Milwaukee, where the vast majority of black citizens live, arguments have long been waged over whether any other major U.S. city has as tight a pattern of racial division or de facto segregation. But no one disputes that residential lines are often tightly drawn between white and black areas of the city. The same is true in Racine and somewhat less so in Madison.

The tabular history of African Americans in Wisconsin begins with the 1840 census that identified 196 blacks in the state, 11 percent of whom were slaves. The black population was far below 1 percent of the state's population then, and it remained below 1 percent for at least a hundred years. The 1960 census for the first time found African Americans to comprise more than 1 percent of the state's population (1.9 percent). That percentage has slowly but steadily risen since then. It now stands at 5.7 percent, which is less than half the percentage of African Americans in the country as a whole. Wisconsin remains a decidedly white state.

Milwaukee was always the center of African American population in Wisconsin. Indeed, in some other parts of Wisconsin, it wasn't until after World War II that it was safe for black Americans to be anywhere in evidence after dark. While Milwaukee was the center of the black population in Wisconsin, its population was tiny during the course of most of Wisconsin's history. As late as 1900 only 862 blacks lived in the city, far below 1 percent of the population of the then-booming industrial city. Even by 1930 only some 7,000 lived there.

By 1945, however, 13,000 African Americans were counted in Milwaukee, for the first time more than 1 percent of the population (actually 2 percent). The wave of African Americans moving north for jobs was well under way. By 1960 the change was clear when blacks made up 8.4 percent of the city's people. By 1970 they were 14.7 percent of the population, and Milwaukee had begun to experience serious racial tensions. Meanwhile Catholic priest James Groppi led protesters who pushed for open housing in the residentially segregated city. In 1967 riots broke out in black areas, and this was followed by major white migration to the suburbs. By 1990 Milwaukee was 30.5 percent African American. Estimates today place the proportion of African Americans (ignoring those who identify themselves as "mixed race") in the city's population at about 40 percent. Milwaukee's movement toward becoming a majority black city is not certain, however, due to the rapid increase in the number of Hispanic residents.

The Civil War era was one of great tension, as there was much hostility both toward the war and toward the minuscule black community in German Milwaukee. There was even a lynching in Milwaukee in 1861. Yet in later years, in the nineteenth century, relations were much more tranquil. There was relatively little conflict or competitive contact with the dominant white communities in the city. The black community was small and self-contained. While some blacks were employed in business or as professionals, most were low-wage manual workers. Many owned their own small frame homes in what has long been the Milwaukee way.

The Great Depression of the 1930s hit the black community in Milwaukee, as in other urban areas, terribly hard, and recovery was slow. As New Deal programs began and then the defense industry of the 1940s led to economic recovery, significant black migration to Milwaukee during and especially after World War II followed. Predictable conflicts developed in the city as blacks sought to move out of their tightly constricted residential areas and began to compete for jobs with white workers.[29]

While other places in Wisconsin now have an African American population, very few are of any size. Racine, south of Milwaukee, is approximately 20 percent African American, Madison 6 percent, and there are a few suburbs of Milwaukee with more than token black populations. A significant example is Brown Deer, which is about 12 percent African American, according to the 2000 census. No more than 5 percent of the Milwaukee area's African

American population lives outside the city limits, as the racial boundaries remain tight in practice in the Milwaukee region.[30]

There is no doubt that the African American community in Milwaukee, as elsewhere, faces great difficulties. Milwaukee is currently beset by a high murder rate, mostly African Americans murdered by other African Americans. Some 11 percent of all black males in Wisconsin are currently in prison, another 11 percent are on probation or parole, and almost 18 percent are unemployed, while 5 percent of white males and 10 percent of Hispanic males are unemployed. The public school system of Milwaukee, which is now largely African American and Hispanic, is in continuing trouble. Most black students do not graduate from high school in the city. Everywhere there is concern about the situation, but solutions are hard to come by.[31]

Study of the voting behavior of African Americans in Wisconsin—in practice in Milwaukee and, of late, Racine—is no simple task. It requires now, as it has in the past, careful comparison of census data and Milwaukee election districts to determine where the African American areas have been and are now. What such studies demonstrate is that African American voting behavior in Milwaukee has changed over time. The legacy of Civil War–based Republican loyalty among black voters still lingered as late as 1932 in a Milwaukee that overall voted 3 to 1 for Roosevelt. Even in this landslide, black voters there gave Roosevelt only 55 percent of their vote, while a plurality of their vote went to the Republican candidate for governor.

That legacy had shifted hugely by 1936 in Milwaukee. Roosevelt received about 80 percent of the African American voters' support in the city and almost that resounding an affirmation in his later two presidential races. African American precincts also demonstrated major support for the La Follettes and other Progressives in the 1930s. The last time a Republican (for governor) carried black precincts (by a plurality) was in 1942.

The post–World War II years were Democratic years in black Milwaukee, generally producing margins of 80 percent or more in years when the Republicans dominated in the state. Black precincts rejected Eisenhower for president in both 1952 and 1956, though Ike got unusually high African American percentages—around 25 percent—of the vote. The Johnson election of 1964 marked the end of just about all Republican support in black areas in Milwaukee. That year and for virtually every statewide election since, the Democratic percentage in black precincts has been more than 90 percent. In sample precincts, Bill Clinton's 1996 vote was the record at 97.2 percent, confirming in Milwaukee as elsewhere his tremendous popularity among African American voters. In the 2000 presidential election John Kerry received 95.6 percent of the vote in black Milwaukee, only slightly down from Clinton's showing four years earlier. In African American areas in Racine Kerry got 92.7 percent. And in 2006 Governor Doyle garnered 92.7 percent in Milwaukee precincts to Green's 6.6 percent and in Racine 92 percent to Green's 7.7 percent.[32]

While the first African American voters appeared at the polls in Wisconsin in 1866, they did not have any major impact on the state or even the City of Milwaukee until the 1960s. The first black member of the state legislature was elected in 1906, and an African American ran for the Milwaukee City Council twice in the middle 1930s. In the (relatively) modern era, Le Roy Simmons, a Democrat, was a black pioneer elected to the Assembly in 1944.

In Milwaukee, however, such tentative beginnings are now ancient history. In the twenty-first century blacks are a major presence on the city council, and Milwaukee sends two black state senators and six members of the Assembly (of ninety-nine) to the state legislature. One other African American member of the Assembly is from Racine. All are Democrats; no Republican African American has appeared in the legislature in the modern era. Milwaukee now has only one congressional seat, and it is held by an African American, Gwendolynne Moore, a former member of the state legislature.[33]

Hispanic or Latino voting participation in any substantial numbers in Wisconsin is an extremely recent phenomenon. While Hispanics have been known to live in Wisconsin at least since 1920, as recently as 1990 the percentage of Hispanics of any race was a mere 1.9 percent. That has now changed decidedly. In the 2000 census that number almost doubled, rising to 3.6 percent, and it will be greater by 2010. The large majority of Wisconsin Hispanics are of Mexican origin, some 65.7 percent; the next largest group, 15.7 percent, is of Puerto Rican background. By far the biggest number of Hispanics in Wisconsin live in the City of Milwaukee, though there are Hispanics now living all over the state. In Milwaukee, 12 percent of the population identified itself as Hispanic in the 2000 census. There the proportion of Mexican background is about the same as in the state as a whole, but the proportion of Puerto Rican background is considerably higher than in the state overall.

Within Milwaukee many Hispanics live in particular areas of the central and central west part of the city, much of which is in the heavily Hispanic Assembly District 8. From selected precincts there it is possible to discern contemporary Hispanic voting behavior, although this quest is problematic since some Hispanics in Milwaukee are also African Americans or live close to or in largely African American areas of the city. Areas that are mostly Hispanic allow us to make reasonable estimates of Hispanic voting behavior in

Milwaukee for most recent elections. They show a consistent pattern. In the governor's race of 2002, 72.4 percent voted Democrat, 21 percent Republican, 1 percent Green, and 5.6 percent Libertarian. For the 2004 presidential election Latinos went 79.8 percent for Kerry and 20.2 percent for Bush, with no sign of the surge of support for Bush that apparently took place in some other Hispanic areas of the country. For 2006 Democrat Doyle received about 73 percent of the vote to 24.8 percent for Green. These figures indicate a Democratic vote that, while overwhelming, is much lower than that in the African American community. Yet the picture painted here offers a pleasant prospect for the Democrats. There will only be more Hispanics voting in the future in Milwaukee and in the state as a whole, and Democrats will decidedly benefit, if past is prologue.[34]

The Milwaukee Suburbs

Superb work has delineated the voting history of suburban Milwaukee electoral units, and the most recent election returns confirm well-documented patterns, defined in part, but only in part, by their relative proximity to the city boundaries. In 2004 the overall Milwaukee suburban vote ran about 64 percent to 36 percent for President Bush, roughly standard in comparison, for example, with the 2000 results. This "normal" division is obviously of tremendous import in Wisconsin elections, not just because of the one-sided margins that Republicans usually roll up but more because suburban Milwaukee now casts about 20 percent of the total vote in Wisconsin, about equal to what Madison and its suburbs and the City of Milwaukee combined cast. This vote and its one-sidedness is absolutely essential to Republican fortunes in Wisconsin today. Without it Wisconsin would be a decidedly one-party Democratic state. Thus when it falls below the "normal" percent, as it did in 2006 (at about 60 percent), Democrats win comfortably statewide.

Milwaukee suburbs vary in character, a factor that must be considered when studying voting behavior. Suburban Milwaukee County itself, while producing fewer votes than the city, is now close to the city's vote totals and comprises about 7 percent of the state's vote. Some suburbs were incorporated as early as 1892, as was the case with Wauwatosa, South Milwaukee, and Whitefish Bay, and most of the closer-in cities and suburbs followed shortly thereafter, as with Cudahy (1895), West Allis (1902), and West Milwaukee (1906). However, it was only in the late 1940s and 1950s that the tremendous expansion of Milwaukee suburbs began, a phenomenon aided in part by Veterans Administration and then Federal Housing Administration (FHA) mortgage financing and one that has continued apace ever since. The growth only accelerated with the movement of whites from the city resulting from the racial upheavals of the 1960s, the increasing deindustrialization of Milwaukee and its surrounding industrial cities, and the growth of significant white-collar employment centers in the suburbs. Growth continues to be the story today, and nowhere more so than in the largest suburban county, Waukesha County, whose population grew by 18.4 percent in the last decade of the twentieth century to 360,767.[35]

Some north and northwest suburbs of the city in Milwaukee County are quite affluent and increasingly are centers of liberal culture. They contain much of suburban Milwaukee's Jewish population and what there is of an African American population outside the city. Bayside, for example, became open to Jewish citizens in the 1920s and 1930s and thereafter when places like Wauwatosa were closed to Jewish people by deed restrictions. All the earliest "north shore" suburbs—such places as Shorewood, Bayside, Brown Deer, and Whitefish Bay—have steadily become more Democratic over the past several decades. They are important examples of why simple class analysis is no neat guide to voting behavior now that cultural issues are often so important. These locales more and more attract younger professionals, singles or families, with high incomes who are committed to social liberalism. Overall in 2004 this section of suburbia voted for Kerry. In 2006 Doyle did better, reaching almost 60 percent.

Another part of Milwaukee's suburbia can be called the New Deal suburbs—working-class cities mostly on the southern side of Milwaukee. They are largely white cities that often grew up as industrial centers and homes for the working class in the late nineteenth century. In some cases they have moved more toward middle-class settings, as is true of the city of Greendale, built in the 1930s as a model New Deal city and once overwhelmingly Democratic. It has turned away from that tradition in part because it has undergone considerable suburban and middle-class development. It voted nearly 59 percent for Bush in 2004. Other places have not seen much suburban growth, but all have taken part in change as industrial Milwaukee has declined. Among these cities are Cudahy, South Milwaukee, and St. Francis. They all used to be intensely Democratic in their voting behavior, but the New Deal–forged allegiance to the Democratic Party waned in good part because the party's positions on social and cultural issues often appeal more to residents of affluent Whitefish Bay than they did, and do, to working-class residents of Cudahy. So in 2004 the old Democratic margins dwindled in the south suburbs to a mere 52 percent for Kerry. St. Francis went 54 percent for Kerry, Cudahy 54.8 percent, and South Milwaukee 52.2 percent, and other places less so. The days of the old New Deal coalition are history in Wisconsin. Doyle did not do much better in 2006, while the marriage referendum he opposed was resoundingly approved in these cities with 63 percent of the vote.

The largest unit of government in the county outside the City of Milwaukee is the City of Wauwatosa. Directly on Milwaukee's west boundary, Wauwatosa is an old, established, middle- and upper-middle-class city. As one goes from east to west in the city, the average family income tends to rise, as does Republican voting. This suggests that voting behavior roughly parallels economic status—a pattern that is often, though far from always, true in suburbia. What is also true about Wauwatosa, however, is that it is today only marginally Republican. More and more it is an example of liberal suburbia, voting like many other close-in, more well-to-do Milwaukee suburbs, and thus actually challenging conventional class analysis of voting in Wisconsin.

The rest of the suburbs in Milwaukee County constitute a first suburban ring around the city, one that takes up the rest of spacious Milwaukee County. Primarily middle-class and white, these suburbs, including such places as Hales Corners and Oak Creek, are Republican, if not by the larger margins of farther-out suburbs. In 2004 they voted 59 percent for Bush and only 41 percent for Kerry, Hales Corners voting 62 percent for Bush and Oak Creek 56 percent. The Republican margins dipped in 2006, but Doyle still did not carry these areas.

Beyond Milwaukee County is the land of more recent suburban growth, and it is a notably Republican world. Now constituting about 12 percent of the state's electorate, its Republican vote margins, combined with suburban Milwaukee County's totals, cancel the Democratic margins from inside the City of Milwaukee today. Here there is little of the liberal voting so characteristic of suburbs outside Boston, New York, or Philadelphia; rather, the voting behavior is closer to that of suburbia in the South and (non-coastal) West.

Waukesha County, directly to the west of Milwaukee County, is filling up rapidly. The largest unit there is the City of Waukesha, an old city now completely surrounded by other newer suburbs, but there are many other places of size in Waukesha County, such as Brookfield (70 percent Bush), New Berlin (65 percent), and Menominee Falls (66 percent). There are communities that even recently were quite rural that are moving into bedroom community status, such as the village of Merton (80 percent Bush), and others that are best described as exurban places, such as Hartland (68 percent) or Oconomowoc (68.8 percent). All are very similar in their voting behavior—

strongly Republican—a reality confirmed in 2006 in the vote for governor. In each place, however, Republican Green did less well than Bush had in 2004, but he still rolled up over 65 percent of the vote in these places, and these areas gave almost 68 percent of their votes to the marriage amendment. A few small places that are at the very top in terms of income in suburbia, such as the villages of Chenequa and Lac La Belle, are usually about 10 percent more Republican than the other, more middle-class suburbs, though in 2004 they were far less eager for Bush than they had been in 2000.

Recent years, however, have seen the rapid expansion of suburbia into and through the two counties north and west of Milwaukee County, Ozaukee and Washington counties. The average governmental unit in Ozaukee County voted 66.4 percent for Bush in the 2004 election, 62 percent for Green in 2006, and 66 percent for the marriage amendment. Home to such popular suburban cities as Mequon and Cedarburg, the Republican reality here is matched by that of Washington County, to the west of Ozaukee, which is rapidly suburbanizing and even more Republican, with the average place voting 70 percent for Bush in 2004, 66 percent for Green, and 73 percent for the marriage amendment in 2006.

The irony here is that both Ozaukee and Washington were once rural counties that were dependably Democratic in the nineteenth century, and often much more Democratic than the rest of the state in the twentieth century. This was because of their substantial German Catholic population. Of course today, given the allegiance to Republicans on the part of rural and small-town German areas, often including Catholic ones, this Democratic allegiance would have softened anyway without the suburban growth. Thus once dependably Democratic, Catholic Belgium in Ozaukee County voted more than 67 percent for Green, the village of Fredonia voted 67 percent for Green, and both led the county in voting 74 percent and 70 percent, respectively, for the marriage amendment. More than anything, however, it is the rise of suburbia that has obliterated Democratic support here. Suburbia has proved to be a powerful agent of electoral change, one that first became noticeable around 1970.

Although it was always more Republican than Ozaukee County because it had more German Protestants, Washington County began to change in 1970, and the process has been steady ever since. Slowly but surely Washington County has gained more and more suburban and exurban residents, and there is no doubt about its subsequent massive shift to the Republicans. The average for Bush in 2004 was 70 percent and for Green 66 percent. This Republican dominance, if it does not diminish, will come to play an ever greater role in Wisconsin voting as Washington County's population, like Ozaukee and Waukesha counties', continues to grow.[36]

The Twins Cities Suburbs

There are many other suburban areas in Wisconsin, though none are as significant as those in the Milwaukee area. One area of increasing, if still modest, significance, however, is that of the suburban (or exurban) growth in Wisconsin from the Twin Cities of St. Paul and Minneapolis, Minnesota. These places are principally in St. Croix County, across the Mississippi River from Minnesota, which is less than an hour commute from the Twin Cities. It is no wonder that St. Croix County has been a fast-growing county in Wisconsin. Between 1990 and 2000 the county grew almost 26 percent. From 2000 to 2005 it went up another 19.8 percent (while the state as a whole increased less than 4 percent). Moreover, the growth has been very specific among the county's thirty-five governmental jurisdictions. Some lost population, for example, but most gained more than 25 percent from 1990 to 2005, and a number of them gained over 50 percent in that fifteen-year period. All of the biggest gainers were close to Minnesota, which is why the area is sometimes called "Winnesota."[37]

In the fairly recent past, St. Croix's voting behavior paralleled the whole state's. This is no longer always true. In some recent state and national elections, St. Croix County has voted more Republican than the state as a whole. Thus in the 2004 presidential election Bush easily carried St. Croix by an almost 10 percent margin. In 2002 the Republican McCallum defeated the state winner, Governor Jim Doyle, by more than 10 percent, carrying the county. In 2006, however, Doyle narrowly won, even winning the growth areas by a bit more than 1 percent, though running 3 percent behind his state showing in this area.

To understand this shift toward the Republicans, sometimes more modest than at other times, it helps to explore the top-ten growth areas in the county. In 1962 half of them were Democratic strongholds. By 2004 and even in 2006 most leaned Republican. The largest exception is the part of River Falls that is in St. Croix County, which Doyle swept in 2006 with 58.5 percent. River Falls is yet another example of a liberal culture center, the location of a branch of the University of Wisconsin System.

It is worth noting that while class measured by income often fails as an indicator of the voting direction of a place in the state as a whole and is a mixed guide in the Milwaukee and Madison suburbs, it is an excellent guide to relative Republican and Democratic strength in the St. Croix growth

areas. There increasing Republican percentage of the vote in a place is associated with ascending median household income. It was the case in 2004
and even more so in 2006.[38] Here class matters, and affluence benefits the
Republicans.

What the future will bring to this region is far from clear. After all, Governor Doyle did well as a Democrat in St. Croix County and even in the growth
towns, cities, and villages. The future will illuminate whether his showing
was the exception or a new development. What is certain is that developments in the voting behavior in Winnesota deserve continuing scrutiny as
suburbia expands there.

Madison and Dane County

The story of Madison's capital city until well into the twentieth century has
been told and illustrated beautifully.[39] Madison and its surrounding suburbs,
towns, and villages in Dane County, which once comprised a small part of
the Wisconsin's electoral story, have become a major part. The main reason
for this is that Madison and Dane County have experienced dramatic growth
in recent years, a process that has propelled Dane County toward being a
greater element in the state's total vote. But growth is not the only factor.
Dane County's population is highly educated, and education closely cor-
relates with voter turnout. These two factors taken together make it no
wonder that the arc of Dane County's percentage of the state vote total has
steadily risen. By the 2006 election it had reached almost 10 percent of the
state's total. In 1950 Dane County cast only 5 percent of the state's vote.

According to the 2000 census, the City of Madison itself had a population
of more than 200,000, up from 170,000 in 1980. It grew 12 percent from
1980 to 1990 and 9 percent from 1990 to 2000. While the City of Madison's
future growth may be more modest because it is running out of space, its
suburbs are booming. The 2000 census showed Dane County (including
Madison) with more than 426,000 people, with the county outside Madison home to more people than the city. By 2007 Dane County had become
the fastest growing county in the state.

The second reason the Madison area looms so large in Wisconsin voting
is that it is so one-sidedly Democratic. Indeed, were Madison and its suburbs to be withdrawn from the state—something critics contend has already
happened in all but a legal sense—Republicans would normally carry the
state. For example, President Bush would have had no trouble winning it
in 2000 and 2004 (though Green would still have lost in the 2006 governor's race). Consider the following: in the 2000 presidential election Al Gore

received 61.6 percent of the votes of Dane County and 66.6 percent of the votes of the City of Madison. Nader received some 5 percent. In 2004 John Kerry got an astounding 66.7 percent of Dane County votes and fully 75 percent of the City of Madison vote and came out of Dane County with a massive 91,000 vote margin. In the 2006 governor's contest the outcome was even more Democratic. Governor Doyle received an overwhelming 70.1 percent of the Dane County ballots while Green was able to gather in only 27.3 percent and Eisman, the Green candidate, 2.6 percent. Doyle came out of Dane County in this nonpresidential year with a staggering 91,000 vote lead. In the City of Madison itself, which cast about half of the county vote, Doyle did even better, picking up 77.3 percent and reducing his Republican opponent to less than 20 percent of the total.

To be sure, as the comparison of the city with the rest of Dane County shows, variations occur. They are not explained, however, by economic variations within the city and the county. Nor can any particular ethnic or religious patterns be isolated in what is an overwhelmingly white but ethnically diverse population. In the city some parts of the west side are less Democratic than the city as a whole, but the most affluent areas of the west side, indeed of the city, are on the near west side, and they are among the most Democratic parts of the entire city. Working-class areas are also heavily Democratic. The least Democratic areas, though usually robustly Democratic, are sometimes the student areas, especially those made up mostly of undergraduates.

The most liberal area is the near east side of Madison, where many older students and many liberal and leftist Madisonians have settled. In some precincts there is scarcely any vote for Republican candidates and occasionally more votes for Left-of-center, third-party candidates than for the Democrats. In any case, this variation and all the others in the city are merely a matter of degree. Democrats routinely carry every precinct in the City of Madison in state and national elections.

Outside the city and in the surrounding towns and villages more variation occurs than is obvious at first glance. The 2004 presidential election reflected well the overall picture displayed in recent elections, one that hardly fits the classic stereotype of Republican suburbs matching or overwhelming central city Democratic margins. To be sure, the area in Dane County outside the City of Madison is less Democratic than the city, and by a fair amount, but it is still consistently Democratic. Thus, for example, Kerry won all nineteen villages in Dane County. The weakest showing he made came in the rapidly growing but distinctly middle-class village of Waunakee. The most surprising was the Democrat's historic victory in the second wealthiest suburb in the county, Maple Bluff. This victory, unprecedented in recent decades, reflected the pervasive Democratic trend in Dane County, including among the upper-income elite. This liberal victory was distinctly underlined in the wealthiest village in Dane County, Shorewood Hills, located near the university, where Democrats routinely win with big margins. In Shorewood Hills Kerry out-did even the usual Democratic vote as he racked up 82 percent of the total, an accurate reflection of widely shared political opinions at the university.

The six other cities in Dane County besides Madison, which are essentially suburbs to Madison, all were carried handily by Kerry, as they usually are carried by the Democrats. The least affluent, Sun Prairie, is the only one sometimes carried by Republican candidates. This picture in the other cities might make a reader finally wonder whether any Republican areas remain in the county, or at least any places that Republicans may win sometimes. The answer is yes, and these places are hidden away in "red" spots, distant (in comparative geographic terms) from the liberal Madison, a few towns that are fairly rural and usually to the north and east of the city. Thus in the Democratic world of Dane County, it is only some small towns and rural areas that are not strongly Democratic, replicating (in a much-reduced fashion) the cultural divisions in the United States at large. It is also in the towns of Dane County (as well as in the villages) that Kerry often lost ground compared with Gore in 2000. This was the opposite of what took place in the City of Madison and such wealthy suburbs as Shorewood Hills and Maple Bluff.

The 2006 election only confirmed 2004, and more. Doyle did run less well outside Madison than in the city itself, getting 62.4 percent of the out city vote. Yet this was still an impressive victory for Doyle; once again, it was only in small locations, usually quite far from Madison, that he did not win big. His landslide everywhere else in the county was sweeping. He won every town, every village, every city, and every precinct in the City of Madison and handily carried such well-to-do areas of Dane County as Shorewood Hills, Maple Bluff, and the town of Middleton.

The current situation in Dane County and Madison is different from the historical record only in degree. Madison and much of Dane County were, from their inception, Democratic strongholds. While Madison was never one of the most non-Yankee communities in Wisconsin, substantial Irish and German American populations in the nineteenth century made their impact. Throughout most of its history Madison also showed a modest class-based pattern of voting with the working-class east side more Democratic than the more affluent west side.

Democrats usually carried the city in state and national elections. For example, Madison did not vote for Abraham Lincoln for president in 1860 or 1864. Occasional exceptions occurred, but the preference for Democrats was maintained up through 1894. After that, with the major realignment of Wisconsin to a Republican state, Madison sometimes voted Republican and sometimes, quite against the reigning norm, went Democratic. During the Woodrow Wilson era it evidenced its Democratic voting tradition. In the 1920s it shifted to the Republicans in the weakest period for the Democrats in Wisconsin history. It supported La Follette in 1924 and returned to Democratic voting by 1932, during the Great Depression. It has stayed a predominantly Democratic city ever since.

The last time the City of Madison voted for a Republican candidate for governor or president was in 1968. In general, this pattern has been replicated in much of Dane County as well, though in the nineteenth century especially voting often turned around the ethnic components of various towns and villages. Thus Cross Plains, a strongly German Catholic area, was unusually Democratic, whereas Stoughton, a Norwegian area, was firmly Republican until the New Deal era. Today these variations rooted in ethnic- and religious-formed traditions have slipped away in the face of suburban penetration of all parts of the county.

While Madison and Dane County were Democratic by tradition and became even more so after the New Deal realignment strengthened the Democrats and eventually brought the demise of the Progressive Party, the margin of Democratic victories showed considerable elasticity. Put another way, although Republicans were generally guaranteed to lose, how badly they lost varied. Thus the immensely popular Republican governor of the 1990s, Tommy Thompson, consistently lost Madison, but he was able on two occasions to hold the Democratic percentage margin down in the 50-percent-plus range. How much elasticity remains is doubtful.

Early in the 1990s there was talk of how a suburbanizing Dane County would soon result in two-party voting behavior. Yet there is no sign of the rise of a suburban Republican electorate in Dane County. On the contrary, the trend is toward an ever more Democratic electorate with the slightly "red" areas of the county being the most marginal sectors, and these are bound soon to receive their own infusion of liberal voters as growth continues. When, about ten years ago, Dane County Democrats began to garner more than 60 percent of the vote, sometimes more in the city (often more than 70 percent there), it was reasonable to wonder if this would continue. Now there is no reason to doubt it. When one considers that Dane County voters now constitute about 10 percent of the state electorate and will make up more as the county grows, this factor is one of considerable significance in speculating about Wisconsin voting behavior in the future.[40]

Wausau and Marathon County

Deserving special consideration are the many counties in Wisconsin that are centered around smaller cities, growing suburbs, and rural farm and non-farm populations. They represent much of Wisconsin, and will represent more as Milwaukee declines and farms disappear. To illustrate this world, which is admittedly highly diverse, consider Marathon County and its principal city, Wausau, in north central Wisconsin.[41]

As of 2000 Marathon County had a population of 126,000, representing a growth rate of 9 percent over 1990. The City of Wausau had a population of 38,000, and it grew about 4 percent over 1990. Like most smaller cities in Wisconsin, and certainly like most suburban and rural areas, Wausau is overwhelmingly white, though it is the home of a Hmong population of around 6,000, the result of an assertive settlement program orchestrated by Wausau churches and the federal government.

Marathon County was organized in 1850 as a center of the lumber business. Wood and paper products are still the leading industries, but there is also a significant white-collar sector to the economy, not just government employees but also the Wausau Insurance Company, which is the largest employer in the county. Farming remains important as well.

Marathon County is pretty evenly balanced in its voting behavior. As with so many places in Wisconsin, class measured by income proves to be a poor predictor of voting behavior. Outside the city there is little association between income and voting behavior, though there is a mild connection within various sections of the city of Wausau, poorer areas being somewhat more Democratic and wealthier areas more Republican. Many places in Marathon County, however, have lower median incomes than Wausau and are more Republican. This explains why there was no statistically significant association between median household income in Marathon County voting units and their 2004 and 2006 votes (Republican and Democratic).[42]

What does matter, however, is the ethnic background of residents of various parts of the county. In areas where Marathon County's considerable Polish American population is concentrated so is Democratic strength, most obviously in the more rural parts of the county. Democratic Party commitment in these mostly stable areas has been passed down through the generations.[43] Thus heavily Polish areas in Marathon County were almost 64 percent for Kerry, while heavily German areas were only 42 percent for him, and places with a considerable mixture fell in between.

One factor that is not illuminating at all in trying to understand Marathon County is the size of place. It is irrelevant in predicting how Marathon County locales vote as compared with how German in ancestry an area's population is. The one exception is the City of Wausau. While a city with far fewer than 50,000 residents is hardly very urban, in the context of Marathon County, and many (even most) places in Wisconsin, it is. Wausau is distinctly more Democratic than the rest of the county. Thus in 2004 Bush did not win the city but carried the county because of votes outside the city. In 2002 and 2006 Democrat gubernatorial candidate Doyle won both the city and the outlying areas but ran far ahead in Wausau compared to the outlying vote, exactly as Kerry did. While there are places of varying size in Marathon County commonly identified as suburban where Republican victories are frequent, the margins are rarely large and hardly compare in one-sidedness with similar areas around Milwaukee in their Republican vote or around Madison in their Democratic vote.

As elsewhere in Wisconsin, Marathon County shows a good deal of electoral stability today. It is closely contested territory leaning slightly Democratic and gives every indication that it, like the state as a whole, will continue that way.

Southwest Wisconsin

The 2000 presidential results were decided by a little more than 5,000 votes in Wisconsin out of a total of 2.6 million cast. Considering the outcome, one where so little might have made so big a difference either way, there turned out to be only one region that seemed to behave far from its historical voting patterns—and that was southwest Wisconsin.[44] What was a surprise in 2000 has now become a trend that has some impact in a state where margins so often matter.

For the purposes of this study southwest Wisconsin encompasses four counties: Green, Iowa, Lafayette, and Grant. These counties are all small in population, none over 50,000 in the 2000 census and none growing rapidly. They are mostly rural places where for many people there is no sign of affluence. Two of them in particular are poor. Lafayette and Grant rank fifty-eighth and fifty-sixth, respectively, among Wisconsin's seventy-two counties in median income. Green is in the middle at thirty-seventh and Iowa is in better shape at twenty-eighth. Overall, however, these are not boom or growth counties—the whole region is not—in population or in economic terms.

What is true, though, is that they have a long history of voting Republican, one rooted in their Yankee past. There are some exceptions, such as the Catholic Swiss areas of Green County and areas in Lafayette County settled early by Cornish miners. The overall Republican tradition was firmly established in the nineteenth century. It continued thereafter and in fact accelerated after World War II.

Republicanism remains the governing way at the local and county levels generally in southwest Wisconsin. But this is no longer the case with state and presidential voting. Southwest Wisconsin has gone Democratic, and it has done so in quite consistent regional fashion, as the table indicates. The 2000 presidential election was when the break took place, but since then a trend has developed and gathered speed. In both the 2004 and 2006 elections, southwest Wisconsin voted more Democratic than the state as a whole.

The question, as always, is why. One thoughtful analyst argues that no single factor explains the shift, but two intersecting realities are especially significant. One is the overall weak economic condition of those counties, seriously true of Grant and Lafayette but also true of much of Green and Iowa counties outside of the Mt. Horeb areas in Green, Mineral Point in Iowa, and the parts of both counties closest to Dane County and Madison. The theory is that economic concerns appear to be edging more and more local residents toward the Democrats, overcoming traditional Republican voting, a view many locals share. As important, and arguably a good deal more so with the counties leading the way toward increased Democratic voting, is the factor of proximity to Madison. Green and Iowa are the two counties most noticeably moving toward the Democrats, and they are the closest to Madison. Moreover, it is the places within these counties—cities aside— that are nearest to Dane County and Madison that are moving most sharply toward Madison's Democratic voting and social liberal political culture.

TABLE 3. Percentage of Democratic Vote in Southwest Wisconsin
    Counties Compared with State as a Whole, 1880–2006

County	1880	1900	1940	1962	2000	2004	2006
Grant	34.5	36.7	40.1	35.1	49.1*	51.3	54.5
Green	29.1	37.2	44.4	35.2	46.8*	53	58.8
Iowa	50.1	34.8	44.7	41.1	55.7	57.1	62.3
Lafayette	49.1	42.3	46.0	41.7	51.3	52.8	57.3
State	46.1	37.5	50.9	50.5	48.3*	50.2	52.8

* Carried with less than 50 percent

This fact was especially obvious in the 2006 vote on the marriage referendum. Still quite culturally conservative Grant and Lafayette supported the amendment at more than 62 percent, but Green, closer to Madison, did so far below that state percentage at 54 percent, and Iowa did so at only 50.7 percent, the lowest county percentage for the amendment in the state except for Dane County. The point here is that Green and Iowa are increasingly penumbra counties to Dane County and its world. Many of their residents are now connected to Madison by their jobs; commuting to Madison is common.[45]

A study of individual units—towns and villages—in Iowa County, for example, shows no close correlation between median household income and percentage of Democratic or Republican voting. This is exactly what one would expect given the two-pronged analysis. While the poor economic situation of many in southwest Wisconsin may be increasing the Democratic vote, the relatively high income of many Dane County workers living in Iowa and Green counties complicates the picture regarding class and voting. But both these factors work in a single direction. Of the two, the movement of population and, so to say, social liberalism and Democratic politics out of Dane County is the most intriguing. Madison and Dane County are expanding—not just in numbers—and counting more and more in the broader picture of Wisconsin voting behavior. This phenomenon is also present in areas north of Dane County, especially in Sauk and Columbia counties, which deserve study in this light. What is certain is that as Dane County expands its reach, the impact in terms of voting behavior will be real—and beneficial for the Democrats.

The future is uncertain for Wisconsin electoral politics. Today Wisconsin is "America's most competitive state," most definitely a classic "purple state."[46] Yet only a fool would make confident predictions about it given its remarkable history. Indeed, a great part of the fascination with voting behavior is that it changes as situations and people change. It may be safe to guess, for now, that Wisconsin will continue to be a closely contested state, and one that is also open to a variety of electoral challenges from outside the two-party system. This means the story of Wisconsin voting will continue to engage the interest of those who follow elections and that there will be new chapters to write in this state's electoral history.

APPENDIX A

Basic Data

1. Wisconsin Vote in Presidential Elections, 1848–2004
2. Wisconsin Canvass Summary, Presidential Election, November 2, 2004
3. U.S. Senators from Wisconsin, 1848–2005
4. Wisconsin Governors since 1848
5. Vote for Governor in General Elections, 1848–2002
6. Wisconsin Canvass Summary, Gubernatorial Election, November 7, 2006
7. Wisconsin Canvass Summary, Statewide Referendum: Definition of Marriage, November 7, 2006
8. Political Composition of the Wisconsin Legislature, 1885–2007

Sources: 1, 3–5: *Wisconsin Blue Book, 2005–2006*, pp. 718–20, 743, 724, 721–23
2, 6, 7: State Elections Board of Wisconsin
8: *Wisconsin Blue Book, 2007–2008*, p. 277

WISCONSIN VOTE IN PRESIDENTIAL ELECTIONS
1848 – 2004

Key:

A – American (Know Nothing)	LF – Labor-Farm/Laborista-Agrario	SL – Socialist Labor
AFC – America First Coalition	Lib – Libertarian	Soc – Socialist
Cit – Citizens	LR – Liberal Republican	SoD – Southern Democrat
Com – Communist	NA – New Alliance	SPW – Socialist Party of Wis.
Con – Constitution	Nat – National	SW – Socialist Worker
CU – Constitutional Union	ND – National Democrat	Tax – U.S. Taxpayers
D – Democrat	NER – National Economic Recovery	TBL – The Better Life
ER – Independents for Economic Recovery	NL – Natural Law	3rd – Third Party
FS – Free Soil	People's – People's (Populist)	U – Union
G – Greenback	Pop – Populist	UL – Union Labor
Gr – Grassroots	PP – People's Progressive	USL – U.S. Labor
Ind – Independent	Prog – Progressive	W – Whig
IP – Ind. Progressive	Proh – Prohibition	WG – Wisconsin Greens
IS – Ind. Socialist	R – Republican	WIA – Wis. Independent Alliance
ISL – Ind. Socialist Labor	Rfm – Reform	Workers – Workers
ISW – Ind. Socialist Worker	SD – Social Democrat	WW – Worker's World

Note: The party designation listed for a candidate is taken from the Congressional Quarterly *Guide to U.S. Elections*. A candidate whose party did not receive 1% of the vote for a statewide office in the previous election or who failed to meet the alternative requirement of Section 5.62, Wisconsin Statutes, must be listed on the Wisconsin ballot as "independent". In this listing, candidates whose party affiliations appear as "Ind", followed by a party designation, were identified on the ballot simply as "independent" although they also provided a party designation or statement of principle.

Under the Electoral College system, each state is entitled to electoral votes equal in number to its total congressional delegation of U.S. Senators and U.S. Representatives.

1848 (4 electoral votes)

Lewis Cass (D)	15,001
Zachary Taylor (W)	13,747
Martin Van Buren (FS)	10,418
TOTAL	39,166

1852 (5 electoral votes)

Franklin Pierce (D)	33,658
Winfield Scott (W)	22,210
John P. Hale (FS)	8,814
TOTAL	64,682

1856 (5 electoral votes)

John C. Fremont (R)	66,090
James Buchanan (D)	52,843
Millard Fillmore (A)	579
TOTAL	119,512

1860 (5 electoral votes)

Abraham Lincoln (R)	86,113
Stephen A. Douglas (D)	65,021
John C. Breckinridge (SoD)	888
John Bell (CU)	161
TOTAL	152,183

1864 (8 electoral votes)

Abraham Lincoln (R)	83,458
George B. McClellan (D)	65,884
TOTAL	149,342

1868 (8 electoral votes)

Ulysses S. Grant (R)	108,857
Horatio Seymour (D)	84,707
TOTAL	193,564

1872 (10 electoral votes)

Ulysses S. Grant (R)	104,994
Horace Greeley (D & LR)	86,477
Charles O'Conor (D)	834
TOTAL	192,305

1876 (10 electoral votes)

Rutherford B. Hayes (R)	130,668
Samuel J. Tilden (D)	123,927
Peter Cooper (G)	1,509
Green Clay Smith (Proh)	27
TOTAL	256,131

1880 (10 electoral votes)

James A. Garfield (R)	144,398
Winfield S. Hancock (D)	114,644
James B. Weaver (G)	7,986

John W. Phelps (A)	91
Neal Dow (Proh)	68
TOTAL	267,187

1884 (11 electoral votes)

James G. Blaine (R)	161,157
Grover Cleveland (D)	146,477
John P. St. John (Proh)	7,656
Benjamin F. Butler (G)	4,598
TOTAL	319,888

1888 (11 electoral votes)

Benjamin Harrison (R)	176,553
Grover Cleveland (D)	155,232
Clinton B. Fisk (Proh)	14,277
Alson J. Streeter (UL)	8,552
TOTAL	354,614

1892 (12 electoral votes)

Grover Cleveland (D)	177,325
Benjamin Harrison (R)	171,101
John Bidwell (Proh)	13,136
James B. Weaver (People's)	10,019
TOTAL	371,581

1896 (12 electoral votes)

William McKinley (R)	268,135
William J. Bryan (D)	165,523
Joshua Levering (Proh)	7,507
John M. Palmer (ND)	4,584
Charles H. Matchett (SL)	1,314
Charles E. Bentley (Nat)	346
TOTAL	447,409

1900 (12 electoral votes)

William McKinley (R)	265,760
William J. Bryan (D)	159,163
John G. Wooley (Proh)	10,027
Eugene V. Debs (SD)	7,048
Joseph F. Malloney (SL)	503
TOTAL	442,501

1904 (13 electoral votes)

Theodore Roosevelt (R)	280,164
Alton B. Parker (D)	124,107
Eugene V. Debs (SD)	28,220
Silas C. Swallow (Proh)	9,770
Thomas E. Watson (People's)	530
Charles H. Corregan (SL)	223
TOTAL	443,014

WISCONSIN VOTE IN PRESIDENTIAL ELECTIONS
1848 – 2004–Continued

1908 (13 electoral votes)

William H. Taft (R)	247,747
William J. Bryan (D)	166,632
Eugene V. Debs (SD)	28,164
Eugene W. Chafin (Proh)	11,564
August Gillhaus (SL)	314
TOTAL	454,421

1912 (13 electoral votes)

Woodrow Wilson (D)	164,230
William H. Taft (R)	130,596
Theodore Roosevelt (Prog)	62,448
Eugene V. Debs (SD)	33,476
Eugene W. Chafin (Proh)	8,584
Arthur E. Reimer (SL)	632
TOTAL	399,966

1916 (13 electoral votes)

Charles E. Hughes (R)	220,822
Woodrow Wilson (D)	191,363
Allan Benson (Soc)	27,631
J. Frank Hanly (Proh)	7,318
TOTAL	447,134

1920 (13 electoral votes)

Warren G. Harding (R)	498,576
James M. Cox (D)	113,422
Eugene V. Debs (Soc)	80,635
Aaron S. Watkins (Proh)	8,647
TOTAL	701,280

1924 (13 electoral votes)

Robert M. La Follette (Prog)	453,678
Calvin Coolidge (R)	311,614
John W. Davis (D)	68,096
William Z. Foster (Workers)	3,834
Herman P. Faris (Proh)	2,918
TOTAL	840,140

1928 (13 electoral votes)

Herbert Hoover (R)	544,205
Alfred E. Smith (D)	450,259
Norman Thomas (Soc)	18,213
William F. Varney (Proh)	2,245
William Z. Foster (Workers)	1,528
Verne L. Reynolds (SL)	381
TOTAL	1,016,831

1932 (12 electoral votes)

Franklin D. Roosevelt (D)	707,410
Herbert Hoover (R)	347,741
Norman Thomas (Soc)	53,379
William Z. Foster (Com)	3,112
William D. Upshaw (Proh)	2,672
Verne L. Reynolds (SL)	494
TOTAL	1,114,808

1936 (12 electoral votes)

Franklin D. Roosevelt (D)	802,984
Alfred M. Landon (R)	380,828
William Lemke (U)	60,297
Norman Thomas (Soc)	10,626
Earl Browder (Com)	2,197
David L. Calvin (Proh)	1,071
John W. Aiken (SL)	557
TOTAL	1,258,560

1940 (12 electoral votes)

Franklin D. Roosevelt (D)	704,821
Wendell Willkie (R)	679,206
Norman Thomas (Soc)	15,071
Earl Browder (Com)	2,394
Roger Babson (Proh)	2,148
John W. Aiken (SL)	1,882
TOTAL	1,405,522

1944 (12 electoral votes)

Thomas Dewey (R)	674,532
Franklin D. Roosevelt (D)	650,413
Norman Thomas (Soc)	13,205
Edward Teichert (Ind)	1,002
TOTAL	1,339,152

1948 (12 electoral votes)

Harry S Truman (D)	647,310
Thomas Dewey (R)	590,959
Henry Wallace (PP)	25,282
Norman Thomas (Soc)	12,547
Edward Teichert (Ind)	399
Farrell Dobbs (ISW)	303
TOTAL	1,276,800

1952 (12 electoral votes)

Dwight D. Eisenhower (R)	979,744
Adlai E. Stevenson (D)	622,175
Vincent Hallinan (IP)	2,174
Farrell Dobbs (ISW)	1,350
Darlington Hoopes (IS)	1,157
Eric Hass (ISL)	770
TOTAL	1,607,370

1956 (12 electoral votes)

Dwight D. Eisenhower (R)	954,844
Adlai E. Stevenson (D)	586,768
T. Coleman Andrews (Ind Con)	6,918
Darlington Hoopes (Ind Soc)	754
Eric Hass (Ind SL)	710
Farrell Dobbs (Ind SW)	564
TOTAL	1,550,558

1960 (12 electoral votes)

Richard M. Nixon (R)	895,175
John F. Kennedy (D)	830,805
Farrell Dobbs (Ind SW)	1,792
Eric Hass (Ind SL)	1,310
TOTAL	1,729,082

1964 (12 electoral votes)

Lyndon B. Johnson (D)	1,050,424
Barry M. Goldwater (R)	638,495
Clifton DeBerry (Ind SW)	1,692
Eric Hass (Ind SL)	1,204
TOTAL	1,691,815

1968 (12 electoral votes)

Richard M. Nixon (R)	809,997
Hubert H. Humphrey (D)	748,804
George C. Wallace (Ind A)	127,835
Henning A. Blomen (Ind SL)	1,338
Frederick W. Halstead (Ind SW)	1,222
TOTAL	1,689,196

1972 (11 electoral votes)

Richard M. Nixon (R)	989,430
George S. McGovern (D)	810,174
John G. Schmitz (A)	47,525
Benjamin M. Spock (Ind Pop)	2,701
Louis Fisher (Ind SL)	998
Gus Hall (Ind Com)	663
Evelyn Reed (Ind SW)	506
TOTAL	1,851,997

WISCONSIN VOTE IN PRESIDENTIAL ELECTIONS
1848 – 2004–Continued

1976 (11 electoral votes)

Jimmy Carter (D)	1,040,232
Gerald R. Ford (R)	1,004,987
Eugene J. McCarthy (Ind)	34,943
Lester Maddox (A)	8,552
Frank P. Zeidler (Ind Soc)	4,298
Roger L. MacBride (Ind Lib)	3,814
Peter Camejo (Ind SW)	1,691
Margaret Wright (Ind Pop)	943
Gus Hall (Ind Com)	749
Lyndon H. LaRouche, Jr. (Ind USL)	738
Jules Levin (Ind SL)	389
TOTAL	2,104,175

1980 (11 electoral votes)

Ronald Reagan (R)	1,088,845
Jimmy Carter (D)	981,584
John Anderson (Ind)	160,657
Ed Clark (Ind Lib)	29,135
Barry Commoner (Ind Cit)	7,767
John Rarick (Ind Con)	1,519
David McReynolds (Ind Soc)	808
Gus Hall (Ind Com)	772
Deidre Griswold (Ind WW)	414
Clifton DeBerry (Ind SW)	383
TOTAL	2,273,221

1984 (11 electoral votes)

Ronald Reagan (R)	1,198,800
Walter F. Mondale (D)	995,847
David Bergland (Lib)	4,884
Bob Richards (Con)	3,864
Lyndon H. LaRouche, Jr. (Ind)	3,791
Sonia Johnson (Ind Cit)	1,456
Dennis L. Serrette (Ind WIA)	1,007
Larry Holmes (Ind WW)	619
Gus Hall (Ind Com)	597
Melvin T. Mason (Ind SW)	445
TOTAL	2,212,018

1988 (11 electoral votes)

Michael S. Dukakis (D)	1,126,794
George Bush (R)	1,047,499
Ronald Paul (Ind Lib)	5,157
David E. Duke (Ind Pop)	3,056
James Warren (Ind SW)	2,574
Lyndon H. LaRouche, Jr. (Ind NER)	2,302
Lenora B. Fulani (Ind NA)	1,953
TOTAL	2,191,612

1992 (11 electoral votes)

Bill Clinton (D)	1,041,066
George Bush (R)	930,855
Ross Perot (Ind)	544,479
Andre Marrou (Lib)	2,877
James Gritz (Ind AFC)	2,311
Ron Daniels (LF)	1,883
Howard Phillips (Ind Tax)	1,772
J. Quinn Brisben (Ind Soc)	1,211
John Hagelin (NL)	1,070
Lenora B. Fulani (Ind NA)	654
Lyndon H. LaRouche, Jr. (Ind ER)	633
Jack Herer (Ind Gr)	547
Eugene A. Hem (3rd)	405
James Warren (Ind SW)	390
TOTAL	2,531,114

1996 (11 electoral votes)

Bill Clinton (D)	1,071,971
Bob Dole (R)	845,029
Ross Perot (Rfm)	227,339
Ralph Nader (Ind WG)	28,723
Howard Phillips (Tax)	8,811
Harry Browne (Lib)	7,929
John Hagelin (Ind NL)	1,379
Monica Mooerhead (Ind WW)	1,333
Mary Cal Hollis (Ind Soc)	848
James E. Harris (Ind SW)	483
TOTAL	2,196,169

2000 (11 electoral votes)

Al Gore (D)	1,242,987
George W. Bush (R)	1,237,279
Ralph Nader (WG)	94,070
Pat Buchanan (Ind Rfm)	11,446
Harry Browne (Lib)	6,640
Howard Phillips (Con)	2,042
Monica G. Moorehead (Ind WW)	1,063
John Hagelin (Ind Rfm)	878
James Harris (Ind SW)	306
TOTAL	2,598,607

2004 (10 electoral votes)

John F. Kerry (D)	1,489,504
George W. Bush (R)	1,478,120
Ralph Nader (Ind TBL)	16,390
Michael Badnarik (Lib)	6,464
David Cobb (WG)	2,661
Walter F. Brown (Ind SPW)	471
James Harris (Ind SW)	411
TOTAL	2,997,007

Note: Some totals include scattered votes for other candidates.

Sources: Official records of the Elections Board and Congressional Quarterly, *Guide to U.S. Elections,* 1994.

APPENDIX A-2. Wisconsin Canvass Summary, Presidential Election, November 2, 2004

	Total Votes Cast	John F. Kerry/ John Edwards (Dem)	George W. Bush/ Dick Cheney (Rep)	Michael Badnarik/ Richard V. Campagna (Lib)	David Cobb/ Patricia LaMarche (WGR)	Ralph Nader/ Peter Miguel Camejo (Ind)	James Harris/ Margaret Trowe (Ind)	Walter F Brown/ Mary Alice Herbert (Ind)	Scattering
Adams County	10,456	5,447	4,890	10	10	79	2	2	16
Ashland County	9,199	5,805	3,313	17	8	55	0	1	0
Barron County	23,937	11,696	12,030	32	14	126	3	3	33
Bayfield County	9,699	5,845	3,754	14	12	70	1	0	3
Brown County	123,294	54,935	67,173	268	91	668	9	44	106
Buffalo County	7,591	3,998	3,502	13	13	62	0	0	3
Burnett County	9,321	4,499	4,743	16	9	43	0	0	11
Calumet County	25,276	10,290	14,721	48	20	161	1	4	31
Chippewa County	30,524	14,751	15,450	58	31	198	1	8	27
Clark County	15,125	6,966	7,966	22	19	132	3	2	15
Columbia County	29,555	14,300	14,956	66	15	158	6	4	50
Crawford County	8,459	4,656	3,680	23	12	57	0	2	29
Dane County	274,249	181,052	90,369	742	331	1,465	19	27	244
Dodge County	44,336	16,690	27,201	78	39	283	5	3	37
Door County	17,491	8,367	8,910	51	24	118	4	2	15
Douglas County	25,187	16,537	8,448	32	25	125	5	3	12
Dunn County	23,172	12,039	10,879	55	11	151	2	7	28
Eau Claire County	55,437	30,068	24,653	158	101	371	8	10	68
Florence County	2,724	993	1,703	3	1	18	0	0	6
Fond du Lac County	53,036	19,216	33,291	98	56	297	9	6	63
Forest County	5,153	2,509	2,608	7	0	24	3	1	1
Grant County	25,264	12,864	12,208	45	19	112	0	3	13

APPENDIX A-2. (Continued)

	Total Votes Cast	John F. Kerry/John Edwards (Dem)	George W. Bush/Dick Cheney (Rep)	Michael Badnarik/Richard V. Campagna (Lib)	David Cobb/Patricia LaMarche (WGR)	Ralph Nader/Peter Miguel Camejo (Ind)	James Harris/Margaret Trowe (Ind)	Walter F. Brown/Mary Alice Herbert (Ind)	Scattering
Green County	18,248	9,575	8,497	32	24	101	0	6	13
Green Lake County	10,178	3,605	6,472	21	10	55	0	0	15
Iowa County	12,542	7,122	5,348	16	6	44	1	0	5
Iron County	3,879	1,956	1,884	7	4	25	0	0	3
Jackson County	9,726	5,249	4,387	18	9	47	1	2	13
Jefferson County	42,115	17,925	23,776	86	29	240	3	5	51
Juneau County	12,379	5,734	6,473	52	18	73	3	1	25
Kenosha County	76,428	40,107	35,587	217	76	366	9	18	48
Kewaunee County	11,273	5,175	5,970	33	12	78	2	0	3
LaCrosse County	62,136	33,170	28,289	129	107	348	5	15	73
Lafayette County	8,388	4,402	3,929	8	8	37	0	1	3
Langlade County	11,074	4,751	6,235	12	5	64	0	0	7
Lincoln County	15,700	7,484	8,024	41	23	112	2	0	14
Manitowoc County	44,160	20,652	23,027	74	50	300	14	6	37
Marathon County	68,059	30,899	36,394	129	68	505	6	9	49
Marinette County	22,270	10,190	11,866	51	10	128	4	0	21
Marquette County	8,477	3,785	4,604	25	7	36	0	0	20
Menominee County	1,710	1,412	288	2	1	6	1	0	0
Milwaukee County	482,236	297,653	180,287	963	319	2,232	142	72	568
Monroe County	19,554	8,973	10,375	58	9	114	1	5	19
Oconto County	19,794	8,534	11,043	43	22	126	1	1	24
Oneida County	22,039	10,464	11,351	63	16	135	1	2	7

County								
Outagamie County	90,050	40,169	48,903	230	85	519	5	11	128
Ozaukee County	53,032	17,714	34,904	108	25	245	1	4	31
Pepin County	4,066	2,181	1,853	4	2	22	0	2	2
Pierce County	21,876	11,176	10,437	41	32	148	5	7	30
Polk County	23,503	11,173	12,095	53	31	134	1	1	15
Portage County	38,961	21,861	16,546	104	95	299	3	11	42
Price County	8,763	4,349	4,312	26	10	56	0	1	9
Racine County	101,569	48,229	52,456	245	62	459	20	41	57
Richland County	9,420	4,501	4,836	21	10	38	2	0	12
Rock County	80,479	46,598	33,151	161	46	409	25	9	80
Rusk County	7,927	3,820	3,985	24	10	74	3	4	7
Sauk County	30,417	15,708	14,415	59	19	184	2	3	27
Sawyer County	9,453	4,411	4,951	12	6	62	0	0	11
Shawano County	20,999	8,657	12,150	26	13	130	3	4	16
Sheboygan County	62,625	27,608	34,458	128	49	323	12	4	43
St. Croix County	41,835	18,784	22,679	99	30	202	2	3	36
Taylor County	9,543	3,829	5,582	16	15	87	1	4	9
Trempealeau County	14,062	8,075	5,878	21	10	71	1	0	6
Vernon County	14,845	7,924	6,774	19	16	87	0	5	20
Vilas County	14,002	5,713	8,155	24	11	76	1	1	21
Walworth County	48,446	19,177	28,754	125	43	278	5	13	51
Washburn County	9,567	4,705	4,762	18	10	60	1	2	9
Washington County	72,467	21,234	50,641	121	43	341	5	7	75
Waukesha County	230,363	73,626	154,926	453	115	966	15	27	235
Waupaca County	26,974	10,792	15,941	39	17	162	3	6	14
Waushara County	12,246	5,257	6,888	11	10	66	3	1	10
Winnebago County	88,596	40,943	46,542	240	103	611	7	19	131
Wood County	40,071	18,950	20,592	100	49	336	8	6	30
	2,997,007	1,489,504	1,478,120	6,464	2,661	16,390	411	471	2,986

U.S. SENATORS FROM WISCONSIN, 1848 – 2005

Class 1		Class 3	
Name	Service	Name	Service
Henry Dodge (D)	1848-1857	Isaac P. Walker (D)	1848-1855
James R. Doolittle (R)	1857-1869	Charles Durkee (UR)	1855-1861
Matthew H. Carpenter (R)	1869-1875	Timothy O. Howe (UR)	1861-1879
Angus Cameron (R)[1]	1875-1881	Matthew H. Carpenter (R)	1879-1881
Philetus Sawyer (R)	1881-1893	Angus Cameron (R)[1]	1881-1885
John Lendrum Mitchell (D)	1893-1899	John C. Spooner (R)	1885-1891
Joseph Very Quarles (R)	1899-1905	William F. Vilas (D)	1891-1897
Robert M. La Follette, Sr. (R)[2]	1906-1925	John C. Spooner (R)	1897-1907
Robert M. La Follette, Jr. (R)[3]	1925-1935	Isaac Stephenson (R)[5]	1907-1915
(P)	1935-1947	Paul O. Husting (D)	1915-1917
Joseph R. McCarthy (R)	1947-1957	Irvine L. Lenroot (R)[6]	1918-1927
William Proxmire (D)[4]	1957-1989	John J. Blaine (R)	1927-1933
Herbert H. Kohl (D)	1989-	F. Ryan Duffy (D)	1933-1939
		Alexander Wiley (R)	1939-1963
		Gaylord A. Nelson (D)	1963-1981
		Robert W. Kasten, Jr. (R)	1981-1993
		Russell D. Feingold (D)	1993-

Note: Each state has two U.S. Senators, and each serves a 6-year term. They were elected by their respective state legislatures until passage of the 17th Amendment to the U.S. Constitution on April 8, 1913, which provided for popular election. Article I, Section 3, Clause 2, of the U.S. Constitution divides senators into three classes so that one-third of the senate is elected every two years. Wisconsin's seats were assigned to Class 1 and Class 3 at statehood.

Key: Democrat (D); Progressive (P); Republican (R); Union Republican (UR)

[1]Not a candidate for reelection to Class 1 seat, but elected 3/10/1881 to fill vacancy caused by death of Class 3 Senator Carpenter on 2/24/1881.

[2]Elected 1/25/1905 but continued to serve as governor until 1/1/1906.

[3]Elected 9/29/1925 to fill vacancy caused by death of Robert La Follette, Sr., on 6/18/1925.

[4]Elected 8/27/1957 to fill vacancy caused by death of McCarthy on 5/2/1957.

[5]Elected 5/17/1907 to fill vacancy caused by resignation of Spooner on 4/30/1907.

[6]Elected 5/2/1918 to fill vacancy caused by death of Husting on 10/21/1917.

Source: Wisconsin Legislative Reference Bureau records.

WISCONSIN GOVERNORS SINCE 1848

Governor[1]	Political Party	Service As Governor[2]		Born	Birthplace	Died	Burial Place
		Began	Ended				
1 Nelson Dewey	Democrat	6-7-1848	1-5-1852	12-19-1813	Lebanon, Conn.	7-21-1889	Lancaster, Wis.
2 Leonard James Farwell	Whig	1-5-1852	1-2-1854	1-5-1819	Watertown, N.Y.	4-11-1889	Grant City, Mo.
3 William Augustus Barstow	Democrat	1-2-1854	3-21-1856	9-13-1813	Plainfield, Conn.	12-13-1865	Cleveland, Ohio
4 Arthur MacArthur[3]	Democrat	3-21-1856	3-25-1856	1-26-1815	Glasgow, Scotland	8-26-1896	Washington, D.C.
5 Coles Bashford	Republican	3-25-1856	1-4-1858	1-24-1816	Putnam Co., N.Y.	4-25-1878	Oakland, Cal.
6 Alexander William Randall	Republican	1-4-1858	1-6-1862	10-31-1819	Ames, N.Y.	7-26-1872	Elmira, N.Y.
7 Louis Powell Harvey[4]	Republican	1-6-1862	4-19-1862	7-22-1820	East Haddam, Conn.	4-19-1862	Madison, Wis.
8 Edward Salomon[4]	Republican	4-19-1862	1-4-1864	8-11-1828	Stroebeck, Prussia	4-21-1909	Frankfurt, Germany
9 James Taylor Lewis	Republican	1-4-1864	1-1-1866	10-30-1819	Clarendon, N.Y.	8-4-1904	Columbus, Wis.
10 Lucius Fairchild	Republican	1-1-1866	1-1-1872	12-27-1831	Kent, Ohio	5-23-1896	Madison, Wis.
11 Cadwallader Colden Washburn	Republican	1-1-1872	1-5-1874	4-22-1818	Livermore, Me.	5-14-1882	La Crosse, Wis.
12 William Robert Taylor	Democrat	1-5-1874	1-3-1876	7-10-1820	Woodbury, Conn.	3-17-1909	Madison, Wis.
13 Harrison Ludington	Republican	1-3-1876	1-7-1878	7-30-1812	Ludingtonville, N.Y.	6-17-1891	Milwaukee, Wis.
14 William E. Smith	Republican	1-7-1878	1-2-1882	6-18-1824	Near Inverness, Scotland	2-13-1883	Milwaukee, Wis.
15 Jeremiah McLain Rusk	Republican	1-2-1882	1-7-1889	6-17-1830	Morgan Co., Ohio	11-21-1893	Viroqua, Wis.
16 William Dempster Hoard	Republican	1-7-1889	1-5-1891	10-10-1836	Stockbridge, N.Y.	11-22-1918	Ft. Atkinson, Wis.
17 George Wilbur Peck	Democrat	1-5-1891	1-7-1895	9-28-1840	Henderson, N.Y.	4-16-1916	Milwaukee, Wis.
18 William Henry Upham	Republican	1-7-1895	1-4-1897	5-3-1841	Westminster, Mass.	7-2-1924	Marshfield, Wis.
19 Edward Scofield	Republican	1-4-1897	1-7-1901	3-28-1842	Clearfield, Pa.	2-3-1925	Oconto, Wis.
20 Robert Marion La Follette, Sr.[5]	Republican	1-7-1901	1-1-1906	6-14-1855	Primrose, Dane Co., Wis.	6-18-1925	Madison, Wis.
21 James O. Davidson[5]	Republican	1-1-1906	1-2-1911	2-10-1854	Sogn, Norway	12-16-1922	Madison, Wis.
22 Francis Edward McGovern	Republican	1-2-1911	1-4-1915	1-21-1866	Elkhart Lake, Wis.	5-16-1946	Milwaukee, Wis.
23 Emanuel Lorenz Philipp	Republican	1-4-1915	1-3-1921	3-25-1861	Honey Creek, Sauk Co., Wis.	6-15-1925	Milwaukee, Wis.
24 John James Blaine	Republican	1-3-1921	1-3-1927	5-4-1875	Wingville, Grant Co., Wis.	4-18-1934	Boscobel, Wis.
25 Fred R. Zimmerman	Republican	1-3-1927	1-7-1929	11-20-1880	Milwaukee, Wis.	12-14-1954	Milwaukee, Wis.
26 Walter Jodok Kohler, Sr.	Republican	1-7-1929	1-5-1931	3-3-1875	Sheboygan, Wis.	4-21-1940	Kohler, Wis.
27 Philip Fox La Follette	Republican	1-5-1931	1-2-1933	5-8-1897	Madison, Wis.	8-18-1965	Madison, Wis.
28 Albert George Schmedeman	Democrat	1-2-1933	1-7-1935	11-25-1864	Madison, Wis.	11-26-1946	Madison, Wis.
29 Philip Fox La Follette	Progressive	1-7-1935	1-2-1939	5-8-1897	Madison, Wis.	8-18-1965	Madison, Wis.
30 Julius Peter Heil	Republican	1-2-1939	1-4-1943	7-24-1876	Duesmond, Germany	11-30-1949	Milwaukee, Wis.
Orland Steen Loomis[6]	Progressive	Died prior to inauguration		11-2-1893	Mauston, Wis.	12-7-1942	Mauston, Wis.
31 Walter Samuel Goodland[6,7]	Republican	1-4-1943	3-12-1947	12-22-1862	Sharon, Wis.	3-12-1947	Racine, Wis.
32 Oscar Rennebohm[7]	Republican	3-12-1947	1-1-1951	5-25-1889	Leeds, Columbia Co., Wis.	10-15-1968	Madison, Wis.
33 Walter Jodok Kohler, Jr.	Republican	1-1-1951	1-7-1957	4-4-1904	Sheboygan, Wis.	3-10-1976	Kohler, Wis.
34 Vernon Wallace Thomson	Republican	1-7-1957	1-5-1959	11-5-1905	Richland Center, Wis.	4-2-1988	Richland Center, Wis.
35 Gaylord Anton Nelson	Democrat	1-5-1959	1-7-1963	6-4-1916	Clear Lake, Wis.	7-3-2005	Clear Lake, Wis.
36 John W. Reynolds	Democrat	1-7-1963	1-4-1965	4-4-1921	Green Bay, Wis.	1-6-2002	Door County, Wis.
37 Warren Perley Knowles	Republican	1-4-1965	1-4-1971	8-19-1908	River Falls, Wis.	4-1-1993	River Falls, Wis.
38 Patrick Joseph Lucey[8]	Democrat	1-4-1971	7-6-1977	3-21-1918	La Crosse, Wis.	———	———
39 Martin James Schreiber[8]	Democrat	7-6-1977	1-1-1979	4-8-1939	Milwaukee, Wis.	———	———
40 Lee Sherman Dreyfus	Republican	1-1-1979	1-3-1983	6-20-1926	Milwaukee, Wis.	———	———
41 Anthony Scully Earl	Democrat	1-3-1983	1-5-1987	4-12-1936	Lansing, Mich.	———	———
42 Tommy George Thompson[9]	Republican	1-5-1987	2-1-2001	11-19-1941	Elroy, Wis.	———	———
43 Scott McCallum[9]	Republican	2-1-2001	1-6-2003	5-2-1950	Fond du Lac, Wis.	———	———
44 James E. Doyle	Democrat	1-6-2003		11-23-1945	Madison, Wis.	———	———

[1] Includes those serving as acting governor when office is vacated. Administrations are numbered.

[2] Article XIII, Section 1 of the Wisconsin Constitution was amended in November 1884 so that the term of office of all state and county officers began in January of odd-numbered years, rather than January of even-numbered years.

[3] Served as acting governor during dispute over who won gubernatorial election.

[4] Salomon became acting governor on death of Harvey on 4/19/62.

[5] Davidson served as acting governor from La Follette's resignation until beginning the terms to which he was elected on 1/7/07.

[6] Goodland became acting governor on death of Governor-elect Loomis and served entire 1943-44 term.

[7] Rennebohm became acting governor on the death of Goodland on 3/1/47.

[8] Schreiber became acting governor when Lucey resigned to become U.S. ambassador to Mexico.

[9] McCallum became acting governor when Thompson resigned to become U.S. Secretary of Health and Human Services.

Sources: "Wisconsin's Former Governors", 1960 Wisconsin Blue Book; Blue Book, pp. 69-206; Blue Book biographies.

VOTE FOR GOVERNOR IN GENERAL ELECTIONS
1848 – 2002

Key:
A – American	IPR – Independent Prohibition Republic	Prog – Progressive
C – Conservative	ISL – Independent Socialist Labor	Proh – Prohibition
Com – Communist	ISW – Independent Socialist Worker	R – Republican
Con – Constitution	IW – Independent Worker	Soc – Socialist
D – Democrat	L – Labor	SD – Social Democrat
DS – Democratic Socialist	LF – Labor Farm/Laborista Agrario	SDA – Social Democrat of America
G – Greenback	Lib – Libertarian	SL – Socialist Labor
Ind – Independent	Nat – National	SW – Socialist Worker
IC – Independent Communist	NR – National Republic	Tax – U.S. Taxpayers
ID – Independent Democrat	People's – People's (Populist)	U – Union
IL – Independent Labor	PLS – Progressive Labor Socialist	UL – Union Labor
IP – Independent Prohibition	PP – People's Progressive	W – Whig
		WG – Wisconsin Greens

Note: Candidates whose party did not receive 1% of the vote for a statewide office in the previous election or who failed to meet the alternative requirement of Section 5.62, Wisconsin Statutes, are listed on the Wisconsin ballot as "independent". When a candidate's party affiliation is listed as "independent" and a party designation is shown in italics, "independent" was the official ballot listing, but a party designation was found by the Wisconsin Legislative Reference Bureau in newspaper reports.

1848
Nelson Dewey (D)[1]	19,875
John Hubbard Tweedy (W)[1]	14,621
Charles Durkee (Ind)[1]	1,134
TOTAL	35,309

1849
Nelson Dewey (D)	16,649
Alexander L. Collins (W)	11,317
Warren Chase (Ind)	3,761
TOTAL	31,759

1851
Leonard James Farwell (W)	22,319
Don Alonzo Joshua Upham (D)	21,812
TOTAL	44,190

1853
William Augustus Barstow (D)	30,405
Edward Dwight Holton (R)	21,886
Henry Samuel Baird (W)	3,304
TOTAL	55,683

1855
William Augustus Barstow (D)[2]	36,355
Coles Bashford (R)	36,198
TOTAL	72,598

1857
Alexander William Randall (R)	44,693
James B. Cross (D)	44,239
TOTAL	90,058

1859
Alexander William Randall (R)	59,999
Harrison Carroll Hobart (D)	52,539
TOTAL	112,755

1861
Louis Powell Harvey (R)	53,777
Benjamin Ferguson (D)	45,456
TOTAL	99,258

1863
James Taylor Lewis (R)	72,717
Henry L. Palmer (D)	49,053
TOTAL	122,029

1865
Lucius Fairchild (R)	58,332
Harrison Carroll Hobart (D)	48,330
TOTAL	106,674

1867
Lucius Fairchild (R)	73,637
John J. Tallmadge (D)	68,873
TOTAL	142,522

1869
Lucius Fairchild (R)	69,502
Charles D. Robinson (D)	61,239
TOTAL	130,781

1871
Cadwallader Colden Washburn (R)	78,301
James Rood Doolittle (D)	68,910
TOTAL	147,274

1873
William Robert Taylor (D)	81,599
Cadwallader Colden Washburn (R)	66,224
TOTAL	147,856

1875
Harrison Ludington (R)	85,155
William Robert Taylor (D)	84,314
TOTAL	170,070

1877
William E. Smith (R)	78,759
James A. Mallory (D)	70,486
Edward Phelps Allis (G)	26,216
Collin M. Campbell (Soc)	2,176
TOTAL	178,122

1879
William E. Smith (R)	100,535
James G. Jenkins (D)	75,030
Reuben May (G)	12,996
TOTAL	189,005

1881
Jeremiah McLain Rusk (R)	81,754
N.D. Fratt (D)	69,797
T.D. Kanouse (Proh)	13,225
Edward Phelps Allis (G)	7,002
TOTAL	171,856

1884
Jeremiah McLain Rusk (R)	163,214
N.D. Fratt (D)	143,945
Samuel Dexter Hastings (Proh)	8,545
William L. Utley (G)	4,274
TOTAL	319,997

1886
Jeremiah McLain Rusk (R)	133,247
Gilbert Motier Woodward (D)	114,529
John Cochrane (People's)	21,467
John Myers Olin (Proh)	17,089
TOTAL	286,368

1888
William Dempster Hoard (R)	175,696
James Morgan (D)	155,423
E.G. Durant (Proh)	14,373
D. Frank Powell (L)	9,196
TOTAL	354,714

1890
George Wilbur Peck (D)	160,388
William Dempster Hoard (R)	132,068
Charles Alexander (Proh)	11,246
Reuben May (UL)	5,447
TOTAL	309,254

1892
George Wilbur Peck (D)	178,095
John Coit Spooner (R)	170,497
Thomas C. Richmond (Proh)	13,185
C.M. Butt (People's)	9,638
TOTAL	371,559

1894
William H. Upham (R)	196,150
George Wilbur Peck (D)	142,250
D. Frank Powell (People's)	25,604
John F. Cleghorn (Proh)	11,240
TOTAL	375,449

1896
Edward Scofield (R)	264,981
Willis C. Silverthorn (D)	169,257
Joshua H. Berkey (Proh)	8,140
Christ Tuttrop (SL)	1,306
Robert Henderson (Nat)	407
TOTAL	444,110

VOTE FOR GOVERNOR IN GENERAL ELECTIONS
1848 − 2002–Continued

1898
Edward Scofield (R)	173,137
Hiram Wilson Sawyer (D)	135,353
Albinus A. Worsley (People's)	8,518
Eugene Wilder Chafin (Proh)	8,078
Howard Tuttle (SDA)	2,544
Henry Riese (SL)	1,473
TOTAL	329,430

1900
Robert Marion La Follette (R)	264,419
Louis G. Bomrich (D)	160,674
J. Burritt Smith (Proh)	9,707
Howard Tuttle (SD)	6,590
Frank R. Wilke (SL)	509
TOTAL	441,900

1902
Robert Marion La Follette (R)	193,417
David Stuart Rose (D)	145,818
Emil Seidel (SD)	15,970
Edwin W. Drake (Proh)	9,647
Henry E.D. Puck (SL)	791
TOTAL	365,676

1904
Robert Marion La Follette (R)	227,253
George Wilbur Peck (D)	176,301
William A. Arnold (SD)	24,857
Edward Scofield (NR)	12,136
William H. Clark (Proh)	8,764
Charles M. Minkley (SL)	249
TOTAL	449,570

1906
James O. Davidson (R)	183,558
John A. Aylward (D)	103,311
Winfield R. Gaylord (SD)	24,437
Ephraim L. Eaton (Proh)	8,211
Ole T. Rosaas (SL)	455
TOTAL	320,003

1908
James O. Davidson (R)	242,935
John A. Aylward (D)	165,977
H.D. Brown (SD)	28,583
Winfred D. Cox (Proh)	11,760
Herman Bottema (SL)	393
TOTAL	449,656

1910
Francis Edward McGovern (R)	161,619
Adolph H. Schmitz (D)	110,442
William A. Jacobs (SD)	39,547
Byron E. Van Keuren (Proh)	7,450
Fred G. Kremer (SL)	430
TOTAL	319,522

1912
Francis Edward McGovern (R)	179,360
John C. Karel (D)	167,316
Carl D. Thompson (SD)	34,468
Charles Lewis Hill (Proh)	9,433
William H. Curtis (SL)	3,253
TOTAL	393,849

1914
Emanuel Lorenz Philipp (R)	140,787
John C. Karel (D)	119,509
John James Blaine (Ind)	32,560
Oscar Ameringer (SD)	25,917
David W. Emerson (Proh)	6,279
John Vierthaler (Ind)	352
TOTAL	325,430

1916
Emanuel Lorenz Philipp (R)	229,889
Burt Williams (D)	164,555
Rae Weaver (Soc)	30,649
George McKerrow (Proh)	9,193
TOTAL	434,340

1918
Emanuel Lorenz Philipp (R)	155,799
Henry A. Moehlenpah (D)	112,576
Emil Seidel (SD)	57,523
William C. Dean (Proh)	5,296
TOTAL	331,582

1920
John James Blaine (R)	366,247
Robert McCoy (D)	247,746
William Coleman (Soc)	71,126
Henry H. Tubbs (Proh)	6,047
TOTAL	691,294

1922
John James Blaine (R)	367,929
Arthur A. Bentley (ID)	51,061
Louis A. Arnold (Soc)	39,570
M.L. Welles (Proh)	21,438
Arthur A. Dietrich (ISL)	1,444
TOTAL	481,828

1924
John James Blaine (R)	412,255
Martin L. Lueck (D)	317,550
William F. Quick (Soc)	45,268
Adolph R. Bucknam (Proh)	11,516
Severi Alanne (IW)	4,107
Farrand K. Shuttleworth (IPR)	4,079
Jose Snover (SL)	1,452
TOTAL	796,432

1926
Fred R. Zimmerman (R)	350,927
Charles Perry (Ind)	76,507
Virgil H. Cady (D)	72,627
Herman O. Kent (Soc)	40,293
David W. Emerson (Proh)	7,333
Alex Gorden (SL)	4,593
TOTAL	552,912

1928
Walter Jodok Kohler, Sr. (R)	547,738
Albert George Schmedeman (D)	394,368
Otto R. Hauser (Soc)	36,924
Adolph R. Bucknam (Proh)	6,477
Joseph Ehrhardt (IL)	1,938
Alvar J. Hayes (IW)	1,420
TOTAL	989,143

1930
Philip Fox La Follette (R)	392,958
Charles E. Hammersley (D)	170,020
Frank B. Metcalfe (Soc)	25,607
Alfred B. Taynton (Proh)	14,818
Fred Bassett Blair (IC)	2,998
TOTAL	606,825

1932
Albert George Schmedeman (D)	590,114
Walter Jodok Kohler, Sr. (R)	470,805
Frank B. Metcalfe (Soc)	56,965
William C. Dean (Proh)	3,148
Fred Bassett Blair (Com)	2,926
Joe Ehrhardt (SL)	398
TOTAL	1,124,502

1934
Philip Fox La Follette (Prog)	373,093
Albert George Schmedeman (D)	359,467
Howard Greene (R)	172,980
George A. Nelson (Soc)	44,589
Morris Childs (IC)	2,454
Thomas W. North (PR)	857
Joe Ehrhardt (ISL)	332
TOTAL	953,797

1936
Philip Fox La Follette (Prog)	573,724
Alexander Wiley (R)	363,973
Arthur W. Lueck (D)	268,530
Joseph F. Walsh (Soc)	27,934
Joseph Ehrhardt (SL)	1,738
August F. Fehlandt (Proh)	1,008
TOTAL	1,237,095

1938
Julius Peter Heil (R)	543,675
Philip Fox La Follette (Prog)	353,381
Harry Wilbur Bolens (D)	78,446
Frank W. Smith (U)	4,564
John Schleier, Jr. (ISL)	1,459
TOTAL	981,560

1940
Julius Peter Heil (R)	558,678
Orland Steen Loomis (Prog)	546,436
Francis Edward McGovern (D)	264,985
Fred Bassett Blair (Com)	2,340
Louis Fisher (SL)	1,158
TOTAL	1,373,754

1942
Orland Steen Loomis (Prog)	397,664
Julius Peter Heil (R)	291,945
William C. Sullivan (D)	98,153
Frank P. Zeidler (Soc)	11,295
Fred Bassett Blair (IC)	1,092
Georgia Cozzini (ISL)	490
TOTAL	800,985

VOTE FOR GOVERNOR IN GENERAL ELECTIONS
1848 – 2002–Continued

1944
Walter Samuel Goodland (R)	697,740
Daniel O. Hoan (D)	536,357
Alexander O. Benz (Prog)	76,028
George A. Nelson (Soc)	9,183
Georgia Cozzini (Ind *ISL*)	1,122
TOTAL	1,320,483

1946
Walter Samuel Goodland (R)	621,970
Daniel W. Hoan (D)	406,499
Walter H. Uphoff (Soc)	8,996
Sigmund G. Eisenscher (IC)	1,857
Jerry R. Kenyon (ISL)	959
TOTAL	1,040,444

1948
Oscar Rennebohm (R)	684,839
Carl W. Thompson (D)	558,497
Henry J. Berquist (PP)	12,928
Walter H. Uphoff (Soc)	9,149
James E. Boulton (ISW)	356
Georgia Cozzini (ISL)	328
TOTAL	1,266,139

1950
Walter Jodok Kohler, Jr. (R)	605,649
Carl W. Thompson (D)	525,319
M. Michael Essin (PP)	3,735
William O. Hart (Soc)	3,384
TOTAL	1,138,148

1952
Walter Jodok Kohler, Jr. (R)	1,009,171
William Proxmire (D)	601,844
M. Michael Essin (Ind)	3,706
TOTAL	1,615,214

1954
Walter Jodok Kohler, Jr. (R)	596,158
William Proxmire (D)	560,747
Arthur Wepfer (Ind)	1,722
TOTAL	1,158,666

1956
Vernon W. Thomson (R)	808,273
William Proxmire (D)	749,421
TOTAL	1,557,788

1958
Gaylord Anton Nelson (D)	644,296
Vernon W. Thomson (R)	556,391
Wayne Leverenz (Ind)	1,485
TOTAL	1,202,219

1960
Gaylord Anton Nelson (D)	890,868
Philip G. Kuehn (R)	837,123
TOTAL	1,728,009

1962
John W. Reynolds (D)	637,491
Philip G. Kuehn (R)	625,536
Adolf Wiggert (Ind)	2,477
TOTAL	1,265,900

1964
Warren P. Knowles (R)	856,779
John W. Reynolds (D)	837,901
TOTAL	1,694,887

1966
Warren P. Knowles (R)	626,041
Patrick J. Lucey (D)	539,258
Adolf Wiggert (Ind)	4,745
TOTAL	1,170,173

1968
Warren P. Knowles (R)	893,463
Bronson C. La Follette (D)	791,100
Adolf Wiggert (Ind)	3,225
Robert Wilkinson (Ind)	1,813
TOTAL	1,689,738

1970
Patrick J. Lucey (D)	728,403
Jack B. Olson (R)	602,617
Leo James McDonald (A)	9,035
Georgia Cozzini (Ind *SL*)	1,287
Samuel K. Hunt (Ind *SW*)	888
Myrtle Kastner (Ind *PLS*)	628
TOTAL	1,343,160

1974
Patrick J. Lucey (D)	628,639
William D. Dyke (R)	497,189
William H. Upham (A)	33,528
Crazy Jim[3] (Ind)	12,107
William Hart (Ind *DS*)	5,113
Fred Blair (Ind *C*)	3,617
Georgia Cozzini (Ind *SL*)	1,492
TOTAL	1,181,685

1978
Lee Sherman Dreyfus (R)	816,056
Martin J. Schreiber (D)	673,813
Eugene R. Zimmerman (C)	6,355
John C. Doherty (Ind)	2,183
Adrienne Kaplan (Ind *SW*)	1,548
Henry A. Ochsner (Ind *SL*)	849
TOTAL	1,500,996

1982
Anthony S. Earl (D)	896,872
Terry J. Kohler (R)	662,738
Larry Smiley (Lib)	9,734
James P. Wickstrom (Con)	7,721
Peter Seidman (Ind *SW*)	3,025
TOTAL	1,580,344

1986
Tommy G. Thompson (R)	805,090
Anthony S. Earl (D)	705,578
Kathryn A. Christensen (LF)	10,323
Darold E. Wall (Ind)	3,913
Sanford Knapp (Ind)	1,668
TOTAL	1,526,573

1990
Tommy G. Thompson (R)	802,321
Thomas A. Loftus (D)	576,280
TOTAL	1,379,727

1994
Tommy G. Thompson (R)	1,051,326
Charles J.Chvala (D)	482,850
David S. Harmon (Lib)	11,639
Edward J. Frami (Tax)	9,188
Michael J. Mangan (Ind)	8,150
TOTAL	1,563,835

1998
Tommy G. Thompson (R)	1,047,716
Ed Garvey (D)	679,553
Jim Mueller (Lib)	11,071
Edward J. Frami (Tax)	10,269
Mike Mangan (Ind)	4,985
A-Ja-mu Muhammad (Ind)	1,604
Jeffrey L. Smith (WG)	14
TOTAL	1,756,014

2002
Jim Doyle (D)	800,515
Scott McCallum (R)	734,779
Ed Thompson (Lib)	185,455
Jim Young (WG)	44,111
Alan D. Eisenberg (Ind)	2,847
Ty A. Bollerud (Ind)	2,637
Mike Mangan (Ind)	1,710
Aneb Jah Rasta Sensas-Utcha Nefer-I (Ind)	929
TOTAL	1,775,349

[1] Votes for Dewey and Tweedy are from *1874 Blue Book;* Durkee vote is based on county returns, as filed in the Office of the Secretary of State, but returns from Manitowoc and Winnebago Counties were missing. Without these 2 counties, Dewey had 19,605 votes and Tweedy had 14,514 votes.

[2] Barstow's plurality was set aside in *Atty. Gen. ex rel. Bashford v. Barstow,* 4 Wis. 567 (1855) because of irregularities in the election returns.

[3] Legal name.

Source: Elections Board records. Totals include scattered votes for other candidates.

	Total Votes Cast	Jim Doyle/ Barbara Lawton (Dem)	Mark Green/ Jean Hundertmark (Rep)	Nelson Eisman/ Leon Todd (WGR)	Scattering
Adams County	7,899	4,416	3,324	150	9
Ashland County	6,258	4,118	1,902	232	6
Barron County	16,333	8,136	7,920	271	6
Bayfield County	7,253	4,653	2,468	129	3
Brown County	93,635	45,046	46,989	1,517	83
Buffalo County	5,362	3,078	2,196	83	5
Burnett County	6,184	3,225	2,900	59	0
Calumet County	19,382	9,059	9,995	320	8
Chippewa County	21,818	11,467	9,839	502	10
Clark County	11,240	5,758	5,152	326	4
Columbia County	22,164	11,662	9,936	521	45
Crawford County	6,331	3,751	2,439	128	13
Dane County	213,940	149,661	58,302	5,645	332
Dodge County	31,049	13,137	17,302	581	29
Door County	14,393	7,592	6,479	319	3
Douglas County	16,284	10,670	5,233	376	5
Dunn County	14,608	8,070	6,208	318	12
Eau Claire County	38,911	22,240	15,733	889	49
Florence County	1,963	865	1,079	19	0
Fond du Lac County	38,226	16,073	21,515	615	23
Forest County	3,614	1,853	1,712	48	1
Grant County	16,952	9,242	7,427	283	0
Green County	13,241	7,769	5,149	304	19
Green Lake County	7,986	3,122	4,714	144	6
Iowa County	9,047	5,630	3,267	145	5
Iron County	2,782	1,560	1,189	30	3
Jackson County	6,938	3,858	2,931	146	3
Jefferson County	30,965	14,247	16,038	640	40
Juneau County	8,289	3,969	4,101	181	38
Kenosha County	51,071	28,338	21,737	938	58
Kewaunee County	9,045	4,354	4,479	211	1
LaCrosse County	43,010	24,663	17,235	1,002	110
Lafayette County	5,846	3,344	2,405	91	6
Langlade County	8,591	4,184	4,276	126	5
Lincoln County	11,083	6,019	4,713	339	12
Manitowoc County	32,463	15,736	16,154	535	38
Marathon County	49,152	25,836	22,186	1,121	9
Marinette County	17,037	8,408	8,455	166	8

	Total Votes Cast	Jim Doyle/ Barbara Lawton (Dem)	Mark Green/ Jean Hundertmark (Rep)	Nelson Eisman/ Leon Todd (WGR)	Scattering
Marquette County	6,108	2,879	3,095	123	11
Menominee County	1,073	886	180	7	0
Milwaukee County	324,068	199,536	118,949	5,019	564
Monroe County	13,446	6,556	6,517	323	50
Oconto County	14,378	6,639	7,497	238	4
Oneida County	16,203	8,372	7,425	389	17
Outagamie County	69,737	34,901	33,511	1,284	41
Ozaukee County	41,274	15,229	25,460	542	43
Pepin County	2,921	1,627	1,256	38	0
Pierce County	14,157	7,829	6,034	284	10
Polk County	15,529	8,128	7,103	291	7
Portage County	28,845	17,754	10,206	858	27
Price County	6,412	3,581	2,737	91	3
Racine County	71,368	34,968	35,286	1,055	59
Richland County	6,413	3,489	2,814	100	10
Rock County	55,129	33,774	20,156	1,115	84
Rusk County	5,743	2,968	2,622	144	9
Sauk County	21,938	12,232	9,148	517	41
Sawyer County	6,283	3,218	2,965	100	0
Shawano County	15,677	7,236	8,227	208	6
Sheboygan County	47,397	21,388	25,257	714	38
St. Croix County	26,896	13,392	13,117	378	9
Taylor County	7,258	3,506	3,551	199	2
Trempealeau County	9,488	5,557	3,725	198	8
Vernon County	10,523	6,034	4,240	234	15
Vilas County	10,630	4,799	5,623	202	6
Walworth County	33,714	14,154	18,781	729	50
Washburn County	6,551	3,323	3,135	87	6
Washington County	53,325	17,219	35,262	803	41
Waukesha County	176,114	61,402	112,243	2,320	149
Waupaca County	19,380	8,767	10,296	307	10
Waushara County	8,926	4,155	4,590	170	11
Winnebago County	64,892	32,765	30,629	1,413	85
Wood County	29,559	16,043	12,711	779	26
	2,161,700	1,139,115	979,427	40,709	2,449

	Total Votes Cast	Yes	No
Adams County	7,883	5,142	2,741
Ashland County	5,958	3,566	2,392
Barron County	15,920	10,958	4,962
Bayfield County	7,142	4,132	3,010
Brown County	92,085	55,780	36,305
Buffalo County	5,349	3,428	1,921
Burnett County	6,104	4,418	1,686
Calumet County	19,324	13,338	5,986
Chippewa County	21,401	13,993	7,408
Clark County	11,173	7,737	3,436
Columbia County	21,889	13,023	8,866
Crawford County	6,407	3,980	2,427
Dane County	212,868	70,377	142,491
Dodge County	30,706	22,552	8,154
Door County	14,202	8,412	5,790
Douglas County	15,557	9,316	6,241
Dunn County	14,459	8,520	5,939
Eau Claire County	37,892	19,595	18,297
Florence County	1,996	1,515	481
Fond du Lac County	37,476	25,745	11,731
Forest County	3,587	2,407	1,180
Grant County	16,867	10,546	6,321
Green County	13,085	7,074	6,011
Green Lake County	7,901	5,850	2,051
Iowa County	8,977	4,553	4,424
Iron County	2,678	1,743	935
Jackson County	6,922	4,418	2,504
Jefferson County	30,605	19,918	10,687
Juneau County	8,342	5,717	2,625
Kenosha County	50,166	29,676	20,490
Kewaunee County	8,849	6,450	2,399
LaCrosse County	42,502	21,327	21,175
Lafayette County	5,773	3,624	2,149
Langlade County	8,580	5,856	2,724
Lincoln County	10,790	7,129	3,661
Manitowoc County	32,014	22,442	9,572
Marathon County	48,729	31,675	17,054
Marinette County	16,746	12,192	4,554
Marquette County	6,155	4,152	2,003
Menominee County	955	507	448
Milwaukee County	314,001	172,548	141,453

	Total Votes Cast	Yes	No
Monroe County	13,396	8,871	4,525
Oconto County	14,387	10,222	4,165
Oneida County	15,834	9,356	6,478
Outagamie County	68,480	42,849	25,631
Ozaukee County	40,830	25,914	14,916
Pepin County	2,995	2,106	889
Pierce County	14,023	8,350	5,673
Polk County	15,352	10,619	4,733
Portage County	28,694	15,409	13,285
Price County	6,203	3,944	2,259
Racine County	68,737	43,869	24,868
Richland County	6,393	3,939	2,454
Rock County	54,307	30,220	24,087
Rusk County	5,764	3,848	1,916
Sauk County	21,704	12,394	9,310
Sawyer County	6,327	4,245	2,082
Shawano County	15,612	11,333	4,279
Sheboygan County	46,803	32,908	13,895
St. Croix County	26,417	16,668	9,749
Taylor County	7,155	4,741	2,414
Trempealeau County	9,462	5,996	3,466
Vernon County	10,154	6,253	3,901
Vilas County	10,339	6,386	3,953
Walworth County	33,153	20,501	12,652
Washburn County	6,562	4,465	2,097
Washington County	52,563	38,759	13,804
Waukesha County	173,901	118,736	55,165
Waupaca County	19,091	13,281	5,810
Waushara County	9,001	6,168	2,833
Winnebago County	64,416	37,188	27,228
Wood County	29,164	19,441	9,723
	2,127,234	1,264,310	862,924

POLITICAL COMPOSITION OF THE
WISCONSIN LEGISLATURE
1885 – 2007

Legislative Session[1]	Senate							Assembly						
	D	R	P	S	SD	M[3]	Vacant	D	R	P	S	SD	M[4]	Vacant
1885	13	20	—	—	—	—	—	39	61	—	—	—	—	—
1887	6	25	—	—	—	2	—	30	57	—	—	—	13	—
1889	6	24	—	—	—	3	—	29	71	—	—	—	—	—
1891	19	14	—	—	—	—	—	66	33	—	—	—	1	—
1893	26	7	—	—	—	—	—	56	44	—	—	—	—	—
1895	13	20	—	—	—	—	—	19	81	—	—	—	—	—
1897	4	29	—	—	—	—	—	8	91	—	—	—	1	—
1899	2	31	—	—	—	—	—	19	81	—	—	—	—	—
1901	2	31	—	—	—	—	—	18	82	—	—	—	—	—
1903	3	30	—	—	—	—	—	25	75	—	—	—	—	—
1905	4	28	—	—	1	—	—	11	85	—	—	4	—	—
1907	5	27	—	—	1	—	—	19	76	—	—	5	—	—
1909	4	28	—	—	1	—	—	17	80	—	—	3	—	—
1911	4	27	—	—	2	—	—	29	59	—	—	12	—	—
1913	9	23	—	—	1	—	—	37	57	—	—	6	—	—
1915	11	21	—	—	1	—	—	29	63	—	—	8	—	—
1917	6	24	—	3	—	—	—	14	79	—	7	—	—	—
1919	2	27	—	4	—	—	—	5	79	—	16	—	—	—
1921	2	27	—	4	—	—	—	2	92	—	6	—	—	—
1923	—	30	—	3	—	—	—	1	89	—	10	—	—	—
1925	—	30	—	3	—	—	—	1	92	—	7	—	—	—
1927	—	31	—	2	—	—	—	3	89	—	8	—	—	—
1929	—	31	—	2	—	—	—	6	90	—	3	—	1	—
1931	1	30	—	2	—	—	—	2	89	—	9	—	—	—
1933	9	23	—	1	—	—	—	59	13	24	3	—	1	—
1935	13	6	14	—	—	—	—	35	17	45	3	—	—	—
1937	9	8	16	—	—	—	—	31	21	46	2	—	—	—
1939	6	16	11	—	—	—	—	15	53	32	—	—	—	—
1941	3	24	6	—	—	—	—	15	60	25	—	—	—	—
1943	4	23	6	—	—	—	—	14	73	13	—	—	—	—
1945	6	22	5	—	—	—	—	19	75	6	—	—	—	—
1947	5	27	1	—	—	—	—	11	88	—	—	—	—	1
1949	3	27	—	—	—	—	3	26	74	—	—	—	—	—
1951	7	26	—	—	—	—	—	24	75	—	—	—	—	1
1953	7	26	—	—	—	—	—	25	75	—	—	—	—	—
1955	8	24	—	—	—	—	1	36	64	—	—	—	—	—
1957	10	23	—	—	—	—	—	33	67	—	—	—	—	—
1959	12	20	—	—	—	—	1	55	45	—	—	—	—	—
1961	13	20	—	—	—	—	—	45	55	—	—	—	—	—
1963	11	22	—	—	—	—	—	46	53	—	—	—	—	1
1965	12	20	—	—	—	—	1	52	48	—	—	—	—	—
1967	12	21	—	—	—	—	—	47	53	—	—	—	—	—
1969	10	23	—	—	—	—	—	48	52	—	—	—	—	—
1971	12	20	—	—	—	—	1	67	33	—	—	—	—	—
1973	15	18	—	—	—	—	—	62	37	—	—	—	—	—
1975	18	13	—	—	—	—	2	63	36	—	—	—	—	—
1977	23	10	—	—	—	—	—	66	33	—	—	—	—	—
1979	21	10	—	—	—	—	2	60	39	—	—	—	—	—
1981	19	14	—	—	—	—	—	59	39	—	—	—	—	1
1983	17	14	—	—	—	—	2	59	40	—	—	—	—	—
1985	19	14	—	—	—	—	—	52	47	—	—	—	—	—
1987	19	11	—	—	—	—	3	54	45	—	—	—	—	—
1989	20	13	—	—	—	—	—	56	43	—	—	—	—	—
1991	19	14	—	—	—	—	—	58	41	—	—	—	—	—
1993[2] ...	15	15	—	—	—	—	3	52	47	—	—	—	—	—
1995[2] ...	16	17	—	—	—	—	—	48	51	—	—	—	—	—
1997[2] ...	17	16	—	—	—	—	—	47	52	—	—	—	—	—
1999	17	16	—	—	—	—	—	44	55	—	—	—	—	—
2001	18	15	—	—	—	—	—	43	56	—	—	—	—	—
2003	15	18	—	—	—	—	—	41	58	—	—	—	—	—
2005	14	19	—	—	—	—	—	39	60	—	—	—	—	—
2007	18	15	—	—	—	—	—	47	52	—	—	—	—	—

Note: The number of assembly districts was reduced from 100 to 99 beginning in 1973.

Key: Democrat (D); Progressive (P); Republican (R); Socialist (S); Social Democrat (SD); Miscellaneous (M).

[1]Political composition at inauguration.

[2]In the 1993, 1995, and 1997 Legislatures, majority control of the senate shifted during the session. On 4/20/93, vacancies were filled resulting in a total of 16 Democrats and 17 Republicans; on 6/16/96, there were 17 Democrats and 16 Republicans; and on 4/19/98, there were 16 Democrats and 17 Republicans.

[3]Miscellaneous = one Independent and one People's (1887); one Independent and 2 Union Labor (1889).

[4]Miscellaneous = 3 Independent, 4 Independent Democrat, and 6 People's (1887); one Union Labor (1891); one Fusion (1897); one Independent (1929); one Independent Republican (1933).

Sources: Pre-1943 data is taken from the Secretary of State, *Officers of Wisconsin: U.S., State, Judicial, Congressional, Legislative and County Officers,* 1943 and earlier editions, and the *Wisconsin Blue Book,* various editions. Later data compiled from Wisconsin Legislative Reference Bureau sources.

APPENDIX B
Methodological Essay

One of the things that made researching and writing this tale of Wisconsin's election history so rewarding was the methodological challenges that were involved. It is one thing to read widely about 150-plus years of Wisconsin history and draw information from it, and it is another to gather and employ the on-the-ground data that allowed me to address empirically my main focus: the story of voting in Wisconsin from 1848 to the present.

My indebtedness to others is real. I acknowledge it in the preface and throughout the book frequently, and it is as much a pleasure as it is a duty to do so. Several scholars' contributions were so substantial that they merit special consideration here. I relied on three scholars in particular, as my notes show, and to them I am extremely grateful.

The first is David Brye. His book *Wisconsin Voting Patterns in the Twentieth Century, 1900–1950,* was immensely valuable to me. While I regularly compared Brye's huge data presentations with my own, and thus rarely relied on his work alone, I found his data, his analyses, and his methodologies consistently of great use. For the period he covered, his work is a version of heaven for the Wisconsin election studies aficionado, and it represents a tremendous effort—valuable and illuminating—on Brye's part. He was also valuable to me because he did a magnificent job of retesting parts of Wyman's study (see below)—and confirming it—and carrying it on over many decades beyond the Progressive Era up to 1950. While 1950 is a long way from the early twenty-first century, Brye covered much ground, and he rooted his work in rigorous quantitative analysis. Though I went my own way too, I am grateful for Brye's splendid work.

The second is Leon Epstein. His *Politics in Wisconsin* along with a series of articles, sometimes coauthored with others, justly established him as the leading academic scholar and student of Wisconsin politics and voting behavior of the 1940s through the 1970s. Epstein's careful, thoughtful work is an integral source for much of my discussion of these decades. I also was influenced by Epstein's "size-of-place" discussion and analysis of Wisconsin voting (see below). Again and again his scholarship was an indispensable source for me in doing this project. He and I often discussed this project in person. In this regard, as in so many others, the recent death of this friend and generous patron was a major loss.

The third individual whose work was essential for my project was Roger E. Wyman, through his Ph.D. dissertation, a masterwork on its subject: "Voting Behavior in the Progressive Era: Wisconsin as a Case Study." I used Wyman's ethnic data work as a valuable source, as I also employed Brye's, in compiling my ethnic longitudinal study. Wyman considered numerous units in detail, as I did, and drew on specific studies of ethnicity in Wisconsin in the period of the late nineteenth and early twentieth century. His discussion of the methods he used to develop samples of particular units notable for their various ethnic concentrations is comprehensive and proved illuminating for me.[1] His work literally overflows with data, and while the period he covers is modest given the entire length of Wisconsin electoral history, it is impossible to imagine matching his superb command of the voting behavior of the period or learning more about it from anyone else.

Brye, Epstein, and Wyman did so much valuable detailed work that any subsequent scholar of Wisconsin voting behavior must acknowledge them with the considerable respect their work deserves. I drew on their work often.

While an important dimension of my work on this book was calling on the insightful efforts of scholars who preceded me, another was the contributions of a number of young student scholars over a period of a decade and more who did research that I sponsored and whose endeavors became a part of this book. Much of their youthful energy and help went into this book, and I am grateful for it. Their names and service appear not just in the preface and notes but sometimes in this Appendix, as they should.

1. The Election Data

My job was to collect election return data and lots of it. This was a time-consuming task. I gathered data on almost 600 separate units—towns, villages, cities—in Wisconsin for various purposes, as explained below in other parts of this Appendix. I gathered the data for most of these units starting from their various dates of legal creation for all presidential and gubernatorial elections from Wisconsin's birth as a state in 1848 through 2006 as well as for a number of key referenda in state history.

The source for election results I mostly used was the *Wisconsin Blue Books,* which almost from the state's beginning provided detailed electoral returns. There were (and continue to be) assorted blank spots there, which required me to explore the world of the Wisconsin Historical Society Archives. It has complete and detailed election reports from every county (and, usually, the units within each county) for every election from 1848 on. Among the lacunae that I had to fill were the detailed returns for the earliest years of the state, almost all referenda votes, and the detailed complete returns for a good many third party candidacies, such as Perot or Anderson, even in recent years. My source in the archives was *Election Return Statements of County Board of Canvassers, 1836–1982*. For more recent results I drew on the outstanding, detailed data of the State Board of Elections. In presenting data on overall state results, I normally included all votes. For all my voting samples, my standard was to include only candidates and parties that received 1 percent or more of the state vote. This judgment caused extra work because it required attention to a lot of minor candidates and parties, but not to use it would have eliminated too many interesting races and would have required me to adopt some other arbitrary standard.

At all times I did the best I could dealing with sometimes missing or obviously erroneous individual results, which sometimes happened for nineteenth-century election reports. The same was true in deciding whether or not to include a place if it was truly a city or a village, if that is what the given sample called for, as distinct from a same-named place listed as "town." I made judgment calls here.

Always my goal was to work from the smallest electoral unit possible. Therefore, I avoided almost completely county results. Of course one learns a lot more about voting behavior when one enters a county and explores the voting of its various particular voting units, its towns, villages, cities, and city precincts. Only then does one encounter the rich variety that inevitably lies beneath a county's overall returns.

Despite my attention to the smallest unit possible with (normally) consistent lines over time, of course I could not avoid ecological fallacy problems. I could not present data on individual voters and how they voted from one election to the next for the 1840s, 1940s, or the 2000s. No one can, as these data do not exist except in isolated instances. Following the example of Wyman and Brye and working with hundreds of mostly small voting units in Wisconsin and comparing their results over time, I could and did get a solid picture of the dimensions and complexities of Wisconsin voting behavior across more than 150 years. This knowledge and this picture underlie a good portion of this book's story.

2. Ethnic Data and Cultural Area Analysis

In constructing and employing samples of ethnic voting units—usually towns and villages—throughout Wisconsin's history, I was determined to work backwards from the most recent U.S. Census, 2000, which reported the claimed ethnic heritage of citizens in every Wisconsin legal locality. My goal was to identify places that were largely of one ethnic ancestry or another and compare them with the work others before me had done identifying such places. Where they were the same I constructed samples of various ethnic places that had not changed in terms of the ancestry of their residents. Doing so allowed me to trace with some confidence the unfolding history of the voting behavior of one ethnic group or another, at least in these locales.

In undertaking this I knew that the well-documented ethnic self-consciousness of the diverse white ethnic groups in Wisconsin's nineteenth and even twentieth centuries is hardly present, if at all, in the twenty-first century. Yet I hypothesized that in much of Wisconsin, while ethnic self-consciousness has dimmed, some cultural distinctiveness remains (whose often unrecognized roots lie in the ethnic history of the areas), and I would continue to find considerable voting solidarity even though its basis now was more cultural and traditional than self-consciously ethnic.

In pursuing this project regarding ethnicity and cultural cohesion in voting I was assisted by the stimulating, relevant discussion in H. S. Lewis's essay "European Ethnicity in Wisconsin: An Exploratory Formulation." And in a classic older form, there was the argument of demographer George Hill on the value of the culture area concept, "The Usage of the Culture-Area Concept in Social Research." A quite fascinating exploration of the concept of "group" in another Wisconsin context is in Lawrence Bobo and Mia Tuan, *Prejudice in Politics,* on consciousness in the recent dispute in Wisconsin over American Indian hunting and fishing rights. I also found valuable broader cultural area analyses that place Wisconsin as a whole and its political culture(s) in the larger picture of the United States. Daniel Elazar and John Fenton's classic arguments in this context are of continuing value in thinking about Wisconsin's ethnic history and diversity.[2] Important on the weakening power of ethnicity among white Euro-Americans are the reflections of Stanley Lieberson and Mary C. Waters in their *From Many Strands.*

The first step was to examine the 1990 and 2000 censuses to locate the places in Wisconsin with the highest concentrations of citizens of various ethnic ancestries. Avraham Fox began this process and pointed the way for me working from the 1990 census. But my major focus became the 2000 census. I used towns and village units because they provided the most consistently established boundaries over time (though there have been changes), unlike many cities that have undergone many boundary and ward line changes over the years. But as this study indicates, for example, by including Milwaukee throughout Wisconsin's history or highly German American or Norwegian American small cities, I also drew on ethnic dimensions present in some Wisconsin urban centers. And in my discussion of the new "ethnics," I plunged into urban area analysis in detail (see below).

In discussing the adventure of developing my ethnic samples, I am thankful for the large help of Clayton Nall, who opened many doors for me. Nall's political sense, passion, and energy, and, far from least, his skill in math and statistics, were of great assistance. He came into the project because of his interest in writing a paper on the Wisconsin senatorial election of 1998. I suggested that he should formulate a serious study of the results by studying ethnic patterns in the contemporary era. While I had begun doing so following the work of Brye and Wyman, Nall proceeded to study the ethnic ancestry data of the 1990 census, deriving from that an updated understanding of which areas of Wisconsin were the most German, Norwegian, etc. He paved the way for my own work on ethnicity and voting behavior in contemporary Wisconsin.

Nall contrived an ancestry index—what I call the Nall Index—on a 0-to-100 scale formed from a weighted average of responses to two ancestry questions on the 1990 census. The first question asked people to name a first ancestry or a sole ancestry; the second asked people to name a second ancestry for themselves. In his index Nall weighted the first ancestry response much heavier than the second, since we assumed it was the most important and also contained reports of the sole ancestry, which in the instance of Wisconsin is relevant since so many listed (and list) only German. Of course the weighting coefficients he developed were not scientific but an intuitive estimate. His index was $(4/3) \times 0.75$ (percent reporting a in the first ancestry response) $+0.25$ (percent reporting a in the second ancestry response) $\times 100$ where a was one of the possible ancestry responses.

I worked from Nall's base as I updated my ancestry samples with the 2000 census data. Working with my 2000 data and his 1990 data, I adjusted his towns and villages to be included in, say, the Norwegian sample by what had happened to the places in it in the intervening ten years. Sometimes a lot had changed. For one thing, ancestry identification had dropped over the ten years among every group. More and more Wisconsinites identify themselves as "other" or nothing. In some cases sharp population shifts rendered inclusion of a town or village no longer relevant in a category. In other cases units were and are included that might not meet the standards established for inclusion—which varied group to group and are described below—on the basis of what I would call tradition. That is, they were and are longtime, say, Swedish American areas but now are, to a large extent, also German areas, a common enough pattern given the consistent dilution of other ethnic groups by the large German American numbers in Wisconsin.

The easiest category to deal with, of course, was German. Wisconsin abounds with places that are overwhelmingly German in ancestry, scores of units where German Americans comprise more than 80 percent of the residents and vastly more if one goes just 5 or 10 percent lower. So it was and is no problem to come up with units that today are indisputably heavily German in ancestry. In fact, in most places in Wisconsin at least one-third of white residents are German in ancestry. In the case of the German units selected for the study, I made a concerted effort to connect them with a historic tradition of German American political behavior that others developed but that I replicated. In this instance it was not difficult to establish a historical continuity that in some cases went back 150 years.

Again, the claim here is not that there is self-conscious German American ethnic voting today (though certainly there was in the past as this book shows) but that cultural and political traditions were established in the past that have consequences in many German American communities today. Indeed, what is striking about the voting today in these communities is how much voting solidarity remains. Following are the German American ancestry places used in this study:

1. Traditionally Protestant (26 places)
   Buffalo County: Lincoln (town)
   Calumet County: Rantoul and Brillion
   Clark County: Fremont
   Dodge County: Herman, Hustisford, Iron Ridge (village), Lebanon, Lowell,
      Williamstown
   Fond du Lac County: Auburn, Eldorado
   Green Lake County: Manchester
   Lincoln County: Pine River
   Manitowoc County: Centerville, Kossuth, Rockland, Schleswig
   Marathon County: Fenwood (village), Frankfort, Hamburg
   Shawano County: Bonduel (village), Grant, Mattoon (village)
   Waupaca County: Dupont, Union

2. Traditionally Catholic (30 places)

    Ashland County: Chippewa (town)

    Calumet County: Brothertown, Charlestown, Chilton (city), Chilton,
       Hilbert (village), Stockbridge (village), Stockbridge, Woodville

    Dodge County: Leroy (town), Rubicon, Shields

    Fond du Lac County: Calumet, Forest, Marshfield, Mt. Calvary (village),
       St. Cloud (village)

    Grant County: Paris

    Manitowoc County: Eaton, St. Nazianz

    Marathon County: Day

    Sauk County: Franklin, Plain (village), Westfield

    Sheboygan County: Russell

    Washington County: Addison

    Wood County: Auburndale, Hewitt (village), Marshfield (city)

In addition to the German samples, I also used the following ethic origins samples for the period from their respective beginnings in Wisconsin to the contemporary period: Belgian, Dutch, Norwegian, Polish, and Swedish. As I explain, the choices I made sought to maximize the use of those places where there were the largest numbers of citizens claiming ancestry in the relevant group with, as sometimes noted, a bow to places of traditional culture. In every case I judged where to draw the line and which places to include, and it is with this in mind that I list in each case the places used in each sample.

Given the large number of Poles and Norwegians who came to Wisconsin from their homelands, it is not surprising that it is still possible to discover in Wisconsin places of high concentration of citizens with these ancestries, and thus it is possible to construct samples of robust numbers of places whose residents are 50 percent or more either Norwegian or Polish in ancestry, only working with towns and villages. Milwaukee and other cities around Milwaukee have considerable Polish American populations, but none anywhere near 50 percent. A future project should explore the areas of Milwaukee that are still largely Polish and connect them with the city's precincts and voting results. Yet the matter of how Polish any place is is relative. The town of Sharon in Portage County is the most Polish American location (of more than 1,000 people) not just in Wisconsin but in the nation, but it is still "only" 63.5 percent Polish American according to the 2000 census.[3] Still, Sharon is far from alone in Wisconsin as a place at least 50 percent Polish in ancestry. I used fourteen places in my Polish sample:

Clark County: Withee (town)
Marathon County: Bevent, Franzen, Hatley (village), Reid
Portage County: Alban, Dewey, Rosholt (village), Sharon, Stockton
Taylor County: Lubin (village)
Trempealeau County: Burnside, Dodge, Independence (city)

The number of locations with large Norwegian American populations is significant, especially in Trempealeau and Vernon counties, including the center of Wisconsin Norwegian ethnicity today, the City of Westby in Vernon County. Once again, my goal was to include those places with the greatest percent of citizens claiming Norwegian ancestry, 50 percent or more. The units in my sample of Norwegian American places in Wisconsin number twenty-seven:

Dunn County: Colfax (village), Sand Creek
Jackson County: Curran, Franklin, Northfield, Taylor (village)
Lafayette County: Blanchard
Trempealeau County: Albion, Blair (city), Eleva (village), Ettrick (village),
    Ettrick, Osseo, Pigeon, Pigeon Falls (village), Preston, Strum (village),
    Sumner, Unity
Vernon County: Christiana, Coon, Coon Valley (village), Franklin, Jefferson,
    Viroqua (village), Viroqua, Westby (city)

In the units I used for my Norwegian and Polish samples, not every unit included met the 50 percent or more standard, though most did. I also selected some places still relatively high in numbers of Norwegian- or Polish-ancestry citizens because of their traditional links to these ethnic origins. I did so only very skeptically and cautiously, always with an eye to current ethnic composition. Thus, for example, "Norwegian" Stoughton in Dane County was not included. It clearly promotes itself as a Norwegian cultural area, but its actual percentage of Norwegian-ancestry citizens is getting lower by the day as the city increasingly becomes a suburb of Madison. In this instance and others I made a judgment call.

In the situation of the other ethnic groups I discuss, and for which I selected a sample for use in the contemporary period as well as the past, it was possible to locate some places with a population greater than 50 percent in the relevant ethnicity, but some of the units included did not meet this test. These samples were regularly composed of the places with the highest percentage of the group, but that did not necessarily mean all of them were

50 percent or more. This was the mixture with my small (seven places) Dutch Protestant sample.

Sheboygan County: Cedar Grove (village), Holland, Oostburg (village)
Fond du Lac County: Alto
Columbia County: Friesland (village), Randolph (village), Randolph

I applied the same criteria to my small Belgian sample, where, again, some locales—for example, Red River in Kewaunee County—still exist where more than 50 percent of the residents identify themselves as of Belgian origin. I used five places in my Belgian ancestry sample.

Door County: Brussels, Union
Kewaunee County: Casco (village), Lincoln, Red River

Overall, my limits for inclusion were strict. I did not construct any samples for the contemporary period for ethnic groups that, despite their historical traditions, were no longer at least 50 percent concentrated in any one place, except as noted below. Thus while discussion of Czech voting behavior in the past was quite possible, it is no longer given that group's geographic dispersal. The same is now true for those of Irish background. While fully 11 percent of the Wisconsin population identifies themselves as Irish, no small percentage and one that may not be casually ignored, Irish Americans are now so thoroughly integrated into the general population that few places in the state have much more than 10 percent of their population of Irish descent, never mind 50 percent. Thus it is no longer possible to get any read on "Irish American voting" absent poll data, which we lack.

A challenging case for the contemporary period is that of Swedish-ancestry areas. The long tradition of geographically concentrated Swedes in Wisconsin has changed, and ended. It is just not possible now to locate places in Wisconsin where Swedish-ancestry citizens dominate, even in such locales as the village of Scandinavia. Nonetheless, I went ahead and selected for a sample those places where there are the greatest percentage of people who claimed Swedish ancestry—rarely more than 30 percent of the population—in the 2000 census and factored them by some of the towns and villages in Wisconsin most traditionally "Swedish" and thus likely to be something of a plausible Swedish cultural area. Arguably, this was not of much value in gaining insight into the current voting preferences of nonurban voters of Swedish ancestry. This justifiable basis for skepticism is accentuated by the fact that most of these places today have more citizens who identify as being of German ancestry than Swedish. And it is true enough that there is nothing particularly distinct today about the voting behavior of the eleven places in my "Swedish" sample. Thus it is probably time—or past time—to retire this ethnic category in contemplating current voting behavior in Wisconsin.

Bayfield County: Port Wing (town)
Burnett County: Anderson, Daniels, Grantsburg (village), Trade Lake,
    Wood River
Pepin County: Stockholm
Polk County: Lake (town), West Sweden
Price County: Hill, Ogema

What is true in the case of every one of the ancestry samples, to be sure, is that the membership of every unit needs to be checked not only as each census comes out but also in terms of the case for its membership in the less rigorous, cultural sense. Thus, for example, the flooding of Calumet County with residents of Appleton and its suburbs and exurbs is transforming many once ethnically and religiously cohesive German American areas and may make their use for purposes similar to mine suspect.

To this point my discussion has focused on how I proceeded in the relatively contemporary situation. However, I used my samples for the entire period of my study. This was possible for two reasons. Again and again when ethnic groups migrated to Wisconsin they tended to settle geographically with fellow nationals (often, in fact, with people from their own region in a country), allowing for ethnic-based discussions of various places in Wisconsin from the start of its voting history. Not only reputational data but also Wisconsin census data, especially the state census of 1905 and some state and federal censuses prior to 1905 (but not after), provided ethic data of all sorts, including nation or place of birth and, often, of parents' birth. It was on this good, invaluable data that previous scholars worked. I depended on their work often in my analysis of individual electoral units among the towns and villages of Wisconsin in the past to achieve my patterns of longitudinal history and behavior.

The scholarship of Brye and Wyman was essential for me here. The amount and quality of their work in isolating places in Wisconsin in their periods that were ethnically homogeneous made a great difference as I set up and employed my ancestry samples. I wanted to employ places in my samples that could be looked at over the course of Wisconsin history, and these scholars' previous work on numerous locations greatly assisted me in this goal. Brye had a great challenge, since he did not have extensive ethnic data that he could count on after the Progressive Era even though he told his story up to 1950, but he made skillful use of what he had, to impressive effect. I used some other useful presentations and discussions of ethnicity in Wisconsin apart from election studies; by far the best of these was the wonderful *Atlas of Ethnic Diversity in Wisconsin* by Kazimierz J. Zaniewski and Carol J. Rosen, who worked with 1990 census data.

I conclude this section by noting again that by looking at selected European group ancestry voting behavior in various locations, I am not arguing that in the present-day they are manifestations of self-conscious ethnic voting, unlike what was so often true in Wisconsin's past. I return to my suggestion that there is a cultural area factor in voting, one that is most obvious in many communities originally founded by one or another ethnic group and still, to a large or small extent, occupied by descendents of those communities.[4]

To put it another way, this study amply demonstrates that plenty of cultural and even issue divides in Wisconsin explain much of the state's ethnic voting in the past. Some of that persists today, an example being African American voting solidarity, but among whites it is almost entirely gone. But what Brye acutely identifies as the "persistence" of the ethnic quality of a place remains a powerful reality, and it is this cultural phenomenon that is so often reflected in rural and small village voting locations in Wisconsin until today. There is nothing self-consciously ethnic about it, but traditions exist and matter, and so often in Wisconsin their roots are firmly ethnic, reminiscent of previous generations.[5]

3. THE "NEW ETHNICS"

Although my discussion of the African American and emerging Hispanic populations in Wisconsin in chapter 9 notes their relatively modest numbers in what is still a very white state, there is no question that the numbers of the "new ethnics" have grown in recent decades. They are now a definite part of the population mix of the state. As a consequence, I had to develop a profile of African American voting behavior especially, but Hispanic as well, insofar as was possible. I also noted American Indian voting, at least in the three most concentrated political units in Wisconsin, Menominee County, which was created in 1961 as a legal county for the Menominee tribe, and the towns of Russell in Bayfield County and Sanborn in Ashland County, homes for the Chippewa. More needs to be done to investigate American Indian voting in other areas of the state.

This task began with the research efforts of Robert Yablon nearly a decade ago. Yablon started the challenge by studying Milwaukee census data, the purpose being to correlate detailed census units from the 1990 census with the particular city voting precincts as they existed then to find precincts largely occupied by African Americans. This was no easy project, but Yablon was successful with it, and I am very grateful to him for showing me the way. His work was my model in repeating the process for subsequent elections, endless precinct redrawings by the city, in both earlier and later censuses. While at times a frustrating and complicated task, this allowed me to make highly plausible estimates of African American voting behavior in Milwaukee for many elections. I was aided in determining African American voting in Milwaukee in the 1930s by the work by of Keith R. Schmitz, "Milwaukee and Its Black Community, 1930–1942." After 2000 I added African American precincts in Racine to broaden my sample, though the results have been about the same in both cities. A list of which precincts I employed in which decade are available on request. For the 2006 election I used the following sample precincts: in Milwaukee 17–19, 104, 106, 111–112, 116, 121–123, 173–177, 188; in Racine 4 and 11.

More difficult is the search for a substantial picture of Hispanic voting behavior in Wisconsin. The numbers of such voters are undoubtedly small, far less than 1 percent of the electorate, but they are bound to grow as more and more Hispanics enter the state and more become citizens. The problem is not locating the areas of Milwaukee in which most Hispanics reside; census data make this inexactly possible. The problem is attempting to separate Hispanics who do also identify themselves as African Americans from the large majority who do not. In any case, study of voting in Hispanic areas makes clear that this group's voting behavior is roughly discernable and need not be simply conflated with neighboring African American areas or precincts. My expectation is that as the number of involved Hispanics grows both in Milwaukee and the rest of Wisconsin, sophistication will grow in discerning Hispanic voting behavior, something I will welcome. Again, the precincts I used varied with Milwaukee's several contemporary redistricting plans; these are available for each recent election on request. For 2006 I used precincts 204–209 in Aldermanic District 8 of the City of Milwaukee, which was the best I could do. Again, this topic is one that requires more work, for example, to locate Hispanic areas outside of Milwaukee where their votes dominate—or will come to dominate as the number of Hispanic voters grows.

One feature of the results of the 2000 census that got a lot of publicity was the rise in the number of U.S. citizens who simply listed their ethnic heritage as "American," up 58 percent from the 1990 census to approximately 20 million people. While still a modest part of the population, this group is no longer insignificant. Its rise reflects the waning European connections as well as the continuing and substantial intermarriage patterns in the United States.[6] My study of the 2000 ethnic census for Wisconsin, however, did not find such a corresponding major rise in the still-modest numbers of citizens who identify themselves simply as Americans. Awareness of people's ethnic origins remains high in Wisconsin.

4. DIFFERENT TYPES OF UNITS IN WISCONSIN AND THE SIZE-OF-PLACE ANALYSIS

I decided that it would be interesting to see if there was any difference in any year and over the years in the average vote margins of a sample of towns, villages, and various types of cities. As the text makes clear, there often was, and it turned out to be valuable to explore this size-of-place dimension of voting.

Leon Epstein was a pioneer in size-of-place analysis. In his work, Epstein explored whether size of place mattered in Wisconsin voting by looking at the governors' races from 1948 through 1954 and the 1957 U.S. Senate race in particular. The basic hypothesis that he developed and confirmed was that the larger the place the more likely it was to vote Democratic, and vice versa, all other things being equal. He noted that the largest cities in the state were decidedly more Democratic, medium-sized cities fell in between, and small cities were distinctly more Republican. Epstein tested to see what variables other than size might explain this pattern. He particularly explored whether the percentage of the local work force employed in manufacturing might be the key and found that it was not.

Size of place seemed to matter on its own. The relevant question was why size of place seemed to be something of an independent variable. Epstein's eventual argument was that smaller cities were much more likely to have absorbed the electoral tradition of Wisconsin in the 1940s and 1950s; that is, they were Republican. Smaller cities were rarely growth areas and were much more a part of the rural and small-town Wisconsin around them. Larger cities, however, and especially the largest, Milwaukee and Madison, had many more residents who had broken away from this world—or had come from outside Wisconsin—and had other values and other loyalties.

The work of David Adamany confirmed Epstein's size-of-place analysis for the late 1950s and early 1960s, drawing a picture of voting in Wisconsin as more Democratic as size of place increased. He underlined what Epstein had already noted, that the size-of-place interpretation did not seem to work in genuinely rural or farm areas because there voting behavior could be quite volatile. He also agreed with Epstein's theory that small cities were so much more likely to be Republican because their residents often embodied the culture and values of the frequently Republican countryside.

There is a considerable literature now on "place" as an independent variable. It takes seriously the impact of the traditions and ethos of particular locations and the effects they may have on all sorts of dimensions of life.[7] It is a variable that is sometimes hard to explain in a tight social science fashion, but at times it is easy enough to show its presence distinct from other variables such as income, religion, or ethnicity in contemporary Wisconsin voting behavior. One should note, though, that it is hardly just small places that reinforce local norms. Even in big places there are many small communities, ones that often have their own powerful norms. Moreover, an atmosphere undoubtedly exists that is culturally enforcing in many bigger cities. Its hold may not be as tight as that in a small town, but in its own way it can be just as central and have just as strong an impact. Thus only focusing on the reality that many or most small towns in Wisconsin have a value set benefiting Republicans should not lead an analyst to overlook the values dominant and reinforced in the liberal culture of Shorewood Hills, Madison, or central city Milwaukee to the benefit of the Democrats.

It is certainly appropriate to ask whether considering size of place is relevant to contemporary Wisconsin electoral analysis. In 2006 Epstein argued with me that the thesis was no longer of much use. One hypothesis about place today is that it is the particular place itself that matters, not its size, appreciating that every place has its specific traditions and culture that inevitably affect local voting behavior. It is difficult to measure variations in what one might term "senses of place," but the factor deserves study and analysis since it undoubtedly does help illuminate the voting behavior of various localities. In the case of Wisconsin, any reasonably informed observer who knows where a voter lives and has any sense of its local culture and traditions can predict with some accuracy that person's electoral behavior. Thus size-of-place analysis, while not necessarily explaining any locale's voting behavior, remains worth studying regarding Wisconsin voting. For example, it is relevant to know that the small cities in Wisconsin continue to be relative bastions of conservative and Republican strength, much more so than larger cities. We know this has long been true; it was the situation, for example, even in the Progressive and Democratic 1930s in Wisconsin when this pattern was well-established and reported by others.[8] However, Wisconsin's villages currently are considerably more Democratic in their voting habits than either small cities (or rural areas), which a strict size-of-place analysis would not predict. While a few villages are actually larger than some small cities, most are quite small in population. This phenomenon may be age-related, as villages are often the place where many rural folks retire, and such retired people tend to have a heightened dependence on government support, from Social Security to Medicare. Such citizens, the argument goes, are more likely to vote for the Democratic Party.

In any case, for this study I developed and employed measures for size-of-place analysis from 1848 to the present, and this is why the text so often employs these categories in discussing Wisconsin's electoral history. Thirty-three towns (often called "townships" in other states) made up my sample, intended to be an unscientific representative sample of the nearly 1,300 towns in Wisconsin today. My test of representativeness was to include a range of towns in terms of population and especially location in the state.

Alamena: Barron County
Caledonia: Waupaca County
Campbell: La Crosse County
Clyde: Iowa County
East Troy: Walworth County
Eastman: Crawford County
Edgewater: Sawyer County
Eisenstein: Price County
Excelsior: Sauk County
Finley: Juneau County
Fredonia: Ozaukee County
Garfield: Polk County
Glendale: Monroe County
Hamburg: Vernon County
Howard: Chippewa County
Johnson: Marathon County
Jordan: Green County
Lake Tomahawk: Oneida County
La Prairie: Rock County
Lima: Grant County
Meeme: Manitowoc County
Mountain (formerly Armstrong): Oconto County
New Chester: Adams County

Neva: Langlade County
Pence: Iron County
Peru: Dunn County
Pilson: Barron County
Rushford: Winnebago County
Summit: Douglas County
Trade Lake: Burnett County
Trego: Washburn County
Unity: Trempealeau County
Worden: Clark County

Villages were mostly a phenomenon that appeared in and then expanded greatly in numbers in the twentieth century. In fact, there were few legally incorporated villages in the nineteenth century. The following thirty-one villages made up my unscientific representative sample of the approximately 400 villages in Wisconsin today.

Almond: Portage County
Auburndale: Wood County
Barneveld: Iowa County
Big Falls: Waupaca County
Bloomington: Grant County
Brokaw: Marathon County
Butternut: Ashland County
Cashton: Monroe County
Coleman: Marinette County
Cottage Grove: Dane County
Deer Park: St. Croix County
Downing: Dunn County
Eleva: Trempealeau County
Elmwood: Pierce County
Fenwood: Marathon County
Gilman: Taylor County
Hewitt: Wood County
Johnson Creek: Jefferson County
Lannon: Waukesha County
Maiden Rock: Pierce County
Milltown: Polk County
Neshkoro: Marquette County

Oliver: Douglas County
Plainfield: Waushara County
Random Lake: Sheboygan County
Rosendale: Fond du Lac County
Siren: Burnett County
Stratford: Marathon County
Union Center: Juneau County
West Milwaukee: Milwaukee County
Winneconne: Winnebago County

It was the city unit that produced the largest and the most varying set of categories over time. I followed Wisconsin law and employed the distinctions it provides among kinds of cities. For example, the 2005–6 *Blue Book* reports the current situation, four official classes of cities: first-class is 150,000 or more citizens; second-class is 39,000–149,999; third-class is 10,000–38,999; and fourth-class is less than 10,000. The idea was to acknowledge the substantial population differences among Wisconsin cities and to assess whether there were any corresponding differences in their voting behavior. However, the categories among cities of today were, as one would realize, not always the same as in the past, nor did where a city was in the various categories necessarily stay constant over time.

Moreover, the number of cities, especially in recent decades, in several classes, but especially the fourth-class (145 currently), required unscientific but roughly representative sampling on my part. Finally, my method in the 1848–90 era, when the "modern" fourfold classification scheme did not effectively exist, led me to use a generic classification of "city" and to use as my cities ones that in the 1990 census were second-class cities (if they existed as cities in the nineteenth century). In practice, this meant I used all the larger cities of Wisconsin as my database for this period. Exactly which cities I used for each ten-year period of elections after 1890 varied by their population and the population specified by law for the several classes of cities. The exact cities in each category in each decade that were employed would take pages to list, but they are available on request. For the 2000 election and subsequent elections, I used the following cities by category:

First class: Milwaukee, Madison
Second class (14): Appleton, Brookfield, Eau Claire, Fond du Lac, Green Bay, Janesville, Kenosha, La Crosse, Oshkosh, Racine, Sheboygan, Superior, Wauwatosa, West Allis

Third class (11): Beloit, DePere, Greenfield, Kaukauma, Marinette, Menasha,
    Neenah, Stevens Point, Waukesha, West Bend, Wisconsin Rapids
Fourth class (19): Altoona, Arcadia, Bloomer, Columbus, Elroy, Gillett, Hurley,
    Ladysmith, Marion, Mayville, Park Falls, Platteville, Rhinelander, Rice Lake,
    Richland Center, Shawano, Sturgeon Bay, Thorp, Washburn

5. ECONOMIC MEASURES

Another problematic realm for my project, one that challenged me over and
over, was addressing what was and is a major gap in much of the electoral
analysis of Wisconsin history: the frequent absence of economic data and
analysis that would allow one to reflect on economic and class factors as an
element in voting behavior. Wyman and, to the extent he could, Brye used
available census data to explore class dimensions of voting. From the late
nineteenth through the early twentieth century, information was available,
though it was no simple task to mobilize it for use. For other periods, however, data were skimpy, and thus discussion of class factors in voting is often
speculative. I knew there was a lot of work to be done in this area, and I did
what I could, though much more needs to be done.

It is best to break down the challenge into several parts, reflecting different historical eras. For the period after 1980 I made use of census data from
the 1980, 1990, and 2000 (actually the years previous) on median income
data. These data are available for every governmental unit in the State of
Wisconsin. This allowed me to do serious comparison of voting behavior in
small units in Wisconsin with income patterns, providing plenty of valuable
data. Within cities data did not come ward by ward but for the whole city,
which presented some problems. That proved to be less of a challenge than it
might have been, because where I wanted more detailed analysis, dedicated
student researchers worked the census unit data with ward data. An example
would be Tom O'Day's perceptive study of the City of Waukesha, "Voting
Pattern and Census Data in the City of Waukesha."

My decision to use median household income as my economic class measure was a judgment call. The income data alternatives were median family
income and mean income. Median family income, in my view, left out too
many people and places, and mean income allowed for some wild distor-
tions depending on income distribution. I found that median household
income portrayed more accurately the state's bell-shaped income distribution. I make no claim that there is a perfect measure to gain a sense of a
place's economic status. But I found median household income usually cap-
tures the economic realities of a location quite well. It is also often close to

median family income, though Wisconsin college towns, where the median household income is much lower than median family income, are a prominent exception.

Once one leaves the 1980 and later censuses, however, and turns to the decades before then but well after 1905, the real problems begin. Census data for some places exist in earlier census reports (for example, the 1970 census) but not the comprehensive data required for comparability. At first I was not certain what to do. The creative and innovative approach I considered for the bulk of the twentieth century before 1980 was formulated by Christopher Chapp and Eric Mussak. In the absence of suitable income data to work with, they attempted to construct an image of a locality's relative economic health by means of other data. What they proposed to do was use data on the reported (for tax purposes) personal and real property in each locality in my representative sample from 1910 on. With these data I then ranked each locale for each decade in terms of its reported affluence.

This measure was and is obviously inexact as a guide to class standing among locations in Wisconsin due to such limitations as putatively different standards of valuation from place to place. To acknowledge the inevitable inexactness and avoid the fallacy of misplaced concreteness, I divided my sample into quintiles. In the process there was no escape from making a judgment call as to where to draw the lines between quintiles for every decade. They could not be drawn purely by numerical fifths, given the ranges in data. The result often did give a decent idea of the relative economic standing of the sample units, or at least one in accord with my reputational knowledge. Applying this test decade by decade, I sometimes found some connection between the relative economic vitality of an area and its voting behavior. Mostly I did not, however. It would be comforting to argue that this was merely a confirmation of what others have found and/or argued, that class or economic standing have rarely proven to be a good guide to Wisconsin voting behavior. But I know I cannot, and I concluded that the measure—ingenious in conception—in my hands did not work.

Not just more income or economic information for earlier and contemporary decades would have aided me in probing class and Wisconsin voting. Certainly it would have been valuable to have employed detailed occupational and educational data for my representative sample, as I did with median household income.

In fact, I did try to use both occupational and educational data to measure locations' relative class standing for elections in the twenty-first century, both for my representative sample and for the suburbs of Milwaukee units.

The data allowing this exists in the 2000 census. For my representative sample, there were no findings of any interest, no correlations of any significance at .05 level, though the use of more precise data regarding occupations might have had more interesting results. The one occupational measure I was especially interested in, percent of workforce employed by the government, a measure that national polls have shown to be associated with Democratic voting, did not yield that result in my representative sample. It did, however, yield a definite positive association with Democratic voting in the Milwaukee suburb sample (2000: .487; 2004: .530; 2006: .511). The educational measures allowed testing by the relative percents in various places with populations who (1) had a high school degree or better; (2) a bachelor's degree or better; and (3) higher than a bachelor's degree. I found few associations with any of these measures except very low positive correlations between high school and better educational attainment and Republican voting, and the reverse for Democratic voting (at .28 for 2004 and 2006). I did not expect to find much with any of these measures, however, as Wisconsin voting behavior simply cannot be grasped by conventional measures of class.

Other scholars have done pieces of economic analysis and reconstruction, attacking the problem from other angles. For example, for his study of the farm vote for governors in the late 1940s and earlier 1950s, Leon Epstein gathered data on the average value per acre of farm lands and buildings for 1,077 farm townships, enabling him to discuss class aspects of farm voting for this period. But this is a rare exception, as few others have ventured to do similar studies of Wisconsin farm townships or any other places.

For the later nineteenth century and very early twentieth century, I sometimes could cite 1905 Wisconsin data, drawing liberally on the use of that data and some other census data that Roger Wyman and David Brye variously employed. A most important data source was farm income information carefully reported in the 1905 census, a data source that covered well most of largely rural Wisconsin. Roger Wyman offers an excellent discussion of the entire issue of use of average farm value and average farm income as a measure of class and in regard to his extensive work on the 1905 census that bears study. For urban areas he employed a measure of class that focused on occupational data from the 1905 census. Here, as elsewhere, it is easy for me to acknowledge how much I learned from Wyman's previous research in his Progressive Era study.[9]

Despite Wyman's and Brye's scholarship, gaps remain, and it is an almost insurmountable task to fill them. This is especially true regarding the nineteenth century before the 1890s and with much of the middle decades of the twentieth century. While earlier censuses do report estimated values for land, farm products, and farm equipment, the huge project of compiling this data in a systematic fashion remains undone. For example, the U.S. Census for 1870 cites both the value of the real estate and the personal estate of all adult male citizens but provides neither totals for any unit nor any median, modal, or mean data for any locality. To explore class analysis seriously in such a circumstance would require completing such work. While it is often said, accurately enough, that ethnicity is a far better guide than anything else to Wisconsin voting behavior in 1870 (and many other times), having actual economic data to correlate with voting behavior remains essential, not least if one wants to test (or undergird) claims of ethnic-religious correlations. And systematically formulated data to explore class for much of the second half of the nineteenth century in Wisconsin are missing, though there are a few exceptions, which I cite in the text.

Nevertheless, we do have some good economic information for today and for recent decades through the census-based median household income data. This is a revealing source of information, and my application of it suggests that we should be skeptical of any assertions that economic standing is a very good guide to the voting behavior of the myriad parts and places of Wisconsin.

6. THE RELIGIOUS ANALYSIS

There is a certain frustration that in our era there is an unmistakable rise of a white Christian evangelical piety that often translates into Republican voting and a parallel growth of a secular mindset that often translates into Democratic voting but no systematic way to track the locations of people of either disposition beyond reputational analysis. At least there was no means to do so for this study. Wisconsin is not a stronghold of white fundamentalist and evangelical Christianity, at least in comparison with many other states. This fact mitigates our ignorance only somewhat, and it cannot be overcome by drawing on general or even, say, county-specific statements about the relative presence of one or another kind of church. This information is too general for my purposes. Moreover, denominationalism is not a guide to conservative or liberal religion and politics today. Nor would such information assist in locating the rising number of secular people.

To be sure, we know some things: Catholic areas are hardly the centers of evangelical politics today; African American areas have many evangelicals, but their politics goes in a different (Democratic) direction from most white evangelicals. Still, most of Wisconsin remains uncharted regarding where evangelicalism is its strongest. The same is largely true regarding secular citizens, though we know that where there are large numbers of young urban professionals or university-affiliated persons or Jewish Americans, we find heartlands of secularism. We badly need a census of religious commitments and a Census Bureau bold enough to undertake it.[10] What we do have is something of a guide to where social liberalism and social conservatism flourish—not to be quickly conflated with a discussion of religion and voting behavior—in the outcomes of the 2006 referendum on marriage, which I discuss at length in chapter 9.

The matter of religious influences in politics and voting cannot be tapped any longer by standard reports of the preferences of Protestants or Catholics, information that once was central to understanding Wisconsin voting behavior. The information about where Catholics and Protestants lived, which was necessary for so many of my historical discussions, is straightforward. In many cases it started with known histories of various locations and the ethnic origins of settlers there. It was sometimes supplemented by documented study, such as the religious census of 1926. It was confirmed in good part by such classics of religion-based voting as the 1928 presidential vote or the 1946 vote on allowing public financing of bus transportation to parochial schools. Rarely was the basis precise, but there are no known instances where it has proven weak. Belgian-settled areas were Catholic and remained so; Polish-settled areas were Catholic and remained so. Granted, there were more complex situations, the classic being in German American areas that had both their Catholic and their Lutheran churches in town, sometimes right across the street from each other. But in general there was little problem in separating Protestant from Catholic when that distinction mattered. But the days when Protestant and Catholic mattered so much in comprehending Wisconsin voting behavior are over. There are new divisions, which are sometimes rooted in America's religious diversity, though our ability to define these differences and their electoral impact in specific local areas is sadly limited.

7. The Representative Sample and the Correlation Data Discussion

In discussing my overall representative sample as well as my general correlation procedures, let me note from the start that all my correlations are Pearson's correlations, r^2, and are at .05 level of significance, unless otherwise noted.

I wanted to develop a representative sample of Wisconsin voting units that I defined as Wisconsin towns, villages, and sometimes cities to get some quantitative perspective on my hypotheses regarding a range of periods in my history. This was especially the case for the Civil War period through the 1880s and from 1950 to the present, where it was most needed.

My representative sample is not a scientific sample or a technically random sample, nor was this my intention. Given the size of the potential number of voting units at my level in Wisconsin—at the start of the twenty-first century there are 190 cities, 402 villages, 1,259 towns—I do not make the claim that my sample is somehow comprehensive. However, given the demands of electoral, ethnic, and economic data collection for any sample covering from 1848 to the present, my sample of 172 units was by no means small. It allowed me to argue that any correlations—when all 172 units were present—had significance at about .140. As always indicated in the text notes, when there were fewer units involved, as in early in the nineteenth century, the standards for significance were higher.

What mattered to me was my sample's putative representativeness, which I defined as (1) the inclusion of a good range of towns, villages, and cities (of differing sizes) and (2) their balanced dispersal over the many geographic areas and regions of Wisconsin. In this quest I selected places largely randomly. Included in the sample are ninety-five towns, thirty-three villages, and forty-four cities, listed by county.

Adams County: Adams, Colburn
Ashland County: Ashland (city), Peeksville
Barron County: Prairie Farm (village), Crystal Lake
Bayfield County: Kelly, Washburn
Brown County: Green Bay (city), Denmark (village), Wrightstown (village)
Buffalo County: Montana, Buffalo
Burnett County: La Follette
Calumet County: Brillion, Chilton, Sherwood (village)
Chippewa County: Chippewa Falls (city), Howard
Clark County: Greenwood (city), Loyal, Thorp (first as a village, then as a city)
Columbia County: Cambria (village), Pardeeville (city), Portage (city)
Crawford County: De Soto (village)
Dane County: Black Earth (village), Blue Mounds (village), Madison (city), Christiana
Dodge County: Ashippun, Chester, Fox Lake (first as a village, then as a city)
Door County: Sturgeon Bay (city)
Douglas County: Superior (city)
Dunn County: Hay River, Ridgeland (village)

Eau Claire County: Eau Claire (city), Fairchild, Fall Creek (village), Otter Creek, Pleasant Valley

Florence County: Fern

Fond du Lac County: Eden, Waupun

Forest County: Crandon, Popple River

Grant County: Fennimore (first as a village, then as a city), Potosi

Green County: Monticello (village), Monroe (city)

Green Lake County: Green Lake, Green Lake (first as a village, then as a city), Princeton (village, city)

Iowa County: Cobb (village), Mineral Point (city)

Iron County: Mercer

Jackson County: Hixton, Irving

Jefferson County: Fort Atkinson (city), Jefferson (city)

Juneau County: Lindina, New Lisbon (first as a village, then as a city), Seven Mile Creek

Kenosha County: Kenosha (city) Paddock Lake (village), Salem

Kewaunee County: Casco

La Crosse County: Greenfield, Medary

Lafayette County: Elk Grove, Monticello

Langlade County: Antigo (city), Neva, Price

Lincoln County: Scott

Manitowoc County: Centerville, Manitowoc Rapids, Two Rivers (city)

Marathon County: Hamburg, Norrie, Ringle, Wausau (city)

Marinette County: Amberg, Stephenson

Marquette County: Endeavor (village), Mecan, Oxford

Milwaukee County: Cudahy (village, city), Greenfield (city), Hales Corners (village), Milwaukee (city), South Milwaukee (city), West Allis (city)

Monroe County: Lafayette, Ridgeville

Oconto County: Maple Valley, Riverview

Oneida County: Newbold, Rhinelander, Sugar Camp

Outagamie County: Appleton (city), Bear Creek (village), Freedom, Osborn

Ozaukee County: Mequon (city), Saukville (village)

Pepin County: Frankfort

Pierce County: Clifton, Gilman

Polk County: Clam Falls, Eureka

Portage County: Lanark, Linwood, New Hope

Price County: Hill, Kennan (village), Knox

Racine County: Mt. Pleasant (village), North Bay (village), Racine (city)

Richland County: Richland Center (city), Rockbridge

Rock County: Beloit (city), Clinton
Rusk County: Bruce (village), Hawkins (village)
St. Croix County: Erin Prairie, Hammond (village), Roberts (village)
Sauk County: Baraboo (city), Spring Green (village), Westfield
Sawyer County: Ojibwa, Weirgor
Shawano County: Bowler (village), Hutchins
Sheboygan County: Sheboygan (city), Scott
Taylor County: Rib Lake, Stetsonville (village)
Trempealeau County: Blair (city)
Vernon County: Bergen, Forest, Viroqua (city)
Vilas County: Eagle River (city), Presque Isle, St. Germain
Walworth County: Lafayette, La Grange
Washburn County: Crystal, Spooner
Washington County: Richfield, West Bend
Waukesha County: Brookfield (city), Butler (village), Chenequa (village),
    Genesee, Lac La Belle (village), Oconomowoc (city), Waukesha (city)
Waupaca County: Caledonia, Scandinavia (village)
Waushara County: Coloma (town), Coloma (village)
Winnebago County: Menasha (city), Oshkosh (town), Oshkosh (city), Rushford
Wood County: Hewitt (village), Saratoga

As the sample worked out in practice, it reported findings that corresponded nicely with the efforts of other scholars when addressing the same times or contests, and otherwise it produced no bizarre findings. So I was comfortable with what this sample offered to this overall project, one part among many.

My correlation analyses both with my representative sample and also with my other various samples referred to in sections 2–6 of this Appendix operated as follows. Following in the footsteps of my scholarly predecessors, for every place I consistently correlated the percent vote for one candidate/party in election x with the percentage in election y. Naturally, I did not correlate individual voters' behavior over time. There are no data with which to do that, though such an approach would, of course, have been preferable. Put in other terms, I correlated, for example, v1 as percent Democratic in year x in unit p with v2 as percent Democratic in year y in unit p, understanding that the higher the correlation toward 1.0 the higher the putative association between the two items, elections, etc. At no time do I make any suggestion that causality is present flowing from any of my correlations that might suggest the same, such as between median household income and percent Republican or Democratic. Association is not causality and is no substitute for the analysis or story I offer. In any case, I was quite cautious in my use of correlation analysis, using it to test some hypotheses but hardly making it the core of my story.

8. PARTICULAR LOCATION DATA PROJECTS

The Marathon County Project

I strove for at least one in-depth study of another county's voting behavior, past and present, besides Dane, Milwaukee and its surrounding suburban counties, and the suburbanizing St. Croix. Marathon County in north central Wisconsin seemed to be an excellent choice since it has a medium-sized and growing city, Wausau, as well as expanding suburbs and a fascinating collection of rural places and villages that are classics in terms of Wisconsin's ethnic heritage. The chance to undertake this part of my project came through the interest of a son of Wausau, Adam Briggs, whose study, "Marathon County Today," was invaluable for my work.

Milwaukee

In gathering electoral information on Milwaukee I was helped tremendously by Sarah C. Ettenheim's work, *How Milwaukee Voted, 1848–1946,* and its detailed data on Milwaukee and the various parts of Milwaukee. Of course 1968 was a long time ago, so Avraham Fox updated the data for me and reconsidered and factored into the picture some minor and not-so-minor parties and candidates. For the most recent several elections I compiled the data. All other aspects of my discussion on Milwaukee came from the many works on Milwaukee and, in the case of African American voting, through a lengthy process begun by Robert Yablon.

The Milwaukee Suburbs

I knew from the beginning that the Milwaukee suburbs were a major and increasing force in Wisconsin voting behavior in the post–World War II era, and especially so in the contemporary age, and that they merited systematic study. Suburban Milwaukee is a considerable and complex world of suburbs—some old, some new, some close in, some increasingly far away, some in Milwaukee County, more and more in surrounding counties, some very Republican, some Democratic, and so on. Under my direction, Erich Mussak performed the original study of the voting behavior of the many suburbs of Milwaukee through the 2000 election, the results of which he published in

"The Unraveling of the New Deal Coalition." I built on his project and brought it up to date for subsequent elections. I also relied on other student studies of individual suburbs, for example the previously cited work of Tom O'Day on Wauwatosa and Michael Felber's work on the North Shore suburbs of Milwaukee.

Today in Wisconsin it seems every city has its suburbs and exurbs, but some are more important to study and understand than others. I explored the suburbs of Madison, and Adam Briggs did the same for Wausau's suburbs. I also investigated St. Croix County, part of which is now a suburb/exurb of Minnesota's Twin Cities.

The Twin Cities Suburbs/St. Croix County

Another region where change is taking place in Wisconsin voting behavior is in St. Croix County on the Minnesota state line. There is potential for this area to change much more drastically, but whether it happens remains to be seen. I decided to pursue this project when I noted the strong Republican results in parts of St. Croix in 2004. As mentioned in the text, I concentrate on the parts of the county experiencing greater or equal growth in population as the county as a whole. The places I include are Baldwin (village), Hudson (city), Hudson, Kinnickinnic, New Richmond (city), River Falls (city), St. Joseph, Somerset (village), Somerset, Star Prairie, Troy, and Warren.

NOTES

Chapter 1. From Statehood to Lincoln's Election

1. Robert C. Nesbit, *Wisconsin: A History*, 89; Mark Wyman, *The Wisconsin Frontier*, 186; Alice E. Smith, *The History of Wisconsin: From Exploration to Statehood*, ch. 14; William H. Hodge, "The Indians of Wisconsin," 119.

2. Robert C. Ostergren, "The Euro-American Settlement of Wisconsin, 1830–1920"; Michael P. Conzen, "The European Settling and Transformation of the Upper Mississippi Valley Lead Region"; Wyman, *Wisconsin Frontier*, 136–37; Nesbit, *Wisconsin*, chs. 8, 9; Nicolaas Mink, "Dynamics of Change: Politics, Ethnicities, and Voting in Wisconsin 1848–1856."

3. Milo M. Quaife, *The Attainment of Statehood*, 337–47, 356–69.

4. See Louise P. Kellogg, "The Alien Suffrage Provision of the Constitution"; Nesbit, *Wisconsin*, 478.

5. Quaife, *Statehood*, 316–19, 394–97.

6. Patty Loew, *Indian Nations of Wisconsin: Histories of Endurance and Renewal*; Robert E. Bieder, *Native American Communities in Wisconsin, 1600–1960*, chs. 2–4; also see Smith, *Exploration to Statehood*.

7. Nancy Oestreich Lurie, *Wisconsin Indians*, 6, 8–12, 22, 36–37; Loew, *Indian Nations*, ch. 8, p. 140; Bieder, *Communities*, 165.

8. Quaife, *Statehood*, 34–35, 95–98, 335, 382–89, 397–400, 408–9.

9. The major source here is Leslie H. Fishel Jr., "Wisconsin and Negro Suffrage."

10. Roger E. Wyman, "Voting Behavior in the Progressive Era: Wisconsin as a Case Study," 33–35; Nesbit, *Wisconsin*, 125, 215, 223, chs. 9, 15; Joseph Schafer, *The Wisconsin Lead Region*; Mink, "Dynamics of Change," 13–15; Smith, *Exploration to Statehood*, 648, chs. 10, 11; Milo M. Quaife, *Wisconsin: Its Identity and Its People, 1634–1924*, 495; Jonathan Kasparek, "Wisconsin's Founding Brothers," 52–58.

11. Some of the many general and Wisconsin-focused discussions of this period include Richard N. Current, *The History of Wisconsin: The Civil War Era: 1848–1873*, ch. 6; Aaron M. Boom, "The Development of Sectional Attitudes in Wisconsin 1848–1861"; George C. Boom, "The Genesis of the Wisconsin Republican Party, 1854," 12; Smith, *Exploration to Statehood*, 616; Jean H. Baker, *Affairs of Party: The Political Culture of Northern Democrats in the Mid-Nineteenth Century*; Joel Sibley, *The Partisan Imperative: The Dynamics of American Politics before the Civil War*.

12. The masterwork on the Whig Party is Michael F. Holt, *The Rise and Fall of the Whig Party*; James L. Sundquist, *Dynamics of the Party System*, chs. 4, 5; Wyman, "Voting Behavior," 35–51; Ronald Formisano, *The Birth of Mass Political Parties*.

13. For the national situation see William G. Shade and Ballard C. Campbell, *American Presidential Campaigns and Elections*, 328–46.

14. Robert Newton Kroncke, "Race and Politics in Wisconsin, 1854–1865," 4; Theodore C. Smith, *The Liberty and Free Soil Parties in the Northwest*.

15. On the Liberty Party see Louis Gerteis, "Anti-Slavery Agitation in Wisconsin, 1836–1848," chs.1, 2; Frederick J. Blue, *The Free Soilers: Third Party Politics, 1848–1854*, 4; Theodore C. Smith, "The Free Soil Party in Wisconsin," 98.

16. Blue, *Free Soilers*, chs. 1–5; Gerteis, "Anti-Slavery Agitation," ch. 5.; Smith, *Liberty and Free Soil*; Steven J. Rosenstone, Roy L. Behr, and Edward H. Lazarus, *Third Parties in America: Citizen Response to Major Party Failure*, 51–56.

17. Smith, *Liberty and Free Soil*; Joseph G. Rayback, *Free Soil: The Election of 1848*. For another valuable national discussion see John Mayfield, *Rehearsal for Republicanism: Free Soil and the Politics of Anti-Slavery*; also see his illuminating "statistical Appendix and maps."

18. Richard H. Sewell, *John P. Hale and the Politics of Abolition*.

19. Among the useful sources are: Michael McManus, *Political Abolitionism in Wisconsin, 1840–1861*; Current, *Civil War Era*, 204–6; Mink, "Dynamics of Change," 16–20; Smith, *Liberty and Free Soil*. Also see Holman Hamilton, "Election of 1848"; Howard P. Nash Jr., *Third Parties in American Politics*, ch. 2. McManus was especially valuable for me, here and elsewhere.

20. Blue, *Free Soilers*, ch. 9; Ernest Bruncken, "The Germans in Wisconsin Politics, Until the Rise of the Republican Party," 237; Smith, *Liberty and Free Soil*.

21. Smith, *Liberty and Free Soil*.

22. Mink, "Dynamics of Change," 23–25; Current, *Civil War Era*, 207; McManus's *Political Abolitionism* is a crucial source here, especially ch. 4; William J. Vollmar, "The Negro in a Midwest Frontier City, Milwaukee: 1835–1870," 20; A. M. Thomson, *A Political History of Wisconsin*, ch. 6.

23. Analysis of the election and election data is mine; Mink, "Dynamics of Change," 21–27. For a range of views on the Compromise of 1850 see the still useful Edwin C. Rozwenc, *The Compromise of 1850*.

24. Roy Nichols and Jeanette Nichols, "Election of 1852," 349–66.

25. William E. Gienapp, *The Origins of the Republican Party, 1852–1856*, ch. 1; also see Sewell, *John Hale*; Mink, "Dynamics of Change," 41; Blue, *Free Soilers*, ch. 9; Smith, *Liberty and Free Soil*; Holt, *Whig Party*, chs. 19, 20.

26. Kenneth John Winkle, "Voters, Issues, and Party: Partisan Realignment in Southern Wisconsin, 1850–1854," 59–64; Boom, "Sectional Attitudes," 83–88; McManus, *Political Abolitionism*, table 6; Current, *Civil War Era*, 216.

27. Smith, *Exploration to Statehood*, 628; Bruncken, "The Germans," 236; La Vern J. Rippley, *The Immigrant Experience in Wisconsin*, 30; William F. Raney, *Wisconsin: A Story of Progress*, 143–44; Frank Byrne, "Maine Law versus Lager Beer: A Dilemma of Wisconsin's Young Republican Party," 115–20; Mink, "Dynamics of Change," 34–40; Peter R. Weisensel, "The Wisconsin Temperance Crusade to 1919," 7–10; Frank Byrne, "Cold Water Crusade: The Anti-Bellum Wisconsin Temperance Movement," chs. 4–7.

28. For correlations see Winkle, "Partisan Realignment," 79–85; correlations all in the negative direction: Milwaukee .896; Kenosha .921; Waukesha .656.

29. Ibid., Yankee positive at .623, German negative at .723.

30. Joseph Schafer, "Prohibition in Early Wisconsin," 281–99; Byrne, "Cold Water Crusade," ch. 8; Wyman, "Voting Behavior," 39.

31. Brown, "The Genesis," 13–14; Boom, "Sectional Attitudes," 24; Joseph A. Ranney, "Suffering the Agonies of their Righteousness: The Rise and Fall of the States Rights Movement in Wisconsin, 1854–1861"; Kroncke, "Race and Politics," 38–40; Mink, "Dynamics of Change," 42–44; Thomson, *Political History*, ch. 9.

32. Brown, "The Genesis," 1–2, 154, chs. 2–3; Gienapp, *The Origins*, ch. 9; Boom, "Sectional Attitudes," ch. 4; Quaife, *Wisconsin*, 552; Nash, *Third Parties*, chs. 3–4; Thomson, *Political History*, ch. 10.

33. Mark Voss-Hubbard, *Beyond Party: Cultures of Antipartisanship in Northern Politics before the Civil War;* Kroncke, "Race and Politics," chs.1, 2, 3; Brown, "The Genesis," 1–2; Boom, "Sectional Attitudes," 188–93; Formisano, *Mass Political Parties;* Baker, *Affairs of Party;* Sibley, *Partisan Imperative;* Nesbit, *Wisconsin,* 245; Gienapp, *The Origins.*

34. Brown, "The Genesis"; Rippley, *Immigrant Experience,* 29; Joseph Schafer, "Know-Nothingism in Wisconsin"; Wyman, "Voting Behavior," 40; Holt, *Whig Party,* chs. 24–26.

35. McManus, *Political Abolitionism,* 96, ch. 6; Nesbit, *Wisconsin,* 239; Boom, "The Genesis," 8; Mink, "Dynamics of Change," 42–44.

36. For an interesting treatment see "Scandal!" 1–2.

37. McManus, *Political Abolitionism,* ch. 7; Byrne, "Maine Law"; Current, *Civil War Era,* 224–30; Boom, "Sectional Attitudes," 117–22; Mink, "Dynamics of Change," 46–49.

38. Gienapp, *The Origins,* 373.

39. Ibid., 347, 365–66, 372, chs. 10, 12; Current, *Civil War Era,* 230–34; McManus, *Political Abolitionism,* ch. 8; Boom, "Sectional Attitudes"; Mink, "Dynamics of Change," 50–54; Jerrold G. Rusk, *A Statistical History of the American Electorate.*

40. See Shade and Campbell, *Campaigns and Elections,* 367–84, for an overview of the 1856 national election.

41. For standard biographies of the principals see Jean H. Baker, *James Buchanan,* and Fredrika S. Smith, *Frémont: Soldier, Explorer, Statesman;* Roy F. Nichols and Philip S. Klein, "Election of 1856."

42. Nesbit, *Wisconsin,* 239; Current, *Civil War Era,* 236, 262–63, 454; McManus, *Political Abolitionism,* ch. 10.

43. Kroncke, "Race and Politics," ch. 3; Fishel, "Negro Suffrage"; Current, *Civil War Era,* 264–66; Boom, "Sectional Attitudes," 157–65.

44. Current, *Civil War Era,* 294–95; Boom, "Sectional Attitudes," 186–88, ch. 7; Gerteis, "Anti-Slavery Agitation," chs. 3, 4.

45. For a consideration of the nation scene in 1860 election see Shade and Campbell, *Campaigns and Elections,* 385–406.

46. In my representative sample Democratic and Republican 1860/1856 Pearson r^2 correlation was .445; between 1860 and 1864 it was .688. All my cited correlations are at a significance level of .05. For a discussion of my sample and correlations see Appendix B.

47. Reinhard Luthin, *The First Lincoln Campaign;* Elting Morison, "Election of 1860."

48. Joseph Schafer, "Who Elected Lincoln?"; McManus, *Political Abolitionism,* ch. 12; Current, *Civil War Era,* 282–88; Wyman, "Voting Behavior," 45; Joseph Schafer, *Four Wisconsin Counties,* 150–57.

49. Winkle, "Partisan Realignment," 58–59, understands this well.

50. Lee Soltow, *Patterns of Wealthholding in Wisconsin since 1850,* 5–8, 34, ch. 3.

51. Winkle, "Partisan Realignment," has an excellent discussion and good data here.

52. See Appendix B for a complete discussion of ethnic issues and this study.

53. For some relevant and valuable general discussions see Richard H. Zeitlin, *Germans in Wisconsin;* Howard W. Kanetzke, "Germans in Wisconsin"; Walter D. Kamphoefner, *Transplanted Westfalians: Chain Migration from Germany to a Rural Midwestern Community;* Kathleen N. Conzen, *Making Their Own America: Assimilation Theory and the German Peasant Pioneer;* Jon Gjerde, *The Minds of the West: Ethnocultural Evolution in the Rural Middle West, 1830–1917.*

54. Fred L. Holmes, *Old World Wisconsin: Around Europe in the Badger State,* ch. 4; Kate E. Levi, "Geographical Origin of German Immigration to Wisconsin"; Paul Kleppner, *The Cross of Culture: A Social Analysis of Midwestern Politics, 1850–1900,* 42–45.

55. See such discussions as Joseph Schafer, *The Winnebago Horicon Basin;* Anton Jarstad, "The Melting Pot in Northeastern Wisconsin"; Robert J. Ulrich, "The Bennett Law of 1889: Education and Politics in Wisconsin," ch. 1; Ernest Bruncken, "How Germans Become Americans," 101–22. A nice discussion of the real-world living situations of immigrants in general is in Gjerde, *Minds of the West.*

56. Harry H. Heming, *The Catholic Church in Wisconsin: A History of the Catholic Church in Wisconsin from the Earliest Time to the Present Day;* Mark Noll, "American Lutherans Yesterday and Today"; Wyman, "Voting Behavior," 507, table 75; Current, *Civil War Era,* ch. 4; Kate A. Everest, "How Wisconsin Came by Its Large German Element"; Louise Phelps Kellogg, "The Bennett Law in Wisconsin"; Holmes, *Old World Wisconsin;* William F. Whyte, "The Settlement of the Town of Lebanon, Dodge County"; Kleppner, *The Cross of Culture,* 38.

57. Noll, "Americans Lutherans"; E. Clifford Nelson, *Lutheranism in North America, 1914–1970;* Kleppner, *The Cross of Culture,* 82.

58. Hans L. Trefousse, *Carl Schurz, a Biography;* Joseph Schafer, *Carl Schurz, Militant Liberal;* Claude M. Fuess, *Carl Schurz, Reformer, 1829–1906;* Robert M. La Follette, *La Follette's Autobiography: A Personal Narrative of Political Experiences,* ch. 6; Wyman, "Voting Behavior," 42–43; Ernest Bruncken, "The Political Activity of Wisconsin Germans, 1854–1860."

59. Wyman, "Voting Behavior," 528; Kleppner, *The Cross of Culture,* 47; W. Hense-Jensen, "The Influence of Germans in Wisconsin."

60. H. S. Lewis, "European Ethnicity in Wisconsin: An Exploratory Formulation"; David L. Brye, *Wisconsin Voting Patterns in the Twentieth Century, 1900–1950,* 114–16; Joseph Schafer, "The Yankee and the Teuton in Wisconsin"; Wyman, "Voting Behavior," 784.

61. On the Dutch see: Joseph R. Bongers, "The Importance of Religion in Regards to the Experience of Nineteenth Century Immigrants to Wisconsin: The Case of the Dutch," 3–8, 11–14, biblio.; Sipko F. Rederus, "The Dutch Settlements of Sheboygan County"; Holmes, *Old World Wisconsin,* ch. 6; Yda Saueressig-Schreuder, "Dutch

Catholic Immigrant Settlement in Wisconsin"; Lewis, "European Ethnicity"; Yda Schreuder, "Urbanization and Assimilation among the Dutch Catholic Immigrants in the Fox River Valley, Wisconsin, 1850–1905"; Rippley, *Immigrant Experience,* 81; Robert P. Swierenga, "Ethnoreligious Political Behavior in the Mid-Nineteenth Century: Voting, Values, Cultures"; Wyman, "Voting Behavior," 40.

62. Wyman, "Voting Behavior," 745–50, ch. 15; Schafer, "Yankee and Teuton"; Holmes, *Old World Wisconsin,* ch. 2; Brye, *Voting Patterns,* 96–98, 186–87; Louis A. Copeland, "The Cornish in Southwest Wisconsin"; Schafer, *Lead Region;* Kleppner, *The Cross of Culture,* 62; *A Merry Britain in Pioneer Wisconsin;* Edward Alexander, "Wisconsin, New York's Daughter State"; James A. Bryden, "The Scots in Wisconsin"; "God Raised Us Up Good Friends: (Letters from) English Immigrants in Wisconsin"; Conzen, "European Settling"; and Ostergren, "Euro-American Settlement."

63. Raney, *Wisconsin,* 749–50.

64. Brye, *Voting Patterns,* 93–94, presents solid data on Yankee voting.

65. David G. Holmes, *Irish in Wisconsin;* Wyman, "Voting Behavior," 732–41; M. J. McDonald, *History of the Irish in Wisconsin in the Nineteenth Century,* 122, chs. 2–6; Kleppner, *The Cross of Culture,* 53–55; "Irish in Wisconsin."

66. Hjalmar R. Holand, *Wisconsin's Belgian Community;* Wyman, "Voting Behavior," 694–702; Xavier Martin, "The Belgians of Northeast Wisconsin"; Brye, *Voting Patterns,* 196; Rippley, *Immigrant Experience,* 82; Holmes, *Old World Wisconsin,* ch. 8; William G. Laatsch and Charles F. Calkins, "Belgians in Wisconsin"; Lee W. Metzner, "The Belgians in the North Country," 280 ff. Voting data are mine.

67. Some nice work on this matter is in McManus, *Political Abolitionism,* table 24.

68. Winkle, "Partisan Realignment," 20.

69. I agree with Wyman, "Voting Behavior," 35, 46, 48.

CHAPTER 2. THE CIVIL WAR AND THE POLITICS IT CREATED

1. Paul Kleppner, *The Cross of Culture,* 13, 15, ch. 2; Brye, *Voting Patterns,* 169; Nesbit, *Wisconsin,* 363.

2. Nesbit, *Wisconsin,* 341–42, chs. 19, 20; Brye, *Voting Patterns,* 84–85; Robert C. Nesbit, *The History of Wisconsin: Urbanization and Industrialization, 1873–1893,* 12, 281–83, ch. 4; Lewis Gould, *Grand Old Party: A History of the Republicans,* chs. 1–3; Randall Rohe, "Lumbering: Wisconsin's Northern Urban Frontier"; Eric Lampard, *The Rise of the Dairy Industry in Wisconsin: A Study of Agricultural Change, 1820–1920.*

3. *Wisconsin Blue Book 1891,* pp. 362–63, has foreign-born data for 1885.

4. Wyman, "Voting Behavior," 20, 52, 66–9, ch. 2; Kleppner, *The Cross of Culture,* 35, 99; Nesbit, *Urbanization and Industrialization,* 264.

5. Kleppner, *The Cross of Culture,* 70, 99, ch. 3; Wyman, "Voting Behavior," 59–62.

6. Kleppner, *The Cross of Culture,* 43, 570, 99, ch. 3.

7. Horace S. Merrill, *Bourbon Democracy of the Middle West, 1865–1896;* Robert J. Ulrich, "The Bennett Law," ch. 2; Brye, *Voting Patterns,* 178–79; Helen J. Williams and Harry Williams, "Wisconsin's Republicans and Reconstruction, 1865–1870"; Robert C. Ostergren, *A Community Transplanted: The Trans-Atlantic Experience of Immigrant Settlement in the Upper Middle West, 1835–1915.*

8. E. Bruce Thompson, *Matthew Hale Carpenter, Webster of the West;* Richard Current, *Pine Logs and Politics: A Life of Philetus Sawyer, 1816–1900.*

9. Kroncke, "Race and Politics," 45–50; Frank L. Klement, *The Copperheads in the Middle West,* 85–87, 115–223, ch. 8.

10. Rusk's *Statistical History* is often used in this study; Kroncke, "Race and Politics," 54.

11. Frank L. Klement, "The Soldier Vote in Wisconsin during the Civil War"; Klement, *Copperheads,* 218–19; Kroncke, "Race and Politics," 5, 56; Current, *Civil War Era,* 401–13.

12. For the national story see Shade and Campbell, *Campaigns and Elections,* 407–28.

13. John C. Waugh, *Reelecting Lincoln: The Battle for the 1864 Presidency;* Harold M. Hyman, "Election 1864"; Current, *Civil War Era,* 401–13; Schafer, *Four Wisconsin Counties,* 163; Frank L. Klement, "Copperheads and Copperheadism in Wisconsin: Democratic Opposition to the Lincoln Administration."

14. This Pearson r² correlation compares Democratic vote with Democratic vote and Republican with Republican in the electoral units in my representative survey of Wisconsin voting units in 1860 and 1864; both are .688 at .05 significance level, as are all correlations reported in this text. For a full consideration of the nature of my representative sample, my approach to correlation analysis, and its limitations, see Appendix B.

15. Sam Ross, *The Empty Sleeve: A Biography of Lucius Fairchild;* Current, *Civil War Era,* 565.

16. Fishel, "Negro Suffrage."

17. For the national scene in 1868 see Slade and Campbell, *Campaigns and Elections,* 429–45.

18. John Hope Franklin, "Election 1868"; Williams and Williams, "Republicans and Reconstruction," 167, 171–73.

19. Democrat 1864 and 1868, .766; Democrat 1860 and 1868, .679; Republican 1864 and 1868, .766; Republican 1860 and 1868, .680. See Appendix B.

20. Albert K. Kelsey, "C. C. Washburn: The Evolution of a Flour Baron"; Nesbit, *Wisconsin,* 307–8. For a description of the politics of the 1870s and 1880s see Nesbit, *Urbanization and Industrialization,* ch. 11.

21. For the complex national situation see Shade and Campbell, *Campaigns and Elections,* 446–64.

22. Richard Current, "The Politics of Reconstruction in Wisconsin, 1865–1873," 100; Herman J. Deutsch, "Disintegrating Forces in Wisconsin Politics of the Early Seventies: The Liberal Republican Movement"; William Gillette, "Election of 1872."

23. Republican 1872 and 1860, .616; Republican 1872 and 1868, .787; Democrat 1860 and 1872, .615; Democrat 1868 and 1872, .787.

24. Allen Ruff and Tracy Will, *Forward! A History of Dane, the Capital County,* 133–34.

25. Current, "Politics of Reconstruction," 102; Nesbit, *Urbanization and Industrialization,* ch. 11; Wyman, "Voting Behavior, 55–58; Herman J. Deutsch, "Disintegrating Forces in Wisconsin Politics of Early Seventies: The Ground Swell of 1873"; Brye, *Voting Patterns,* 168–69; Nesbit, *Wisconsin,* 384; Graham A. Cosmas, "The Democracy in Search of Issues: The Wisconsin Reform Party, 1873–1877"; Current, *Civil War Era,* 593–94; Nash, *Third Parties,* ch. 5.

26. Nesbit, *Wisconsin,* 370, 386; Herman J. Deutsch, "Disintegrating Forces in Wisconsin Politics of the Early Seventies: Railroad Politics"; Cosmas, "The Democracy," 105; Kleppner, *The Cross of Culture,* 112.

27. The governor votes for 1871 to 1875 in my representative sample: Democrats .717, Republicans .719; slight variations here and elsewhere are due to rounding. See Appendix B.

28. Roy Morris, *Fraud of the Century: Rutherford B. Hayes, Samuel Tilden, and the Stolen Election of 1876;* William H. Rehnquist, *Centennial Crisis: The Disputed Election of 1876;* Sidney I. Pomerantz, "Election of 1876."

29. Nathan Fine, *Labor and Farmer Parties in the United States, 1828–1928,* 60–72; Nesbit, *Urbanization and Industrialization,* 576–77; Ellis B. Usher, *The Greenback Movement of 1875–1884 and Wisconsin's Part in It;* Nesbit, *Wisconsin,* 387–89; Sundquist, *Dynamics,* 98–99; Richard M. Doolan, "The Greenback Party in the Great Lakes Midwest"; Rosenstone, Behr, and Lazarus, *Third Parties,* 63–67; Irwin Unger, *The Greenback Era: A Social and Political History of American Finance, 1865–1879,* chs. 9–11; Fred E. Haynes, *Third Party Movements Since the Civil War with Special Reference to Iowa,* pt. 3; Nash, *Third Parties,* 148–70; Thomson, *Political History,* 414–16, ch. 18.

30. Based on my samples of these areas; see Appendix B.

31. See Appendix B for a discussion of my German American samples.

32. Cosmas, "The Democracy," 107; Nesbit, *Urbanization and Industrialization,* 107–8.

33. For the national scene see Shade and Campbell, *Campaigns and Elections,* 483–503.

34. Usher, *Greenback Movement;* Doolan, "Greenback Party"; David M. Jordan, *Winfield Scott Hancock: A Soldier's Life;* Leonard Dinnerstein, "Election of 1880."

35. Henry Casson, *"Uncle Jerry": Life of General Jeremiah M. Rusk.*

36. Weisensel, "Temperance Crusade," ch. 1; Rippley, *Immigrant Experience,* ch. 8; Rosenstone, Behr, and Lazarus, *Third Parties,* 75–78; Thomson, *Political History,* ch. 19.

37. Weisensel, "Temperance Crusade," 4–5, 25, 96–112, 85–87, 79, chs. 2–3; Nesbit, *Urbanization and Industrialization,* 593; David P. Thelen, "La Follette and the Temperance Crusade"; Theodora Youmans, "How Wisconsin Women Won the Ballot," 14–15; Rosenstone, Behr, and Lazarus, *Third Parties,* 77–78; Jack S. Blocker Jr., *Retreat from Reform: The Prohibition Movement in the United States, 1890–1913.*

38. Weisensel, "Temperance Crusade," 86–95, ch. 5.

39. The national election is well-covered in Shade and Campbell, *Campaigns and Elections,* 504–24.

40. Mark W. Summers, *Rum, Romanism, and Rebellion: The Making of a President, 1884;* Mark D. Hirsch, "Election of 1884."

41. Nesbit, *Urbanization and Industrialization,* 588; Rusk, *Statistical History.*

42. Based on my samples; see Appendix B.

43. Milton M. Small, "The Biography of Robert Schilling"; Thomas W. Gavett, *Development of the Labor Movement in Milwaukee,* 68–71; Nesbit, *Wisconsin,* 392–94; Rusk, *Statistical History;* Casson, *"Uncle Jerry."*

44. Olympia Brown, *Acquaintances, Old and New, among Reformers;* Charles Neu, "Olympia Brown and the Woman's Suffrage Movement"; Lawrence Graves, "The Wisconsin Woman Suffrage Movement, 1846–1920," 28–31, 41, 48, 54–62; Youmans, "How Women Won"; Genevieve G. McBride, *On Wisconsin Women: Working for Their Rights from Settlement to Suffrage,* 46–48, 100–106, 113, chs. 2, 3. For a full-length biography of Olympia Brown see Charlotte Coté, *Olympia Brown: The Battle for Equality.*

45. Marilyn Grant, "The 1912 Suffrage Referendum: An Exercise in Political Action," 107; Graves, "Wisconsin Woman," 19.

46. Based on my samples; see Appendix B.

47. McBride, *Wisconsin Women*, 123–25; Graves, "Wisconsin Woman," 51–54; Nesbit, *Urbanization and Industrialization*, 465–69; David Mollenhoff, *Madison: A History of the Formative Years*, 354–55; Stuart Levitan, *Madison: The Illustrated Sesquicentennial History, 1856–1931*, 150.

48. 1888 and 1868, Republican .699 and Democratic .714; 1888 and 1860, Republican .533 and Democratic .551; 1888 and 1872, Republican .672 and Democratic .716. See Appendix B.

49. Charles W. Calhoun, *Benjamin Harrison;* Shade and Ballard, *Campaigns and Elections*, 525–42.

50. Robert F. Wesser, "Election of 1888"; Wyman, "Voting Behavior," 227, 411, 219, 91; George W. Rankin, *The Life of William Dempster Hoard;* Kleppner, *The Cross of Culture*, 21–22.

51. Wyman, "Voting Behavior," 219; Herman Deutsch, "Yankee-Teuton Rivalry in Wisconsin Politics of the Seventies."

52. The best source for Norwegian American politics in Wisconsin is the splendid Jørn Brøndal, *Ethnic Leadership and Midwestern Politics: Scandinavian Americans and the Progressive Movement in Wisconsin, 1890–1914.*

53. Merle Curti, *The Making of an American Community: A Case Study of Democracy in a Frontier County;* Guy-Harold Smith, "Notes on the Distribution of Foreign Born Scandinavians in Wisconsin in 1905"; Ulrich, "The Bennett Law," ch. 1; Gjerde, *Peasants to Farmers.*

54. William H. Tishler, "Norwegians in Wisconsin"; Peter A. Munch, "Segregation and Assimilation of Norwegian Settlements in Wisconsin" and "Social Adjustment among Wisconsin Norwegians"; Wyman, "Voting Behavior," 605–10; Lewis, "European Ethnicity"; Kazimierz J. Zaniewski and Carol J. Rosen, *The Atlas of Ethnic Diversity in Wisconsin;* Rippley, *Immigrant Experience*, 74; Richard J. Fapso, *Norwegians in Wisconsin;* Ann Marie Legreid, "Community Building, Conflict, and Change: Geographic Perspectives on the Norwegian-American Experience in Frontier Wisconsin," ch. 15.

55. Herman A. Preus, "History of Norwegian Lutheranism in America to 1917"; Kleppner, *The Cross of Culture*, 86–87; Wyman, "Voting Behavior," 605–11; Nelson, *Lutheranism;* Gjerde, *Minds of the West*, ch. 4; Brøndal, *Ethnic Leadership*, ch. 2.

56. Brøndal, *Ethnic Leadership*, 54.

57. The data from my Norwegian sample are very uniform; see Appendix B.

58. Rippley, *Immigrant Experience*, 36; Wyman, "Voting Behavior," 611–20; Jon M. Wefald, "From Peasant Ideals to the Reform State: A Study of Norwegian Attitudes toward Reform in the American Midwest, 1890–1917," chs.1, 3, 4; Bayrd Still, "Norwegian-Americans and Wisconsin Politics in the Forties."

59. See Ostergren, *A Community Transplanted.*

60. Frederick A. Hale, *Swedes in Wisconsin;* Brye, *Voting Patterns*, 123–26; Wyman, "Voting Behavior," 650, 108; Kleppner, *The Cross of Culture*, 52; Erik Ehn, "The Swedes in Wisconsin."

61. Wyman, "Voting Behavior," ch. 12.

62. See Appendix B for a consideration of my Swedish places sample. Also see Brøndal, *Ethnic Leadership*, 73–81, ch. 3, which notes that despite their deep orientation to the

Republicans, Swedes did not play a prominent role in the Yankee-controlled Republican Party of this era.

63. Based on my samples; also see Wyman, "Voting Behavior," 103, 219.

64. *Poles in Wisconsin;* Zaniewski and Rosen, *Ethnic Diversity;* Richard Carter Smith, "Church Affiliation as Social Differentiator in Rural Wisconsin," 78–79; Michael J. Goc, *Native Realm: The Polish-American Community of Portage County, 1857–1992,* 91, 146, passim; Geoffrey M. Gyrisco, "Polish Flats and Farmhouses: What Makes a House Polish"; John Tomkiewicz, "Polanders in Wisconsin"; Donald Pienkos, "Politics, Religion, and Change in Polish Milwaukee, 1900–1930"; Leo Rummel, *History of the Catholic Church in Wisconsin;* Lewis, "European Ethnicity"; Ladislas J. Siekaniec, "The Poles of Upper North Wisconsin"; Albert H. Sanford, "Portage County Poles"; Nesbit, *Urbanization and Industrialization,* 301; Brye, *Voting Patterns,* 131; Wyman, "Voting Behavior," 717, 722; Judith T. Kenny, "Polish Routes to Americanization."

65. Wyman, "Voting Behavior," 61.

66. Wyman, "Voting Behavior," 68–69, 106–8; Rippley, *Immigrant Experience,* 53, 43.

67. Based on my samples; see Appendix B.

68. Wyman, "Voting Behavior," 91.

69. Kleppner, *The Cross of Culture,* 35.

70. Wyman, "Voting Behavior," 60; Kleppner, *The Cross of Culture,* 17–34; Current, *Pine Logs,* 237.

71. Jane Marie Pederson, *Between Memory and Reality: Family and Community in Rural Wisconsin, 1870–1970.*

CHAPTER 3. THE DECISIVE 1890S

1. John D. Buenker, *The History of Wisconsin: The Progressive Era, 1993–1914,* ch. 2. Robert F. Fries, *Empire in Pine: The Story of Lumbering in Wisconsin, 1830–1900,* is one fascinating part of the economic history.

2. Brye, *Voting Patterns,* 84, 88; Buenker, *Progressive Era,* 182, 13, 231, 127, chs. 1, 4.

3. John I. Kolehmainen and George W. Hill, *Haven in the Woods; The Story of the Finns in Wisconsin;* Arnold R. Alanen, "Homes on the Range: Settling the Penokee-Gogebic Iron Ore District of Northern Wisconsin and Michigan"; Brye, *Voting Patterns,* 269; Rippley, *Immigrant Experience* 11; Holmes, *Old World Wisconsin,* ch. 13; William F. Thompson, *The History of Wisconsin: Continuity and Change, 1940–1965,* 52–53.

4. Kleppner, *The Cross of Culture,* 99; Heming, *Catholic Church in Wisconsin;* Rummel, *History of the Catholic Church.*

5. Smith, "Church Affiliation," 34; Wyman, "Voting Behavior" 128–53.

6. Wyman, "Voting Behavior," 100–101, 111–13, 89; Gould, *Grand Old Party,* 109–10; Janet C. Wegner, "The Bennett Law Controversy in Wisconsin 1889–1891," 122–23; Alfred S. Harvey, "The Background of the Progressive Movement in Wisconsin," 60.

7. Some accounts of the whole event include: Thomson, *Political History,* ch. 20; Roger E. Wyman, "Wisconsin Ethnic Groups and the Election of 1890"; Wyman, "Voting Behavior," ch. 3; Kleppner, *The Cross of Culture,* 158 ff; Ulrich, "The Bennett Law," ch. 3.

8. Luther B. Otto, "Catholic and Lutheran Political Cultures in Medium-Sized Wisconsin Cities," 145; Wegner, "Bennett Law," ch. 5. A good example of a contemporary

celebration is Norman K. Risjord, "From the Plow to the Cow: William D. Hoard and America's Dairyland," 40–49.

9. Bennett Law, ch. 519, *Laws of 1889* (Madison: Wisconsin Department of Public Instruction, 1890).

10. For a broader perspective on such "social" issues of the time see Gjerde, *Minds of the West.*

11. Brøndal, *Ethnic Leadership*, 154.

12. William F. Whyte, "The Bennett Law Campaign in Wisconsin," 377, 375, 390; Dorothy G. Fowler, *John C. Spooner, Defender of Presidents*, 153.

13. Rankin, *William Dempster Hoard*, 131, ch. 3; Nesbit, *Urbanization and Industrialization*, 607–8; Whyte, "Bennett Law"; Thomson, *Political History*, 331–33.

14. My sample of Irish areas at the time does not show Republican gains, though Wyman argues otherwise in "Voting Behavior"; see Appendix B.

15. Whyte, "Bennett Law," 388, 386; Brye, *Voting Patterns*, 172; Wegner, "Bennett Law," 114, 33–34.

16. Rippley, *Immigrant Experience*, 14–47; Wyman, "Voting Behavior," 83; Rasmus B. Anderson, *The Life of Rasmus B. Anderson*, 595; Whyte, "Bennett Law," 386; Kellogg, "Bennett Law"; Wegner, "Bennett Law," 118; Ulrich, "Bennett Law," chs. 4, 5.

17. Thomson, *Political History*, 338–40; Wyman, "Voting Behavior," 82; Buenker, *Progressive Era*, 408. For some of Peck's tales see George Peck, *Peck's Bad Boy and His Pa* and *Peck's Bad Boy in an Airship.*

18. Correlated with 1890 my representative sample yields Democrats .781, Republicans .702. Again, all correlations are significant at the .05 level using Pearson's rho; see Appendix B. Ulrich, "Bennett Law," ch. 6; Wyman, "Voting Behavior," 84–114; Roger T. Johnson, *Robert M. La Follette Jr. and the Decline of the Progressive Party in Wisconsin*, 72; Wegner, "Bennett Law," 132. Most of the analysis is based on my correlations.

19. See, for example, Wyman, "Voting Behavior," 107–8.

20. Horace S. Merrill, *William Freeman Vilas: Doctrinaire Democrat.*

21. Wyman, "Voting Behavior," ch. 4.

22. In "Voting Behavior" Wyman did extensive work on this election, work whose results are of great value; see, for example, pages 411, 449, 227, 407, 219 and figure 5.3.

23. The German data are mine; see Appendix B.

24. Two good general introductions to Populism are William F. Holmes, *American Populism*, and Lawrence Goodwyn, *Democratic Promise: The Populist Movement in America.* Also see Roger E. Wyman, "Agrarian or Working-Class Radicalism? The Electoral Basis of Populism in Wisconsin," 825, 827, 830, 832–35, 840–44, 846; Kleppner, *The Cross of Culture*, 140, 203; Wyman, "Voting Behavior," 153–62; Rosenstone, Behr, and Lazarus, *Third Parties*, 67–75. For a comparative perspective see Haynes, *Third Party Movements*, pt. 4.

25. Wyman, "Populism in Wisconsin," 837, 831.

26. In this context it is puzzling to reflect on Walter Dean Burnham's discussion accompanying his valuable data collection, *Presidential Ballots 1836–1892.* It would seem Burnham never heard of ethnic- or religious-based voting.

27. David P. Thelen, *The Early Life of Robert M. La Follette, 1855–1884;* Nancy C. Unger, *Fighting Bob La Follette: The Righteous Reformer*, ch. 1, passim; Buenker, *Progressive Era,*

433–39; David P. Thelen, "The Boss and the Upstart: Keyes and La Follette, 1880–1884"; La Follette, *Autobiography,* chs. 4, 5. One gets some range in Robert S. Maxwell, *La Follette;* Bernard Weisberger, *The La Follettes of Wisconsin: Love and Politics in Progressive America;* David P. Thelen, "Robert La Follette's Leadership, 1891–1896"; and Albert O. Barton, *La Follette's Winning of Wisconsin, 1894–1904.*

28. Belle C. La Follette and Fola La Follette, *Robert M. La Follette,* ch. 8; Buenker, *Progressive Era,* 438–39; Kenneth Acrea, "The Wisconsin Reform Coalition, 1892–1900: La Follette's Rise to Power," 133–34.

29. Brøndal, *Ethnic Leadership,* 146–47, 159; Buenker, *Progressive Era,* 438–39.

30. For example, see Fowler, *Spooner,* 168–69; Acrea, "La Follette's Rise"; La Follette, *La Follette's Autobiography;* Brøndal, *Ethnic Leadership,* 165–79, 181.

31. Brøndal, *Ethnic Leadership,* 164.

32. Sundquist, *Dynamics,* chs. 6–7.

33. Harlan W. Hein Jr., "William Henry Upham."

34. Kleppner, *The Cross of Culture,* 254–56, 188; Wyman, "Voting Behavior," 449, 407, 219, 128–53, 158.

35. Wyman, "Voting Behavior," 202, ch. 5; Kleppner, *The Cross of Culture,* ch. 7; Sundquist, *Dynamics,* ch. 7; Lewis, *Grand Old Party,* ch. 3; Buenker, *Progressive Era,* 424–25. For a dissenting take on realignments see David Mayhew, *Electoral Realignments: A Critique of an American Genre.*

36. Stanley L. Jones, *The Presidential Election of 1896;* Paul Glad, *The Trumpet Soundeth: William Jennings Bryan and His Democracy, 1896–1912;* Kevin Phillips, *William McKinley;* William Diamond, "Urban and Rural Voting in 1896."

37. Wyman, "Voting Behavior," 168, 165, 121; Sundquist, *Dynamics,* 137. Also see Merrill, *William Freeman Vilas,* ch. 17, for the response of "orthodox" Democrats in Wisconsin; Shade and Campbell, *Campaigns and Elections,* 543–74.

38. Sundquist, *Dynamics,* 152–54; Wyman, Voting Behavior," 186, 172, 196, 198, 201–204. Much of my analysis here is based on my ethnic samples (see Appendix B); Brye, *Voting Patterns,* 184–85, 165–66.

39. Kleppner, *The Cross of Culture,* 286, 321; Wyman, "Voting Behavior," 173–76, figure 5.3.

40. Kleppner makes the case; see *The Cross of Culture,* 333–35, 291, for his discussion on rural voting. My sample of Norwegian towns and villages does not support his claim; see Appendix B.

41. Kleppner, *The Cross of Culture,* 333–35, 291; Sundquist, *Dynamics,* 151.

42. Wyman, "Voting Behavior," 449; Buenker, *Progressive Era,* 409; Brye, *Voting Patterns,* 163–65, 177.

43. Wyman, "Voting Behavior," 173–76.

44. These claims are based on my various ethnic, town, and village samples; see Appendix B.

CHAPTER 4. THE LA FOLLETTE PROGRESSIVE ERA THROUGH 1914

1. The literature on the Progressive Era is vast. Some of the many titles worth exploring are: John D. Buenker and Joseph Buenker, *Encyclopedia of the Gilded Age and Progressive Era;* Elizabeth Burt, *The Progressive Era: Primary Documents on Events from 1890 to 1914;* John Milton Cooper, *Pivotal Decades: The United States, 1900–1920* and

Warrior and Priest: Woodrow Wilson and Theodore Roosevelt; Robert Crunden, *Ministers of Reform: The Progressives' Achievement in American Civilization, 1889–1920;* Steven J. Diner, *A Very Different Age: Americans in the Progressive Era;* Robert Booth Fowler, *Carrie Catt: Feminist Politician;* John A. Gable, *The Bull Moose Years: Theodore Roosevelt and the Progressive Party;* Richard Hofstadter, *The Age of Reform: From Bryan to F.D.R.* and *The Progressive Historians;* Michael McGerr, *A Fierce Discontent: The Rise and Fall of the Progressive Movement in America, 1870–1920;* Norman Risjord, *Populists and Progressives;* Russell Nye, *Midwestern Progressive Politics: A Historical Study of its Origins and Development, 1870–1958;* Dorothy Schneider and Carl J. Schneider, *American Women in the Progressive Era, 1900–1920.*

2. Brye, *Voting Patterns,* ch. 5; Wyman's "Voting Behavior" is the master work.

3. Buenker, *Progressive Era,* 25–38; Wyman, "Voting Behavior," 743, 515–6; Brye, *Voting Patterns,* 85; Richard Bernard, *The Melting Pot and the Altar: Marital Assimilation in Early Twentieth Century Wisconsin.*

4. Unger, *Fighting Bob;* La Follette, *Autobiography;* Nesbit, *Wisconsin,* ch. 25; Buenker, *Progressive Era,* ch. 10; David P. Thelen, *Robert M. La Follette and the Insurgent Spirit;* Raney, *Wisconsin,* ch. 15; Alice H. Van Deburg, *La Follette and His Legacy;* La Follette and La Follette, *Robert M. La Follette;* Weisberger, *The La Follettes.*

5. Barton, *Winning;* Thelen, "La Follette's Leadership."

6. Harvey, "Background," 68–69, 88–89, passim; Youmans, "How Women Won," 3; La Follette, *Autobiography,* ch. 3; Wyman, "Voting Behavior," 241; Fowler, *John C. Spooner,* ch. 10; Barton, *Winning;* Ellen Torelle, *The Political Philosophy of Robert M. La Follette.*

7. Torelle, *Philosophy of La Follette;* Allen F. Lovejoy, *La Follette and the Establishment of the Direct Primary in Wisconsin, 1890–1904;* Youmans, "How Women Won"; Thomas W. Gavett, "The Development of the Labor Movement in Milwaukee," chs. 1, 2; Buenker, *Progressive Era,* ch. 11; John E. Miller, "Fighting for the Cause: The Rhetoric and Symbolism of the Wisconsin Progressive Movement," 17–18.

8. Brøndal, *Ethnic Leadership, 1890–1914,* 145.

9. Robert S. Maxwell, "La Follette and the Progressive Machine in Wisconsin"; another frank analysis is found in Unger, *Fighting Bob.*

10. Belle's remark is in La Follette, *Autobiography,* 44, 107–9; see also Karl E. Meyer, "The Politics of Loyalty from La Follette to McCarthy in Wisconsin: 1918–1952," ch. 1; Gwyneth K. Roe, "Two Views of the La Follettes: Madison, the 90s"; Unger, *Fighting Bob,* 73; Carrol P. Lahman, "Robert Marion La Follette as Public Speaker and Political Leader, 1855–1905."

11. For example, see Lucy Freeman, Sherry La Follette, and George Zabriskie, *Belle: The Biography of Belle Case La Follette;* and Nancy Unger, "The Two Worlds of Belle Case La Follette."

12. Herbert F. Margulies, *Senator Lenroot of Wisconsin: A Political Biography, 1900–1929;* Herbert F. Margulies, "Robert M. La Follette Goes to the Senate, 1905," 214–25.

13. Unger, *Fighting Bob,* 3, 101, ch. 5; Harvey, "Background," 108. There is another perspective presented in Stuart D. Brandes, "Nils P. Haugen and the Wisconsin Progressive Movement."

14. Miller, "Fighting for the Cause," 17; Isaac Stephenson, *Recollections of a Long Life, 1829–1915;* Emanuel Philipp, *Political Reform in Wisconsin: A Historical Review of the*

Subjects of Primary Election, Taxation, and Railway Regulation. For a perspective far kinder but not unperceptive see Weisberger, *La Follettes.*

15. For example, Anderson, *Rasmus B. Anderson,* ch. 1; Unger, *Fighting Bob,* ch. 12; Thelen, "Temperance Crusade," 299.

16. John Milton Cooper, "Robert M. La Follette: Political Prophet," 93.

17. John D. Buenker, "Bob La Follette at 150 Years," 53.

18. Cooper, "Political Prophet," 101–2, provides an excellent contemporary and balanced assessment; Unger, *Fighting Bob* is tougher.

19. Wyman, "Voting Behavior," 492.

20. Ibid., 254, 241.

21. Current, *Pine Logs;* Thomson, *Political History,* 302–4.

22. Fowler, *John C. Spooner.*

23. Philipp, *Political Reform;* Robert S. Maxwell, *Emanuel L. Philipp: Wisconsin Stalwart.*

24. Wyman, "Voting Behavior," 820, 424.

25. Ibid., 219–27, 407; Brye, *Voting Patterns,* 378.

26. Harvey, "Background," 123. For the national picture of the 1900 election see Shade and Campbell, *Campaigns and Elections,* 575–91.

27. Most of this data is from Wyman, "Voting Behavior," 407–11, 219, 343–50, 942, 726, 809, 822, 865, table 5.5; also see Brye, *Voting Patterns,* 332–33, 378.

28. Wyman, "Voting Behavior," 204. My data roughly confirm the general conclusions here regarding various groups; see Appendix B.

29. Ibid., 407, 422; Meyer, "Loyalty," 15, 19.

30. For the 1904 national scene see Shade and Campbell, *Campaigns and Elections,* 592–607.

31. Buenker, *Progressive Era,* 476–81; Wyman, "Voting Behavior," 422, 452, 851, 942, 880–83, which my representative sample and group data support (see Appendix B); Brye, *Voting Patterns,* 227.

32. Gary D. Wekkin, *Democrat versus Democrat: The National Party's Campaign to Close the Wisconsin Primary,* 47–50; Lovejoy, *Direct Primary;* Jørn Brøndal, *The Quest for a New Political Order: Robert M. La Follette and the Genesis of the Direct Primary, 1891–1904,* 106–8, passim; Brye, *Voting Patterns,* 229; Wyman, "Voting Behavior," 457, 268–73.

33. Margulies, *Senator Lenroot;* Gertrude L. Morris, "The Administration of Governor Davidson of Wisconsin"; Padriac M. Kennedy, "Lenroot, La Follette, and the Campaign of 1906"; Buenker, *Progressive Era,* 495–512; Brøndal, *Ethnic Leadership,* 185–203; Brye, *Voting Patterns,* 225; Wyman, "Voting Behavior," 277; Rippley, *Immigrant Experience,* 58.

34. Paolo E. Coletta, "Election of 1908"; Shade and Campbell, *Campaigns and Elections,* 608–25.

35. Stephenson, *Recollections;* Robert Griffith, "Prelude to Insurgency: Irvine Lenroot and the Republican Primary of 1908"; Wyman, "Voting Behavior," 454, 469; Buenker, *Progressive Era,* 498–500; Thomson, *Political History,* 392–94.

36. David G. Ondercin, "The Early Years of Francis Edward McGovern, 1866–1910"; Wyman, "Voting Behavior," 471, 298; Buenker, *Progressive Era,* 521–25, 624–25, chs. 12, 14; Nesbit, *Wisconsin,* 425.

37. James Chace, *1912: Wilson, Roosevelt, Taft, and Debs—The Election That Changed the Country,* chs. 4, 11; Shade and Campbell, *Campaigns and Elections,* 626–45.

38. Herbert F. Margulies, "The Background of the La Follette-McGovern Schism"; Wyman, "Voting Behavior," 435–36, 301; Buenker, *Progressive Era,* 614; Brye, *Voting Patterns,* 248; Unger, *Fighting Bob,* 224. For the full 1912 story from a national perspective see Chace, *1912;* James A. Cavanaugh, "Dane and Milwaukee Counties and the Campaign of 1912."

39. Data on 1912 are drawn from my samples; see Appendix B. For a broader look at Roosevelt's effort see Rosenstone, Behr, and Lazarus, *Third Parties,* 81–88.

40. Wyman, "Voting Behavior," 436; Margulies, "Background"; Thompson, *Continuity and Change,* 163; Buenker, *Progressive Era,* 614–21.

41. Graves, "Wisconsin Woman," 78–95; Buenker, *Progressive Era,* 346; McBride, *Wisconsin Women,* 198.

42. Three general overviews are Grant, "Suffrage Referendum"; McBride, *Wisconsin Women,* ch. 7; Graves, "Wisconsin Woman," ch. 3.

43. Fowler, *Carrie Catt,* ch. 4; Graves, "Wisconsin Woman," ch. 6.

44. Graves, "Wisconsin Woman," 115–20, 288–92.

45. McBride, *Wisconsin Women,* 213; Graves, "Wisconsin Woman," 144–45; Grant, "Suffrage Referendum," 113.

46. Brown, *Acquaintances;* Neu, "Olympia Brown"; Kelly Morrow, "Calculating Progress, Constructing Identity: Ethnicity and the 1912 Wisconsin Women's Suffrage Campaign," 6. Also see Kelly Morrow, "Fighting for Rights, Fighting for Citizenship: The Impact of Ethnicity on the 1912 Wisconsin Women's Suffrage Referendum"; Morrow's work is excellent, and I am very grateful for her help. Grant, "Suffrage Referendum," 110–11; Buenker, *Progressive Era,* 345, 349–50; Graves, "Wisconsin Woman," 109–10, 141–44; Youmans, "How Women Won," 11.

47. Morrow, "Calculating Progress," 15.

48. Youmans, "How Women Won"; Graves, "Wisconsin Woman," 113, 115, 182, 188; Grant, "Suffrage Referendum," 114; McBride, *Wisconsin Women,* 219–23; Morrow, "Calculating Progress," 30, 38.

49. Buenker, *Progressive Era,* 347–51; Graves, "Wisconsin Woman," 195; McBride, *Wisconsin Women,* ch. 6.

50. Graves, "Wisconsin Woman," 293.

51. Morrow, "Calculating Progress," 4, 17; Graves, "Wisconsin Woman," 122–29, 159, 355; Buenker, *Progressive Era,* 351;

52. Fowler, *Carrie Catt,* chs. 5, 6; Morrow, "Calculating Progress," 10, 31, 41–65.

53. For the discussion of the overall situation see Morrow, "Calculating Progress," 21–26, 31–33; Graves, "Wisconsin Woman," 200–203, 363; Wyman, "Voting Behavior," 337. Morrow's "Fighting for Rights" is also a superb source of information on this subject.

54. Based on my data; see Appendix B.

55. My data. For the Socialist vote in Milwaukee see McBride, *Wisconsin Women,* 229.

56. My data. Also see Morrow, "Fighting for Rights," 9.

57. McBride, *Wisconsin Women,* 249, 271; Graves, "Wisconsin Woman," 213, 234, ch. 4; Youmans, "How Women Won," 13.

58. Controversy still exists over whether Illinois or Wisconsin was actually the first state to ratify the Nineteenth Amendment. Youmans, "How Women Won," 13–14.

59. Maxwell, *Philipp;* Wyman, "Voting Behavior," 442–47; Philipp, *Political Reform.*

60. Brøndal, *Ethnic Leadership,* 247.

61. Ibid., 247–48; Herbert F. Margulies, "Anti-Catholicism in Wisconsin Politics, 1914–1920"; Wyman, "Voting Behavior," 338–39, 479–80.

62. La Follette and La Follette, *Robert M. La Follette,* 505–9; Wyman, "Voting Behavior," 442–43; Buenker, *Progressive Era,* 658–60; Bill Christofferson, *The Man from Clear Lake: Earth Day Founder Senator Gaylord Nelson,* 13.

63. Frederick Olson, "The Socialist Party and the Union in Milwaukee, 1900–1912"; Gavett, *Labor Movement in Milwaukee,* 3, 41–46, ch. 3, passim; Austin King, "Wisconsin Socialism"; Leon Fink, *Workingmen's Democracy: The Knights of Labor and American Politics,* ch. 7; Joseph A. Gasperetti, "The 1910 Social-Democratic Mayoral Campaign in Milwaukee," chs. 2, 3.

64. Marvin Wachman, *History of the Social-Democratic Party of Milwaukee 1897–1910,* ch. 1; Gasperetti, "Mayoral Campaign," ch. 1; King, "Wisconsin Socialism"; Roderick Nash, "Victor L. Berger: Making Marx Respectable"; Gavett, *Labor Movement in Milwaukee,* 90; Rosenstone, Behr, and Lazarus, *Third Parties in America,* 88–92.

65. Edward Kerstein, *Milwaukee's All-American Mayor: Portrait of Daniel Webster Hoan,* ch. 11; Buenker, *Progressive Era,* 517; King, "Wisconsin Socialism"; Floyd J. Stachowski, "The Political Career of Daniel Webster Hoan," 22–23.

66. Wachman, *Social-Democratic Party,* chs. 2, 4; King, "Wisconsin Socialism"; Gasperetti, "Mayoral Campaign," ch. 2; Bernard E. Fuller, "Voting Patterns in Milwaukee," ch. 2.

67. Wachman, *Social-Democratic Party,* ch. 6; Gasperetti, "Mayoral Campaign"; Brye, *Voting Patterns,* 267; King, "Wisconsin Socialism"; Gavett, "The Development of the Labor Movement," 253.

68. Gasperetti, "Mayoral Campaign," ch. 5.

69. Sally Miller, *Victor Berger and the Promise of Constructive Socialism, 1910–1920;* Gasperetti, "Mayoral Campaign," 8.

70. Edward J. Muzik, "Victor L. Berger: Congress and the Red Scare," 309–18; Buenker, *Progressive Era,* 470; Miller, *Victor Berger,* 76, 81, chs. 2, 7–9; King, "Wisconsin Socialism."

71. Stachowski, "Daniel Hoan," 3–10, chs. 3–7, 11, 13; Brye, *Voting Patterns,* 267–69; Clifford Nelson, *German-American Political Behavior in Nebraska and Wisconsin 1916–1920,* 38–39; Kerstein, *Daniel Hoan,* 169–70, chs. 1, 3–6, 15; Robert C. Reinders, "Daniel W. Hoan and the Milwaukee Socialist Party during the First World War"; Olson, "Socialist Party and the Union."

72. Stachowski, "Daniel Hoan," ch. 11; Brye, *Voting Patterns,* 267; Kerstein, *Daniel Hoan,* ch. 26.

73. Fuller, "Voting Patterns in Milwaukee 1896–1920," 139–40; Wyman, "Voting Behavior," 391–97, 839; Olson, "Socialist Party and the Union"; Pienkos, "Politics, Religion, and Change"; Brye, *Voting Patterns,* 268, 385–91; King, "Wisconsin Socialism."

74. Miller, *Victor Berger.*

75. Brye, *Voting Patterns,* 385–91, lays out the data well; my own samples' data support his well-developed ranges. James J. Lorence, "'Dynamite for the Brain': The Growth and Decline of Socialism in Central and Lakeshore Wisconsin, 1910–1920"; Wyman, "Voting Behavior," 586, 833–34, 397.

76. Stachowski, "Daniel Hoan," ch. 10; Gavett, "Labor Movement in Milwaukee," 305–8, chs. 8, 9; John H. M. Laslett and Seymour M. Lipset, *Failure of a Dream? Essays in the History of American Socialism*, chs. 8–10.

77. Gavett, *Labor Movement in Milwaukee*, 209. See discussion by Laslett and Lipset, *Failure of a Dream?*; James Weinstein, *The Decline of American Socialism, 1912–1925*; Ira Kipnis, *The American Socialist Movement, 1897–1912*, 699–701. For an older excellent discussion of the Socialist Party and movement in the United States see Fine, *Labor and Farmer Parties*, chs. 7–11.

78. Jorgen Weiball, "The Wisconsin Progressives, 1900–1914"; see also rural data in Wyman, "Voting Behavior," chs. 16–20.

79. Wyman, "Voting Behavior," chs. 16–17.

80. Gavett, "Labor Movement in Milwaukee," 290.

81. Hofstadter, *Age of Reform*; Wyman, "Voting Behavior," 820, 916, 911, 321, 809, 822–23; Brye, *Voting Patterns*, 235.

82. Buenker, *Progressive Era*, 413–14; Wyman, "Voting Behavior," 387–89.

83. Wyman, "Voting Behavior," 217, 343, 530, 388, 726–29, 596–644, 352, 590, 815, 581, 625, 697–700, 709, 770, 738, 915, 942–44, chs. 13–14. Wyman's data are superb and detailed; my findings based on my samples confirm his findings regarding voting in ethnic areas.

84. Based on my samples of Swedish, rural, and German American voting in the Progressive Era; see Appendix B.

85. Brøndal, *Ethnic Leadership*, 245.

86. Ibid., 253.

Chapter 5. Turbulent Years

1. Buenker, *Progressive Era*, ch. 6, appendix; Walter L. Slocum, "Ethnic Stocks as Cultural Types in Rural Wisconsin: A Study of Differential Native-American, German and Norwegian Influence on Certain Aspects of Man and Land Adjustment in Rural Localities," ch. 4; Ostergren, "Euro-American Settlement"; Paul Glad, *The History of Wisconsin: War, a New Era, and Depression, 1914–1940*, ch. 6.

2. Wyman's "Voting Behavior" takes us to the beginning of this period and provides useful background.

3. Glad, *A New Era*, 19–21; Maxwell, *Philipp*, ch. 9.

4. Arthur S. Link and William M. Leary Jr., "Election of 1916"; Shade and Campbell, *Campaigns and Elections*, 646–62.

5. Nelson, *German-American Political Behavior*, ch. 2; Rippley, *Immigrant Experience*, 104.

6. Wefald, "Peasant Ideals," 169–76; Nelson, *German-American Political Behavior*, ch. 2; Clifton J. Child, *The German-Americans in Politics, 1914–1917*, chs. 6, 7.

7. Data are based on my sample; see Appendix B. See also Brye, *Voting Patterns*, 249–51, 256, 268, 382–89; Rippley, *Immigrant Experience*, 105.

8. Philip La Follette, *Adventure in Politics: Memoirs of Philip La Follette*, chs. 4, 5.

9. Nelson, *German-American Political Behavior*, ch. 3; Glad, *A New Era*, 33–44; Karen Falk, "Public Opinion in Wisconsin during World War I"; Meyer, "Loyalty," ch. 2; Rippley, *Immigrant Experience*, ch. 7; Child, *German-Americans in Politics*, chs. 1, 2, 4, 5; Lorin L. Carey, "The Wisconsin Loyalty Legion, 1917–1918."

10. Herbert F. Margulies, "Cautiously Constructive: The Congressional Career of John Jacob Esch of Wisconsin."

11. Meyer, "Loyalty," 61, ch. 2; La Follette, *Autobiography,* ch. 53.

12. Brye, *Voting Patterns,* 391, 267–68; Gould, *Grand Old Party,* 213; Meyer, "Loyalty," 54, ch. 2; Glad, *A New Era,* 45–54.

13. Maxwell, *Philipp,* ch. 11.

14. Richard C. Haney, "The Rise of Wisconsin's New Democrats: A Political Realignment in the Mid–Twentieth Century," 92; Brye, *Voting Patterns,* 226.

15. Donald R. McCoy, "Election of 1920"; Shade and Campbell, *Campaigns and Elections,* 663–81; Rusk, *Statistical History;* Brye, *Voting Patterns,* 383–86, 264.

16. Brye, *Voting Patterns,* 382, 260–63. The data from my ethnic samples completely support this; see Appendix B.

17. Brye, *Voting Patterns,* 390, does a nice job of locating some of the key precincts; also see Fuller, "Voting Patterns in Milwaukee," for a discussion of voting in Milwaukee in this period.

18. Brye, *Voting Patterns,* 246; Glad, *A New Era,* ch. 1, which has one lively view of the many political clashes of the period.

19. Herbert F. Margulies, "The Election of 1920 in Wisconsin: The Return to 'Normalcy' Reappraised."

20. Brye, *Voting Patterns,* 246–7; Meyer, "Loyalty," 63.

21. Nesbit, *Wisconsin,* 465.

22. Ibid., 468–69; Meyer, "Loyalty," 14.

23. My samples' results demonstrate how sweeping all this was; see Appendix B. Brye, *Voting Patterns,* 247; Meyer, "Loyalty," 65; Glad, *A New Era,* 272–73.

24. Wayne E. Laufenberg, "The Schmedeman Administration in Wisconsin: A Study of Missed Opportunities," 2; Haney, "New Democrats," 92.

25. Kenneth C. MacKay's *The Progressive Movement of 1924* is a useful standard work. See also David Bruner, "Election of 1924"; Karen Hurt, "The Presidential Election of 1924: A Wisconsin Overview"; James H. Shideler, "The La Follette Progressive Party Campaign of 1924"; La Follette, *Autobiography,* chs. 70–71; La Follette, *Adventure in Politics,* ch. 8; Brye, *Voting Patterns,* 392–95. Weisberger, *The La Follettes,* ch. 7, provides an interesting take on this and other "last" campaigns of La Follette. Rosenstone, Behr, and Lazarus, *Third Parties,* 93–97; Glad, *A New Era,* 278–83.

26. Meyer, "Loyalty," 22.

27. James Weinstein, "Radicalism in the Midst of Normalcy."

28. Data are from my samples and examples; see Appendix B.

29. Based on my samples; see Appendix B. Also see Brye, *Voting Patterns,* 275–80, 301; Michael Rogin, *The Intellectuals and McCarthy: The Radical Specter,* 73; MacKay, *Progressive Movement,* 143, ch. 8; Samuel Lubell, *Revolt of the Moderates,* ch. 3.

30. The case here is strong, though the actual data are too weak to use; see Appendix B for details.

31. Glad, *A New Era,* 300–307.

32. Two good treatments of La Follette are Thelen, *Insurgent Spirit,* and Maxwell, *La Follette.*

33. La Follette, *Adventure in Politics,* 114–15; Miller, "Fighting for the Cause," 21; Van Deburg, *Legacy;* Weisberger, *The La Follettes,* ch. 8, Epilogue.

34. Albert Erlebacher, "Herman L. Ekern: The Quiet Progressive."

35. Meyer, "Loyalty," 65; Herbert F. Margulies, "Irvine L. Lenroot and the Republican Vice Presidential Nomination of 1920"; Glad, *A New Era,* 103.

36. Jeffrey Lucker, "The Politics of Prohibition in Wisconsin 1917–1933," esp. chs. 2–4; Raney, *Wisconsin,* 319–21; Kelly Morrow, "The Connections of Ethnicity, Women's Suffrage, and Prohibition in Wisconsin: The Results of Analysis of the 1912 and 1926 Referenda" and "1926 Referendum: Repealing the Volstead Act."

37. Based on my samples of the relevant categories cited; see Appendix B.

38. The correlation between the two referenda of 1912 and 1926 was .415 in a negative direction; see Appendix B. Also see Morrow, "Volstead Act"; and data in Brye, *Voting Patterns,* 395.

39. Based on my representative sample, Smith's vote in 1928 correlated with the 1926 referendum at .475 with .05 significance and with the 1946 referendum at .524 at .05. For other discussions of the 1928 campaign and results, see also Brye, *Voting Patterns,* 301–9; Andrew R. Baggaley, "Religious Influence on Wisconsin Voting, 1928–1960"; Edmund Moore, *A Catholic Runs for President: The Campaign of 1928*; Glad, *A New Era,* 321. Allan J. Lichtman, *Prejudice and the Old Politics: The Presidential Election of 1928,* skillfully analyzes the relevant issues nationally. Lawrence H. Fuchs, "Election of 1928."

40. Data are based on my ethnic and urban samples; see Appendix B. See also Brye, *Voting Patterns,* 395, 307.

41. Gregory A. Fossedal, *Kohler: A Political Biography of Walter J. Kohler, Jr.;* Thomas C. Reeves, *Distinguished Service: The Life of Wisconsin Governor Walter J. Kohler, Jr.,* chs. 2 and 3; Glad, *A New Era,* 311–12, 319–21; La Follette, *Adventure in Politics,* ch. 11.

42. See La Follette's own story in La Follette, *Adventure in Politics,* 101, passim, chs. 1–6, 12; Jonathan Kasparek's *Fighting Son: A Biography of Philip F. La Follette* is an excellent guide to Phil La Follette.

43. See 1930 in Rusk, *Statistical History.*

44. All these figures are based on my ethnic samples; see Appendix B.

CHAPTER 6. THE NEW DEAL AND WAR

1. For an overall perspective on Wisconsin in this era, see Workers of the Writers' Program of the Works Progress Administration, *Wisconsin: A Guide to the Badger State.*

2. An excellent treatment of industry in Wisconsin in 1940–65 is Thompson, *Continuity and Change,* 160–65, ch. 5.

3. Harold F. Gosnell and Morris H. Cohen, "Progressive Politics: Wisconsin an Example"; Thompson, *Continuity and Change,* 161–65, 16–17, 40, 36; John Miller, *Governor Philip F. La Follette, the Wisconsin Progressives, and the New Deal,* 188; Brye, *Voting Patterns,* Appendix B.

4. Leon D. Epstein, *Politics in Wisconsin,* 43–44; Richard C. Haney, "A History of the Democratic Party of Wisconsin since World War Two," 12; David Adamany, "The 1960 Election in Wisconsin," ch. 2; Sundquist, *Dynamics,* chs. 10, 11; Charles H. Backstrom, "The Progressive Party of Wisconsin, 1934–1936," 1:288–89.

5. Backstrom, "Progressive Party," 1:45–54, vol. 2; also see Lester F. Schmidt, "The Farmer-Labor Progressive Federation: The Study of a 'United Front'"; Donald R. McCoy, "The Formation of the Wisconsin Progressive Party in 1934."

6. On the Phil La Follette story see La Follette, *Adventure in Politics;* Kasparek, *Fighting Son,* 207, 214, chs. 4, 5; Miller, "Fighting for the Cause"; Backstrom, "Progressive Party," 2:411–34, 531; Francis J. Moriarty, "Philip F. La Follette: State and National Politics, 1937–1938," chs. 1, 3; Donald R. McCoy, *Angry Voices: Left of Center Politics in the New Deal Era,* 162–77; Haney, "Democratic Party," 11. For a highly sympathetic account of Phil's effort see Glad, *A New Era,* 438–42, 524–52; Patrick J. Maney, *"Young Bob" La Follette.*

7. An excellent treatment is in Backstrom, "Progressive Party," 2:469–93.

8. Robert E. Long, "Thomas Amlie: A Political Biography."

9. James J. Lorence, *Gerald J. Boileau and the Progressive-Farmer-Labor Alliance.*

10. Alfred R. Schumann, *No Peddlers Allowed.*

11. Harold C. Gosnell, *Grass Roots Politics: National Voting Behavior of Typical States,* ch. 4; John E. Miller, "The Election of 1932 in Wisconsin," ch. 4.

12. Frank Freidel, "Election of 1932"; Shade and Campbell, *Campaigns and Elections,* 720–37.

13. Miller, "Election of 1932"; Nesbit, *Wisconsin,* 489. My discussion with Leon Epstein on Schmedeman, like so many others over the years, was also very helpful.

14. Miller, *Governor La Follette,* ch. 2; Kasparek, *Fighting Son,* 135; Glad, *A New Era,* 400–401. Kasparek offers an excellent treatment of Phil's governorship and the Progressive Party.

15. Meyer, "Loyalty," 112–18, ch. 3; Glad, *A New Era,* ch. 10.

16. The figure was .014; see Appendix B.

17. See Appendix B.

18. This data are based on my various samples; see Appendix B. See also Brye, *Voting Patterns,* 310–11, 295, 301, 394, 396.

19. See Laufenberg, "Schmedeman Administration."

20. Jonathan Kasparek, "FDR's 'Old Friends' in Wisconsin: Presidential Finesse in the Land of La Follette."

21. Kasparek, *Fighting Son,* 161; Laufenberg, "Schmedeman Administration," 11, chs. 2, 3; McCoy, *Angry Voices,* 46; La Follette, *Adventure in Politics,* ch. 17; Robert E. Long, "Wisconsin State Politics 1932–1934: The Democratic Interlude," 443–47.

22. William Leuchtenburg, "Election of 1936"; Shade and Campbell, *Campaigns and Elections,* 738–56.

23. Gosnell and Cohen, "Progressive Politics"; Brye, *Voting Patterns,* 317–18; Gosnell, *Grass Roots,* 42–43; Kristi Andersen, *The Creation of a Democratic Majority, 1928–1936;* Glad, *A New Era,* 477–82; see Appendix B for a discussion of my samples.

24. Based on my data, see Appendix B. Brye, *Voting Patterns,* 396–97, also makes the point well.

25. Edward C. Blackorby, *Prairie Rebel: The Life of William Lemke;* David O. Powell, "The Union Party of 1936: Campaign Tactics and Issues"; David H. Bennett, *Demagogues in the Depression: American Radicals and the Union Party, 1932–1936;* Rosenstone, Behr, and Lazarus, *Third Parties,* 98–102.

26. Richard C. Haney, *A Concise History of the Modern Republican Party of Wisconsin, 1925–1975,* 1, 20.

27. Thompson, *Continuity and Change,* 401–2, 620; Nesbit, *Wisconsin,* 493–94; McCoy, *Angry Voices,* 181; Schmidt, "The Farmer-Labor Federation," 322; Lorence,

Boileau, 238; Gosnell, *Grass Roots,* 44–57; Moriarty, "Philip La Follette," 110; John B. Chapple, *La Follette Road to Communism—Must We Go Further Down That Road? A Book of Facts, Evidence, and Photographs;* Backstrom, "Progressive Party," 1:262–78, 287–307; Glad, *A New Era,* 553–58.

28. Christofferson, *The Man from Clear Lake,* 39; on the 1940 election see Shade and Campbell, *Campaigns and Elections,* 757–74.

29. Based on my ethnic samples; see Appendix B.

30. Based on my data; see Appendix B.

31. Samuel Lubell, *The Future of American Politics,* first presented the reality of the classic German switch to me; Adamany, "1860 Election," 18–20; Thompson, *Continuity and Change,* 35. See Gosnell, *Grass Roots,* for a classic on this election that is totally out of touch with ethnic realities.

32. In my representative sample the Republican and Democratic votes in 1940 just did not correlate with the same in 1932 at a .05 level of significance. By 1940 the parties' constituencies had dramatically altered over the protest year of 1932. See Appendix B; also note Brye, *Voting Patterns,* 317–20.

33. The classic "class voting" study on 1940 is Paul Lazarsfeld, Bernard Berelson, and Hazel Gaudet, *The People's Choice.*

34. My calculations could not confirm this class reality for Wisconsin. Any claims concerning economic well-being and voting behavior in 1940 and similar years prior to 1970 deserve skepticism in the absence of data. See Appendix B.

35. Thompson, *Continuity and Change,* 403–4, 433; Brye, *Voting Patterns,* 397.

36. Thompson, *Continuity and Change,* 402, 426, 437.

37. Sundquist, *Dynamics,* 224; Nesbit, *Wisconsin,* 527; Thompson, *Continuity and Change,* 434–39.

38. General treatments include Meyer, "Loyalty," ch. 4, passim; Haney, "Democratic Party," 49–50; Michael Kades, "Incumbent without a Party: Robert M. La Follette, Jr., and the Wisconsin Republican Primary of 1946"; Thompson, *Continuity and Change,* 441–59; on the end of the line see Weisberger, *The La Follettes,* ch. 8, epilogue; Maney, *"Young Bob" La Follette.*

39. Thomas C. Reeves, *The Life and Times of Joe McCarthy: A Biography,* ch. 6.

40. Kades, "Incumbent without a Party," 5–6, 11–12; Johnson, *Robert M. La Follette, Jr.*

41. Kades, "Incumbent without a Party," 15–19; La Follette, *Adventure in Politics,* 276–77; Backstrom, "Progressive Party," 2:461–63; Reeves, *McCarthy,* ch. 6.

42. Discussion and controversy over the patterns of voting in the 1946 Republican primary are endless. For example, see Lubell, *Revolt,* ch. 3; Brye, *Voting Patterns,* 322, 328, 399; Gavett, *Labor Movement in Milwaukee,* chs. 15, 16; La Follette, *Adventure in Politics,* 276–77; Kades, "Incumbent without a Party"; Meyer, "Loyalty," 206–9, ch. 4. Much of the debate once turned around the claims in Rogin, *Intellectuals and McCarthy,* but this controversy has long since faded away; for a reply to Rogin's argument that is far more rooted in actual Wisconsin voting data than Rogin's see Robert R. Dykstra and David R. Reynolds, "In Search of Wisconsin Progressivism, 1904–1952: A Test of the Rogin Scenario."

43. John H. Fenton, *Midwest Politics,* 49. On McCarthy see Reeves, *McCarthy,* ch. 6; Richard H. Rovere, *Senator Joe McCarthy;* David M. Oshinsky, *A Conspiracy So Immense: The World of Joseph McCarthy;* Michael O'Brien, *McCarthy and McCarthyism in Wisconsin.*

44. Thompson, *Continuity and Change,* 620.

45. Approval was eventually granted by the voters in 1967. The vote was 497,236 yes and 377,107 no; Nesbit, *Wisconsin,* 518.

46. Correlation is Brye's, *Voting Patterns,* 303. Thompson, *Continuity and Change,* 518–27; Nathan B. Scovronick, "The Wisconsin 'School Bus' Campaign of 1946."

47. For both my city samples discussion and my size of place analysis, see Appendix B; also see Brye, *Voting Patterns,* 483.

48. The data used in this discussion of the elements of the vote are almost entirely mine; see Appendix B.

49. A highly quantitative and equally plausible interpretation of Wisconsin voting behavior in this period set in the context of the entire first half of the century's electoral history is Dykstra and Reynolds, "Wisconsin Progressivism."

CHAPTER 7. THE EMERGENCE OF THE MODERN DEMOCRATIC PARTY AND MODERN VOTING PATTERNS

1. This correlation data are from Brye, *Voting Patterns,* 330; Sundquist, *Dynamics,* 222–38; Epstein, *Politics in Wisconsin,* 51, 147; Leon Epstein, "Size of Place and the Division of the Two Party Vote in Wisconsin."

2. Thompson, *Continuity and Change,* 528.

3. Haney, *A Concise History,* 8–10.

4. Ibid., 408–15, ch. 11; Haney, "New Democrats."

5. Haney, "Democratic Party," ch. 4; Thompson, *Continuity and Change,* ch. 11; Haney, "New Democrats."

6. Haney, "New Democrats," 98–99.

7. Haney, "Democratic Party," 16, ch. 2; Brye, *Voting Patterns,* 327–28; Epstein, *Politics in Wisconsin,* 51–52; Backstrom, "Progressive Party," 1:228–35, 2:375–76.

8. Haney, "Democratic Party," 21.

9. Fenton, *Midwest Politics,* 59; Haney, "New Democrats," 22–28, 66, 93–94.

10. Christofferson, *The Man from Clear Lake,* ch. 6; Haney, "New Democrats," 94–98; Haney, "Democratic Party," 61–69, 85; Fenton, *Midwest Politics,* 55–56; Thompson, *Continuity and Change,* 567–68.

11. Haney, "New Democrats," 102; Haney, "Democratic Party," ch. 8.

12. Lubell, *The Future.* On the 1948 campaign see Irwin Ross, *The Loneliest Campaign: The Truman Victory of 1948.* On Henry Wallace see John C. Culver and John Hyde, *American Dreamer: The Life and Times of Henry A. Wallace.* Kades, "Incumbent without a Party"; Rippley, *Immigrant Experience,* 139; Brye, *Voting Patterns,* 330; Rosenstone, Behr, and Lazarus, *Third Parties,* 103–7. See Appendix B.

13. Haney, "Democratic Party," 91; Epstein, *Politics in Wisconsin,* 49. Occasionally a Republican breaks through, as was the case in the early 2000s with the office of sheriff.

14. Reeves, *Distinguished Service,* 16. See also chs. 2, 4, 6, and 7, pp. 203–6, 209–23.

15. Fossedal, *Kohler,* vii, chs. 2–6; Thompson, *Continuity and Change,* 620; Haney, "Democratic Party," 121–29; Brye, *Voting Patterns,* 330–33.

16. Jay G. Sykes, *Proxmire.*

17. The correlation figure is from Dykstra and Reynolds, "Wisconsin Progressivism," 326; also see Christofferson, *The Man from Clear Lake,* ch. 7. For an insightful, even bold, analysis of the whole story see Meyer, "Loyalty," ch. 5; also see Michael O'Brien,

"The Anti-McCarthy Campaign in Wisconsin, 1951–1952"; Fossedal, *Kohler,* ch. 2; Reeves, *Distinguished Service,* chs. 8–10.

18. Haney, "Democratic Party," ch. 5; David Oshinsky, "Wisconsin Labor and the Campaign of 1952."

19. Haney, "Democratic Party," 229–44; Sykes, *Proxmire,* ch. 7. For a discussion of the early and middle 1950s voting patterns see Andrew R. Baggaley, "Patterns of Voting Change in Wisconsin Counties, 1952–1957."

20. Reeves, *Distinguished Service,* chs. 11–13; Epstein, *Politics of Wisconsin,* 46; Haney, "Democratic Party," 247–59; Sykes, *Proxmire,* ch. 8.

21. To be sure, Merlin Hall, a former Progressive, had won a congressional seat in northern Wisconsin as a Democrat in 1953 and had held on, but this was no more a guide to statewide Democratic success than were Democratic victories in Milwaukee's congressional seats.

22. Haney, "New Democrats," 100; Haney, "Democratic Party," 275–303; Thompson, *Change and Continuity,* 560; Fossedal, *Kohler,* ch. 8; Reeves, *Distinguished Service,* ch. 14; election analysis is mine.

23. Sykes, *Proxmire,* chs. 2–5, 9.

24. Haney, "New Democrats," 102–3; Fenton, *Midwest Politics,* 66, ch. 3; Sundquist, *Dynamics,* 225; Haney, "New Democrats," 103–4; Haney, "Democratic Party," 2, ch. 9; Thompson, *Continuity and Change,* 659.

25. Christofferson, *The Man from Clear Lake,* 55–57, chs. 2, 3, 5, 8.

26. The deservedly most admired treatment is Theodore H. White, *The Making of the President 1960.*

27. White, *1960,* ch. 4; Haney, "Democratic Party," 2:ch. 10; Adamany, "1960 Election," 70, chs. 3, 4.

28. Adamany, "1960 Election," 110, 127; Harry M. Scoble and Leon D. Epstein, "Religion and Wisconsin Voting in 1960"; Jane Cittenda, "The 1960 Democratic Campaign."

29. Based on my representative sample, JFK correlated with Smith at .257 at a .05 significance level; see Appendix B.

30. Fenton, *Politics,* 60; Adamany, "1960 Election," 112; Baggaley, "Religious Influence"; Haney, "New Democrats," 104; Christofferson, *The Man from Clear Lake,* 123–28.

31. Christofferson, *The Man from Clear Lake,* 123–26, chs. 9, 10, 13–15.

32. Ibid., ch. 16; Haney, "Democratic Party," 491–503, ch. 11; Fenton, *Midwest Politics,* 60.

33. Haney, "Democratic Party," 533–53.

34. Two interesting treatments are Marshall Frady, *Wallace,* and Stephan Lesher, *George Wallace: American Populist.*

35. Margaret Conway, "The White Backlash Re-examined: Wallace and the 1964 Primaries"; Richard C. Haney, "Wallace in Wisconsin; The Presidential Primary of 1964"; Michael Rogin, "Wallace and the Middle Class: The White Backlash in Wisconsin"; Frady, *Wallace;* Leon D. Epstein and Austin Ranney, "Who Voted for Goldwater? The Wisconsin Case"; Haney, "Democratic Party," 543, 541, 536.

36. Leon D. Epstein and Austin Ranney, "The Two Electorates: Voters and Nonvoters in a Wisconsin Primary"; Philip E. Converse, Aage R. Clausen, and Warren E.

Miller, "Electoral Myth and Reality: The 1964 Election"; Gary Donaldson, *Liberalism's Last Hurrah: The Presidential Campaign of 1964.*

37. Thompson, *Continuity and Change,* 735–36; Haney, "Democratic Party," 533–53.

38. Fenton, *Midwest Politics,* 54.

39. Epstein, "Size of Place"; Leon D. Epstein, "The Wisconsin Farm Vote for Governor, 1948–1954," 4, 11–14. An interesting discussion of urban political culture in Wisconsin in this period from a quite different angle appears in Robert Alford, *Bureaucracy and Participation: Political Cultures in Four Wisconsin Cities.*

40. Fenton, *Midwest Politics,* 70.

41. This nice comparison is in Brye, *Voting Patterns,* 332–33.

42. This analysis is derived from my samples of the relevant categories. For consideration of my samples, see Appendix B.

CHAPTER 8. ELECTORAL STABILITY IN A TWO-PARTY POLITICS

1. Edwin S. Gaustad and Philip L. Barlow, *New Historical Atlas of Religion in America.*

2. For a valuable discussion of Wisconsin politics and voting behavior in the 1980s and 1990s see John Bibby, "Political Parties and Elections in Wisconsin," ch. 4.

3. John H. Fenton, "Programmatic Politics in Wisconsin," 168–75; Nesbit, *Wisconsin,* 525; James R. Donoghue, *Voting in the 1990 General Election: A Review of Wisconsin Voting Trends; Wisconsin Legislative District Almanac.*

4. Daniel J. Elazar, "The American Cultural Matrix."

5. For example, see Thomas Holbrook and Craig Svoboda, "Wisconsin among the States"; and Joel Lieske, "Regional Subcultures in the U.S."

6. Jacob Stampen, "Rise of Block Voting in the Wisconsin State Legislature One Reason for Public Policy Lull," www.wisopinion.com/index.iml?mdl = article.mdl&article = 9333.

7. Haney, *A Concise History,* 16–17; Haney, "Democratic Party," ch. 13.

8. On Wallace see Frady, *Wallace;* and Jody Carlson, *George C. Wallace and the Politics of Powerlessness.* See Rosenstone, Behr, and Lazarus, *Third Parties,* 110–15.

9. For the national picture in 1968 see Shade and Campbell, *Campaigns and Elections,* 885–904.

10. A good biography of Lucey is much needed.

11. Wekkin, *Democrat versus Democrat,* 119.

12. Leon D. Epstein and Austin Ranney, "Who Voted for McGovern? The Wisconsin Case"; James R. Donoghue, *How Wisconsin Voted, 1848–1972: 1974 Election Supplement.* For the national picture in 1972 see Shade and Campbell, *Campaigns and Elections,* 905–22.

13. Donoghue, *How Wisconsin Voted.*

14. Nixon in 1972 and Dyke in 1974, .638; McGovern in 1972 and Lucey in 1974, .615; Carter/Earl Democrat 1976/74, .531; and Ford/Dyke Republican 1976/74, .585. All correlations are Pearson's at .05 significance. For a discussion of my correlation analysis see Appendix B.

15. My thanks to Crawford Young, who raised this topic with me.

16. For the national story see Gerald Pomper, *The Election of 1976;* Shade and Campbell, *Campaigns and Elections,* 923–40.

17. Examples and other data are based on my samples; see Appendix B.

18. For 1976 and 1972: Carter and McGovern, .653; Ford and Nixon, .661. For my correlation approach see Appendix B.

19. For the national picture in 1980 see Richard Harwood, *The Pursuit of the Presidency 1980.*

20. Christofferson, *The Man from Clear Lake,* ch. 32. When some voters (always presumed to be Democrats) left the polls upon hearing that Ronald Reagan had won the presidency, the consoling idea arose among some of Nelson's longtime supporters that their departure was the explanation for Nelson's narrow loss. There is no systematic evidence to support this, nor does it alter the basic conditions of weakness that faced Nelson in 1980.

21. Rosenstone, Behr, and Lazarus, *Third Parties,* 116–19.

22. James R. Donoghue, *Voting in the State General Election.*

23. For the national story see Ellis Sandoz and Cecil V. Crabb Jr., *Election 84;* for Wisconsin see James R. Donoghue, *The 1984 Elections: A Survey of Wisconsin Voting Trends;* "Post Election Survey February 1985."

24. Earl's vote correlated in my sample with Carter's in 1980 at .537; Thompson's with Reagan's in 1980 at .585; see Appendix B.

25. Tom Loftus, *The Art of Legislative Politics,* 7.

26. James R. Donoghue, *Voting in the 1990 General Election: A Review of Wisconsin Voting Trends.* For Thompson's active government philosophy, see Thompson, *Power to the People.*

27. For the national perspective on 1992 see Gerald M. Pomper, *The Election of 1992;* Micah L. Sifry, *Spoiling for a Fight: Third Party Politics in America,* chs. 3–5.

28. A nice comparison of the national polling data on presidential elections 1976 through 1992 is in the *New York Times,* Nov. 5, 1992, B9.

29. For a solid introduction to the subject of presidential elections in the United States see Nelson W. Polsby, *Presidential Elections: Strategies of American Electoral Politics.*

30. For the national 1994 story see Everett Carl Ladd, *America at the Polls 1994;* and Clyde Wilcox, *The Latest American Revolution? The 1994 Elections and Their Implications for Governance.*

31. Thompson 1994 and Bush 1988, .552; and Thompson 1994 and Thompson 1990, .567. See Appendix B for a consideration of my correlation analyses.

32. Based on my Milwaukee precinct analysis; see Appendix B

33. The correlation between the Thompson vote in my representative sample of places and rising median household income in 1990 was a positive .179, a situation of low significance at .05. The association in the 1994 landslide was, predictably, not there at all. See Appendix B for discussion of my economic measure.

34. The definitive and superb discussion of the 1998 Feingold race is in Clayton Nall, "Battle of the Mavericks: The 1998 Wisconsin Senate Race."

35. Based on my examples and data; see Appendix B. For a picture of Wisconsin religious patterns in this general era see Stephen J. Tordella, *Religion in Wisconsin: Preferences, Practices, and Ethnic Composition.*

36. See Appendix B for a discussion of how I developed the data on African American voting in Milwaukee.

37. The data and examples cited here are from the 2000 census as discussed in the section on class measures in Appendix B.

CHAPTER 9. THE CURRENT SCENE

1. For a valuable and detailed discussion of local governmental units and more see Edward Miller and Brett Hawkins, "Local Government," ch. 3.

2. Three sources here are the *Wisconsin Blue Books 2001–2002* and *2005–2006*, and the *Wisconsin State Journal*, May 19, 2002, A4. An interesting discussion of Wisconsin populations is in Myron Orfield and Thomas Luce, *Wisconsin Metropatterns*. By far the best single-authored book on contemporary Wisconsin government is James Conant, *Wisconsin Politics and Government: America's Laboratory of Democracy*.

3. For the national picture see Paul R. Abramson, John H. Aldrich, and David W. Rohde, *Change and Continuity in the 2004 Elections;* Michael Nelson, *The Elections of 2004.*

4. Gore and Kerry correlated at .813 and Bush with himself at .815.

5. Based on my analysis and data; see also Sifry, *Spoiling for a Fight.*

6. At .424 in my sample of fourth-class cities, significant at .05 level; see Appendix B for a discussion of my cities samples.

7. John C. Green and Mark Silk, "Why Moral Values Did Count."

8. See Appendix B's discussion of economic measures.

9. Republican 2000 vote for president and median household income places in my representative sample: .252; for same in 2004: .251, both in a positive direction. Equivalent Democratic correlations were .245 and .250, both in a negative direction.

10. Nader's vote did not reach a correlation of significance (.05) with either rising or falling median household income; see Appendix B.

11. David Canon suggested this as a possibility. Canon was helpful in my thinking about the Wisconsin results.

12. See "Consortium Exit Polls for the 2004 Presidential Election: Comparing Wisconsin and the U.S." www.CNN.com/election/2004.

13. The arrangement for this situation was established by an amendment to the Wisconsin Constitution in 1979.

14. See Abramson, Aldrich, and Rohde, *Change and Continuity.*

15. McCallum .294 (positive), Doyle .186 (negative) with increasing median household income; see Appendix B for relevant discussion.

16. Green in 2006 and Bush vote in my sample of places 2004, .752; Doyle and Kerry, .737. Neither Green nor Doyle's vote pattern in the places in my representative sample came close to a level of statistical association at .05 with Ed Thompson's showing.

17. Green positively at .245 with rising median household income and Doyle negatively at .239.

18. Scott McDonell made the best case for this view in conversation.

19. Neither the Democratic nor the Republican vote patterns in my representative sample in the vote for president in 2000 and 2004 or the vote for governor in 2006 came close to achieving a statistically significant association at .05 with their respective presidential votes in 1900. See Appendix B for a discussion of my correlation process.

20. Neither the Democratic nor the Republican vote in my representative sample in the vote for president in 2000 and the vote for governor in 2006 achieved a statistically significant association at .05 with their respective 1940 presidential votes. See Appendix B for discussion of my correlation procedures.

21. Democratic voting in my representative sample for president in 2000 and 2004 and for governor in 2006 and Republican voting in the same elections did not correlate statistically at .05 significance with their respective votes in the 1942 governor's election; nor did any significant correlations emerge with the Progressive vote in 1942 or the Progressive plus Democratic vote of 1942. See Appendix B for a consideration of my correlation procedures.

22. By 1962, at least with the presidential election of 2004, there was a very low association in my representative sample: Republican 1962 and 2004, .176; Republican 1962 and 2006, .137; Democrat 1962 and 2004, .174; Republican 1962 and 2006, .137; and Democrat 1962 and 2006, .121 don't really reach the .05 level for significance, however. Overall, the association between the 1960s and the present is very, very weak to say the least.

23. All correlations here and elsewhere in this chapter are mine; see Appendix B.

24. See Abramson, Aldrich, and Rohde, *Change and Continuity,* and Larry J. Sabato, *Midterm Madness: The Elections of 2002,* on contemporary issues.

25. Mark Silk, "Faith and Values Down the Tube."

26. On Milwaukee see Richard Prestor, *Images of America: Milwaukee, Wisconsin;* Roger D. Simon, "The Expansion of an Industrial City: Milwaukee, 1880–1910"; Goodwin Berquist and Paul C. Bowers Jr., *Byron Kilbourn and the Development of Milwaukee;* Bayrd Still, *Milwaukee: The History of a City;* John Gurda, *The Making of Milwaukee;* Gavett, *Labor Movement in Milwaukee;* Robert W. Wells, *This Is Milwaukee;* Kathleen N. Conzen, *Immigrant Milwaukee, 1836–1860: Accommodation and Community in a Frontier City.*

27. On Milwaukee voting history see Sarah C. Ettenheim, *How Milwaukee Voted, 1848–1968;* Wyman, "Voting Behavior"; Brye, *Voting Patterns.* My own data on Milwaukee voting were started by Avraham Fox, who was a great help.

28. See Ellen Langill, *Milwaukee 150;* Sandra Ackerman, *Milwaukee Then and Now;* Harry H. Anderson and Frederick I. Olson, *Milwaukee: At the Gathering of the Waters.* Still, *Milwaukee;* Frank Aukofer, *City with a Chance;* one of the best sources on contemporary Milwaukee is *Milwaukee Magazine,* a monthly. Also see Alan J. Borsuk, "Frank Zeidler, 1912–2006: Mayor Served 'The Public Welfare,'" *Milwaukee Journal Sentinel,* July 9, 2006, A1, A18, A19.

29. Paul H. Green, introduction by Reuben K. Harpole, *Milwaukee's Bronzeville: 1900–1950;* Thomas R. Buchanan, "Black Milwaukee, 1890–1915"; Thomas P. Imse, "The Negro Community in Milwaukee"; Joe W. Trotter Jr., *Black Milwaukee: The Making of an Industrial Proletariat, 1915–1945;* Keith R. Schmitz, "Milwaukee and Its Black Community, 1930–1942."

30. As usual I draw on the 2000 census data to develop these figures.

31. See Part J, *Wisconsin State Journal,* July 31, 2005, for a depressing discussion and the data.

32. Largely based on my data, partially created with the help of Robert Yablon; see Appendix B.

33. Schmitz, "Milwaukee," 90–97, for some relevant historical information.

34. For a consideration of my Hispanic calculations see Appendix B. For a good introduction to the subject of the history of Hispanics in the United States, see George Ochoa, *Atlas of Hispanic-American History.*

35. For a definitive treatment see Erich N. Mussak, "The Unraveling of the New Deal Coalition: A Typological Study of Suburban Milwaukee Voting Behavior."

36. On Milwaukee suburbia, the 2004 and 2006 figures are mine. The best guide to this entire subject is to be found in Mussak's article, "The Unraveling of the New Deal Coalition"; Mussak's work is splendid in its conceptual creativity, location description, and data acquisition and presentation. On Wauwatosa, see especially Tom O'Day, *Voting Patterns and Census Data in the City of Wauwatosa;* Mussak, "The Unraveling of the New Deal Coalition"; and *Wauwatosa.*

37. A good discussion is in the *Milwaukee Journal Sentinel,* Feb. 19, 2006, 1A, 18A.

38. Republican vote and rising median household income in units: 2004 .682; 2006 .764 at .05; see Appendix B.

39. Two excellent accounts of Madison history are Mollenhoff, *Madison,* and Levitan, *Madison.*

40. All data here are mine. See Ira Sharkansky, "One Party Suburb," for a nice discussion of the story of Monona, a close suburb of Madison.

41. My discussion depends on the excellent work done by Adam C. Briggs, "Marathon County Today" and Howard Klueter and James Lorence, *Woodlot and Ballot Box;* I provided the post-1998 analysis and data.

42. Testing Republican and Democratic vote in my sample for president in 2004 and governor in 2006 and median household income of units in the county, I found no association at the .05 level of significance; see Appendix B.

43. See Briggs, "Marathon County," 21.

44. I first noted this due to a conversation in 2001 with Ray Taffora and Mike Felber, friends of differing political persuasions who are sharp analysts of Wisconsin politics and elections.

45. David Boyd very much helped me develop this analysis.

46. Thomas Schaller, *Whistling Past Dixie,* 152, 148–51.

APPENDIX B: METHODOLOGICAL ESSAY

1. Wyman, "Voting Behavior," 1073–77.

2. Elazar, "Cultural Matrix"; Daniel J. Elazar and Joseph Zikmund II, *American Federalism: A View from the States,* ch.1; Fenton, "Programmatic Politics."

3. *Wisconsin State Journal,* June 7, 2002, B5.

4. George W. Hill, "The Use of Cultural-Area Concept in Social Research."

5. Brye, *Voting Patterns,* ch. 2.

6. *USA Today,* June 5, 2002, 1; *New York Times,* June 8, 2002, 19.

7. For example, see Mary Luthert Wingert, *Claiming the City: Politics, Faith, and the Power of Place in St. Paul.*

8. Gosnell, *Grass Roots,* 50.

9. Wyman's work is explained and detailed at length in his impressive methodological appendix and at pp. 1078–81 in his "Voting Behavior in the Progressive Era."

10. For a discussion of the subject of religion and voting in the United States today see Robert Booth Fowler, Allen Hertzke, Laura Olson, and Kevin den Dulk, *Religion and Politics in America.*

BIBLIOGRAPHY

Abramson, Paul R., John H. Aldrich, and David W. Rohde. *Change and Continuity: The 2000 and 2002 Elections.* Washington, D.C.: CQ Press, 2003.

———. *Change and Continuity in the 2004 Elections.* Washington, D.C.: CQ Press, 2005.

Ackerman, Sandra. *Milwaukee Then and Now.* San Diego: Thunder Bay Press, 2003.

Acrea, Kenneth. "The Wisconsin Reform Coalition, 1892 to 1900: La Follette's Rise to Power." *Wisconsin Magazine of History* 52 (Winter 1968–69): 132–57.

Adamany, David. "The 1960 Election in Wisconsin." M.A. thesis, University of Wisconsin, 1963.

———. "The Size-of-Place Analysis Reconsidered." *Western Political Quarterly* 17 (September 1964): 477–87.

Alanen, Arnold R. "Homes on the Range: Settling the Penokee-Gogebic Iron Ore District of Northern Wisconsin and Michigan." In Ostergren and Vale, eds., *Wisconsin Land and Life,* 241–62.

Alexander, Edward. "Wisconsin, New York's Daughter State." *Wisconsin Magazine of History* 30 (September 1946): 11–30.

Alford, Robert. *Bureaucracy and Participation: Political Cultures in Four Wisconsin Cities.* Chicago: Rand McNally, 1969.

Allen, James Paul, and Eugene James Turner. *We the People: An Atlas of America's Ethnic Diversity.* New York: Macmillan, 1988.

Andersen, Kristi. *The Creation of a Democratic Majority, 1928–1936.* Chicago: University of Chicago Press, 1979.

Anderson, Harry H., and Frederick I. Olson. *Milwaukee: At the Gathering of the Waters.* Tulsa, Okla.: Continental Heritage Press, 1981.

Anderson, Rasmus B. *The Life of Rasmus B. Anderson.* Madison: n.p., 1915.

Aukofer, Frank. *City with a Chance.* Milwaukee: Bruce Publishing Co., 1968.

Backstrom, Charles H. "The Progressive Party of Wisconsin, 1934–1936." 2 vols. Ph.D. dissertation, University of Wisconsin, 1956.

Baggaley, Andrew R. "Patterns of Voting Change in Wisconsin Counties, 1952–1957." *Western Political Quarterly* 12 (March 1959): 141–44.

———. "Religious Influence on Wisconsin Voting, 1928–1960." *American Political Science Review* 56 (March 1962): 66–69.

Baker, Jean H. *Affairs of Party: The Political Culture of Northern Democrats in the Mid-Nineteenth Century.* Ithaca, N.Y.: Cornell University Press, 1983.

——. *James Buchanan*. New York: Times Books, 2004.

Barton, Albert O. *La Follette's Winning of Wisconsin, 1894–1904*. Madison: Barton, 1922.

Bennett, David. H. *Demagogues in the Depression: American Radicals and the Union Party, 1932–1936*. New Brunswick, N.J.: Rutgers University Press, 1969.

Bernard, Richard. *The Melting Pot and the Altar: Marital Assimilation in Early Twentieth Century Wisconsin*. Minneapolis: University of Minnesota Press, 1980.

Berquist, Goodwin, and Paul C. Bowers, Jr. *Byron Kilbourn and the Development of Milwaukee*. Milwaukee: Milwaukee County Historical Society, 2001.

Bibby, John. "Political Parties and Elections in Wisconsin." In Weber, ed., *Crane and Hagensick's Wisconsin Government and Politics*.

Bicha, Karen B. "The Czechs in Wisconsin History." *Wisconsin Magazine of History* 53 (Spring 1970): 194–230.

——. "Karel Jonas of Racine: First Czech in America." *Wisconsin Magazine of History* (Winter 1979–80): 122–41.

Bieder, Robert E. *Native American Communities in Wisconsin 1600–1960*. Madison: University of Wisconsin Press, 1995.

Blackorby, Edward C. *Prairie Rebel: The Public Life of William Lemke*. Lincoln: University of Nebraska Press, 1963.

Blocker, Jack S., Jr. *Retreat from Reform: The Prohibition Movement in the United States, 1890–1913*. Westport, Conn.: Greenwood Press, 1976.

Blue, Frederick J. *The Free Soilers: Third Party Politics, 1848–1854*. Urbana: University of Illinois Press, 1973.

Bobo, Lawrence D., and Mia Tuan. *Prejudice in Politics: Group Position, Public Opinion, and the Wisconsin Treaty Rights Dispute*. Cambridge, Mass.: Harvard University Press, 2006.

Bongers, Joseph R. "The Importance of Religion in Regards to the Experience of Nineteenth Century Immigrants to Wisconsin: The Case of the Dutch." Unpublished paper, 1997.

Boom, Aaron Morey. "The Development of Sectional Attitudes in Wisconsin, 1848–1861." Ph.D. dissertation, University of Chicago, 1948.

Brandes, Stuart D. "Nils P. Haugen and the Wisconsin Progressive Movement." M.S. thesis, University of Wisconsin, 1965.

Briggs, Adam C. "Marathon County Today: A Study of Recent Voting Patterns and Changing Sociopolitical Trends." Hilldale Research Project, University of Wisconsin–Madison, 2000.

Brøndal, Jørn. *Ethnic Leadership and Midwestern Politics: Scandinavian-Americans and the Progressive Movement in Wisconsin, 1890–1914*. Northfield, Minn.: Norwegian-American Historical Association, 2004.

——. *The Quest for a New Political Order: Robert M. La Follette and the Genesis of the Direct Primary 1891–1904*. Madison: State Historical Society Photocopy Manuscript, 1990.

Brown, George Clifford. "The Genesis of the Wisconsin Republican Party, 1854." M.A. thesis, University of Wisconsin–Madison, 1978.

Brown, Olympia. *Acquaintances, Old and New, among Reformers*. Milwaukee: S. E. Tate, 1911.

Brown, Ray A. "The Making of the Wisconsin Constitution: Part II." *Wisconsin Law Review* (1952): 23–63.

Bruncken, Ernest. "The Germans in Wisconsin Politics, Until the Rise of the Republican Party." Milwaukee: Parkman Club Papers, 1896. 225–38.

——. "How Germans Become Americans." *Proceedings of the State Historical Society of Wisconsin* (1897): 101–22.

——. "The Political Activity of Wisconsin Germans, 1854–60." *Proceedings of the State Historical Society of Wisconsin* (1901): 190–211.

Bruner, David. "Election of 1924." In Schlesinger, ed., *History of American Presidential Elections,* 2459–81.

Bryden, James A. "The Scots in Wisconsin." *Proceedings of the State Historical Society of Wisconsin* (1901): 153–58.

Brye, David L. *Wisconsin Voting Patterns in the Twentieth Century, 1900–1950.* New York: Garland, 1979.

Buchanan, Thomas R. "Black Milwaukee, 1890–1915." M.A. thesis, University of Wisconsin–Milwaukee, 1973.

Buenker, John D. "Bob La Follette at 150 Years." *Wisconsin Magazine of History* 88 (Summer 2005): 52–53.

——. *The History of Wisconsin.* Vol. 4: *The Progressive Era, 1893–1914.* Madison: State Historical Society of Wisconsin, 1998.

——. "Wisconsin as Maverick, Model and Microcosm." In Madison, ed., *Heartland,* 59–85.

Buenker, John D., and Joseph Buenker, eds. *Encyclopedia of the Gilded Age and Progressive Era.* Armonk, N.Y.: Sharpe, 2005.

Burnham, Walter Dean. *Presidential Ballots 1836–1892.* Baltimore: Johns Hopkins University Press, 1955.

Burt, Elizabeth V. *The Progressive Era: Primary Documents and Events from 1890 to 1914.* Westport, Conn.: Greenwood Press, 2004.

Byrne, Frank. "Cold Water Crusade: The Anti-Bellum Wisconsin Temperance Movement." M.S. thesis, University of Wisconsin, 1951.

——. "Maine Law versus Lager Beer: A Dilemma of Wisconsin's Young Republican Party." *Wisconsin Magazine of History* 42 (Winter 1958–59): 115–20.

Calhoun, Charles W. *Benjamin Harrison.* New York: Henry Holt, 2005.

Carey, Lorin L. "The Wisconsin Loyalty Legion, 1917–1918." *Wisconsin Magazine of History* 53 (Autumn 1969): 33–50.

Carlson, Jody. *George C. Wallace and the Politics of Powerlessness.* New Brunswick, N.J.: Transaction Books, 1981.

Casson, Henry. *"Uncle Jerry": Life of General Jeremiah M. Rusk.* Madison: Junius W. Hill, 1895.

Cavanaugh, James A. "Dane and Milwaukee Counties and the Campaign of 1912." M.A. thesis, University of Wisconsin, 1969.

Chace, James. *1912: Wilson, Roosevelt, Taft and Debs: The Election That Changed the Country.* New York: Simon and Schuster, 2004.

Chapple, John B. *La Follette Road to Communism: Must We Go Further Down that Road? A Book of Facts, Evidence, and Photographs.* Ashland, Wisc.: n.p., 1936.

Child, Clifton James. *The German-Americans in Politics, 1914–1917.* Madison: University of Wisconsin Press, 1939.

Christofferson, Bill. *The Man from Clear Lake: Earth Day Founder Senator Gaylord Nelson.* Madison: University of Wisconsin Press, 2004.

Cittenda, Jane. "The 1960 Democratic Campaign." M.A. thesis, University of Wisconsin, 1961.

Coletta, Paolo E. "Election of 1908." In Schlesinger, *History of American Presidential Elections,* 2048–131.

Conant, James. *Wisconsin Politics and Government: America's Laboratory of Democracy.* Lincoln: University of Nebraska Press, 2006.

Converse, Philip E, Aage R. Clausen, and Warren E. Miller. "Electoral Myth and Reality: The 1964 Election." *American Political Science Review* 59 (June 1965): 321–36.

Conway, Margaret. "The White Backlash Re-examined: Wallace and the 1964 Primaries." *Social Science Quarterly* 49 (December 1968): 710–19.

Conzen, Kathleen N. *Immigrant Milwaukee, 1836–1860: Accommodation and Community in a Frontier City.* Cambridge, Mass.: Harvard University Press, 1976.

———. *Making Their Own America: Assimilation Theory and the German Peasant Pioneer.* New York: Berg, 1990.

Conzen, Michael P. "The European Settling and Transformation of the Upper Mississippi Valley Lead Region." In Ostergren and Vale, eds., *Wisconsin Land and Life,* 163–96.

Cooper, John M. *Pivotal Decades: The United States, 1900–1920.* New York: Norton, 1920.

———. "Robert M. La Follette: Political Prophet." *Wisconsin Magazine of History* 69 (Winter 1985): 91–105.

———. *Warrior and Priest: Woodrow Wilson and Theodore Roosevelt.* Cambridge, Mass.: Harvard University Press, 1983.

Copeland, Louis A. "The Cornish in Southwest Wisconsin." *Collections of the State Historical Society of Wisconsin* (1898): 301–34.

Cosmas, Graham A. "The Democracy in Search of Issues: The Wisconsin Reform Party, 1873–1877." *Wisconsin Magazine of History* 46 (Winter 1962–63): 93–108.

Coté, Charlotte. *Olympia Brown: The Battle for Equality.* Racine: Mother Courage Press, 1988.

Crunden, Robert. *Ministers of Reform: The Progressives' Achievement in American Civilization, 1889–1920.* New York: Basic Books, 1982.

Culver, John C., and John Hyde. *American Dreamer: The Life and Times of Henry A. Wallace.* New York: Norton, 2000.

Current, Richard N. *The History of Wisconsin.* Vol. 2: *The Civil War Era, 1848–1873.* Madison: State Historical Society of Wisconsin, 1976.

———. *Pine Logs and Politics: A Life of Philetus Sawyer 1816–1900.* Madison: State Historical Society of Wisconsin, 1950.

———. "The Politics of Reconstruction in Wisconsin, 1865–1873." *Wisconsin Magazine of History* 60 (Winter 1976–77): 83–108.

Curti, Merle. "Isaac P. Walker: Reformer in Mid-Century Politics." *Wisconsin Magazine of History* 34 (Autumn 1950): 3–6, 58–62.

———. *The Making of an American Community: A Case Study of Democracy in a Frontier County.* Stanford, Calif.: Stanford University Press, 1959.

Derleth, August. *The Wisconsin: River of a Thousand Isles.* Madison: University of Wisconsin Press, 1985.

Deutsch, Herman J. "Disintegrating Forces in Wisconsin Politics of the Early Seventies: The Liberal Republican Movement." *Wisconsin Magazine of History* 15 (December 1931): 168–81.

———. "Disintegrating Forces in Wisconsin Politics of the Early Seventies: Railroad Politics." *Wisconsin Magazine of History* 15 (June 1932): 391–411.

———. "Disintegrating Forces in Wisconsin Politics of the Early Seventies: The Ground Swell of 1873." *Wisconsin Magazine of History* 15 (March 1932): 282–96.

———. "Yankee-Teuton Rivalry in Wisconsin Politics of the Seventies." *Wisconsin Magazine of History* 14 (March 1931): 262–82.

———. "Yankee-Teuton Rivalry in Wisconsin Politics of the Seventies." *Wisconsin Magazine of History* 14 (June 1931): 403–18.

Diamond, William. "Urban and Rural Voting in 1896." *American Historical Review* 46 (January 1947): 218–305.

Diner, Steven J. *A Very Different Age: Americans in the Progressive Era.* New York: Hill and Wang, 1998.

Dinnerstein, Leonard. "Election of 1880." In Schlesinger, ed., *History of American Presidential Elections,* 1491–558.

Donaldson, Gary. *Liberalism's Last Hurrah: The Presidential Campaign of 1964.* Armonk, N.Y.: M. E. Sharpe, 2003.

Donoghue, James R. *The 1984 Elections: A Survey of Wisconsin Voting Trends.* Madison: Department of Governmental Affairs, University of Wisconsin–Extension, 1984.

———. *How Wisconsin Voted, 1848–1972: 1974 Election Supplement.* Madison: University of Wisconsin–Extension, Institute of Governmental Affairs, 1975.

———. *Voting in the 1988 General Election: A Survey of Wisconsin Voting Trends.* Madison: University of Wisconsin–Madison, Department of Governmental Affairs, 1988.

———. *Voting in the 1990 General Election: A Review of Wisconsin Voting Trends.* Madison: University of Wisconsin–Madison, Department of Governmental Affairs, 1990.

———. *Voting in the State General Election.* Madison: University of Wisconsin–Extension, Department of Governmental Affairs, 1982.

Doolan, Richard M. "The Greenback Party in the Great Lakes Midwest." Ph.D. dissertation, University of Michigan, 1969.

Durand, Loyal, and Leavelva M. Bradbury. *Home Regions of Wisconsin: A Geography of the State.* New York: Macon, 1933.

Dykstra, Robert R., and David R. Reynolds. "In Search of Wisconsin Progressivism, 1904–1952: A Test of the Rogin Scenario." In Joel H. Sibley, Allan G. Bogue, and William H. Flanigan, eds., *The History of American Electoral Behavior.* Princeton, N.J.: Princeton University Press, 1998. 299–326

Ehn, Erik. "The Swedes in Wisconsin." *Swedish Pioneer Historical Quarterly* 19 (April 1968): 116–29.

Elazar, Daniel J. "The American Cultural Matrix." In Elazar and Zikmund, eds., *American Federalism,* ch. 1.

Elazar, Daniel J., and Joseph Zikmund II, eds. *American Federalism: A View from the States.* New York: Crowell, 1972.

———. *The Ecology of American Political Culture.* New York: Thomas Crowell, 1975.

Epstein, Leon D. *Politics in Wisconsin.* Madison: University of Wisconsin Press, 1958.

———. "Size of Place and the Division of the Two Party Vote in Wisconsin." *Western Political Quarterly* 9 (March 1956): 138–50.

———. *The Wisconsin Farm Vote for Governors, 1948–1954.* Madison: University of Wisconsin–Extension, 1956.

Epstein, Leon D., and Austin Ranney. "The Two Electorates: Voters and Non-Voters in a Wisconsin Primary." *Journal of Politics* 28 (August 1966): 598–616.

———. "Who Voted for Goldwater? The Wisconsin Case." *Political Science Quarterly* 81 (March 1966): 82–94.

———. "Who Voted for McGovern? The Wisconsin Case." *American Politics Quarterly* 1 (October 1973): 465–77.

Erlebacher, Albert. "Herman L. Ekern: The Quiet Progressive." Ph.D. dissertation, University of Wisconsin, 1965.

Ettenheim, Sarah C. *How Milwaukee Voted, 1848–1968.* Milwaukee: Institute of Governmental Affairs, 1970.

Everest, Kate A. "How Wisconsin Came by Its Large German Element." *Collections of the State Historical Society of Wisconsin* (1892): 299–334.

Falk, Karen. "Public Opinion in Wisconsin during World War I." *Wisconsin Magazine of History* 25 (June 1942): 389–407.

Fapso, Richard J. *Norwegians in Wisconsin.* Madison: State Historical Society of Wisconsin, 2001.

Felber, Michael J. "Presidential Voting in Milwaukee's North Shore Suburbs." Unpublished manuscript, 1981.

Fenton, John H. *Midwest Politics.* New York: Holt, Rinehart and Winston, 1966.

———. "Programmatic Politics in Wisconsin." In Elazar and Zikmund, eds., *The Ecology of American Political Culture,* 168–75.

Fine, Nathan. *Labor and Farmer Parties in the United States, 1828–1928.* New York: Russell and Russell, 1961.

Fink, Leon. *Workingmen's Democracy: The Knights of Labor and American Politics.* Urbana: University of Illinois Press, 1983.

Fishel, Leslie H., Jr. "Wisconsin and Negro Suffrage." *Wisconsin Magazine of History* 46 (Spring 1963): 180–96.

Fite, Gilbert. "Election of 1896." In Schlesinger, ed., *History of American Presidential Elections,* 1787–874.

Formisano, Ronald. *The Birth of Mass Political Parties.* Princeton, N.J.: Princeton University Press, 1971.

Fossedal, Gregory A. *Kohler: A Political Biography of Walter J. Kohler, Jr.* New Brunswick, N.J.: Transaction Books, 2003.

Fowler, Dorothy G. *John C. Spooner, Defender of Presidents.* New York: University Publishers, 1961.

Fowler, Robert Booth. *Carrie Catt: Feminist Politician.* Boston: Northeastern University Press, 1986.

Fowler, Robert Booth, Allen Hertzke, Laura Olson, and Kevin den Dulk, eds. *Religion and Politics in America.* Boulder, Colo.: Westview Press, 2004.

Frady, Marshall. *Wallace.* New York: New American Library, 1976.

Franklin, John Hope. "Election of 1868." In Schlesinger, ed., *History of American Presidential Elections,* 1247–300.

Freeman, Lucy, Sherry La Follette, and George Zabriskie. *Belle: The Biography of Belle Case La Follette.* New York: Beaufort Books, 1986.

Freidel, Frank. "Election of 1932." In Schlesinger, ed., *History of American Presidential Elections,* 2707–806.

Fries, Robert F. *Empire in Pine: The Story of Lumbering in Wisconsin, 1830–1900*. Madison: State Historical Society of Wisconsin, 1951.

Fuchs, Lawrence H. "Election of 1928." In Schlesinger, ed., *History of American Presidential Elections*, 2585–704.

Fuess, Claude M. *Carl Schurz, Reformer, 1829–1906*. New York: Dodd, Mead, 1932.

Fuller, Bernard E. "Voting Patterns in Milwaukee, 1896–1920." M.A. thesis, University of Wisconsin–Milwaukee, 1973.

Gable, John A. *The Bull Moose Years: Theodore Roosevelt and the Progressive Party*. Port Washington, N.Y.: Kennikat, 1978.

Gasperetti, Joseph A. "The 1910 Social-Democratic Mayoral Campaign in Milwaukee." M.A. thesis, University of Wisconsin–Milwaukee, 1970.

Gaustad, Edwin S., and Philip L. Barlow. *New Historical Atlas of Religion in America*. New York: Oxford University Press, 2001.

Gavett, Thomas W. "The Development of the Labor Movement in Milwaukee." Ph.D. dissertation, University of Wisconsin, 1957.

———. *Development of the Labor Movement in Milwaukee*. Madison: University of Wisconsin Press, 1965.

Geenen, Paul H. *Milwaukee's Bronzeville, 1900–1950*. Charleston: Arcadia, 2006.

Gerteis, Louis. "Anti-Slavery Agitation in Wisconsin, 1836–1848." M.A. thesis, University of Wisconsin, 1966.

Gienapp, William E. *The Origins of the Republican Party, 1852–1856*. New York: Oxford University Press, 1987.

Gillette, William. "Election of 1872." In Schlesinger, ed., *History of American Presidential Elections*, 1303–75.

Gjerde, Jon. *From Peasants to Farmers: The Migration from Balestrand, Norway, to the Upper Midwest*. New York: Cambridge University Press, 1985.

———. *The Minds of the West: Ethnocultural Evolution in the Rural Middle West, 1830–1917*. Chapel Hill: University of North Carolina Press, 1997.

Glad, Paul. *The History of Wisconsin*. Vol. 5: *War, a New Era, and Depression, 1914–1940*. Madison: State Historical Society of Wisconsin, 1990.

———. *The Trumpet Soundeth: William Jennings Bryan and His Democracy, 1896–1912*. Lincoln: University of Nebraska Press, 1960.

Goc, Michael J. *Native Realm: The Polish-American Community of Portage County, 1857–1992*. Stevens Point, Wisc.: Worzalla Publishing, 1992.

"God Raised Us Up Good Friends: (Letters from) English Immigrants in Wisconsin." *Wisconsin Magazine of History* 47 (Summer 1964): 224–37.

Goldman, Eric. *Rendezvous with Destiny: A History of Modern American Reform*. New York: Knopf, 1952.

Goodwyn, Lawrence. *Democratic Promise: The Populist Movement in America*. New York: Oxford University Press, 1976.

Gosnell, Harold C. *Grass Roots Politics: National Voting Behavior of Typical States*. New York: Russell and Russell, 1970.

Gosnell, Harold F., and Morris H. Cohen. "Progressive Politics: Wisconsin an Example." *American Political Science Review* 34 (October 1940): 920–35.

Gould, Lewis. *Grand Old Party: A History of the Republicans*. New York: Random House, 2003.

Grant, Marilyn. "The 1912 Suffrage Referendum: An Exercise in Political Action." *Wisconsin Magazine of History* 64 (Winter 1980–81): 107–18.

Graves, Lawrence. "The Wisconsin Woman Suffrage Movement, 1846–1920." Ph.D. dissertation, University of Wisconsin, 1954.

Green, John, and Mark Silk. "Why Moral Values Did Count." *Religion in the News* 8 (Spring 2005): 5–8.

Griffith, Robert. "Prelude to Insurgency: Irvine Lenroot and the Republican Primary of 1908." *Wisconsin Magazine of History* 49 (Autumn 1965): 16–28.

Gurda, John. *The Making of Milwaukee.* Milwaukee: Milwaukee Historical Society, 1999.

Gyrisco, Geoffrey M. "Polish Flats and Farmhouses: What Makes a House Polish." *Wisconsin Magazine of History* 84 (Spring 2001): 23–33.

Hale, Frederick A. *Swedes in Wisconsin.* Madison: Wisconsin Historical Society Press, 2002.

Hamilton, Holman. "Election of 1848." In Schlesinger, ed., *History of American Presidential Elections,* 865–918.

Haney, Richard C. *A Concise History of the Modern Republican Party of Wisconsin, 1925–1975.* Madison: Kramer Printing, 1976.

———. "A History of the Democratic Party of Wisconsin since World War Two." Ph.D. dissertation, University of Wisconsin, 1970.

———. "The Rise of Wisconsin's New Democrats: A Political Realignment in the Mid-Twentieth Century." *Wisconsin Magazine of History* 58 (1974–75): 91–106.

———. "Wallace in Wisconsin: The Presidential Primary of 1964." *Wisconsin Magazine of History* 61 (Summer 1978): 259–78.

Harvey, Alfred S. "The Background of the Progressive Movement in Wisconsin." M.A. thesis, University of Wisconsin, 1933.

Harwood, Richard, ed. *The Pursuit of the Presidency 1980.* New York: Berkeley Books, 1980.

Haynes, Fred E. *Third Party Movements since the Civil War with Special Reference to Iowa.* Iowa: State Historical Society of Iowa, 1916.

Hein, Harlan W., Jr. "William Henry Upham." Unpublished paper, 1976. College of Education, University of Wisconsin–La Crosse, 1976.

Heming, Harry H. *The Catholic Church in Wisconsin: A History of the Catholic Church in Wisconsin from the Earliest Time to the Present Day.* La Crosse: Brookhaven Press, 1998.

Hense-Jensen, W. "The Influence of the Germans in Wisconsin." *Proceedings of the State Historical Society of Wisconsin* (1901): 144–47

Hill, George W. "The Use of the Culture-Area Concept in Social Research." *American Journal of Sociology* 47 (July 1941): 39–47.

Hirsch, Mark D. "Election of 1884." In Schlesinger, ed., *History of American Presidential Elections,* 1561–611.

Hodge, William H. "The Indians of Wisconsin." In *Wisconsin Blue Book 1975,* 95–192. Madison: Legislative Reference Bureau, 1976.

Hofstadter, Richard. *The Age of Reform: From Bryan to FDR.* New York: Knopf, 1955.

———. *The Progressive Historians.* New York: Knopf, 1968.

———. *The Progressive Movement, 1900–1915.* Englewood Cliffs: Prentice-Hall, 1963.

Holand, Hjalmar R. "Wisconsin's Belgian Community." *Peninsula Historical Review* 7 (1933).

———. *Wisconsin's Belgian Community*. Sturgeon Bay: Door County Historical Society, 1933.

Holbrook, Thomas, and Craig Svoboda. "Wisconsin among the States." In Ronald E. Weber, ed. *Crane and Hagensick's Wisconsin Government and Politics*. New York: McGraw-Hill, 1996.

Holmes, David G. *Irish in Wisconsin*. Madison: Wisconsin Historical Society Press, 2004.

Holmes, Fred L. *Old World Wisconsin: Around Europe in the Badger State*. Eau Claire: E. M. Hale, 1944. Reprinted, Madison: Wisconsin House, 1974.

Holmes, William F., ed. *American Populism*. Lexington, Mass.: D. C. Heath, 1994.

Holt, Michael F. *The Rise and Fall of the Whig Party*. New York: Oxford University Press, 1999.

Hurt, Karen. "The Presidential Election of 1924: A Wisconsin Overview." Unpublished paper, 2001.

Hyman, Harold M. "Election 1864." In Schlesinger, ed., *History of American Presidential Elections*, 1155–244.

Imse, Thomas P. "The Negro Community in Milwaukee." M.A. thesis, Marquette University, 1942.

"Irish in Wisconsin." *Badger History* 31 (March 1978): 1–49.

Jarstad, Anton. "The Melting Pot in Northeastern Wisconsin." *Wisconsin Magazine of History* 26 (June 1943): 426–32.

Johnson, Roger T. *Robert M. La Follette Jr. and the Decline of the Progressive Party in Wisconsin*. Madison: University of Wisconsin Press, 1964.

Jones, Stanley L. *The Presidential Election of 1896*. Madison: University of Wisconsin Press, 1964.

Jordan, David M. *Winfield Scott Hancock: A Soldier's Life*. Bloomington: Indiana University Press, 1988.

Kades, Michael. "Incumbent without a Party: Robert M. La Follette, Jr., and the Wisconsin Republican Primary of 1946." *Wisconsin Magazine of History* 80 (Autumn 1996): 3–35.

Kamphoefner, Walter D. *Transplanted Westfalians: Chain Migration from Germany to a Rural Midwestern Community*. Princeton, N.J.: Princeton University Press, 1987.

Kanetzke, Howard W. "Germans in Wisconsin." *Badger History* 27 (March 1974): 1–64.

Karabell, Zachary. *The Last Campaign: How Harry Truman Won the 1948 Election*. New York: Knopf, 2000.

Kasparek, Jonathan. "FDR's 'Old Friends' in Wisconsin: Presidential Finesses in the Land of La Follette." *Wisconsin Magazine of History* 84 (Summer 2001): 17–25.

———. *Fighting Son: A Biography of Philip F. La Follette*. Madison: Wisconsin Historical Society Press, 2006.

———. "Fighting Son: A Biography of Philip F. La Follette." *Wisconsin Magazine of History* 89 (Summer 2006): 48–51.

———. "Wisconsin's Founding Brothers." *Wisconsin Academy Review* 50 (Fall 2004): 52–58.

Kellogg, Louise Phelps. "The Alien Suffrage Provision of the Constitution." *Wisconsin Magazine of History* (June 1918): 422–25.

———. "The Bennett Law in Wisconsin." *Wisconsin Magazine of History* 2 (September 1918): 3–25.

Kelsey, Albert K. "C. C. Washburn: The Evolution of a Flour Baron." *Wisconsin Magazine of History* 88 (Summer 2005): 38–51.

Kennedy, Padraic M. "Lenroot, La Follette, and the Campaign of 1906." *Wisconsin Magazine of History* 42 (Spring 1959): 163–74.

Kenny, Judith T. "Polish Routes to Americanization." In Ostergren and Vale, eds., *Wisconsin Land and Life,* 263–81.

Kerstein, Edward. *Milwaukee's All-American Mayor: Portrait of Daniel Webster Hoan.* Englewood Cliffs, N.J.: Prentice-Hall, 1966.

King, Austin. "Wisconsin Socialism." Unpublished paper, 2001.

Kipnis, Ira. *The American Socialist Movement 1897–1912.* Westport, Conn.: Greenwood Press, 1968.

Klement, Frank L. "Copperheads and Copperheadism in Wisconsin: Democratic Opposition to the Lincoln Administration." *Wisconsin Magazine of History* 42 (Spring 1959): 182–88.

———. *The Copperheads in the Middle West.* Gloucester, Mass.: Peter Smith, 1972.

———. "The Soldier Vote in Wisconsin during the Civil War." *Wisconsin Magazine of History* 28 (September 1944): 37–47.

Kleppner, Paul. *The Cross of Culture: A Social Analysis of Midwestern Politics, 1850–1900.* New York: Free Press, 1970.

Klueter, Howard, and James Lorence. *Woodlot and Ballot Box: Marathon County in the Twentieth Century.* Wausau: Marathon County Historical Society, 1977.

Kolehmainen, John I., and George W. Hill. *Haven in the Woods: The Story of the Finns in Wisconsin.* New York: Arno Press, 1979.

Krabbendem, Hans, and Larry J. Wagenaar, eds. *The Dutch-American Experience: Essays in Honor of Robert P. Swierenga.* Amsterdam: VU Uitgeverij, 2000.

Kroncke, Robert Newton. "Race and Politics in Wisconsin, 1854–1865." M.A. thesis, University of Wisconsin, 1968.

Laatsch, William G., and Charles F. Calkins. "Belgians in Wisconsin." In Noble, ed., *To Build in a New Land,* 195–210.

Ladd, Everett Carl. *America at the Polls 1994.* Storrs: The Roper Center, 1995.

LaFeber, Walter. "Election of 1980." In Schlesinger, ed., *History of American Presidential Elections,* 1877–902.

La Follette, Belle C., and Fola La Follette. *Robert M. La Follette.* New York: Macmillan, 1953.

La Follette, Philip. *Adventure in Politics: The Memoirs of Philip La Follette.* Ed. Donald Young. New York: Holt, Rinehart and Winston, 1970.

La Follette, Robert M. *La Follette's Autobiography: A Personal Narrative of Political Experiences.* Madison: Robert M. La Follette Co., 1913.

Lahman, Carrol P. "Robert Marion La Follette as Public Speaker and Political Leader, 1855–1905." Ph.D. dissertation, University of Wisconsin, 1939.

Lampard, Eric. *The Rise of the Dairy Industry in Wisconsin: A Study of Agricultural Change, 1820–1920.* Madison: State Historical Society of Wisconsin, 1963.

Langill, Ellen. *Milwaukee 150.* Milwaukee: Milwaukee Publishing Group, 1996.

Laslett, John H. M., and Seymour M. Lipset, eds. *Failure of a Dream? Essays in the History of American Socialism.* Garden City, N.J.: Doubleday, 1974.

Laufenberg, Wayne E. "The Schmedeman Administration in Wisconsin: A Study of Missed Opportunities." M.S. thesis, University of Wisconsin, 1965.

Lazarsfeld, Paul, Bernard Berelson, and Hazel Gaudet. *The People's Choice.* New York: Duell, Sloan, and Pearce, 1944.

Legreid, Ann Marie. "Community Building, Conflict, and Change: Geographic Perspectives on the Norwegian-American Experience in Frontier Wisconsin." In Ostergren and Vale, eds., *Wisconsin Land and Life,* 300–319.

Lesher, Stephan. *George Wallace: American Populist.* Reading, Mass.: Addison-Wesley, 1994.

Leuchtenburg, William E. "Election of 1936." In Schlesinger, ed., *History of American Presidential Elections,* 2809–914.

Levi, Kate E. "Geographical Origin of German Immigration to Wisconsin." *Collections of the State Historical Society of Wisconsin* (1898): 341–93.

Levitan, Stuart. D. *Madison: The Illustrated Sesquicentennial History, 1856–1931.* Vol. 1. Madison: University of Wisconsin Press, 2006.

Lewis, H. S. "European Ethnicity in Wisconsin: An Exploratory Formulation." *Ethnicity* 5 (March 1978): 174–88.

Lichtman, Allan J. *Prejudice and the Old Politics: The Presidential Election of 1928.* Charlotte: University of North Carolina Press, 1979.

Lieberson, Stanley, and Mary Waters. *From Many Strands: Ethnic and Racial Groups in Contemporary America.* New York: Russell Sage, 1990.

Lieske, Joel. "Regional Subcultures in the United States." *Journal of Politics* 55 (1993): 888–913.

Link, Arthur S. *Woodrow Wilson and the Progressive Era, 1910–1917.* New York: Harper and Row, 1963.

Link, Arthur S., and William M. Leary, Jr. "Election of 1916." In Schlesinger, ed., *History of American Presidential Elections,* 2245–345.

Loftus, Tom. *The Art of Legislative Politics.* Washington, D.C.: CQ Press, 1994.

Long, Robert E. "Thomas Amlie: A Political Biography." Ph.D. dissertation, University of Wisconsin, 1969.

———. "Wisconsin State Politics, 1932–1934: The Democratic Interlude." M.A. thesis, University of Wisconsin, 1962.

Lorence, James J. "'Dynamite for the Brain': The Growth and Decline of Socialism in Central and Lakeshore Wisconsin, 1910–1920." *Wisconsin Magazine of History* 66 (Summer 1983): 251–73.

———. *Gerald J. Boileau and the Progressive-Farmer-Labor Alliance.* Columbia: University of Missouri Press, 1994.

Lovejoy, Allen F. *La Follette and the Establishment of the Direct Primary in Wisconsin, 1890–1904.* New Haven, Conn.: Yale University Press, 1941.

Loew, Patty. *Indian Nations of Wisconsin: Histories of Endurance and Renewal.* Madison: Wisconsin Historical Society Press, 2001.

Lubell, Samuel. *The Future of American Politics.* New York: Harper, 1952.

———. *Revolt of the Moderates.* New York: Harper, 1956.

Lucker, Jeffrey. "The Politics of Prohibition in Wisconsin, 1917–1933." M.A. thesis, University of Wisconsin, 1968.

Lurie, Nancy Oestrich. *Wisconsin Indians.* Madison: Wisconsin Historical Society Press, 2002.

Luthin, Reinhard H. *The First Lincoln Campaign.* Cambridge, Mass.: Harvard University Press, 1944.

MacKay, Kenneth C. *The Progressive Movement of 1924*. New York: Octagon, 1966.

Madison, James H., ed. *Heart Land: Comparative Histories of the Midwestern States*. Bloomington: Indiana University Press, 1988.

Maney, Patrick J. *"Young Bob" La Follette: A Biography of Robert M. La Follette Jr., 1895–1953*. Columbia: University of Missouri Press, 1978.

Margulies, Herbert F. "Anti-Catholicism in Wisconsin Politics, 1914–1920." *Mid-America* 44 (January 1962): 51–56.

———. "The Background of the La Follette-McGovern Schism." *Wisconsin Magazine of History* 40 (Autumn 1956): 21–29.

———. "Cautiously Constructive: The Congressional Career of John Jacob Esch of Wisconsin." *Wisconsin Magazine of History* 83 (Winter 1999): 111–37.

———. "The Election of 1920 in Wisconsin: The Return to 'Normalcy' Reappraised." *Wisconsin Magazine of History* 41 (Autumn 1957): 15–22.

———. "Irvine L. Lenroot and the Republican Vice Presidential Nomination of 1920." *Wisconsin Magazine of History* 61 (Autumn 1977): 21–31.

———. "Robert M. La Follette Goes to the Senate, 1905." *Wisconsin Magazine of History* 59 (Spring 1976): 214–25.

———. *Senator Lenroot of Wisconsin: A Political Biography: 1900–1929*. Columbia: University of Missouri Press, 1977.

Martin, Xavier. "The Belgians of Northeast Wisconsin." *Collections of the State Historical Society of Wisconsin* (1895): 375–96.

Maxwell, Robert S. *Emanuel L. Philipp: Wisconsin Stalwart*. Madison: State Historical Society of Wisconsin, 1959.

———. "La Follette and the Progressive Machine in Wisconsin." *Indiana Magazine of History* 48 (March 1952): 55–70.

———, ed. *La Follette*. Englewood Cliffs: Prentice-Hall, 1969.

Mayfield, John. *Rehearsal for Republicanism: Free Soil and the Politics of Anti-Slavery*. Port Washington, N.Y.: Kennikat Press, 1980.

Mayhew, David. *Electoral Realignments: A Critique of an American Genre*. New Haven, Conn.: Yale University Press, 2002.

McBride, Genevieve G. *On Wisconsin Women: Working for their Rights from Settlement to Suffrage*. Madison: University of Wisconsin Press, 1993.

McCoy, Donald R. *Angry Voices: Left of Center Politics in the New Deal Era*. Lawrence: University of Kansas, 1958.

———. "Election of 1920." In Schlesinger, ed., *History of American Presidential Elections*, 2349–450.

———. "The Formation of the Wisconsin Progressive Party in 1934." *Historian* 14 (Autumn 1951): 70–90.

McDonald, M. J. *History of the Irish in Wisconsin in the Nineteenth Century*. Washington, D.C.: Catholic University Press, 1954.

McGerr, Michael. *A Fierce Discontent: The Rise and Fall of the Progressive Movement in America, 1870–1920*. New York: Free Press, 2003.

McManus, Michael. *Political Abolitionism in Wisconsin, 1840–1861*. Kent, Ohio: Kent State University Press, 1998.

Merrill, Horace S. *Bourbon Democracy of the Middle West, 1865–1896*. Baton Rouge: Louisiana State University Press, 1953.

——. *William Freeman Vilas: Doctrinaire Democrat.* Madison: University of Wisconsin Press, 1954.

A Merry Briton in Pioneer Wisconsin. Madison: State Historical Society of Wisconsin, 1950.

Metzner, Lee W. "The Belgians in the North Country." *Wisconsin Magazine of History* 26 (March 1943): 280–88.

Meyer, Karl E. "The Politics of Loyalty from La Follette to McCarthy in Wisconsin: 1918–1952." Ph.D. dissertation, Princeton University, 1956.

Miller, Edward, and Bret Hawkins. "Local Government." In Weber, ed., *Crane and Hagensick's Wisconsin Government and Politics.*

Miller, John E. "The Election of 1932 in Wisconsin." M.A. thesis, University of Wisconsin, 1968.

——. "Fighting for the Cause: The Rhetoric and Symbolism of the Wisconsin Progressive Movement." *Wisconsin Magazine of History* 87 (Summer 2004): 14–25.

——. *Governor Philip F. La Follette, the Wisconsin Progressives, and the New Deal.* Columbia: University of Missouri Press, 1982.

Miller, Sally. *Victor Berger and the Promise of Constructive Socialism, 1910–1920.* Westport, Conn.: Greenwood, 1973.

Mink, Nicolaas. "Dynamics of Change: Politics, Ethnicities, and Voting in Wisconsin 1848–1857." Unpublished paper, 2001.

Mollenhoff, David. *Madison: A History of the Formative Years.* 2d ed. Madison: University of Wisconsin Press, 2003.

Moore, Edmund A. *A Catholic Runs for President: The Campaign of 1928.* New York: Ronald Press, 1956.

Morgan, H. Wayne. "Election of 1892." In Schlesinger, ed., *History of American Presidential Elections,* 1703–84.

Moriarty, Francis J. "Philip F. La Follette: State and National Politics, 1937–1938." M.S. thesis, University of Wisconsin, 1960.

Morin, Richard. "Trading the Souls at the Polls: Religiously Affiliated Voters Split along Traditional Lines in the 2000 Election." *Washington Post National Edition,* February 26–March 4, 2001.

Morison, Elting. "Election of 1860." In Schlesinger, ed., *History of American Presidential Elections,* 1097–152.

Morris, Gertrude L. "The Administration of Governor Davidson of Wisconsin." B.A. thesis, University of Wisconsin, 1922.

Morris, Roy. *Fraud of the Century: Rutherford B. Hayes, Samuel Tilden, and the Stolen Election of 1876.* New York: Simon and Schuster, 2003.

Morrow, Kelly. "Calculating Progress, Constructing Identity: Ethnicity and the 1912 Wisconsin Women's Suffrage Campaign." Honors thesis, University of Wisconsin-Madison, 2003.

——. "The Connections of Ethnicity, Women's Suffrage, and Prohibition in Wisconsin: The Results of Analysis of the 1912 and 1926 Wisconsin Referenda." Unpublished paper, 2001.

——. "Fighting for Rights, Fighting for Citizenship: The Impact of Ethnicity on the 1912 Women's Suffrage Referendum." Unpublished paper, 2001.

——. "1912 Referendum: Extending the Right of Suffrage to Women." Unpublished paper, 2000.

——. "1926 Referendum: Repealing the Volstead Act." Unpublished paper, 2000.

Mowry, George E. "Election of 1912." In Schlesinger, ed., *History of American Presidential Elections,* 2135–242.

Munch, Peter A. "Segregation and Assimilation of Norwegian Settlements in Wisconsin." *Norwegian-American Studies and Records* 18 (1954): 102–40.

——. "Social Adjustment among Wisconsin Norwegians." *American Sociological Review* 14 (December 1949): 780–87.

Mussak, Erich N. "The Unraveling of the New Deal Coalition: A Typological Case Study of Suburban Milwaukee Voting Behavior." *The Michigan Journal of Political Science* 32 (Fall 2001): 1–70.

——. "The Unraveling of the New Deal Coalition: A Typological Case Study of Suburban Milwaukee Voting Behavior (1950–2000)." Honors thesis, University of Wisconsin–Madison, 2001.

Muzik, Edward J. "Victor L. Berger: Congress and the Red Scare." *Wisconsin Magazine of History* 47 (Summer 1964): 309–18.

Nall, Clayton. "Battle of the Mavericks: The 1988 Wisconsin Senate Race." Unpublished paper, 1999. Available from author.

Nash, Howard P., Jr. *Third Parties in American Politics.* Washington, D.C.: Public Affairs Press, 1959.

Nash, Roderick. "Victor L. Berger: Making Marx Respectable." *Wisconsin Magazine of History* 47 (Summer 1964): 301–7.

Nelson, E. Clifford. *German-American Political Behavior in Nebraska and Wisconsin 1916–1920.* Lincoln: University of Nebraska Press, 1972.

——. *Lutheranism in North America 1914–1970.* Minneapolis: Augsburg Press, 1972.

Nelson, Michael, ed. *The Elections of 2004.* Washington, D.C.: CQ Press, 2005.

Nesbit, Robert C. *The History of Wisconsin.* Vol. 3: *Urbanization and Industrialization, 1873–1893.* Madison: State Historical Society of Wisconsin, 1985.

——. *Wisconsin: A History.* Madison: University of Wisconsin Press, 1973.

Neu, Charles. "Olympia Brown and the Woman's Suffrage Movement." *Wisconsin Magazine of History* 43 (Summer 1960): 277–87.

Nichols, Roy F., and Philip S. Klein. "Election of 1856." In Schlesinger, ed., *History of American Presidential Elections,* 1007–94.

Nichols, Roy F., and Jeanette Nichols. "Election of 1852." In Schlesinger, ed., *History of American Presidential Elections,* 921–1003.

Noble, Allen, G., ed. *To Build in a New Land.* Baltimore: Johns Hopkins University Press, 1992.

Noll, Mark. "American Lutherans Yesterday and Today." In *Lutherans Today,* ed. Richard Cimino, 3–25. Grand Rapids, Mich.: Eerdmans, 2003.

——, ed. *Religion and American Politics.* New York: Oxford University Press, 1990.

Nye, Russell. *Midwest Progressive Politics: A History of Its Origins and Development, 1870–1958.* East Lansing: Michigan State University Press, 1959.

O'Brien, Michael. "The Anti-McCarthy Campaign in Wisconsin, 1951–1952." *Wisconsin Magazine of History* 56 (Winter 1972–73): 91–108.

——. *McCarthy and McCarthyism in Wisconsin.* Columbia: University of Missouri Press, 1980.

Ochoa, George. *Atlas of Hispanic-American History.* New York: Checkmate Books, 2001.

O'Day, Tom. "Voting Patterns and Census Data in the City of Wauwatosa." Unpublished paper, 1995.

Olson, Frederick. "The Socialist Party and the Union in Milwaukee, 1900–1912." *Wisconsin Magazine of History* 44 (Winter 1960–61): 110–16.

Ondercin, David G. "The Early Years of Francis Edward McGovern, 1866–1910." M.A. thesis, University of Wisconsin–Milwaukee, 1967.

Orfield, Myron, and Thomas Luce. *Wisconsin Metropatterns.* Minneapolis: Metropolitan Area Research Corporation, 2002.

Oshinsky, David M. *A Conspiracy So Immense: The World of Joseph McCarthy.* New York: Free Press, 1983.

——. "Wisconsin Labor and the Campaign of 1952." *Wisconsin Magazine of History* 56 (Winter 1972–73): 109–18.

Ostergren, Robert C. *A Community Transplanted: The Trans-Atlantic Experience of a Swedish Immigrant Settlement in the Upper Middle West, 1835–1915.* Madison: University of Wisconsin Press, 1988.

——. "The Euro-American Settlement of Wisconsin, 1830–1920." In Ostergren and Vale, eds., *Wisconsin Land and Life,* 137–62.

Ostergren, Robert C., and Thomas R. Vale, eds., *Wisconsin Land and Life.* Madison: University of Wisconsin Press, 1997.

Otto, Luther B. "Catholic and Lutheran Political Cultures in Medium-Sized Wisconsin Cities." M.A. thesis, University of Wisconsin, 1963.

Otto, Max C. "Two Views of the La Follettes: Washington, the 20s." *Wisconsin Magazine of History* 42 (Winter 1958–59): 109–14.

Peck, George. *Peck's Bad Boy and His Pa.* Chicago: Belford, Clarke, 1883.

——. *Peck's Bad Boy in an Airship.* Chicago: Belford, Clarke, 1908.

Pederson, Jane Marie. *Between Memory and Reality: Family and Community in Rural Wisconsin, 1870–1970.* Madison: University of Wisconsin Press, 1992.

Philipp, Emanuel. *Political Reform in Wisconsin: A Historical Review of the Subjects of Primary Election, Taxation, and Railway Regulation.* Milwaukee: E. L. Philipp, 1910.

Phillips, Kevin. *William McKinley.* New York: Henry Holt, 2003.

Pienkos, Donald. "Politics, Religion, and Change in Polish Milwaukee, 1900–1930." *Wisconsin Magazine of History* 61 (Spring 1978): 179–209.

Plumb, Ralph G. *Badger Politics, 1836–1930.* Manitowoc: Brandt Printing, 1930.

Poles in Wisconsin. Madison: State Historical Society of Wisconsin, 1979.

Polsby, Nelson W. *Presidential Elections: Strategies of American Electoral Politics.* Lanham, Md.: Rowman and Littlefield, 2003.

Pomerantz, Sidney I. "Election of 1876." In Schlesinger, ed., *History of American Presidential Elections,* 1379–487.

Pomper, Gerald R., ed. *The Election of 1976.* New York: David McKay, 1977.

——. *The Election of 1992.* Chatham, N.J.: Chatham House, 1993.

"Post Election Survey February 1985." Madison: University of Wisconsin Survey Research Laboratory, 1985.

Powell, David O. "The Union Party of 1936: Campaign Tactics and Issues." *Mid-America* 46 (April 1964): 126–41.

——. "The Union Party of 1936." Ph.D. dissertation, Ohio State University, 1962.

Prestor, Richard. *Images of America: Milwaukee, Wisconsin.* Milwaukee: Arcadia Publishing Co., 2000.

Preus, Herman A. "History of Norwegian Lutheranism in America to 1917." *Concordia Historical Institute Quarterly* 40 (October 1967): 99–118.

Quaife, Milo M. *The Attainment of Statehood.* Madison: State Historical Society of Wisconsin, 1928.

———. *Wisconsin: Its Identity and Its People, 1634–1924.* Vol. 1. Chicago: S. J. Clarke, 1924.

Raney, William F. *Wisconsin: A Story of Progress.* New York: Prentice-Hall, 1940.

Rankin, George W. *The Life of William Dempster Hoard.* Fort Atkinson, Wisc.: The Press of W. D. Hoard and Sons, 1925.

Ranney, Austin, and Leon D. Epstein. "The Two Electorates: Voters and Non-Voters in a Wisconsin Primary." *Journal of Politics* 28 (August 1966): 598–616.

Ranney, Joseph A. "Suffering the Agonies of Their Righteousness: The Rise and Fall of the States Rights Movement in Wisconsin, 1854–1861." *Wisconsin Magazine of History* 75 (Autumn 1991): 82–116.

Rayback, Joseph G. *Free Soil: The Election of 1848.* Lexington: University of Kentucky Press, 1970.

Reaves, Shiela. *Wisconsin: Pathways to Prosperity.* Northridge, Calif.: Windsor, 1988.

Rederus, Sipko F. "The Dutch Settlements of Sheboygan County." *Wisconsin Magazine of History* 1 (March 1918): 256–65.

Reeves, Thomas C. *Distinguished Service: The Life of Wisconsin Governor Walter J. Kohler, Jr.* Milwaukee: Marquette University Press, 2006.

———. *The Life and Times of Joe McCarthy: A Biography.* New York: Stein and Day, 1982.

Rehnquist, William H. *Centennial Crisis: The Disputed Election of 1876.* New York: Knopf, 2004.

Reidinger, David. "Ethno-Religious Myth, Economic Realities: The Social Foundations of Lincoln's Electoral Support in Two Wisconsin Counties, 1860." Unpublished Paper, 1992.

Reinders, Robert C. "Daniel W. Hoan and the Milwaukee Socialist Party during the First World War." *Wisconsin Magazine of History* 36 (Autumn 1952): 48–55.

Rippley, La Vern J. *The Immigrant Experience in Wisconsin.* Boston: Twayne, 1985.

Risjord, Norman K. "From the Plow to the Cow: William D. Hoard and America's Dairyland." *Wisconsin Magazine of History* 88 (Spring 2005): 40–49.

———. *Populists and Progressives.* Lanham, Md.: Rowman and Littlefield, 2005.

Roe, Gwyneth King. "Two Views of the La Follettes: Madison, the 90s." *Wisconsin Magazine of History* 42 (Winter 1958–59): 102–8.

Rogers, Lindsay, and Parker Thomas Moon. "Record of Political Events." *Political Science Quarterly* 40 (March 1925): 51–57.

Rogin, Michael. *The Intellectuals and McCarthy: The Radical Specter.* Cambridge, Mass.: MIT Press, 1967.

———. "Wallace and the Middle Class: The White Backlash in Wisconsin." *Public Opinion Quarterly* 30 (Spring 1966): 98–108.

Rohe, Randall. "Lumbering: Wisconsin's Northern Urban Frontier." In Ostergren and Vale, eds., *Wisconsin Land and Life,* 221–40.

Rosenstone, Steven J., Roy L. Behr, and Edward H. Lazarus. *Third Parties in America: Citizen Response to Major Party Failure*. Princeton, N.J.: Princeton University Press, 1984.

Ross, Irwin. *The Loneliest Campaign: The Truman Victory of 1948*. Westport, Conn.: Greenwood Press, 1968.

Ross, Sam. *The Empty Sleeve: A Biography of Lucius Fairchild*. Madison: State Historical Society of Wisconsin, 1964.

Rovere, Richard H. *Senator Joe McCarthy*. New York: Harcourt, Brace, 1959.

Rozwenc, Edwin C. *The Compromise of 1850*. Boston: D. C. Heath, 1957.

Ruff, Allen, and Tracey Will. *Forward! A History of Dane, the Capital County*. Cambridge, Wisc.: Woodhenge Press, 2000.

Rummel, Leo. *History of the Catholic Church in Wisconsin*. Madison: Knights of Columbus, 1976.

Rusk, Jerrold G. *A Statistical History of the American Electorate*. Washington, D.C.: CQ Press, 2001.

Sabato, Larry J., ed. *Midterm Madness: The Elections of 2002*. New York: Rowman and Littlefield, 2003.

Sandoz, Ellis, and Cecil V. Crabb Jr., eds. *Election 84*. New York: New American Library, 1985.

Sanford, Albert H. "Portage County Poles." *Proceedings of the State Historical Society of Wisconsin* (1907): 259–88.

Saueressig-Schreuder, Yda. "Dutch Catholic Immigrant Settlement in Wisconsin." In *The Dutch in America,* ed. Robert P. Swierenga, 105–24. New Brunswick: Rutgers University Press, 1985.

"Scandal!" *Historic Madison Newsletter* (Winter 2003): 1–4.

Schafer, Joseph. *Carl Schurz, Militant Liberal*. Madison: State Historical Society of Wisconsin, 1930.

———. *Four Wisconsin Counties*. Madison: State Historical Society of Wisconsin, 1927.

———. "Know-Nothingism in Wisconsin." *Wisconsin Magazine of History* 8 (September 1924): 3–21.

———. "Prohibition in Early Wisconsin." *Wisconsin Magazine of History* 8 (March 1925): 281–99.

———. "Who Elected Lincoln?" *American Historical Review* 47 (October 1941): 51–63.

———. *The Winnebago Horicon Basin*. Madison: State Historical Society of Wisconsin, 1937.

———. *The Wisconsin Lead Region*. Madison: State Historical Society of Wisconsin, 1932.

———. "The Yankee and the Teuton in Wisconsin." *Wisconsin Magazine of History* 6 (1922–23): 125–45, 261–79, 386–402.

Schaller, Thomas F. *Whistling Past Dixie*. New York: Simon and Schuster, 2006.

Schlesinger, Arthur M., Jr., ed. *History of American Presidential Elections, 1789–1968*. New York: McGraw-Hill, 1971.

Schmidt, Karl M. *Henry A. Wallace: Quixotic Crusade 1948*. Syracuse, N.Y.: Syracuse University Press, 1960.

Schmidt, Lester F. "The Farmer-Labor Progressive Federation: The Study of a 'United Front.'" Ph.D. dissertation, University of Wisconsin, 1954.

Schmitz, Keith Robert. "Milwaukee and Its Black Community, 1930–1942." M.A. thesis, University of Wisconsin–Milwaukee, 1979.

Schneider, Dorothy, and Carl J. Schneider. *American Women in the Progressive Era, 1900–1920.* New York: Anchor, 1994.

Schreuder, Yda. "Americans by Choice and Circumstance, Dutch Protestant and Dutch Roman Catholic Immigrants in Wisconsin, 1850–1965." In Ostergren and Vale, eds., *Wisconsin Land and Life,* 320–30.

———. "Urbanization and Assimilation among the Dutch Catholic Immigrants in the Fox River Valley, Wisconsin, 1850–1905." In Krabbendam and Wagenaar, eds., *The Dutch-American Experience.*

Schumann, Alfred R. *No Peddlers Allowed.* Appleton: C. C. Nelson, 1948.

Scoble, Harry M., and Leon D. Epstein. "Religion and Wisconsin Voting in 1960." *Journal of Politics* 26 (May 1964): 381–96.

Scovronick, Nathan B. "The Wisconsin 'School Bus' Campaign of 1946." M.A. thesis, University of Wisconsin, 1967.

Sewell, Richard H. *John P. Hale and the Politics of Abolition.* Cambridge, Mass.: Harvard University Press, 1965.

Shade, William G., and Ballard C. Campbell, eds. *American Presidential Campaigns and Elections.* Armonk, N.Y.: Sharpe, 2003.

Shafer, Byron. *Two Majorities and the Puzzle of Modern American Politics.* Lawrence: University of Kansas Press, 2003.

Sharkansky, Ira. "One Party Suburb." M.A. thesis, University of Wisconsin, 1961.

Shideler, James H. "The La Follette Progressive Party Campaign of 1924." *Wisconsin Magazine of History* 33 (June 1950): 444–57.

Sibley, Joel. *The Partisan Imperative: The Dynamics of American Politics before the Civil War.* New York: Oxford University Press, 1965.

Siekaniec, Ladislas J., OFM. "The Poles of Upper North Wisconsin." *Wisconsin Magazine of History* 39 (Spring 1956): 195–98.

Sifry, Micah L. *Spoiling for a Fight: Third Party Politics in America.* New York: Rutledge, 2002.

Silk, Mark. "Faith and Values Down the Tube." *Religion in the News* (Winter 2007): 1–4.

Simon, Roger D. "The Expansion of an Industrial City: Milwaukee, 1880–1910." Ph.D. dissertation, University of Wisconsin, 1971.

Slocum, Walter Lucius. "Ethnic Stocks as Culture Types in Rural Wisconsin: A Study of Differential Native American, German and Norwegian Influences on Certain Aspects of Man-Land Adjustment in Rural Localities." Ph.D. dissertation, University of Wisconsin, 1940.

Small, Milton M. "The Biography of Robert Schilling." M.A. thesis, University of Wisconsin, 1953.

Smith, Alice E. *The History of Wisconsin.* Vol. 1: *From Exploration to Statehood.* Madison: State Historical Society of Wisconsin, 1973.

Smith, Fredrika S. *Frémont: Soldier, Explorer, Statesman.* New York: Rand McNally, 1966.

Smith, Guy-Harold. "Notes on the Distribution of the Foreign Born Scandinavian in Wisconsin in 1905." *Wisconsin Magazine of History* 14 (June 1931) 417–36.

———. "Notes on the Distribution of the German Born in Wisconsin in 1905." *Wisconsin Magazine of History* 13 (September 1929): 107–20.

Smith, Richard C. "Church Affiliation as Social Differentiator in Rural Wisconsin." Ph.D. dissertation, University of Wisconsin, 1942.

Smith, Theodore C. "The Free Soil Party in Wisconsin." *Proceedings of the State Histori-cal Society of Wisconsin* (1895): 97–162.

———. *The Liberty and Free Soil Parties in the Northwest.* New York: Longmans, Green, and Co., 1897.

Soltow, Lee. *Patterns of Wealthholding in Wisconsin since 1850.* Madison: University of Wisconsin Press, 1971.

Stachowski, Floyd J. "The Political Career of Daniel Webster Hoan." Ph.D. dissertation, Northwestern University, 1966.

Stedman, Murray S., Jr., and Susan W. Stedman. *Discontent at the Polls: A Study of Farm and Labor Parties, 1827–1948.* New York: Columbia University Press, 1950.

Stephenson, Isaac. *Recollections of a Long Life, 1829–1915.* Chicago: R. R. Donnelley and Sons, 1915.

Stewart, James Brewer. *Joshua R. Giddings and the Tactics of Radical Politics.* Cleveland, Ohio: Case Western Reserve University Press, 1970.

Still, Bayrd. *Milwaukee: The History of a City.* Madison: State Historical Society of Wisconsin, 1965.

———. "Norwegian-Americans and Wisconsin Politics in the Forties." *Norwegian-American Studies and Records* 8 (1934): 58–64.

Summers, Mark W. *Rum, Romanism, and Rebellion: The Making of a President, 1884.* Chapel Hill: University of North Carolina Press, 2000.

Sundquist, James L. *Dynamics of the Party System.* Washington, D.C.: The Brookings Institution, 1973.

The Swedes in Wisconsin. Madison: State Historical Society of Wisconsin, 1983.

Swierenga, Robert P. "Ethnoreligious Political Behavior in the Mid–Nineteenth Cen-tury: Voting, Values, Cultures." In Noll, ed., *Religion and American Politics,* 146–71.

Sykes, Jay G. *Proxmire.* New York: R. B. Luce, 1972.

Thelen, David P. "The Boss and the Upstart: Keyes and La Follette, 1880–1884." *Wiscon-sin Magazine of History* 47 (Summer 1964): 103–15.

———. *The Early Life of Robert M. La Follette, 1855–1884.* Chicago: Loyola University Press, 1966.

———. "La Follette and the Temperance Crusade." *Wisconsin Magazine of History* 47 (Summer 1964): 291–300.

———. "Robert La Follette's Leadership, 1891–1896." *Pacific Northwest Quarterly* 62 (July 1971): 97–109.

———. *Robert M. La Follette and the Insurgent Spirit.* Madison: University of Wisconsin–Madison Press, 1985.

———. "Social Tensions and the Origins of Progressivism." *Journal of American History* 56 (September 1969): 323–41.

Thompson, E. Bruce. *Matthew Hale Carpenter, Webster of the West.* Madison: State His-torical Society of Wisconsin, 1954.

Thompson, Tommy. *Power to the People: An American State at Work.* New York: Harper-Collins, 1996.

Thompson, William F. *The History of Wisconsin.* Vol. 6: *Continuity and Change, 1940–1965.* Madison: State Historical Society of Wisconsin, 1988.

Thomson, A. M. *A Political History of Wisconsin.* Milwaukee: E. C. Williams, 1900.

Tishler, William H. "Norwegians in Wisconsin." In Noble, ed., *To Build in a New Land*, 226–41.

Tomkiewicz, John. "Polanders in Wisconsin." *Proceedings of the State Historical Society of Wisconsin* (1902): 148–52.

Tordella, Stephen J. *Religion in Wisconsin: Preferences, Practices, and Ethnic Composition*. Madison: Department of Rural Sociology, University of Wisconsin–Madison, 1979.

Torelle, Ellen, ed. *The Political Philosophy of Robert M. La Follette*. Madison: Robert M. La Follette, 1920.

Trefousse, Hans L. *Carl Schurz, a Biography*. Knoxville: University of Tennessee Press, 1982.

Trotter, Joe W., Jr. *Black Milwaukee: The Making of an Industrial Proletariat, 1915–45*. Urbana: University of Illinois Press, 1985.

Ulrich, Robert J. "The Bennett Law of 1889: Education and Politics in Wisconsin." Ph.D. dissertation, University of Wisconsin–Madison, 1965.

Unger, Irwin. *The Greenback Era: A Social and Political History of American Finance, 1865–1879*. Princeton, N.J.: Princeton University Press, 1964.

Unger, Nancy C. *Fighting Bob La Follette: The Righteous Reformer*. Chapel Hill: University of North Carolina Press, 2000.

———. "The Two Worlds of Belle Case La Follette." *Wisconsin Magazine of History* 83 (Winter 1999–2000): 83–110.

Usher, Ellis B. *The Greenback Movement of 1875–1884 and Wisconsin's Part in It*. Milwaukee: Meisenheimer, 1911.

Van Deburg, Alice H. *La Follette and His Legacy*. Madison: Robert M. La Follette Institute of Public Affairs, 1984.

Vollmar, William J. "The Negro in a Midwest Frontier City, Milwaukee: 1835–1870." M.A. thesis, Marquette University, 1968.

Voss-Hubbard, Mark. *Beyond Party: Cultures of Antipartisanship in Northern Politics before the Civil War*. Baltimore: Johns Hopkins University Press, 2002.

Wachman, Marvin. *History of the Social-Democratic Party of Milwaukee 1897–1910*. Urbana: University of Illinois Press, 1945.

Wahl, John R. "A Statistical Analysis of Gubernatorial Election Results for Madison, Wisconsin, 1934–1950." M.S. thesis, University of Wisconsin, 1952.

Waugh, John C. *Reelecting Lincoln: The Battle for the 1864 Presidency*. New York: Crown, 1997.

Wauwatosa. Wauwatosa: Wauwatosa Historical Society, 2004.

Weber, Ronald E., ed. *Crane and Hagensick's Wisconsin Government and Politics*. 6th ed. New York: McGraw-Hill, 1996.

Wefald, Jon M. "From Peasant Ideals to the Reform State: A Study of Norwegian Attitudes toward Reform in the American Middle West, 1890–1917." Ph.D. dissertation, University of Michigan, 1965.

Wegner, Janet Carole. "The Bennett Law Controversy in Wisconsin, 1889–1891." M.A. thesis, Brown University, 1966.

Weibull, Jorgen. "The Wisconsin Progressives, 1900–1914." *Mid-America* 47 (July 1965): 191–221.

Weinstein, James. *The Decline of Socialism in America, 1912–1925*. New Brunswick, N. J.: Rutgers University Press, 1984.

———. "Radicalism in the Midst of Normalcy." *Journal of American History* 52 (March 1966): 773–90.

Weisberger, Bernard A. *The La Follettes of Wisconsin: Love and Politics in Progressive America.* Madison: University of Wisconsin Press, 1994.

Weisensel, Peter R. "The Wisconsin Temperance Crusade to 1919." M.S. thesis, University of Wisconsin, 1965.

Wekkin, Gary D. *Democrat versus Democrat: The National Party's Campaign to Close the Wisconsin Primary.* Columbia: University of Missouri Press, 1984.

Wells, Robert W. *This Is Milwaukee.* Milwaukee: Renaissance Books, 1970.

Wesser, Robert F. "Election of 1888." In Schlesinger, ed., *History of American Presidential Elections,* 1615–700.

White, Theodore H. *The Making of the President 1960.* New York: Atheneum, 1961.

Whyte, William F. "The Bennett Law Campaign in Wisconsin." *Wisconsin Magazine of History* 10 (June 1927): 363–90.

———. "The Settlement of the Town of Lebanon, Dodge County." *Proceedings of the State Historical Society of Wisconsin* (1915): 99–110.

Wilcox, Clyde. *The Latest American Revolution? The 1994 Elections and Their Implications for Governance.* New York: St. Martin's, 1995.

Williams, Helen J., and Harry Williams. "Wisconsin's Republicans and Reconstruction, 1865–1870." *Wisconsin Magazine of History* 23 (September 1939): 17–39.

Wingert, Mary Lethert. *Claiming the City: Politics, Faith, and the Power of Place in St. Paul.* Ithaca, N.Y.: Cornell University Press, 2001.

Winkle, Kenneth John. "Voters, Issues, and Parties: Partisan Realignment in Southeastern Wisconsin, 1850–1854." M.A. thesis, University of Wisconsin–Madison, 1977.

Wisconsin Legislative District Almanac. Madison: State of Wisconsin Legislative Reference Bureau, 1994.

Workers of the Writers' Program of the Work Progress Administration. *Wisconsin: A Guide to the Badger State.* New York: Duell, Sloan, and Pearce, 1941.

Wyman, Mark. *The Wisconsin Frontier.* Bloomington: Indiana University Press, 1998.

Wyman, Roger E. "Agrarian or Working-Class Radicalism? The Electoral Basis of Populism in Wisconsin." *Political Science Quarterly* 89 (Winter 1974–75): 825–47.

———. "Voting Behavior in the Progressive Era: Wisconsin as a Case Study." Ph.D. dissertation, University of Wisconsin, 1970.

———. "Wisconsin Ethnic Groups and the Election of 1890." *Wisconsin Magazine of History* 51 (Summer 1968): 269–93.

Youmans, Theodora W. "How Wisconsin Women Won the Ballot." *Wisconsin Magazine of History* 5 (September 1921): 3–32.

Zaniewski, Kazimierz J., and Carol J. Rosen. *The Atlas of Ethnic Diversity in Wisconsin.* Madison: University of Wisconsin Press, 1998.

Zeitlin, Richard H. *Germans in Wisconsin.* Madison: State Historical Society of Wisconsin, 2000.

INDEX